VICĀRADĪPA OF BHAGAVATKAVI
(A CRITICAL STUDY)

VICĀRADĪPA
OF
BHAGAVATKAVI

(A CRITICAL STUDY)

With Critical Edition, Introduction, Translation and Notes

DR. NINA BHAVNAGARI

BKP

BHARATIYA KALA PRAKASHAN
DELHI (INDIA)

First Published : 2006

Published by **C.P. Gautam**
BHARATIYA KALA PRAKASHAN
3421-A, IInd Floor, Narang Colony, Tri Nagar,
Delhi-110035. Phone : (O) 27393083, 30967505 (R) 27522129

ISBN : 81-8090-098-3

Laser Type Setting by
A-ONE GRAPHICS
JD-18C, IInd Floor, Pitampura, Delhi-110088
Phone : 55640278, Mob. : 9811167357

Printed by
BDH Printer at Salasar Imaging Systems
Delhi, Ph. 31045804

DEDICATED

to

Parama Pujya

NARAYANA SWAMI

With

Regards.

अज्ञानतिमिरान्धस्य ज्ञानाञ्जनशलाकया।
चक्षुरुन्मीलितं येन तस्मै श्रीगुरवे नमः॥

CONTENTS

	अभिमतम्	(ix)
	Foreward	(xi)
	Welcome	(xiii)
	Preface	(xv)
	Acknowledgements	(xvii)
	Abbreviations	(xix)
I	INTRODUCTION	1-26
	(i) The tradition and Bhagavatkavi	1
	(ii) Manuscript Material	6
	(a) Description	
	(b) Peculiarities	
	(c) Types of Errors	
	(iii) The Author: His life, date and works	12
	(iv) Bhagavatkavi's scholarship	17
II	THE TEXT	27-90
	(i) Principles of Text-editing	27
	(ii) Constitution of the Text and emendations therein	28
	(iii) The Text विचारदीप:	31-90
III	TRANSLATION	91-146
IV	DISCUSSION OF CONTENTS	147-242
	(i) *Maṅgala śloka*	148
	(ii) The Title-Vicāradīpa	152
	(iii) Discussion of *śabda* 'the word' as a *śāstra*	156

(iv) The Theory of *sphoṭa* 160
(v) The Word *śāstra*-a polysemic word 166
(vi) *vṛtti* 177
(vii) *śakti (abhidhā)* 179
(viii) *lakṣaṇā* 185
(ix) *vyañjanā* 210
(x) Concluding verses and the colophon 236
V NOTES 243-267
VI NŪTANTATARĪ: HIS OTHER WORK 268-279
VII CONCLUSION 280-289
Bhagavatkavi : His Contribution
Appendix-I 290-328
Xerox copy of the Manuscript
Appendix-II 329-333
Verses Quoted in the Text
Appendix-III 334
Pāṇinīya Sūtras Quoted in the Text
Appendix-IV 335
Vārttikādi Quoted in the Text
Appendix-V 336
Works Mentioned in the Text
Appendix-VI 337
Authors Mentioned in the Text
CONSPECTUS 338
Topic Discussed in the work
GENERAL INDEX 340
GLOSSARY 343
MAP SHOWING LĀLĪGRĀMA 346
BIBLIOGRAPHY 347

श्रीहरिः

अभिमतम्

विद्वद्बहुला, शास्त्रबहुला, विचारबहुला च भूरियं भारतस्येति चतुर्दिक्षु स्थितेषु सर्वेषु प्रदेशेष्वसंख्याका संस्कृतग्रन्थाः प्रकाशनमपेक्षमाणा वरीवृत्यन्ते। तेष्वन्यतमोऽयं ग्रन्थः सर्वशास्त्रमतपुरस्सरं शब्दशक्तिविचारं विदधानः, लघुकलेवरोऽपि महद्गौरवं भजमानः, विचारान् दीपयमानः, काव्यशास्त्रार्थान् प्रकाशयमानः, दीपक इव 'विचारदीपः, केनापि रैक्वज्ञातीयानन्दरामभट्टात्मजेनाथ चाशाधरशिष्येण भगवन्नाम्ना विदुषा विरचितः 'वादग्रन्थः' सूरतनगराल्लब्धः। अस्मिन् ग्रन्थे वादरीत्या 'शास्त्र' इति शब्दस्य विवादः कृतः।

श्रीमद्गुरोः पादयुगं प्रणम्य नत्वा च साम्बं तपनं गजास्यम्।
शास्त्रेति शब्दस्य विचारदीपं कुर्वे विवादं भगवान् सुबोधम्॥

इत्येक एव श्लोको माङ्गलिकोऽत्र ग्रन्थकारेणानेन विरचितः। अस्यैव श्लोकस्य वादरीत्या वितानं कुर्वाणो ग्रन्थकारः प्राधान्येन 'शास्त्र' इति शब्दस्य विचारं करोति। अथ च सर्वेषां शास्त्राणां शास्त्रत्वस्य परीक्षां कुर्वन्नयं सप्रमाणं व्याकरणस्य शास्त्रत्वं स्थापयति। यथा–मङ्गलाचरण एव 'पादयुगं प्रणम्य' इत्यत्र चतुर्थी स्याद्, द्वितीया वा, इति प्रश्नमुत्थापयति। एवमेव कथं 'शास्त्र' इति शब्दस्याविभक्ति को निर्देशः, कथञ्च 'विचारदीप' इत्यत्रासमर्थसमासः, कोऽर्थः शास्त्रशब्दस्य, सामान्यविशेषण-वल्लक्षणं शास्त्रं कीदृशमित्यादीन् प्रश्नानुत्थाप्य महता वैदुष्येण शास्त्रार्थपुरस्सरं तान् समादधाति।

तर्कादिषु षट्संख्याकेषु शास्त्रेष्वेन शास्त्रत्वमान्येष्विति वचनमसहमानो ग्रन्थकारः याज्ञवल्क्योपदिष्टेषु चतुर्दशसु विद्यास्थानेषु प्रधानवेदाङ्गत्वात्, भगवतो वेदस्य मुखत्वाच्च कौमुदीमनोरमाशेखरादिग्रन्थपुरस्सरं व्याकरणस्य शास्त्रत्वं महता कण्ठेन घटाटोपैः प्रतिपादयति। उपदेशकत्वाच्च काव्यस्यापि। वस्तुतस्तु व्याकरणस्य शास्त्रत्वप्रति-पादनायैवानेन वादोऽयमुत्थापितः।

शब्दशास्त्रं प्रति महता पक्षपातेन पाणिनीयप्रमाणैः विवादं प्रस्तुवन्नयं महान् वैयाकरणः प्रतिभाति। 'यथा नैयायिकानां पृथिव्यप्तेजोवाय्वाकाशादीनां लक्षणानि तथा वैयाकरणानां सूत्राणीत्यवधेयम्' इति ब्रुवाणो ग्रन्थकारः स्वीयं वैयाकरणत्वं व्यनक्ति। अतः हठात् प्रसङ्गमुत्थाप्य शब्दस्य नित्यत्वं, स्फोटस्य चाष्टविधत्वमपि निरूपयति। हरेऽव, विष्णोऽव, इत्यादौ पदयोः स्पष्टमज्ञानेऽपि समुदायशक्त्या

बोधात् समुदायस्यैव विशिष्टवाक्यार्थे शक्तिरिति नागेशमतानुसारेण वाक्यस्फोटस्य नित्यत्वं च प्रतिपादयति।

यद्यपि ग्रन्थस्य विभागस्त्रिषु शब्दशक्तिषु कृत इव प्रतिभाति, किन्तु प्राधान्येनायं ग्रन्थः पाणिनीयशास्त्रविषयकान् वादानेव प्राधान्येन पूर्वपक्षोपन्यासपूर्वकं प्रस्तौति। यथा–सामान्यशास्त्रं प्रति विशेषशास्त्रस्य बलवत्त्वं, पूर्वं प्रति परशास्त्रस्यासिद्धत्वं, उणादिषु बाहुलकं, शास्त्रसिद्धत्वं, कार्यासिद्धत्वमित्यादीन्।

महाभाष्यवाक्यपदीयशब्दकौस्तुभमनोरमादयो बहवो व्याकरणग्रन्थाः, काव्यप्रकाशरसविलासादयोऽलंकारशास्त्रग्रन्थाः, श्रीमद्भागवतादयः पुराणग्रन्थाः, वेदान्तपरिभाषादयो वेदान्तग्रन्थाः, कुमारसम्भवनैषधादयः काव्यग्रन्था, अन्ये च बहवो ग्रन्था अनेन महत्या नैपुण्यास्मिन् ग्रन्थे वादार्थमुद्धृताः। यद्यपि व्याकरणन्याय-मीमांसाप्रभृतिषु सर्वेषु शास्त्रेषु शब्दशक्तिमधिकृत्य बहु वितर्कितं, किन्तु वादरीत्या शब्दशक्तिविचारं कुर्वन्नयं 'विचारदीपः' कामपि नूत्नां विच्छित्तिमाविष्करोति।

पाण्डुलिपिरूपेण लब्धस्यास्य ग्रन्थस्य सम्पादनं महता श्रमेणाथ च महता वैदुष्येण कुर्वत्या डॉ. नीना सी. भावनगर्या महदुपकृतं शास्त्राध्येतॄणाम्। पाण्डुलिप्यामस्यां सन्ति बहवो वर्णा व्यत्यस्ता, तेषां शोधनं सम्पादनावसरे सम्पादयित्र्या यथा कृतं, तत् सर्वथाश्चर्यावहं, बुधजनामोदवहञ्च। यथा–पाण्डुलिप्यां स्थितस्य 'जगास्यम्' इत्यस्य स्थाने 'गजास्यम्', 'कुम्भयंद्व' इत्यस्य स्थाने 'कुम्भद्वयं', 'कर्वे' इत्यस्य स्थाने 'कुर्वे', 'द्विजायतः' इत्यस्य स्थाने 'द्विजातयः' 'तांजग्ना' इत्यस्य स्थाने 'नाञ्जसा', तन्वत्र' इत्यस्य स्थाने 'नन्वत्र' इत्यादीनि संशोधनानि वस्तुतश्चित्तं रञ्जयन्ति। संशोधनपूर्वकं हस्तलेखस्य देवनागर्यां मुद्रणं कृत्वा, ग्रन्थस्यांग्लभाषायामनुवादं च साधु विधाय, स्वकीयं वैदुष्यमयं विवरणमप्यनया तथा प्रस्तुतं येनैकमेव शब्दमाश्रित्य प्रवर्तिता वादस्य रीतिरियमितरेषामपि ज्ञानविषया भविष्यतीति।

कार्येऽस्मिन् सम्पादयित्र्याः प्रखरप्रतिभा प्रतिपदं प्रस्फुटति। गुजरातप्रदेशे पाण्डुलिप्यवस्थायां स्थिता अन्ये ग्रन्था अप्येवमेव प्रकाशमानीयन्तामनयेत्याशासे। ईदृश्यः पाण्डुलिपयो भारतस्य सम्पत्तिरिति यो यो यत्र यथा यतते स सर्वः साधुवादार्हः, प्रशंसार्हश्चास्ति।

अस्य दुर्लभग्रन्थरत्नस्य सम्पादनेन डॉ. नीनाया यशो वरीवृध्यतामथ च कृतिरियं शास्त्ररसपानलोलुपानां विदुषां मध्ये चकास्तुतरामिति कामयते।

–दीक्षितपुष्पा
पूर्वाचार्या, संस्कृतविभागस्य
बिलासपुरस्थशासकीयन्यामहाविद्यालयस्य
अध्यक्षा, पाणिनीयशोधसंस्थानस्य

FOREWORD

It gives me great pleasure in writing this foreword. This work contains the critically edited Sanskrit text with English translation and notes. Dr. Nina Bhavnagari has also added a detailed introduction to it.

The text called *Vicāradīpa of* Bhagavatkavi is a text of the category called *vāda-grantha*. In a *vāda-grantha* a topic is chosen for discussion and the writer develops the discussion by critically examining the opinions of the other scholars on the same issue. Such texts can be appropriately called texts on 'Analytical Discourse.

It is, therefore, heartening to see that *Vicāradīpa* is being brought to light by Dr. Nina Bhavnagari for which she has been awarded the degree of Ph. D. by the M.S University of Baroda.

The central issue in this text is to arrive at the concept of the referent of the term *śāstra*. While engaging himself in the discourse the author of the text, Bhagavatkavi has dealt with various other relevant issues such as the relationships between a morpheme and its referent namely. *śakti, lakṣaṇā* and *vyañjanā*. The text is indeed most valuable from the point of view of the śāstric tradition of Sanskrit.

Dr. Nina Bhavnagari has added additional utility features to this work by adding a detailed study which contains rich informations on the study of *MS* of the text, date and works of Bhagavatkavi, summary of the contents of the text, English translation and notes on the text and very useful indices.

Dr. Bhavnagari has followed scientific principles of editing a text and hence the text accepted by her is dependable. English translation of the text and notes are lucid, readable and authentic. This reflects good command of Dr. Bhavnagari over the language. logic, style and subject matter of the śāstric Sanskrit text. It also reflects that she is familiar with various branches of śāstric Sanskrit learning such as *Vyākaraṇa, Nyāya, Mīmāṁsā* etc.

I congratulate her for this good work and hope that scholars of Indian Intellectual Traditions will welcome it.

I wish that Dr. Bhavangari continues to work in the field of analytic Sanskrit traditions.

V. N. JHA

(DIRECTOR, CASS)

WELCOME

Āśādhara Bhaṭṭa was a doyen of Sanskrit Studies in the eighteenth century Gujarat. He taught at the *pāṭhaśālā* of a small town called Vaso (Dist. Kheda) in central Gujarat. He has written two treatises on *śabda-śakti, Triveṇikā* for students and *Kovidānanda* for scholars. A third one coming from a student of his, Bhaṭṭa Bhagavatkavi of Lālīgrāma (a village about 30 km. north-west from Vaso), offers an interesting variety. Bhagavat-kavi, though much less known than his *guru*, was a scholar in his own right, quite independent in his thinking. In the tract *vicāradīpa,* he approaches the problem from an entirely different angle and treats the topic of *śabda-śakti* in an original way. Here, he is writing a *vāda-grantha,* an interdisciplinary work in a sense, bringing in fresh deliberations from *śāstras* like grammar, *mīmāṁsā* etc. to bear upon the subject. To edit this work from a single and sufficiently corrupt manuscript, to translate it and to explain its various śāstraic nuances and intricacies-it was a hard nut to crack. Dr. Nina has cracked it successfully. During the progress of the project, when non-*ālaṅkārika* zones appeared in the text, she, basically a student of *alaṅkāra-śāstra,* cultivated the other needed disciplines and very often traversed the track independently. And no short cuts. Her resolute sincerity was exemplary. During the process, I have witnessed Nina develop independent faculties and grow into a mature scholar. That is what any research worth the name is expected to achieve.

Nina has been among the very few of my better students. She has often reminded me of that famous teacher who avers

yad yat prayoga-viṣaye bhāvikam upadiśyate mayā tasyai/
tat tad viśeṣakaraṇāt pratyupadiśatīva me bālā//

In this edition of *Vicāra-dīpa*, she has unearthed and presented to the scholarly world a small but shining gem of Sanskrit Scholarship from Gujarat. I am happy that scholars like Prof.V.N. Jha and Dr. Pushpa Dixit have liked it and praised it. I am sure that the work in its published form also will receive approbation of scholars it so richly deserves.

May Nina follow her own example and, in times to come, present some more of such gems.

My best wishes.

—R.I. Nanavati

PREFACE

Gujarat has substantially contributed in all the areas of Sanskrit literature-poetry, drama, history, philosophy, grammar, criticism, linguistics and so on. A series of scholars hailed from Gujarat we can be proud of. Āśādhara Bhaṭṭa was one of them. He has given at least six works inclusive of those on grammar, poetics, Vedānta etc. The name of Āśādhara Bhaṭṭa is quite well-known to Sanskrit scholars due to his scholarship. An equally erudite student of his, namely Bhagavatkavi Bhaṭṭa has given a small but compact and peculiar *vādagrantha* named Vicāradīpa on *śabdaśakti*. The only manuscript (*codex unicum*) of this work, on which this study is based, is registered in Chunilal Gandhi Vidyabhavan, Surat. The text of the manuscript is quite corrupt, the work of restoring the correct text on the basis of transcriptional and contextual probability would be quite interesting and instructive in the field of manuscriptology. Besides, no other work of this Bhagavatkavi Bhaṭṭa who hailed from Gujarat has been brought to light so far. This publication of his small but erudite work, therefore, will hopefully be found interesting to the scholors.

Vicāradīpa is a *śāstraic* work on *śabdaśakti*. It treats the topic with a different viewpoint from that of his *guru* Āśādhara who himself has given two *prakaraṇa* works on the same subject which are already published. Unlike Āśādhara, Bhagavatkavi Bhaṭṭa gives a *vādagrantha* which includes a number of *śāstraic* discussions from grammatical point of view. He also brings in other *śāstras* like *Mīmaṁsā* and *Nyāya*. An attempt therefore, has been made here to prepare the critical edition of the text of Vicāradīpa and to make its detailed study in view of Bhagavatkavi's contribution to Sanskrit literature. I hope this research work will throw a new light on the meritorious contribution of Gujarat to Sanskrit *śāstra* literature. It will also bring recognition and fame to the erudite and learned contributor, Bhagavatkavi himself who has hitherto remained unknown to the world of Sanskrit scholars. It is hoped that this small research work will prepare ground for further exploration in the field of manuscriptology that can bring out our still uncovered, voluminous treasure of *śāstra* literature.

SURAT
Date : 25.1.2005

Nina Bhavnagari
M.T.B. Arts College

ACKNOWLEDGEMENTS

This research project could not have been complete without invaluable co-operation and help of many scholars and friends. I hereby take the opportunity to express a sense of gratitude towards them. Dr. R. I. Nanavati, the ex-director of Oriental Institute Baroda, the most revered teacher and guide of mine, cultivated a systematic discipline for research work and critical aptitude in me since the beginning of my academic career. He kept a constant watch and extended every kind of help from the inception to the accomplishment of this difficult research-project. I find no words to express heart-felt gratitude towards him. Esha and Prof. Mrs. L.R.Nanavati always entertained me warmly during my stay at Baroda for the project. I thank them heartily. Dr. Ramesh Oza, the then honorary director of Chunilal Gandhi Vidyabhavan allowed me to make use of the only manuscript of Vicāradīpa and took personal interest in my research work. I am heartily grateful to such a loving and revered teacher of mine. My thanks are also due to Prof. B.R. Bhatt, Dr. M.V. Meghani and Late Dr. Arunodaya N. Jani who helped me to solve some problems with the text and *śāstraic* discussions in the work at the very initial stage. I feel honoured that Dr. Pushpa Dikṣit a renouned scholar in Sanskrit-Grammar and Dr. V.N. Jha, a stalwart in so many branches of Sanskrit learning, have favoured me with a few words of welcome to this publication. I thank Dr. Jha with earnest regards also for some valuable clues and modifications he suggested. The authorities of the M.S. University of Baroda gave me permission to publish this thesis. I offer my thanks towards them. Prof D.D. Vaidya and Dr. Sharifa Vijliwala, close friends of mine supported me morally in moments of frustration. All the members of my family stood by me at every step in unfavourable circumstances. It has been always my privilege to have their support. Last, but not the least, I must thank Dr. Sweta Prajapati and Shri C.P. Gautamji of Bharatiya Kala Prakashan without whose help, this work could not have been brought to light.

Nina Bhavnagari

ABBREVIATIONS

अमर०	अमरकोश
उदा०	उदाहरण
का०प्र०	काव्यप्रकाश
कुमार०	कुमारसंभवम्
नै०च०/नै०म०	नैषधचरितम्, नैषधमहाकाव्यम्
परि०	परिभाषा
परि०शे०	परिभाषेन्दुशेखर
पा०अ०	पाणिनिअष्टाध्यायी
पा०म०भा०	पातञ्जलमहाभाष्य
भट्टि०	भट्टिकाव्यम्
भरतना०शा०	भरतप्रणीतनाट्यशास्त्र
रघु०	रघुवंशम्
ल०सि०कौ०	लघुसिद्धान्तकौमुदी
वा०	वार्त्तिक
वा०प०	वाक्यपदीय
वा०रा०	वाल्मीकिरामायण
वै०भू०सार	वैयाकरणभूषणसार
वै०सि०का०	वैयाकरणसिद्धान्तकारिका
शिशु०	शिशुपालवधम्
शु०यजु०	शुक्लयजुर्वेद
श्रीधरी०	श्रीधरीटीका–श्रीमद्भागवतपुराण
श्री०भ०गीता	श्रीमद्भगवद्गीता

श्री०भा०पु०	श्रीमद्भागवतपुराण
सु०र०भा०	सुभाषितरत्नभाण्डागार
AB	Āśādhara Bhaṭṭa
ABM	Abhidhāvṛttimātṛkā
AND	Aṣṭanāyikādarpaṇa
BKB	Bhagavatkavi Bhaṭṭa
BP	Bhāgavatapurāṇa
cent.	Century
Ch.	Chapter
K.	Kuvalayānanda
KND	Kovidānanda
KP	Kāvyaprakāśa
NT/NTN	Nūtanatarī
P.	Pāṇini Aṣṭādhyāyī
Pāt.Mbh.	Pātañjala Mahābhāṣya
TRN	Triveṇikā
V.	Vārttika
VD	Vicāradīpa
Vṛtti.	Vṛttivārttika

CHAPTER - I

INTRODUCTION

The tradition and Bhagavat Kavi

The investigation in the power of words, the *śabdaśakti,* has been engaging the attention of our philosophers since millenia. The relation between the word and its meaning is inseparable and co-existent. The Vaiyākaraṇas, the Naiyāyikas, the Mīmāṁsakas and the Ālaṅkārikas have tried to explain this relation in their own ways. As the grammarians concentrated their studies on correct formation of words, grammar is known as पदशास्त्र. The Naiyāikas defined the word-पद-as शक्तं पदम्। and discussed the nature of the individual words only. The Mīmāṁsā system of philosophical thought is known as वाक्यशास्त्र as it was the Mīmāṁsā school which started a detailed and systematic study of sentences. However, their principles of interpretation and their study was also based on words and their meanings and was principally limited to Vedic language. At the same time, the Vaiyākaraṇas had had a sound tradition pertaining to the meaning of the word in their *sphoṭa* theory.

While the Mīmāṁsakas were busy discussing on the meaning of Vedic rites and rituals with reference to Vedic statements, Sanskrit literary works were being composed and comprehensive works on Sanskrit poetics were also being written independently. The Sanskrit poeticians were not satisfied with that much portion of the total meaning of a word which is precise and accurate, and which can be objectively studied. The poets, poeticians and linguists were closely concerned thus with that vast area of language behaviour which covers the problem of change or development in the meaning of the word. This led to the discussion of the powers-functions of the word-levels of meaning. In the discussion of *nirūḍhā lakṣaṇā* such two levels of meaning, primary and secondary, can be seen. The फल (i.e. प्रयोजन)-motive of *lakṣaṇā* was included into its acceptance and this led to the admission of *vyañjanā* i.e. suggestion. In philosophical systems, however, the Naiyāyikas accept two forms of *vṛttī-śabdāśakti*-namely *abhidhā* (=śakti) and *lakṣaṇā*. Poeticians like Bhāmaha (7th-8th cent.) and Udbhaṭa considered twofold functions of poetic word viz. *abhidhā* and *lakṣaṇā* (*gauṇī-guṇavṛtti*).

It was Ānandavardhana (9th cent.) who advocated and systematically established *vyañjanā* as the third independent function of the poetic word. He took the cue from Bhartṛhari and the *sphoṭa* theory of the Vaiyākaraṇas which is quite well-known. Known as Dhvanikāra, Ānandavardhana extended the meaning of the term *artha* (अर्थ) to include not only the cognitive and logical meaning but also the emotive elements and social-cultural significance of the utterances depending upon various contextual factors. Ānandvardhana, however, does not discuss about *abhidhā* and *lakṣaṇā,* taking them as quite well-known. But since his time, the subject of *śabdaśakti*-the power of poetic word came to be a regular topic to be treated as an integral part of the comprehensive systems of the Sanskrit poetics-Alaṅkāraśāstra. Mahimabhaṭṭa (11th cent.) in his Vyaktiviveka controverts the theory of *dhvani-vyañjanā* and propounds that words have a single power *abhidhā* and the so-called suggested sense is conveyed by the expressed sense through the process of inference (अनुमान); but he could not shake the sound foundations of *dhvani* theory strongly established by the support of Abhinavagupta; and *vyañjanā* was almost unanimously admitted by most of the poeticians as an independent function-*vṛtti*-power-of the poetic word. Mammaṭa (11thcent.) has elaborated the subject of *śabdaśakti* in the IInd and IIIrd chapters of Kāvyaprakāśa (KP). Viśvanātha (14th cent.) in his Sāhityadarpaṇa gives a detailed discussion of *śabdaśakti* in the IInd chapter. But very few works deal with the subject independently. Vācaspati Miśra gave a treatise named Tattvabindu in the 9th century. Mukulabhaṭṭa (883-925 A.D.) in his Abhidhāvṛttimātṛkā (AVM) has treated the topic of *śabdaśakti* exclusively. His is the first *prakaraṇagrantha* on the subject of powers of the word. However, Mukulabhaṭṭa does not consider *vyañjanā,* the suggestive power, to be a distinctive function of the poetic word, and avoids to mention and discuss it at all. Mammaṭa's Śabdavyāpāravicāra (SVV) is a small, independent work on the same subject. But it is very likely that Mammaṭa himself, should have, for some specific purpose, only summarised the discussion of the topic from KP, his own famous textbook-like treatise on poetics, and should have put it in the form of a separate compilation with illustrations and have entitled it as SVV. Still another such treatise on the subject is Vṛttivārttika (VV) by Appaya Dikṣita. He proposes to treat all the three powers of the word, namely, *abhidhā, lakṣaṇā* and *vyakti (vyañjanā),* independently of the other topics of poetics. His *Pratijñāśloka* runs like this:

वृत्तयः काव्यसरणावलङ्कारप्रबन्धृभिः।
अभिघालक्षणाव्यक्तिरिति तिस्त्रो निरूपिताः।।
तत्र काचित्क्वचिद्वृद्धैर्विशेषानस्फुटीकृतान्।
निष्टङ्कयितुमस्माभिः क्रियते वृत्तिवार्त्तिकम्।।[1]

Unfortunately, the third *parichheda* of his work, supposed to be dealing with *vyakti (vyañjanā)* is not available to us so far. Had it been complete, VV would perhaps have been the best epitome on the subject.

In this lean tradition of expositions on the topic of *śabdāśakti,* appears Āśādharabhaṭṭa from Gujarat. He has given us two works on *śabdāśakti,* namely, Kovidānanda (KN) and Triveṇikā (Trn.) the independent identity of Gujarat[2] as a state had already become discernible from the time of Hemacandrācārya when Āśādhara appeared on the sphere. Among many other *śāstras* like philosophy, commentaries, grammar, musicology etc.; it had already made contribution to Sanskrit poetics also. Hemachndrācārya (Kāvyānuśāsana), Ramachandra-Guṇacandra (Nāṭyadarpaṇa), Vāgbhaṭa (Vāgbhaṭālaṅkāra), Deveśvara (Kavikalpalatā) and Āśādharabhaṭṭa are some such important contributors to Sanskrit Poetics. Particularly remarkable is Āśādharabhaṭṭa in the present context. As it is already mentioned, he has given us two independent works KN. and Trn. on *śabdaśakti*. Both of these small works solely deal with the same topic. The former in the verse form with an autocommentary in prose and the latter in purely simplified prose. It must be pointed out that Āśādhara is the first and the only scholar from Gujarat to offer two *prakaraṇa* works on the topic both complete and now available in printed form. He has done full justice to the subject in a some-what complex style in KN. and in a scientific but simplified style in Trn.

In the same line comes one Bhagavat Kavi Bhaṭṭa (BKB), a learned and worthy pupil of Āśādharabhaṭṭa. He has also made contribution in his own small way to the field of Sanskrit Poetics. He is known to have written three works and all of them related to one or the other aspect of Sanskrit poetics. A work called Aṣṭanāyikādarpaṇa is ascribed to him; and as the title suggests, it should be dealing with the types of Nāyikās. Nūtanatarī, (NT) another work of his, is a commentary on Bhānudatta's famous Rasataraṅgiṇī. This work aims at elucidating that well-known and popular work on the topic of *rasa* theory. The Vicāradīpa (VD) is a brief but compact and peculiar work of BKB, which deals with the same subject of *śabdaśakti,* but the approach of the author is somewhat different from that of his predecessors. He calls VD a विवाद, a वाद work which is peculiarly different from a *prakaraṇagrantha*. The latter are mainly expository in nature whereas the former aims at scholarly discussions of the minute and controversial issues related to the topic. The VD thus closely examines and discusses some topics connected with *śabdāśakti* from grammatical point of view. BKB's specific interest is in giving detailed discussions and elaborate explanations of debatable issues. his attempt to establish this work as a *śāstra,* his strong advocacy of the *sphota theory and vyañjanā,* his discussions of certain grammatical formations and prominent issues go a long way in establishing the VD as a *vādagrantha.* This aspect is discussed in some detail while speaking of the author's scholarship.

The VD is found in an only manuscript (ms.)- the *codex unicum* in the Chunilal Gandhi Vidyabhavan, Surat, This single ms. has been neither listed in new Catalogus Calalogorum (NCC) nor mentioned by even P.V. Kane and S.K.De in their historical works on Sanskrit poetics. The VD reveals its author's thorough knowledge of various *śāstras* like *Mimāṃsā, Nyāya, Pāṇinian Grammar, Alaṅkāraśāstra, Dharmaśāstra, Purāṇas* and so on. He not only does full justice to his subject but also gives detailed explanations of grammatical formations of words quoted by way of illustrations, He does this with a sound support of Pāṇinisūtras, Mahābhāṣya, and Vārttikas in a lucid style. Eventhough, the topic of *śabdaśakti* has been treated (twice!) excellently by his *guru* Āśādhara, BKB's approach towards, and treatment of the subject are quite different and novel, of course, he has taken inspiration from the preceding works of his *guru.* He has also added some discussions like those on *sphoṭa* or *nipāta-dyotakatvā-vācakatva.* He explains illustrations elaborately, differs in some ways from his *guru,* he proves, too, how this *śāstra* on *śabda* is as important as other philosophical systems. Thus, this small but significant work by a comparatively unknown scholar from Gujarat should be brought to the notice of the world of scholars in Sanskrit, as it is not noticed so far, and it is a *vādagrantha.*

It is, therefore, intended here to critically edit and to make a minute and detailed study of the work-VD. It is also interesting to surmise why the student should at all write a book on the same subject as has been already treated quite satisfactorily by his own teacher! It appears that BKB's approach to the subject is grammar-oriented and it is his intention to make this work a *vādagrantha,* He, therefore, adopts *bhāṣya* style in the treatment of his subject-matter. His interest extends from discussions on seemingly ungrammatical formations to salient problems like variant readings. There are points on which he differs from his *guru,* Āśādhaṛa. It will be, therefore, interesting to compare and contrast the treatment of the same topic given by both the teacher and the taught.

I. ii. Manuscript material:-

(a) Description:-

The manuscript (ms.) of the work VD belongs to the Chunilal Gandhi Vidyabhavan (Sarvajanik Education Society), Surat. It is the only ms (*codex unicum*) of the work VD. It is registered with serial no. 115 and accession No. 1555. It is written in Devanāgarī Script on paper. The date when this work was accomplished by the author is noted in the ms. as V.S. 1860, i.e. 1804 A.D. The ms. is 10.5" × 5.5" in size, with side margins of 2.5 c.m.s. A space of 2.00 c.m.s. is left out on the top as well as at the bottom. The ms. consists of twenty folios. The number of lines written on each side varies between thirteen and sixteen. The last folio has, however, only ten lines. The folios 9 to 17 and 19 to 20 are not numbered. The condition of the ms. is comparatively good. Ink is spread on some letters but the legibility of those letters is not affected thereby. On F_{15}R, some part of the page is spoiled but not torn or moth-eaten, the edges are, however, broken.

The writing is fairly legible but the text is corrupt. There are fourteen cases of marginal additions of letters or words left out while copying. The text is complete with five concluding verses and the colophon which contains the names of the author Bhagavat Kavi Bhaṭṭa, his father Ānandarāma Bhaṭṭa, his inhabitance and the date when this work was completed.

(b) Peculiarities:-

The text is written in a continuous form. Double *daṇdas* are generally put at the end of the sentences. Single *daṇdas* are rearely used. *Kākapadas* are used to indicate marginal additions. At two places (F_{10}R and F_{19}O) the order of letters is corrected by putting numbers 1 and 2 upon the letters like this:

(1) तथा[२]द्य[१] (F_{10}R)=तद्यथा

(2) कुम्भय[२]द्व[१]ं (F_{19}0)=कुम्भद्वयं

Avagrahas are not at all used. त्त्व is always written as त्व, च्छ as छ, ष्ट as ष्ठ. Rules of *sandhi* are not sometimes observed. Such examples like स्फुरत् घनघनागमे............(F_{19}O) are often found. The suitable *anunāsikas* are never used, the scribe puts only *anuswāras* even at the end of sentences. The *pṛṣṭhamātrās* are not used. Occasionally, *anuswāras* and the initial vowels of the succeeding word are placed side by side, without observing the *sandhi*. Final म् is also written as *anuswāra*. e.g.

श्रीमद्गुरोः पादयुगं प्रणम्य
श्रीशं च सांबं तपनं जगास्यं 1 (F_1O)

Irregularity in the use of *visarga* is often observed. it is often introduced when not necessary and dropped when necessary. e.g.

द्वौ चकै (तर्कौ) द्वि (द्वे) च मीमांसे द्वौ योगाविति षट् बुधा (।:) (F_1R)

The sign 'j' is used to indicate उ.

e.g. विस्तरस्क्त=विस्तरस्तु (F_{12}O)

and बाहुल्याद् बहुवचनम्। = बाहुल्याद्बहुवचनम्। (F_{12}O)

Erasures are marked by two or three strokes crossing the unrequired sign or letter; e.g. to correct निःशेषाच्युत etc. it is written as :

निःशेष E च्युतचन्दनं.........(F_{14}O)

(c) Types of Errors:-

The thorough analysis of the ms. brings the student to the

general opinion that most of the corruption in the text has resulted due to the scribe's slip of pen or carelessness or misunderstanding. Such corruption is involuntary. In other words. most of the errors found in the text are scribal errors. They are analysed here according to the guidelines given by S.M. Katre in his book.[3]

(1) Confusion of letters:-

This kind of corruption in the text can be settled by palaeographical evidences, as some similar signs of certain letters in the Devanagari script frequently interchange. Such signs are: ब्द-ष्ट, न-त, र-द etc. Such examples in this ms. are:

शब्दस्य	>	शब्टस्य	[p.31]
नन्वत्र	>	तन्वत्र	[p.32]
नाञ्जसा	>	तांजग्ना	[p.38]
सम्यज्ज्ञातः	>	सम्यक्जातः	[p.41]
मुरोभेदं	>	मुदोभेदं	[p.56]
समदेशे	>	यमदेशे	[p.60]
तिस्रो	>	त्रिस्रो	[p.61]

(2) Sometimes letters or syllables are omitted, particularly the superscript vowelsigns are dropped. the examples in this ms. are as under:

कुर्वे	>	कर्वे	[p. 31]
विशेषणमात्र	>	विशेषमात्र	[p. 32]
शितिकण्ठायेत्यादौ	>	शितिकंठात्यादौ	[p. 31]
क्रियार्थोपपदेत्यादिना	>	क्रियार्थेपपदेत्यादिना	[p. 32]
तत्स्मृतम्	>	तस्मृतम्	[p. 32]
तात्स्थ्यादिति	>	तात्स्थादिति	[p. 37]
दोषोत्सारणस्य	>	दोषात्सारणस्य	[p. 38]

Such cases are innumerable in this manuscript.

(3) Transposition of letters and syllables is also frequently found. It is described as anagrammatism. Here are some examples from the ms. of VD:

गजास्यं > जगास्यं [p. 31]

रथ्यायामारोपितस्य > रथ्यायारामोपितस्य [p. 32]

कथंचन > कथंनच [p. 40]

वर्णयोराश्रययोर्भेदा...... > वर्णयोराश्रयोयभेदा...... [p. 42]

द्विजातय: > द्विजायत: [p. 40]

(4) Sometimes letters or vowel-signs are added due to various causes like hurried writing or slip of pen, or the effect of adjoining letters. e.g.

सामर्थ्यात् > सामार्थ्यात् [p. 33]

(5) **Confusion of words:** Any word in language may be confused if its general similarity to some other word is sufficient to overcome its unlikeness to it in some particular. Such examples in this ms. are:

मानाभाव: > भानाभाव: [p. 36]

परिसंख्येति गीयते > परिसंख्या निगद्यते [p. 60]

(6) **Homolographon:-**Such kind of corruption occurs in the text when there is loss of letters, syllables, words or even lines sometimes. This is on account of similarity or writitng. Sometimes Similar letters stand next to eachother or similar lines are repeated. Such similarity create trouble for the scribe while copying. He tends to drop such similar letters, syllables or words and sometimes lines also. Such instances are found in the present ms also:

न्याय्या > न्याया [p. 35]

प्राचीनमतमवमत्य > प्राचीनमतमवत्य [p. 35]

युगपदवतरितंतत्र श्लेषा > युगपदवतरितत्रशेषा... [p. 43]

बहुवचनस्वीकारेण > बहुवचस्वीकारेण [p. 59]

(7) **Dittography:-**Letters, group of letters, words or even lines are often repeated-written twice when they are supposed to be written once. Such a mistake occurs due to the scribe's carelessness or absentmindedness. e.g.

वाक्यपदीयवचनं > वाक्यपदीयपदीयंवचनं......[p. 52]

दध्युपघातकमात्रे > दध्युपघतकतकमात्रे.......[p. 54]

षड्विधमधिकरणम् > षद्विधमधिमधिकरणं.... [p. 54]

(8) Occasionally, groups of letters, words, even lines are omitted due to similarity or through simple negligence. This ms. contains a number of such instances:

मुख्यार्थबाधे > मुख्याबाधे [p. 57]

व्यञ्जनाख्यव्यापार > व्यंजनाख्यापार [p. 57]

प्रथमंतावद्वि > प्रमंतावद्वि [p. 19]

(9) Some corruption in the text seems to be semivoluntary or voluntary. This is explained thus: Phonetic confusions are likely to occur when the copyist transcribes his ms. at someone's dictation. he tends to make mistakes while listening. Such examples are:

गर्वेणेर्ष्यया > गर्वेणेर्षया [p. 40]

तदधिष्ठानमस्त्येषामिति > तदधिष्ठानमस्तेषामिति [p. 56]

प्राणापहरणं > प्राणाप्रहरणं [p. 56]

(10) Transposition of one or more lines. This is an explanation of such errors: A copyst finds that he has accidentally omitted a line or a number of lines; and rather than disfigure his page or waste his material or time, he writes the omitted portion in the margin or at the foot, or at the top of the page, usually adding a sign to show where it should occur.

The succeeding copyist may easily overlook this sign, and thus permanently misplace the passage. One such example is found in this manuscript:

मल्लिनाथेनाप्येतदभिप्रायेण 'सापेक्षत्वेऽपि गमकत्वान्न समास' इति उक्तं भवति॥ तेन 'रतेर्गृहीतानुनयेन कामं'

'चैत्रस्य शिष्यकुलं मैत्रस्य गुरुकुल' मितिमाख्यातम्। [p. 33]

In these sentences 'सापेक्षत्वेऽपि.......etc. is Malllinātha's commentary on 'रतेर्गृहीता....' (रघु. VI-2). The order of the sentences as it is, does not fit in the context. It seems to be such a case of transposition of lines as should be settled with contextual support.

(11) **False Recollections:-** It may sometimes happen that something in a passage before a scribe may suggest to him something else and he will write down what is in his mind, rather than what is before his eyes. One such case is detected in this ms. where the author quotes a verse from the Vākyapadīya. The original verse runs like this:

सम्बन्धिशब्दः सापेक्षो नित्यं सर्वः प्रयुज्यते।
वाक्यवत्सा व्यपेक्षा हि वृत्तावपि न हीयते॥

(वा.प. III, xiv,48)

The scribe has written this verse as :

सम्बन्धिशब्दः सापेक्षो नित्यं सर्वः समस्यते।
वाक्यवशा व्यपेक्षा हि वृत्तावपि न हीयते॥ [p. 33]

Such quotations are to be restored on the basis of their origin.

In some cases, however they are rare, the corruption seems to be beyond explanation and since, emendation. e.g.

(1) नीलरूपवत् परोषम् (सरोजम्?) [p. 45]

(2) .....वामनपदेन सहान्वस्यन् विवक्षा

शब्दाद्बाहुशब्देन सामर्थ्याभावान्न समासः।....[p. 54]

It is, very difficult, here, to conjecture the correct reading. However, such cases are only two. In most of the cases, the text is contextually settled easily.

I. iii. The Author : His Life, date and works :

P.V. Kane and S.K. De give us a wealth of information about various major and minor writers and their works on Alaṅkāraśāstra. However, Bhagavatkavi Bhaṭṭa (BKB), as the author of the Vicāradīpa (VD) is not mentioned by either cf them. Aufrecht[4] and Kane[5] mention one Bhagavatkavi as the author of Aṣṭanāyikādarpaṇa (AND). A commentary called the Nūtanatarī (NT) on Bhānudatta's famous work Rasataraṅgiṇī, by BKB is also mentioned by S. K. De[6], and by P.V. Kane[7]; But the VD is not mentioned by any of them.

The problem here, appears to be about the identity of the author of all the three works viz. AND, NT and VD. NT has been mentioned by BKB as his own work in the VD but AND is mentioned neither in NT nor in the VD and therefore, whether the author of AND is the same as that of the VD and NT is difficult ot assert.

BKB gives many personal details about himself in the VD and the NT. They are reproduced below:

(1) In the *maṅgala'sloka* of the VD itself he mentions his own name as the author of this work:

विचारदीपं कुर्वे विवादं भगवान् सुबोधम्।

and comments thereon:

भगवन्नामा कविरहं शास्त्र इति शब्दस्य सुबोधं विचारदीपाख्यं विवादं कुर्वे....। [p. 31]

(2) The colophon of the VD runs thus:

इतिश्रीरैक्वज्ञातीयानन्दरामभट्टात्मजेन भगवता रचितोऽयं ग्रन्थः संपूर्णतामगमत्।। [p. 89]

(3) The last three of the six concluding verses of the VD are as follows:

आनन्दराममविबुधात्मजतामुपेत :
शास्त्रार्थशोधनपरो भगवान् बुधोऽहं।
याचे क्षमां विबुधवृन्दमथात्र मन्तौ
यत्साध्वसाधुचरितं मयकानिबन्धे॥४॥
लालीग्रामस्थितिजुषा नाम्ना भगवताधुना।
विप्रेणेदं विरचितं गंगाधरमुदेऽस्तु तत्॥५॥
संवदष्टादशे षष्टितमेऽब्धे मासि चाश्विने।
शुक्ले सोमे च पञ्चम्यां प्राप्तः संपूर्णतामयम्॥६॥ [p. 89]

(4) During the discussion of the types of *lakṣaṇā,* he once mentions his *guru* thus:

विस्तरस्तु आशाधरगुरुकृतत्रिवेणिकायां द्रष्टव्यः।

(5) He mentions his other work Nūtanatarī during the discussion of *rasadhvani* in the following words:

विस्तरस्तु मत्कृते रसतरङ्गिणीव्याख्यानरूपनूतनतरीयनाम्नि ग्रन्थे द्रष्टव्यः। [p. 71]

(6) Of the five various interpretations of the verse सत्यासक्तमनाः......, the example of शब्दशक्तिमूला व्यञ्जना, he refers to one Gaṅgādhara Śāstrī under whose obligation BKB seems to be in someway. he has probably mentioned his name in concluding verses also.

(7) Conversely in the Nūtanatarī, many of these details are coroborated. e.g. The uniform colophon at the end of all the *taraṅgas* runs like this:

इतिश्री महोपाध्यायावटङ्कानन्दरामभट्टात्मज-
भगवद्भट्टविरचितायां रसतरङ्गिणीव्याख्यायां
नूतनतरीसमाख्यायां स्थायिभावनिरूपणे
प्रथमस्तरङ्गः।

(8) Even in NT he refers to Āśādharabhaṭṭa as his *guru*, vide:

अधीताशाधरगुरोर्यथा रसतरङ्गिणी।
तथैव रचिता तस्याष्टीकेयं कृतिनां मुदे॥

(NT ms. F_{97}O)

and

श्रीमदाशाधरगुरोः प्रसादात्क्रियते मया।
तरी रसतरङ्गिण्याष्टीकेयं नातिविस्तरा॥

(NT ms. F_{1}O)

From the above excerpts mentioning his personal details, the following information about Bhagavat Kavi is gathered.

(1) His belonged to the caste of *Raikva* Brahmins.

(2) His father's name was Ānandarāma Bhaṭṭa. He was Mahāmahopādhyāya. His surname (अवटङ्क) was **Bhaṭṭa.**

(3) He resided at Lālīgrāma, most probably situated near Ahmedabad in Gujarat.

(4) Aśdhara Bhaṭṭa, a famous scholar from Gujarat, the author of Kovidānanda and Triveṇikā was his teacher, who taught him various *śāstras* like poetics and Rasataraṅgiṇī.

(5) The reference to Gaṅgādhara Śāstri shows that the author is indebted to him in some way or the other because even at the end of the VD, reference is again made to this Gaṅgādhara in dedicatory tone :

विप्रेणेदं विरचितं गंगाधरमुदेऽस्तु तत्। [p. 89]

(6) His religious inclinations are also conveyed here.

In two *maṅgala'slokas* of a couple of his works BKB refers to various deities:

श्रीमद्गुरोः पादयुगं प्रणम्य श्रीशं च साम्बं तपनं गजास्यम्।
शास्त्रेति शब्दस्य विचारदीपं कुर्वे विवादं भगवान् सुबोधम्॥
[p. ३१]

and

गौरीं त्रिलोकजननीं जनकं जगत्याः
शम्भुंशशाङ्ककलया च विराजमानम्।
हृत्पुण्डरीककुहरे स्थिरभावयोग-
गम्यं नमामि भगवानहमर्थसिद्धयै॥१॥

(NT ms F_1O)

Thus in the VD, he refers to the पञ्चायतन gods, while in the other, he shows his devotion towards Gaurī and Śaṅkara. However, during the discussions, he evinces a strong inclination towards Bhāgavatapurāṇa. he must be a *śaiva* brahmin, but his salutations to पञ्चायतन gods and his inclinations towards Bhāgavata reveal him to be a broad-minded brahmin. That may be due to his आश्रयदाता, probably Gaṅgādhara Śāstri, or under the influence of his *guru*. Such kind of religious tolerance was prevailing in Gujarat even in those days.

(7) So far as BKB'S native place is concerned. It can be said with certainty that BKB was from Gujarat. There are many reasons for this assertion:

(a) The single manuscripts of both his works viz. the Vicāradīpa and Nūtanatarī (a commentary on Rasataraṅgiṇī) are traced from Surat and Vadodara respectively.

(b) He is a direct pupil of Āśādharabhaṭṭa who hailed from Gujarat.

(c) *Lālīgrāma,* the place, he has mentioned as his native

village, is situated some 25 Kms. away from Ahmedabad; and his *vidyāguru* Āśādharabhaṭṭa is a prominent writer in Sanskrit from Gujarat.

(d) Linguistic Confirmations:- There are some linguistic expressions which appear to be quite unusual in Sanskrit. They are very likely to have been either under the influence of Gujarati idioms or back formations or peculiarly Gujarati verb-roots. here are the examples:

(i) **नियमविधेः सकाशात् परिसंख्यायाः भेदोऽवगन्तव्यः।**

[p. 62]

The use of the word सकाशात् here indicates the influence of Gujarati language.

(ii) Another example of such an impact is this:

ब्रह्मलोके ब्रह्मणामेव सत्त्वात्तैः कृत्वा शोभितविग्रहः।

[p. 72]

In Gujarati it is an idiomatic expression, as it is said: *temnā vaḍe karīne.........*

(iii) BKB has used the root परि+√विश् in the words : अत्रौदनं परिवेशयन्तीम् तरुणीं प्रति...... [p. २७]

In परिवेशयन्तीं and परिवेशित–परि+√विश् is used in sense of 'to distribute food', the Gujarati word for it being-*pīrasatī*. The words परिवेशयन्तीं and परिवेशित can be explained as the backformations of the word *pīrasatī* in Gujarati.

(8) **His date:-**

The date of BKB can be fixed with accuracy as he has clearly mentioned the time when he accomplished the VD. One of the concluding verses runs thus :

संवदष्टादशे षष्टितमेऽब्दे मासि चाश्विने।
शुक्ले सोमे च पञ्चम्यां प्राप्तः संपूर्णतामयम्॥ [p. 89]
(VD F_{20}O)

This book was completed on Monday *Āśvin śukla pañcamī* in V.S. 1860 (i.e. Monday, 8th October 1804).

This date is corroborated by the other evidence of the time of his *guru* Āśādhara Bhaṭṭa. Āśādhara lived in the last quarters of eighteenth and the first two quarters of the nineteenth century. He was the protege of the famous Diwan Lallubhai of Bharuch who died in 1799 A.D.[8] He wrote one work Rasikānanda at the instance of Lallubhai perhaps in his younger days. After Lallubhai's death, he seems to have moved towards upper-middle Gujarat and he is said to have lived in Vaso, a village near Ahmedabad.[9] Again, the village Vaso and *Lālīgrāma* are situated quite near each other. The statement, therefore, that he was the direct teacher of BKB is well-corroborated by the available factual details.

(9) **Bhagavat Kavi's Works :**

As already mentioned, the Vicāradīpa and Nūtanatarī are definitely the works by BKB. Since we have concentrated this study on the VD which has already been introduced heretofore, we shall not dwell upon it at length once again.

Aufrecht refers to a Bhagavatkavi as the author of Aṣṭanāyikādarpaṇa.[10] P.V. Kane also has mentioned that work but only in the index.[11] As this work-Aṣṭanāyikādarpaṇa is unavailable, it is difficult to confirm the identitiy of the two Bhagavatkavis. The title of the work suggests that it should be a work on poetics.

A detailed note on BKB's another work Nūtanatarī, a commentary on Bhānudatta's Rasataraṅgiṇī, is given in a separate chapter. No other work of BKB has come to light either in a ms. form. or in a printed form.

I. iv, Bhagavatkavi's Scholarship :

A thorough study of BKB's works definitely leads the

reader to say that he is an eminent scholar and that would not be an exaggerated statement. He quotes from literary works, *stotrakāvyas, śruti* literature, *smṛtis, purāṇas*, various texts on Pāṇinian grammar, *mīmāṁsā* and *nyāya* texts, from a variety of other *śāstras* and he does it with ease and spontaneity. He proposes to treat the subject of *śabdāśakti,* a topic on poetics, but as he intends to make his work a *vādagrantha,* he is supposed to enter into the discussion of debatable and controversial issues. This demands a thorough acqaintance with various other *śāstras* on the part of the author. BKB fulfils the demand aptly.

The VD contains ample evidence to show his close study of the works on various *śāstras* and poetics. His treatment of the topic is generally based on the works of his predecessors from some of whom he borrows definitions and examples. However, he holds independent views on some matters and does not hesitate to criticise his predecessors such as Āśādhara-bhaṭṭa, his own teacher.

Here is a detailed account of his scholarship revealed in various branches of learning especially in the VD.

(1) Grammar : In ancient India, the education of a *paṇḍit* began with Pāṇinian grammar. The *Vyākaraṇaśāstra-pada-jñāna*-formed the foundation on which stood the structure of specialization in any other *śāstra*. It is already stated that the VD contains detailed discussions on grammatical formations. BKB supports such discussions by Pāṇinian *sūtras, paribhāṣās, vārttikas, mahābhāṣya* and so on and so forth. Here are some representative examples:

In the *maṅgalaśloka* BKB uses accusative case and supports the usage by the *paribhāṣā-*

उपपदविभक्तेः कारकविभक्तिर्बलीयसी।

(Paribhāṣenduśekhara p.92) [p.31]

In the same context he quotes *Pāṇini sūtra*-क्रियार्थोपपदस्य कर्मणि स्थानिनः। (P.II, iii, 14) [p. 32]

He has quoted Pāṇini more often than not (cf. App. II). while discussing the compound-विचारदीप, he brings in the प्रदीप by Kaiyaṭa on Mahābhāṣya:

सम्बन्धिशब्दः सापेक्षो नित्यं सर्वः प्रयुज्यते।
वाक्यवत्सा व्यपेक्षा हि वृत्तावपि न हीयते।।

(प्रदीप on P.II, i1) [p. 33]

BKB clarifies the derivation of the word शास्त्र and boldly refutes the explanation of that word given in Manoramā:

यद्यपि मनोरमायामुपदिश्यतेऽनेनेति करणव्युत्पत्त्या शास्त्रमुपदेश इति भाष्यवृत्त्यादिषु व्याख्यातं तथापि तत्प्रौढिवादमात्रम्। करणे घञो दुर्लभत्वात्। ल्युटा बाधादित्युक्तं तथापि शास्त्रशब्दे तु शास्धातोरौंणादिके ष्ट्रन्प्रत्यये उणादयो बहुलमिति बाहुलकात्करणे व्युत्पत्तिरेव न्याय्या। [p.35]

It can be seen here that BKB cites from grammatical texts with ease and spontaneity, thereby bringing his profound, erudite knowledge of these texts to help.

He quotes as authority Patañjali's Mahābhāsya and Bhartṛhari's Vākyapadīya. While discussing *vyākaraṇa* as a *śāstra* he quotes from Mahābhāṣya :

तात्स्थ्यात्ताच्छब्द्यम् इत्यनुशासनात्........

(Mahābhāṣya on P.v. iv.50) [p.37]

BKB has brought in the controversial topic of निपातानाम् वाचकत्वम् द्योतकत्वम्.......and then he quotes a statement from the Vākyapadīya to support that the grammarians are not insistent upon the suggestiveness or denotativeness of the *nipātas*:

स वाचको विशेषाणां संभवाद्द्योतकोऽपि वा।

(Vākyapadīya, II, 188 p.48) [p.52]

And such quotations from the grammatical works are not less in number as it will be seen in the text. (ch.II)

(2) Vedic Literature : The VD is enriched by a number

of citations from vedic literature ranging from the Ṛgveda and Yajurveda Saṁhitās to the Upaniṣads. While explaining the verse सत्यासक्तमना.......he quotes a *mantra* from *Ṛgveda* :

सहस्राक्षः सहस्रपात्। (ऋ. x, 90.1) [p.82]

In the discussion of विधि, नियम and परिसंख्या, he quotes a *mantra* from Yajurveda: इमामगृभ्णन् रशनामृतस्य........(२२,२) [p.61]

* Giving interpretation of the verse- सत्यासक्तमनाः...... he quotes from Taittirīya Āraṇyaka also: ईशानः सर्वविद्यानाम्। ....(x, 47.1) [p.80]
* Establishing *śabda as brahman* and science of *śabda* as a *śāstra,* he quotes from Maitrāyaṇī Upaniṣad:

  द्वे ब्रह्मणी वेदितव्ये शब्दब्रह्म परञ्च यत् (मै. ३.६, २२)
* He has also cited from Muṇḍaka Upaniṣad to support his interpretation of सत्यासक्तमनाः.........etc. as applicable to Viṣṇu:

  यः सर्वज्ञः स सर्वविद्। ....(1-9) [p. 81]

(3) Mīmāṁsāśāstra: It is BKB's practice that he explains each and every example given by him in the light of particular *śāstra* connected with it. He illustrates *lakṣaṇā* with the example न जातु ब्राह्मणं हन्यात्। He discusses whether this is विधि, नियम or परिसंख्या so far as Mīmāṁsā system is concerned. In this connection, he quotes the definitions of these terms from Tantravārttika:

विधिरत्यन्तमप्राप्तौ नियमः पाक्षिके सति।
तत्र चान्यत्र च प्राप्तौ परिसंख्येति गीयते॥ [p.60]

He not only quotes the verse but also discusses in detail and that reveals his acquaintance with the Mīmāṁsā system and its terminology. He has also supported the *sphoṭa* theory of the grammarians refuting the protest of the Mīmāṁsakas against that theory. (cf ch.II p. 41-43) and ch. IV Discussion of contents.

(4) Nyāyaśāstra: BKB has not missed to quote from the *Nyāyaśāstra* more than once. While putting the *sphoṭa* theory on strong grounds, he refuted the *nyāya* arguments against it. He cites their opinion as the *pūrvapakṣa*:

ननु पूर्वपूर्ववर्णव्याहारजन्यसंस्कारसहकृतेन चरमवर्णेनार्थः स्फुटीभविष्यति किं स्फोटकल्पनयेति चेत्। [p.41]

He quotes the opinion of the *Naiyāyikas* and the illustration thereof during the discussion of *śakti* (*abhidhā*):

किञ्च तार्किकाणां मते तु शक्तं पदम् चतुर्धा। रूढम्। यौगिकम्। योगरूढम्। यौगिकरूढश्चेति। गौः। पाचकः। पङ्कजम्। उद्भिदिति। [p. 55]

The quotation is based on Nyāsiddhāntamukāvalī.

(5) Works on Poetics : The subject of the VD is *śabdaśakti,* directly related to Sanskrit poetics-Alaṅkāraśāstra. BKB, both of whose works are on poetics, is an eminent poetician who seems to have studied all the works on poetics before him. Here are some evidences to exemplify his acquintance with them:

He quotes *kārikās* on *rasa* theory from the Nāṭyaśāstra while incidentally touching असंलक्ष्यक्रमव्यङ्ग्यध्वनि as a subtype of ध्वनिकाव्य cf.

रतिर्हासश्च शोकश्च.........etc. (ना. शा. VI. 17) [p.70]

He also lists out all the nine *rasas, vyabhicāribhāvas* etc. from the Nātyaśāstra. (p.70-71)

He gives more than one quotations from Dhvanyāloka (कस्य न वा... I-iv or भ्रम धार्मिक.....I. iv) [p. 76-77] His discussion of the *vyañjanā vṛtti* is mainly based on that of the Dhvanyāloka and Kāvyaprakāśa. For most of his treatment of *śabdaśakti* he seems to be indebted to Mammaṭa and his Kāvyaprakāśa from which he quotes frequently. The definition of poetry, three types of poetry, *lakṣaṇā, abhidhāmūla vyañjanā, rasa* theory, *types of dhvani*—all these are quoted in VD from the Kāvyaprakāśa.

But it does not mean that BKB's study is limited to these texts of poetics only. He quotes the definition of मुद्रालङ्कार from the Kuvalayānanda:

सूच्यार्थसूचनं स मुद्रा। (K. 139) [p. 86]

He quotes abundantly from Rasavilāsa by Bhūdeva Śukla. While discussing the nature of *rasa,* his diction seems to be based on that found in the Rasagaṅgādhara by Jagannātha.

In most of the theoretical aspects of *śabdaśakti.* i.e. definitions and types of *abhidhā, lakṣaṇā* and *vyañjanā,* BKB follows his teacher Āśādharabhaṭṭa who has treated the topic thoroughly in Kovidānanda and Triveṇikā. In other words, he quotes from the two works abundantly. The detailed comparision of the two is given in the IVth chapter. His thorough study of these two works is revealed where he differs from his teacher on subtle points in the interpretations of certain examples.

(6) Śrīmadbhagavadgitā: An important point about BKB's scholarship should specifically be noted where he touches even a subtle problem of variant reading in the Bhagavadgītā, incidentally from which he quotes only once! His sharp, accurate and subtle-pointed acumen must be taken into note there; he states:

सहयज्ञाः प्रजाः सृष्ट्वा पुरोवाच प्रजापतिः।
अनेन प्रसविष्यध्वमेष वोऽस्त्विष्टकामधुक्॥ इति॥ (III, 10)

ब्रह्मणः क्रतूनां फलदातृत्वं चोक्तं भगवद्गीतायाम्–

प्रसविष्यध्वमिति सार्वत्रिकः पाठस्तु चिन्त्यः। स्य प्रत्यये लोटोऽसम्भवात्। लङि् अडागमणस्य दुर्वारत्वाच्च। [p. 82-83]

He raises doubt against the reading 'प्रसविष्यध्वम्' perhaps for the first time on the basis of grammatical regulation.

(7) The Bhāgavatapurāṇa: BKB has given at least eleven quotations from the Bhāgavatapurāṇa and almost everytime alongwith the Śrīdharītīkā. Each of these quotations is given in one way or the other in support of some technical discussion, whether it be a problem of a variant reading or a grammatical formation like सुभ्रु. He appears to be *parama bhāgavata* as he develops almost all the discussions about Bhāgāvata with ease, fluency and spontaneity. He also quotes from Viṣṇupurāṇa once: राघवत्वेऽभवत्सीता रुक्मिणी कृष्णजन्मनि। [p. 50]

(8) Classical Sanskrit Literature- BKB must have carefully studied the principal works comprising the classical Kāvya literature and *subhāṣita-saṅgrahas*. He quotes more than twenty five stanzas either in parts or completly as illustrations for various topics dealt with in his work. Works of Kālidāsa, Subhāṣita-saṅgrahas and Amaruśataka appear to be his special favourites. Verses from Śiśupālavadham, Naiṣdhacaritam and Bhaṭṭikāvyam are also cited, which are less quoted by poeticians. BKB also quotes from Anargharāghava by Murāri, rarely quoted by other authors, by way of illustration.

The most noticeable point about these quotations is, wherever necessary, they are subtly analysed and so suitably selected as to bring out the crux of the complicated point under discussion, and it is here that BKB's sharp acumen is put to work. Let us take a single verse from Śiśupālavadham, the author has quoted to prove how a गजवशीकरणग्रन्थ also is a *śāstra*. The verse is cited in this context:

किञ्च न्यायादिषट्संख्याकेष्वेव तत्त्वे (=शास्त्रत्वे) तच्छास्त्राध्ययने ब्राह्मणानामेवाधिकारात्तेषां यथा शास्त्रित्वं तथा गजवशीकरणग्रन्थाध्ययने-नाधोरणस्य अपि शास्त्रित्वमस्तीति। अन्यथा–

निर्धूतवीतमपि बालकमुल्ललन्तं
यन्ता क्रमेण परिसान्त्वनतर्जनाभिः।
शिक्षावशेन शनकैर्वशमानिनाय
शास्त्रं हि निश्चितधियां क्व न सिद्धिमेति॥

(शिशु ५. ४७)

इत्यादौ सामान्येन विशेषसमर्थनरूपार्थान्तरन्यासालङ्कारो न स्यात्। गजवशीकरणस्याशास्त्रत्वे तत्पाठकस्याघोरणस्यापि तत्त्वाभावात् सामान्याभावः। [p. 39]

It can be seen here, that the author selects a citation from a *śāstrakāvya* (as are Śiśupālavadham etc. described) in order to support his discussion which is purely technical *(śāstrīya)* and such examples are not few.

(9) Miscellaneous works: In addition to the works and *śāstras* mentioned, the text of the VD is abundantly filled with quotations from a number of miscellaneous works namely Amarkośa, the Rāmāyaṇa, Yājñavalkyasmṛti, Manusmṛti, Śiva-mahimnastotra, Caurapañcāśikā-Bilhaṇacarita and other stray verses from popular works. Evenwhen, BKB does not give actual quotations, he refers to various works without mentioning the names. The whole discussion of *sphoṭa* theory and *vyañjanā vṛtti* are such examples, where he has refuted the arguments of the Mīmāṁsakas and the Naiyāyikas with ease and spontaneity in *bhāṣya* style mostly suited to such treatment. Nor has he avoided elaborating on the *rasamīmā-ṁsā* where he sweepingly refers to Bharata, Abhinavagupta and Jagannātha! He declares his disagreement even with his *guru* Āśādhara on some points where logic demands. cf:

यत्तु त्रिवेणिकायां न जातु ब्राह्मणं हन्यादित्यत्र व्यक्तिपरेण ब्राह्मणशब्देन तत्समवेता जातिर्लक्ष्यते इति प्राचीनमतानुसारेणोक्तं भविष्यति। परन्तु न तत्समञ्जसं प्रतिभाति। तथा हि–अत्र लक्षणा व्यक्त्या जातिबोधाभ्युगमेऽपि जातेर्हननायोगात्पुनरपि व्यक्तौ लक्षणापेक्षा। यथा–क्षत्रजातिरुदियाय भुजाभ्यां यस्तवेह सृजतोर्भुवनं प्रागित्यत्र जातिशब्देन तदाश्रयीभूता व्यक्तयो लक्ष्यन्ते जातेरुत्पत्त्यभावे मुख्यार्थबाधत्वात्तद्वदिहापीति। तद्दोषस्तावदवश्यमेव। तस्मात् ब्राह्मणशब्दोत्तरद्वितीयैकवचनांशपरित्यागेनाशक्यद्वितीयाबहुवचनस्वीकारेण लक्षणायाः प्रवृत्तिर्न तु जाताविति। [p. 59]

Such bold frankness reveals his clarity of thought and logical approach which the topic demands especially in a *vādagrantha*.

Apart from all these citations from other *śāstras*, writers and works, BKB's originality is revealed in his exposition and discussion of certain subtle, controversial and debatable points and issues. They should be listed here:

(1) He starts the work VD with a systematic discussion to prove that this *vādagrantha* on *śabdāśakti* is a śāstra.

(2) He shows in detail how *jñāpaka* is reliable in rare grammatical formations.

(3) He elaborately explains how the formation of सुभ्रु in vocative singular is completely justified with a strong support from grammatical texts.

(4) He extends more arguments than his predecessors in support of *vyañjanā vṛtti*.

(5) His approach in the treatment of the subject of *śabdāśakti* is altogether different. He intends to make his work a *vādagrantha* unlike the *prakaraṇagranthas* of his *guru* Āśādharabhaṭṭa, and therefore, at every step, he stops for technical discussions which may be either grammatical or about the interpretation or about some variant reading; and such discussions bring in complexities in his work.

It can be seen, thus, that BKB not only follows his teacher's tradition in scholarship, acumen and originality, but also extends it further. He undoubtedly establishes himself as an eminent scholar in Sanskrit poetics from Gujarat. Such an important contribution of his to Sanskrit literature, therefore, must be taken note of.

FOOTNOTES

1. *Vṛttivārttika*—Introductory verses.
2. 'Contribution of Gujarat to Sk. Lit'., Dr.M.I. Prajapati Felicitation volume. Gen Ed. Dr. Gautam Patel.
3. Katre S.M. 'Introduction to Indian Textual Criticism.' (Ch. V to VII)

4. Index No. 7 Asiatic Society Cat. 1838.8.
5. Index of authors and works. 'History of Sanskrit Poetics.' p. 405.
6. 'History of Sk. Poetics.' V. I, p. 454.
7. Index of authors and works. 'History of Sk. Poetics'. p. 426.
8. '*Bharuch no itihās*' p. 453, Bharuch Gazetteer, p. 485. Vol. II Oriental Memoirs Vol. 1 p. 233.
9. See Introduction, *Triveṇika* Ed. Kālikā Prasād Shukla.
10. *Sucipatra*. 7 Asiatic Society,Cat. 1838.8.
11. 'History of Sk. Poetics.' p. 405.

CHAPTER - II

THE TEXT

II. i. Principles of text-editing

The text as presented here is in a modernly acceptable and corrected form in *devanāgarī* script. The characteristics of the ms. and the written form of the text have already been shown before in section ii of chapter 1. Hence we need not repeat it here. We present below the changes in the method of the presentation of the text so as to make it more comprehensible.

(1) The corrected and systematised text is written on the upper part of the pages.

(2) The text in the manuscript being corrupt, the original text has to be presented side by side with the constituted text. necessity of this lies in the fact that very often the correction is bound to be subjective and the scholars may differ on various points of the restoration and emendation of the text. The erred textual readings found in the ms. are, therefore, given continuously in the footnotes.

(3) Thus, in the place of the continuous *anusvaras* given in the ms. we have introduced the appropriate *anunāsikas*.

(4) The *avagrahas* which have been dropped by the scribe in the ms. are restored here wherever necessary following the rules of coalition.

(5) There are no punctuation marks except one or two *daṇḍas*. We, in our presentation have, besides keeping *daṇḍa* (s)

to mark full stop or paragraphs, introduced all modern punctuation marks to facilitate an easy grasping of the movement and development of the arguments.

(6) The paragraphs are formed according to the necessity of the argument of the topic.

(7) This being a *vādagrantha* the author has adopted the *bhāṣya* style. So the *pūrvapakṣa,* the arguments of the opposition are given in indention.

(8) As already noted before in chapter-I, the *codex unicum* gives a very corrupt text of the work. Hence the editor had to resort to emendations at a few places. Such emendations are clearly indicated by putting them in round brackets like these:().

(9) Similarly, there have remained some three passages in the text which are beyond even emendation. These are indicated by square brackets.

(10) There are two types of numericals shown in the text. The *devanāgarī* numerals refer to the corrupt readings of the ms. which are given in the footnotes on the respective pages. They are pagewise. The roman numerals indicate words and technical terms or maxims on which explanatory notes are given in chapter V.

(11) The verses quoted in the text are indented and presented in bold types. All the quotations are printed in bold types with their sources indicated in round brackets at the same place.

II. ii. Constitution of the text and emendations therein:

For the emendation and constitution of the text, the procedure directed in the 'Introduction to Indian Textual Criticism' by S. M. Karte is followed. thus, wherever the text is corrupt, correction or emendation is attempted on the basis of intrinsic and extrinsic possibility. As it is already stated in the first chapter, most of the errors found in the text are scribal. A complete analysis of these errors is also attempted there. Confusion of letters; letters, syllables or vowel signs omitted or added; transposition of letters; dittography and all such errors are easily corrected on the ground of a palaeographical evidence. Transposition of words or lines is settled with contextual supoort. Corruptions in the quotations are emended as far as possible by referring to their original source.Since the corrected text and its corrupt readings are given one above the other on the same pages, it will be easy for the reader to see how the proposal made for the emendation possesses transcriptional probability.

Thus, for example, on the very first page, the transposition of letters in the case of जगास्यं for गजास्यं is corrected. Such cases of anagrammatism are quite frequently seen and corrected. Corrections are also made to satisfy the demands of sense, context, grammar or style i.e. depending upon intrinsic possibility. In most of such cases the text is corrected with contextual support. Thus conjuncts like त्त्व (forत्व), च्छ (for छ), the proper *anunāsikas* (for constant *anusvaras*) etc. needed to be restored in the corrected text. While presenting the text, all such corrections are carried out.

The sentences or portion which do not seem to be either relevant or original, are put into square brackets. Attention is particularly drawn to the following three portions, which, to the best understanding of the present editor, appear to be totally irrelevent and interpolated. they seem to be totally unrelated in the context, and are shown within square brackets. They are as follows:

(1) Such a portion of distorted text is found on page no. 33 (मल्लिनाथेन.........गुरुकुलमित्याख्यातम्।) The sentence- चैत्रस्य शिष्यकुलं मैत्रस्य गुरुकुलमित्याख्यातम्।- does not seem to relate itself with the preceding or succeeding sentences. Perhaps, some phrase or sentence seems to be missing here.

(2) Page no. 38-39 (इदानीं शरीरभूतस्य.......व्यवहारो न स्यात्।) This is almost a verbative reproduction from the seventh

stabaka of Rasavilāsa. Evenif we neglect the whole portion, the continuity of the discussion in the text is not broken, This may be an interpolation.

(3) One such sentence is found on page no. ३८ (इमं लक्षणा।) It does not fit in the context. hence, may be an interpolation.

भगवत्कविभट्टविरचितः
विचारदीपः

॥ श्री गणेशाय नमः॥

श्रीमद्गुरोः पादयुगं प्रणम्य श्रीशं च साम्बं तपनं गजा[१]स्यम्।
शास्त्रेति शब्द[२]स्य विचारदीपं कु[३]र्वे विवादं भगवान् सुबोधम्॥

अत्र[४] मन्त्रशास्त्रोक्तगुरुचतुष्टय[1] पादद्वयं श्रीशादीन् पञ्चदेवान् च नत्वा भ[५]गवन्नामा कविरह[६] शास्त्र इति शब्दस्य सुबोधं विचारदीपाख्यं विवादं कुर्वे इत्यन्वयः[७]। अत्र **प्रणम्य शितिकण्ठाये**[८] (**कुमार० ६, ८१**) त्यादाविव गुरु[९]पादयुगादिषु चतुर्थी स्या[१०]न्न द्वितीयेति **चेदुपपदविभक्तेः कारकविभक्तिर्बलीयसी**[2] (परि.शे०परि. ९४)ति परिभाषया कारकविभक्तिः द्वितीया उपपदविभक्तिं चतुर्थीं बाधत इति। शितिकण्ठाये[११]त्यादौ तु

---

१. जगा°।
२. °ष्ट°।
३. क°।
४. °त्रं।
५. न्न°।
६. कविहरं।
७. कुर्वेत्यन्वयः।
८. °कंता°।
९. गुरुं।
१०. स्ता°।
११. °कंठात्यां।

[3]**क्रियार्थो**[12]**पपदे** (पा.अ. २,३,१४) त्यादिना चतुर्थी। साम्बेति विशेषणमात्र-प्रयोगाद्विशेष्यस्य[13] शक्तियुक्तशिवस्योपलब्धिर्बोध्या[14]। विशेष[15]णमात्रप्रयोगो विशेष्यप्रतिपत्तौ सागराम्बरादिवदिति।

अत्र शास्त्र इति शब्दस्य रामेति लोकरमणादि (श्री. भा. पु. १०, २, १३) तिवदविभक्तिको निर्देशः।

भूसत्ताया (पा. अ. धातुपाठ:१) मितिवदनुकरणत्वात्। उक्तञ्च-

अत एव गवित्याह भूसत्तायामितीदृशम्।
न प्रातिपदिकं नापि पदं साधु तु तत्स्मृ[16]तमिति॥

(वै.भू. सार ४, २७)

विचाराणां दीप इव दीपः प्रकाशकः। अत्र दीपशब्देन वृत्तौ साध्यवसाना लक्षणा।

ज्ञेया साध्य[17]वसाना सा विषयी यत्र केवलः

(कोविदानन्द २, ११)

इति तल्ल[18]क्षणात्। अन्यथा दीपकालङ्कार इव विचारदीपकमिति स्यात्। यथा तत्र प्रा[19]सादशोभार्थं रथ्यायामारो[20]पितस्य दीपस्यानेकोप-कारकत्वे[21]न साम्यादिवार्थे[4] कन्विधानस्य तथा दर्शनात्।

[22]नन्वत्र विचारपदं शास्त्रपदेन सह साकाङ्क्षं, तथा सति **साकाङ्क्ष-**

---

१२. °र्थे।
१३. विशेणमात्र......द्विशेष्यस्त।
१४. °ध्यां।
१५. °षे°।
१६. तस्मृत°।
१७. साध्यं°।
१८. तप्ल°।
१९. प्र°।
२०. रामोपि°।
२१. त्वें°।
२२. त°।

मसमर्थवद्वाच्यमिति[5] वार्त्तिकेणासाम[२३]र्थ्यात्**समर्थः पदविधि**[6] (पा.अ. २,१,१) रिति सूत्रस्याप्रवृत्तौ, समासविधायकसूत्रान्तराभावा[२४]न्न समास इति चेत्।

न भ[२५]वति वै नित्यसापेक्षस्यापि वृत्तिरिति भाष्यवार्त्तिकोक्तेः सर्वत्र समासदर्शनात्। उक्तञ्च कैयटेन-

सम्बन्धिशब्दः सापेक्षो नित्यं सर्वः[२६] **प्रयुज्यते**[२७]।[7]
वाक्यवत्सा[२८] **व्यपेक्षा हि वृत्तावपि न हीयत।।** इति।

(भाष्यप्रदीप पा०अ० २, १, १)

मल्लिनाथेनाप्येतदभिप्रायेण सापेक्ष[8]त्वे[२९] ऽपि **गमकत्वात्स**[३०]**मासः** (मल्लिनाथप्रणीतसञ्जीविनी रघु० ६, २) इति उक्तं भवति। तेन- **'रतेर्गृहीतानुनयेन कामं'** (रघु० ६, २) [चैत्रस्य शिष्यकुलं मैत्रस्य गुरुकुलमित्या[३१]ख्यातम्।]

इत्थं च- **'क्षत्रस्य शब्दो भुवनेषु रूढ'** (रघु० २, ५३) इति पाठमनार्हत्य 'क्षत्रेति शब्दो भुवनेष्वि'ति पाठोऽङ्गी[३२]कार्यः।

कुर्वे इत्युक्त्यो[३३]त्तमपुरुषस्त्वहमित्य[३४] ध्याहारेण बोध्यः। वाक्येष्वाकाङ्क्षितैकदेशपूरणमध्याहारः। आकाङ्क्षितत्वं चार्थस्यैवा[३५]न्वयस्यार्थनिष्ठ[३६] त्वात्। यथा **'भवानपीदं परवानवैती**[३७] (रघु० २, ५६) त्यत्र युष्मच्छब्दार्थस्याध्याहार

२३. मा°।
२४. °भान्न।
२५. भा°।
२६. व।
२७. समस्यते।
२८. °वशा।
२९. °त्वो°।
३०. न्स°।
३१. °मितिमा°।
३२. पाठोगी°।
३३. क्तो°।
३४. °स°।
३५. °व°।
३६. ष्ट°।
३७. °मी°।

इति। अन्यथा शब्दाध्याहारेऽवैतीत्यत्र प्रथमपुरुषो न स्यात्। युष्मच्छब्दस्य विशेषे[३८]ण प्रा[३९]धान्यात्। भवच्छब्दस्य तु न प्रा[४०]धान्यम्। भातीति भवानिति व्युत्पत्तेर्विशेषणत्वानुगमात्। तेन-**तत्त्वं निवर्त्त[४१]स्व विहाय लज्जां गुरोर्भवान् दर्शितशिष्यभक्ति** (रघु० २, ४०) रित्यत्र न पुनरुक्तिः। भवति भिक्षां देहीत्यादौ तु युष्मच्छब्दस्यैवाध्याहारः भवच्छब्दस्य सम्बोध्यतया चरितार्थत्वात्। अन्यथा देहीत्यत्र मध्यमपुरुषो न स्यात्।

नन्वर्थाना[४२]मेवान्वये शब्दाध्याहारो न युक्तः इति चेत्। न।

शाब्दबोधे शब्दोऽपि भासते इति पक्षे शब्दद्वारेणै[४३]वार्थानामन्वयस्वीकारात् तोयमात्रस्यैव पिपासतेऽपि कलशद्वारेणैव[४४] तदानयनवदिति।

अत्रादौ निषिद्धगणादिदोषनि[४५] रसनार्थ श्रीशब्दप्रयोगः कृतो भवति। प्रथमं तावच्छिष्ट[४६] संप्रदायार्थं[४७] नमस्क्रियारूपं मङ्गल[४८] निबध्नन् कर्तुमिष्टं प्रतिजानीते–

वेदस्तु भगवान्साक्षात्तस्य व्याकरणं मुखम्।
यत्तयोर्वचनं शास्त्रं तात्स्थ्यात्तत्त्वं परेष्वपि[४९]॥

यत्तु–

द्वौ तर्कौ[५०] द्वे च मीमांसे द्वौ योगाविति षड्[५१] बुधाः।
वेदार्थदर्शकत्वेन दर्शनानि प्रचक्षते[५२]॥

---

३८. °ष्ये°।
३९. °प्र°।
४०. °प्र°।
४१. °त्त°।
४२. °र्थता°।
४३. °नै°।
४४. द्वारैव।
४५. °णि°।
४६. °ष्टं°।
४७. °र्थ।
४८. °ल।
४९. °ष्टतु।
५०. चकै।
५१. °ट्।
५२. °क्षंते।

इति तर्का[५३] दिषटसङ्ख्याकेष्वेव शास्त्रत्वन्नान्येषु निबन्धे[५४]ष्विति विनानुशासनं[9] ये प्रलपन्ति तान्निराचष्टे वेद इत्यादिना। वेदो हि साक्षाद्-भगवान्नारायण इत्यर्थः। तस्य भगवतो मुखमास्यं व्याकरणशास्त्रं स्मृतम्। शिक्षायां तथोक्तत्वादिति भावः। तयोर्यद्वचनमुपदेशो[५५] निदेश इति यावत्। तच्छ्‌ास्त्रं शास्त्रशब्दवाच्यमित्यर्थः। तथा[५६] चोक्तं उपदेशः शास्त्रमिति प्राचां वाचां विचारणादिति। यद्यपि मनोरमा[10]**यामुपदिश्यतेऽनेनेति करण[५७] व्युत्पत्त्या शास्त्रमुपदेश इति भाष्यवृत्त्या[५८]दिषु व्याख्यातं[५९] तथापि तत्प्रौढिवादमात्रम्। करणे घञो[६०] दुर्लभ[६१] त्वात्। ल्यु[६२]टा बाधादित्युक्तं[६३]** (प्रौढमनोरमा) तथापि शास्त्रशब्दे तु शास्‌धातोरौणादिके ष्ट्रन्प्रत्यये **उणादयो बहुल**[11]**मि** (पा०अ० ३, ३, १)ति बाहुलकात्करणे व्युत्पत्तिरेव न्याय्या[६४]। **निदेश-ग्रन्थयोः**[६५] **शास्त्र** (अमर० ३, ३, ९) मित्यमरव्याख्याने[६६]। निदेश आज्ञा। शास्यतेऽनेनेति शास्त्रम्। करणार्थे ष्ट्रन्निति क्षीरस्वामिना[12] तथोपपादितत्वात्। यद्यपि नवीनैः प्राचीनमतमवम[६७] त्य करण[६८]व्युत्पत्तिर्निराकृता तथापि बाहुलक[13]स्याप्यगतिकगतत्वेन[६९] स्वीकाराद्विचारात्प्राचीनमतं सम्यगेव प्रतिभातीति। एवं

---

५३. कर्ता।
५४. °न्ध°।
५५. °शे।
५६. °या।
५७. °णा।
५८. °त्ता।
५९. °नं।
६०. द्ययो।
६१. °भे।
६२. प्लु।
६३. °धात्युक्तं।
६४. °या।
६५. °यथोः।
६६. °श्ख्याने।
६७. °मव°।
६८. कारेण°।
६९. व्यगतिकगत्वेन।

च सर्वेषां निदेशानां ग्रन्थानां च शास्त्रत्वे सिद्धे सति व्याकरणस्य तदन्तर्गतानां सूत्राणां च तत्त्वं नि[७०] ष्पन्नमेव।

शाब्दिकानां शास्त्रपक्षविचारे शास्त्रं सूक्तमित्युक्तत्वात् सूत्राणामेव सिद्धत्वासिद्धत्वमिति। उक्तञ्च–

सामान्यशास्त्रतो नूनं विशेषो बलवान्[७१] भवेत्।
परेण पूर्वबाधो वा प्रायशो दृश्यतामिहेति।।

अस्य व्याख्याने माधवोऽप्याह–

'सामान्यमुत्सर्गस्तस्य शास्त्रं सूक्तं लक्षणमि'ति यावत्। एतेन यथा नैयायिकानां पृथिव्यप्तेजोवाय्वाकाशादीनां लक्षणादि तथा वैयाकरणानां सूत्राणी[७२] त्यवधेयम्।

शब्दशास्त्रमनधीत्य यः पुमान्
वक्तुमिच्छति वचः सभान्तरे।
हस्तिनं कमलनालतन्तुना
बद्धु[७३]मिच्छति मदोत्कट[७४] बने।

(सु. र. भा. वैयाकरणप्रशंसा श्लोक. ८)

इत्यादिश्लोकेष्वपि व्याकरणस्य शास्त्रशब्दव्यवहारः। न च व्याकरणस्य तत्त्वे मा[७५] नाभाव इति वाच्यम्। शास्त्रासिद्धपक्षे सामान्यशास्त्रतो नून[७६]मित्यादौ च सिद्धत्वासिद्धत्वयोर्दर्शन[७७] स्यैव मानत्वात् इतरेतराण्यपि कार्याणि शास्त्रेण प्रकल्प्य[७८]न्ते अभेदका इह शास्त्रे गुणा इत्यादिवचनस्यापि[७९] मानत्वाच्च।

---

७०. °त्वन्नि°।
७१. बवान्।
७२. °णि।
७३. बंधु°।
७४. °त्कंठ।
७५. भा°।
७६. न्यू°।
७७. °स्न°।
७८. °ल्पं°।
७९. °चस्यादि।

ननु व्याकरणस्यैव मुरव्यत्वेन तत्त्वे न्यायादिषु तत्प्रति सिद्धिभङ्गापत्तिः स्यादित्याशङ्कायामाह–

तात्स्थ्यादिति[८०]। **तात्स्थ्यात्ताच्छब्द्य[14]मि** (पा०म०भा० पा० अ०. ५, ४, ५० वा, ३) त्यनु[८१]शासनात्तस्मिंस्तिष्ठतीति तत्स्थस्य भाव–[८२] स्तात्स्थ्यं[८३] तस्मात् परेषु न्यायमीमांसावेदान्ताष्टादशस्मृतिकाव्या लङ्काररस-नाटकसङ्गतकामगजशास्त्रादिषु तत्त्वं शास्त्रत्वमङ्गिकृतं शिष्टैरिति शेषः। सर्वेष्वपि निबन्धेषु व्याकरणस्य प्रकृतिप्रत्ययोत्सर्गापवादसूत्रनिष्पन्नाशेषरूपेण स्थित-संभवाच्छास्त्रत्व[८४]मिति भावः।

एवं च–

> **पुराणन्यायमीमांसाधर्मशास्त्राङ्गमिश्रिताः।**
> **वेदाः[८५] स्थानानि विद्यानां ध[८६]र्मस्य चतुर्दशेति॥**

(याज्ञवल्क्यस्मृति १, ३)

याज्ञवल्क्योक्तचतुर्दशविद्यानिवासस्थलभूतेषु वेदेष्वथ च पुराणन्याय-मीमांसाधर्मशास्त्रशिक्षाकल्पव्याकरण[८७]निरुक्तच्छन्दो[८८]ज्योतिःष्वि[८९]ति चतुर्दशसु तत्त्वमविरुद्धमस्तीति।

अत्रेदमवधेयम्–शरीरिणां हस्तपादाद्यङ्गे[९०]षु मुखस्येवैवं वेदस्या[९१]पि शिक्षाकल्पाद्यङ्गेषु व्याकरणस्यैव मुख्यत्वम्। यज्ञकर्मणि वैयाकरणानां प्राधान्यदर्शनात्। तथा हि–

---

८०. °त्स्थादित्यादिति।
८१. तात्स्थात्ताछक्ष्यादितय°।
८२. °वा°।
८३. °त्स्थंस्त°।
८४. °ध्व°।
८५. °दा।
८६. धार्मस्यापि।
८७. °णा।
८८. °न्दसु°।
८९. °तिष्वि°।
९०. °ङ्गे°।
९१. °स्यां°।

नाञ्जसा[९२] निगदितं विभक्तिभि-
र्व्यक्तिभिश्च निखिलाभिरागमे[९३]।
तत्र कर्मसु विपर्यणीनम-
न्मन्त्रमूह[15] कुशलाः प्रयोगिणः॥ इति

(शिशु० १४, २३)

इत्थं च काव्यस्याप्युपदेशकत्वाच्छास्त्रत्वम्। अस्योपदेशकत्वं चोक्तमालङ्कारिकैः।

तथा हि–

काव्यं यशसेऽर्थकृते व्यवहारविदे शिवेतरक्षतये।
सद्यः परनिर्वृतये कान्तासम्मिततयोपदेशयुजे[९४]॥

(का० प्र० १, २)

इति। काव्यलक्षणं तू[९५]क्तं रसविलासे काव्यप्रकाशे च। इत्थं निरूपितः[९६] सपरिकरो रसरूपः काव्यस्यात्मा [इदानीं शरीरभूतस्य[९७] काव्यपदप्रतिपाद्यस्व[९८] रूपलक्ष्य[९९]तावच्छेदकाक्रान्तस्य (तस्य) लक्षणमुच्यते-**तददोषौ शब्दार्थौ सगुणावनलङ्कृती पुनः क्वापी[१००]ति** (का० प्र० १, ४अ)। निर्दोष[१०१] त्वादिविशेषणविशिष्टौ शब्दार्थौ काव्य[१०२]पदवाच्यौ (रसविलासः-सप्तमः स्तबकः)। अदोषावित्यत्रानुदरा कन्येतिवन्नञो[१०३] ऽल्पार्थत्वम्[१०४]। यावद्दो[१०५]-

---

९२. तांजग्ना।
९३. निखिलागमे।
९४. °ज्यत।
९५. सू°।
९६. °ता।
९७. °भूत°।
९८. °त्व°।
९९. °क्ष।
१००. °पि°।
१०१. °दो°।
१०२. °ष्ठा।
१०३. °यों°।
१०४. °त्व°।
१०५. °दोषा°।

षोत्सारणस्य दुःसाध्य[१०६]त्वात्। (रसविलासः-सप्तमः स्तबकः।) तस्य यावद्दोषाभावे का[१०७]व्यं दुष्टमिति व्यवहारो न स्यात्।]

काव्यस्य शास्त्रत्वे तादृक् प्रसिद्धिर्नास्तीति चेत् पुराणेऽपि समानम्।

इदं भागवतं नाम पुराणं ब्रह्मसम्मितमि (कौशिकसंहितीयं भागवत-माहात्म्यम् १, २, ७१) ति भागवतस्य पुराणतया[१०८] प्रसिद्धिसत्त्वेऽपि संक्षेपतो विस्तरतश्चेति द्वेधा चास्य श्रीभागवतस्य शास्त्रस्य प्रवृत्तिरिति श्रीधरस्वामिनोक्तमस्तीति तेन पुराणेऽपि तथा व्चवहारदर्शनात्तत्त्वमेवेति[१०९] भावः। अन्यथा याज्ञवल्क्योक्तेषु चतुर्दशसु तत्त्वतया केषाञ्चित्त्या[११०]गे केषाञ्चितस्वीकारेर्ध[१११] जरतीया[16] पत्तिः स्यात्।

किञ्च न्यायादिषट्सङ्ख्याकेष्वेव तत्त्वे तच्छास्त्राध्ययने ब्राह्मणा-नामेवाधिकारात्तेषां यथा शास्त्रित्वं तथा गजवशीकरणग्रन्थाध्ययनेनाघोरणस्य अपि शास्त्रित्वमस्तीति। अन्यथा–

निर्धूतवीतमपि बालकमुल्ललन्तं
यन्ता क्रमेण परिसान्त्वनतर्जनाभिः।
शिक्षावशेन शनकैर्वश[११२]मानिनाय
शास्त्रं हि[११३] निश्चितधियां क्व न सिद्धि[११४]मेती॥

(शिशु० ५, ४७)

त्यादौ सामान्येन विशेषसमर्थनरूपार्थान्तरन्यासालङ्कारो न स्यात्। गजवशीकरणग्रन्थस्याशास्त्रत्वे तत्पाठकस्याघोरणस्यापि तत्त्वाभावात् सामान्यत्वा-भावः।

---

१०६. °ध°।

१०७. को°।

१०८. °यां।

१०९. °पि।

११०. °त्या।

१११. °द्धर्जरति°।

११२. °शममानियाय।

११३. सु°।

११४. °धि°।

तथा सति--

'निर्विशेषं न सामान्यं विशेषा न तदुक्तितः[११५]।' इति न्यायात् सामान्येन विशेषसमर्थन[११६]मिति। विशेषार्थे वर्णनीये तेन सहाप्रस्तुतसामान्यरूपार्थान्तरारोपे[११७] अथवा सामान्यार्थे वर्णनीये तेन सहावर्णनीयार्थान्तरारोपे अर्थान्तरन्यास[११८] इति सिद्धान्तात्।

वस्तुतस्तु कोकगजवशीकरणग्रन्थादिषु[११९] शास्त्रमिव शास्त्रमिति गौण्या-वृत्त्या[१२०] तद्व्यवहारः। यथा शास्त्रमध्येतृ[१२१] णां फलदायकं तथा तत्तत्त्वपा[१२२] ठकानां तत्तत्फलदायकमिति बोध्यम्। एतेन वयमत्त्युत्तमाः शास्त्रिणः एते पौराणिकाः काव्यालङ्काररसनाटकाध्येतारश्च सामान्या इति वैधेयसमाजे गर्वेणेर्ष्य[१२३]या च स्वप्रौढिं नाटयन्तः प्रत्युक्ताः। किञ्च यत्कीर्तनाच्छुकमैत्रेयादयो यच्छ्रवणात्परीक्षि[१२४] द्विदुरादयश्च ब्रह्मपदवीं प्राप्तास्तद्विकत्थनं दोषावहमिति। तस्य वेदार्थत्वात्। उक्तञ्च–

कपिलादुग्धपानेन ब्राह्मणीगमनेन च।
वेदाक्षरविचारेण शूद्रश्चाण्डालतां व्रजेत्॥
न तस्माच्छुणुयाच्छुद्रो ज्ञात्वा वेदं कथञ्चन[१२५]।
तदर्थं च पुराणेषु श्रुणुयान्मुनिभिः स्मृतमिति॥

(quoted in रसविलास)

एवं च–

पौराणीं वृत्तिमाश्रित्य ये जीवन्ति द्विजातयः[१२६]।

---

११५. °दुरिता।
११६. °र्थंन°।
११७. °रोवा।
११८. °अर्थांन्यास।
११९. दिाशु।
१२०. °त्या।
१२१. °तृ°।
१२२. तत्पा°।
१२३. °र्ष°।
१२४. °रिक्षि°।
१२५. कथं न च।
१२६. °यतः।

ते सूर्यमण्डलं भित्त्वा[१२७] **यान्ति ब्रह्म सनातनमिति** स्मृत्या पुराणानुवाचनात्पौराणिकानामिव पदार्थज्ञानान्नै[१२८] यायिकानामिव शब्दार्थज्ञाना[१२९] द्वैयाकरणानां मोक्षो भवतीति। तथा च श्रुतिः–

एकः शब्दः सुष्ठुप्रयुक्तः सम्यग्ज्ञा[१३०]**तः स्वर्गेलोके कामधुग्भ**[१३१]**वती** (महाभाष्य-प्रदीप-पस्पशाह्निक) ति। शब्दानां ब्रह्मरूपत्वात्। उक्तञ्च–

द्वे ब्रह्मणी वेदितव्ये शब्दब्रह्म परं च यत्।
शब्दब्रह्मणि निष्णा[१३२]**तः परं ब्रह्माधिगच्छतीति॥**

(मैत्रायण्युपनिषत्, ६, २२)

स्मृतिः।

स्फोटसत्त्वे[१३३] प्रमाणमपि प्रसङ्गाद्दर्शितम्। वैयाकरणानां स्फोटो ध्व[१३४]निश्चेति द्विविधः शब्दः। यस्मादर्थः स्फुटीभवति स स्फोटः। यस्मात् स्फोटः स्फुटीभवति स ध्वनिर्लिपिवत्स्फोटानुस्मारकः।

ननु पूर्वपूर्ववर्णव्याहारजन्यसंस्कारसहकृतेन चरमवर्णेनार्थः स्फुटीभविष्यति किं

स्फोटकल्पनयेति। चेत्।

(न।) तयोरुभयोरपि संकेताभावाद[१३५] र्धजरतीयापत्तेः। स्फोटो यदि न स्यात्तर्हि स एवायं मन्त्र इति प्रत्य[१३६] भिज्ञापि न स्यात्। न चेयं प्रत्यभिज्ञा[17]

---

१२७. °त्वा।
१२८. °नांनै°।
१२९. °नां°।
१३०. °क्जा°।
१३१. °धुद्भ°।
१३२. °ष्ठा°।
१३३. °त्वे।
१३४. °स्फोटोर्ध्व°।
१३५. °भादार्ध°।
१३६. °ज्ञ°।

स[१३७] जात्यालम्बनौषधवदिति वाच्यम्। कृतपुरश्चरणवदन्यमन्त्रस्य फलवत्त्वा[१३८]-पत्तेः, स्फोटं विना पुरश्चरणजन्यसिद्धेर्निर्विष[१३९] यतापत्तेश्च। किञ्च मंत्रमूर्त्तीनां देवानां विनाशित्वं प्रसज्येत।

तस्मात्स्फोटकल्पना समञ्जसैव। यदि शब्दे न[१४०]ष्टे तत्संस्कारस्यार्थ-वत्त्वं[१४१] स्यात्तदा घटे नष्टे तदनुभवजन्यसंस्कारस्य तदीयध्वंसस्य वा ज[१४२]लाहरणयोग्यता दुर्वारैव। अन्यच्च पूर्वसंस्कारान्त्य[१४३]वर्णयोराश्रय[१४४] योर्भेदादेककार्यकारित्वासंभवः।

ननु संकेताभावेऽर्थिव्यक्तिर्न स्यादिति चेद्वर्णस्फोटो न सिध्येदिति चेत्।

राम इत्यादौ भवती[१४५]त्यादौ च पर्यायेणैकैकवर्णविपर्यये बोधविपर्यया-दन्वयव्यतिरेकाभ्यां वर्णानामपि वाचक[१४६]त्वाद्वर्णस्फोटसिद्धिः। सरो रस इत्यादौ वर्णानुपूर्व्य[१४७]वच्छिन्नपदस्य संकेतगोचरत्वात्पदस्फोटसिद्धिः। केवलात् पदात्प्रवृत्तिनिवृत्तिरूपव्यवहा[१४८] रानुत्पत्तेर्वा[१४९] क्यस्फोटसिद्धिः। वर्णस्फोटानङ्गी-कारे बीजानां देवतावाचकत्वं न सिध्येत्।

ननु स्फोटः कः पदार्थ इति। वर्णानां प्रध्वंसाभावः स्फोट इति चेत्।

(न।) अभावस्य भावकार्यकारित्वासंभवात्। तस्माच्छब्दब्रह्माख्यः स्फोटो

---

१३७. सा°।
१३८. °त्वा°।
१३९. °विं°।
१४०. त°।
१४१. °त्वं।
१४२. जं°।
१४३. °त्य।
१४४. °श्रंयोयभे°।
१४५. °ती°।
१४६. °कर्णत्वा°।
१४७. °र्व।
१४८. °व्यहार°।
१४९. °वा।

भावपदार्थः। यद्यपि वर्णव्यक्तिस्फोटः, सखण्डपदव्यक्तिस्फोटः, अखण्डपदव्यक्तिस्फोटः, (सखण्डवाक्यव्यक्तिस्फोटः), अखण्डवाक्यव्यक्तिस्फोटः, अखण्डवर्णजातिस्फोटः, अखण्डपदजातिस्फोटः, अखण्डवाक्यजातिस्फोट इत्यष्टौ स्फोटपक्षाः सिद्धान्तग्रन्थेषूक्ता[१५०] स्तथापि वाक्यस्फोटे तात्पर्यम्। तत्रापि जातिस्फोटे इति। इत्थं च ध्वनिव्यङ्ग्यत्वे सति संकेता[१५१]र्थबोधकत्वं स्फोटस्य लक्षण[१५२]मिति।

प्रकृतमनुसरा[१५३]मः।

किञ्च शास्त्रशब्दस्यानेकार्थित्वाद्योगरूढ्या स[१५४]मकालं सर्वेऽर्थाः प्रतिपाद्यन्ते क्वचिदिति[१५५] विप्रतिपत्तिः। तत्रैककालावच्छेदेन सर्वार्थबोधनं तु न भवति। सकृदुच्चरितः शब्दः सकृदर्थं गमयतीति न्यायात्। यथा सकृत्प्रयुक्तः शरः सकृल्लक्ष्यं[१५६] भिनत्तीति तद्वदित्यर्थः। यथाने[१५७]काश्वस्य राज्ञो न युगपत् सर्वाश्वारोहणं किन्तु पर्यायेण तद्वित्यर्थः।

आलङ्कारिकास्तु[१५८] सकृ[१५९]दुच्चरित इत्यस्यानित्यत्वमाश्रित्य नानार्थेषु यत्र यत्र तात्पर्यग्रहणं प्रक[१६०]रणादिकं युगपदवतरितं[१६१] तत्र श्ले[१६२]षालङ्कारः। यत्र क्रमेण तात्पर्यं[१६३] तत्रावृत्तिरिति। इत्थं च सर्वत्र तात्पर्यग्राहकं[१६४] प्रकरणादिकमेव। उक्तं च काव्यप्रकाशे–

---

१५०. °क्तां°।

१५१. °त°।

१५२. °णा°।

१५३. °रसा°।

१५४. °सां°।

१५५. कश्चिद्देति।

१५६. °क्षं°।

१५७. °से°।

१५८. °स्तां।

१५९. °त्त°।

१६०. °का°।

१६१. °तरि°।

१६२. शे°।

१६३. °र्यं°।

१६४. °णं°।

अनेकार्थस्य शब्दस्य वाचकत्वे[१६५] नियन्त्रिते।
संयोगाद्यैरवाच्यार्थधीकृद्व्यापृतिरञ्जन[१६६]म्।

(का० प्र० २, १९)

संयोगो विप्रयोगश्च साहचर्यं विरोधिता।
अर्थः प्रक[१६७]रणं लिङ्गं शब्दस्यान्यस्य सन्निधिः॥
साम[१६८]र्थ्यमौचिती देशः कालो व्यक्तिः स्वरादयः।
शब्दार्थस्यानवच्छेदे विशेषस्मृतिहेतवः॥

(वा० प० २, ३१५, ३१६)

इति। अनेकार्थस्य शब्दस्य कतमोऽर्थोऽत्र विवक्षित इति सन्देहे प्राप्ते सति विशेषः प्रकृतार्थस्तस्य स्मृतिकारणानि संयोगादी[१६९]नीत्यर्थः। संयोगादीनामुदाहरणानि तु विस्तरभिया नोच्यते।

प्रकरणोदाहरणं तु-'सर्वगुणवान् सर्वं जानाति देव' इति राजानां प्रति दूतवचनम्। देवशब्दस्यानेकार्थत्वं तु '**राजा भट्टारको देव**' (अमर० १, ७, १३) इति कोशात्।

ननु सर्वगुणवानित्यत्र न कर्मधारया[१७०] न्मत्वर्थीयो, बहुव्रीहिश्चेदर्थप्रत्यायक इति निषेधात्।

सर्वे गुणा यस्य सर्वगुण इति बहुव्रीहिणैवार्थनिर्वाहे किमर्थ कर्मधारयान्मत्वर्थीन (य) प्रत्ययेन वृत्तिद्वयकल्प[१७१]नगौरवमि[१७२]ति पूर्वपक्षः।

अत्रोच्यते-कृष्णसारङ्ग इत्यत्र **वर्णो वर्णेनेति**[18] (पा० अ० २, १,

---

१६५. °त्वे।
१६६. °रं।
१६७. °का°।
१६८. °मे°।
१६९. °दिनी°।
१७०. याम°।
१७१. °ल्पे°।
१७२. °भि°।

६९) सूत्रेण कृष्णेन सारङ्गः कृष्णसारङ्ग इति यद्वा कृष्णः सारङ्गः कृष्णसारङ्ग इति। कश्चात्र विशेष इति प्रसङ्गाद्बहुव्रीहिकर्मधारयोः प्राप्तौ निर्णयमाह भाष्यकारः। अत्र–

समानाधिकरण[१७३]समासाद्बहुव्रीहिर्भवति विप्रतिषेधेन[19]।

(पा० म० भा० पा० अ० २, १, ६८ वा० ४)

क[१७४]दाचित्कर्म[१७५]धारयः सर्वधनाद्यर्थः।

(पा० म० भा० पा० अ० २, १, ६८ वा० ५) इति।

अत्र यद्यपि विप्रतिषेधेन वृत्तिद्वयकल्पनगौरवनिरासार्थं बहुव्रीहेः प्राप्तिः[१७६]।

सर्वश्चायमेवमर्थो[१७७] यत्नः कर्मधारयप्रकृतिभिर्मत्वर्थीये निषेधश्चास्ति। (पा० म० भा० पा० अ०, २, १, ६८ वा० ५) वृत्तिद्वयकल्पनगौरवनिरासा[१७८]र्थं मत्वर्थीयप्रत्यय[१७९]स्य सर्वथा निषेधेऽपि **किञ्चिदाचार्याः कार्यबुद्धिं कृत्वा पठन्ति।**

अस्ति चात्र विशेषः।

मत्वर्थीयप्रत्ययैर्भूमनिन्दादयः[20] सप्तार्थनिर्देशा बहुव्रीहिणा न ज्ञायन्ते। तस्मात्फलमुखं गौरवं न दोषायेति सि[१८०]द्धान्तात् वृत्तिद्वयकल्पनगौरवम[१८१]प्यङ्गीकृतमिति। एवं सति सर्वधनी, सर्वबीजी, सर्वकेशी, गाढानुरागी, एकदेशी, गौरखरवदरण्यम्, कृष्णसर्पवान् व[१८२]ल्मीकः, लोहितशालिमान् ग्रामः, नीलरूपवत् पुरी[१८३]षम् (सरोजम्?) हंसचिह्नदुकूलवानित्यादिप्रयोगाणां

---

१७३. °णे°।

१७४. कु°।

१७५. °म°।

१७६ °तिः।

१७७. °र्थ।

१७८. °गौरवार्थं।

१७९. °त्यस्य।

१८०. रा°।

१८१. °मं°।

१८२. वा°।

१८३. परो°।

भूमनिन्दाविशेषार्थप्रतीत्यर्थ मत्वर्थीय एव न्याय्यः। किम् बहुव्रीहेः प्रयोजनम्। किञ्च–

विप्रतिषेधे परमि (पा० अ० १, ४, २) त्यत्रेष्ट[१८४]वाची परशब्दः। **विप्रतिषेधे परं यदिष्टं** (तद्) **भवतीति** (पा० म० भा० पा० अ० १, २, ३ वा० ६) व्याख्यानादिष्टत्वाभावान्न बहुव्रीहिरिति।

केचित्तु कृष्णसर्पवान् व[१८५]ल्मीक (पा० म० भा० पा० अ० २, १, ६८ वा० ५) इति भाष्यवचन ज्ञापका[21]न्मत्वर्थीयोऽस्तीति वदन्ति तन्मतं चारुतरं[१८६] भाति इति।

न ह्येकेन ज्ञापकेननिखिलप्रयोगाणां निष्पत्तिः किन्तु अगतिकस्य[१८७] कस्यचित्प्रयोगस्य। **ज्ञापकसिद्धं न सर्वत्रे**[22] (परि० शे० पृ० १२६) ति निषेधात्। न हि सार्वत्रिकाणां[१८८] प्रयोगाणां ज्ञापकेन प्रामादिकत्वेन[23] वा समाधानम्। किन्तु क्वाचित्कस्यैव। इत्थं च–

सुभ्रूशब्दस्य **नेयङुव[१८९]ङ्स्थानावस्त्री**[24] (पा० अ० १, ४, ४) ति नदी[25] संज्ञाप्रतिषेधा**दम्बार्थनद्योर्ह्रस्व**[26] (पा० अ० ७, ३, १०७) इति सम्बु[१९०]द्धौ[27] ह्रस्वत्वं नास्ति। तेन ह्रस्वप्रयोगः प्रा[१९१]मादिक इति। तेनः–

हा पितः क्वासि हे सुभ्रु (भट्टि० ६, ११) इ[१९२]ति भट्टिप्रयोगसमाधानं कैश्चि[१९३]त्कृतमस्ति न तत्समञ्जसम्। सुभ्रूशब्दस्य सम्बुद्धौ ह्रस्वान्तस्यैव सर्वत्र प्रयोगदर्शनम्, न तु दीर्घान्तस्य कुत्रापी[१९४]ति प्रा[१९५]मादिकः प्रयोगः क्वाचित्को भवति विश्वजनीनः। बहुप्रयोगदर्शनं तु–

---

१८४. °ष्ठ°।

१८५. वा°।

१८६. °तो°।

१८७. °गस्या।

१८८. °त्रिणां।

१८९. °य°।

१९०. °म्बुद्यौ।

१९१. °प्र°।

१९२. रि°।

१९३. श्चिकृ°।

१९४. °पि°।

१९५. °प्र°।

वयं कलादा इव दुर्विदग्धं
त्वद्गौरिमस्पर्धि[१९६] दहेम हेम।
प्रसूननाराचशरासनस्य
सहैकवंशप्रभवभ्रु बभ्रु॥

(नै० म० ८, ९९)

इति नैषधे।

सुभ्रु त्वं कुपितेत्यपास्तमशनं त्याक्ताः कथा योषितामिति (चौरपञ्चाशिका-बिल्हणचरित ७६) रसविलासे (?)। काव्यप्रकाशे (?) च–

राजभ्यो बिभ्यतः सुभ्रु समुद्रं शरणं गताः।

(श्री०भा०पु० १०, ६०, १२)

इति। तथा–

आस्थिताः पदवीं सुभ्रु प्रायः सीदन्ति योषितः।

(श्री०भा०पु० १०, १६, १३)

इति श्रीमद्भागवते।

विमानना सुभ्रु कुतः पितुर्गृहे (कुमार० ५, ४३) इति
कुमारसम्भवे कालिदासप्रयोगश्चेति।

अत्र

सुभ्रूः कुतस्तातगृहेऽवमाननेति

पाठान्तरं विधाय शब्दान्तर[28]त्वमापाद्य[१९७] कश्चित्समाधानं करोति स देवप्रिय एव मूर्ख इति यावत्। वंशस्थवृत्ते पादादौ जगणभङ्गप्रसङ्गात्। वंशस्थलक्षणं तूक्तं वृत्तरत्नाकरे–

जतौ तु वंशस्थमुदीरि[१९८]तं जराविति। (वृत्तरत्नाकर, ३, १३२)

---

१९६. °स्पर्द्धि°।

१९७. °द°।

१९८. °र°।

वस्तुतः समाधानं तु–

अप्राणिजातेश्चारज्ज्वा[१९९]**दीनामि** (पा०अ० ४, १, ६६, वा० १)[29] **त्यत्र** अलाबूः कर्कन्धूरित्यूकारादप्यूङ्प्रत्ययमुदाजहार भाष्यकारः। यथाह वामनः[30]–

ऊकारान्तादप्यूङ्प्रवृत्ते[२००]**रिति।** (काव्यालङ्कारसूत्रवृत्ति, ५, २, ४८)

तेन सुभ्रूशब्दस्याप्यूङ्प्रत्ययान्तत्वं विधाय शब्दान्तरत्वमापादनीयम्। यद्वा–

ऊ[२०१]**ङुत** (पा०अ० ४, १, ६६) इति सूत्रे ऊङ्इति योगो विभज्यते। तत्र चार्थवशान्मण्डूकप्लुत्या[31] बहुव्रीहेरित्यनुवर्तनीयम्। तेन क्वचित् बहुव्रीहेरूङ्स्यादित्यर्थे सिद्धे सुभ्रूशब्दस्योङ्प्रत्ययान्तत्वेन शब्दान्तरत्वान्नदीसंज्ञासद्भावे[२०२] **अम्बार्थनद्योर्ह्र**[२०३]**स्व** (पा०अ० ७, ३, १०७) इति ह्रस्वत्वम्।

तेन हे सुभ्रु इत्य[२०४]विरुद्धमेव।

बहुव्रीहेरननुवृत्तिपक्षेऽपि क्वचिदित्यर्थो[२०५] लभ्यते[२०६] तेन अलाबूः कर्कन्धूरनयोरप्यूङ्प्रत्ययः साधुरेव। एतदुदाहरणद्वये दीर्घादप्यूङ्प्रत्ययं कुर्वता भाष्यकारेणायं योगविभागो[32] ज्ञा[२०७]प्यते। उत इति तपरकरण[33]स्यातन्त्रत्वं[34] वा अप्राणिजातेरित्यादिवार्त्ति[२०८] के ह्रस्वोकाराननुवृत्तिर्वा **चकारोऽनुक्त**[35]-**समुच्चयार्थ** इति वा। तेन दीर्घोदाहरणज्ञापितेन योगविभागेनैवास्योङ्प्रत्ययान्तत्वं सुवचमिति शब्दान्तरत्वे नदीसंज्ञासद्भावात्सम्बुद्धौ ह्रस्वो भवत्येवेति सङ्क्षेपः।

---

१९९. °ज्वा°।

२००. °त्ति°।

२०१. °उ°।

२०२. °वै।

२०३. °ह्र°।

२०४. °त्या°।

२०५. °र्थ।

२०६. भ्यंतेन।

२०७. ज्ञो.।

२०८. °र्ति°।

भवत्येवे[२०९]ति प्रसंङ्गादेवकारार्थोऽपि निरूप्यते। एवकारार्थस्त्रिधा भवति। एक: क्रियासङ्गत: द्वितीयो विशेषणसङ्गत: तृतीयो विशेष्यसङ्गत: इति। तत्र क्रियासङ्गतस्यैवकारस्यात्यन्तयोगव्यवच्छेदोऽर्थ: यथा नीलं सरोजं भवत्येव। विशेषणसङ्गतस्यायोगव्यवच्छेदोऽर्थ:। यथा शङ्ख: पाण्डु[२१०]र एवेति। विशेष्य-सङ्गतस्यान्ययोगव्यवच्छेदोऽर्थ:। यथा पार्थ एव धनुर्धर इतिं तेनानेकार्थत्वमस्य बोध्यम्। एवं सति–

अस्यैव भार्या भवितुं रुक्मिण्यर्हति नापरा।
असावप्यनवद्यात्मा भैष्म्या: समुचित: पति॥

(श्री०भा०पु० १०, ५३, ३७)

रित्यत्रा[२११]नेकार्थस्याप्येकस्यैवकारस्य अस्यैव रुक्मिण्येव अर्ह[२१२]त्येवेति पूर्वार्द्धेऽवधारण[36]त्रयम्। असावेव भैष्म्या एव समुचितो भवत्येवेत्यवधारण-त्रयमुत्तरार्द्धे इति कथं युगपत् षड्भि: सहान्वयेन षडवधारणानीति चेच्छ्र[२१३]व्यम्।

अत्र श्रीधरस्वामिनोऽयमाशय:। अस्येति पदसमभिव्या[37]हृतैवकार: पर्यायेणान्वेति। न तु युगप[२१४]दिति। सकृदुच्चरित: शब्द: सकृदर्थं बोधयति सकृदेवान्वेति चेति न्यायात्। हर्यादिशब्दानामनेकार्थत्वेऽपि संयोगाद्यैर्वाचकत्व-नियन्त्रणात्पर्यायेणार्थबोधकत्वम्। न ह्यनेकाश्वाधिपतेर्युगपत् सर्वाश्वारोहणं किं[२१५]त्वनुक्रमेणेति त्रिस्वामिन एकाश्वस्य वा। न हि युगपत्त्र[२१६]याणामारोहणमिति वा।

इत्थं च यद्यपि सर्वत्रायोगव्यवच्छेदार्थकोऽन्ययोगव्यवच्छेदार्थकोऽ-त्यन्तायोगव्यवच्छेदार्थक इति अर्थत्रयवाच्य[२१७] एवकारो भवति तथाप्यत्र तु

२०९. °वै°।
२१०. पीठु°।
२११. °त्र°।
२१२. °ह°।
२१३. छ्रू°।
२१४. °पे°।
२१५. क्रि°।
२१६. पत्र°।
२१७. °च्यैव°।

अन्ययोगव्यवच्छेदार्थक एक एवैवकारः पर्यायेण षड्भिः षोढान्वेति। युगपदुल्लेखः न तु (ननु) अन्वययोग्यतासूचनार्थमिति। रुक्मिणी अस्यैव कृष्णस्यैव भार्या भवितुमर्हति नान्यस्येत्यर्थः लभ्यः तेन श्रीकृष्णादन्यस्य चे[२१८]द्यादेरेवकारेण व्यवच्छेदो बोध्यः। कुत इत्यपेक्षायामाह–नापरेति इयं अपरा न भवति किन्तु

'राघवत्वेऽभव[२१९]त्सीता रुक्मिणी कृष्णजन्मनी (विष्णुपुराण १, ९, १४४)'ति पुराणवचनात् या पूर्वजन्मनि[२२०] सीता सैव रुक्मिणी नान्ये[२२१]ति सुज्ञानामयमाशयः। यद्वा नास्ति अपरः श्रीकृष्णादन्यो वरणीयत्वेन यस्या इति। स्वस्य (यं) श्रीकृष्णासाधारणगुणरवणात्। यद्वा नास्ति आस[२२२] मन्तात् परा उत्कृष्टा यस्याः सकाशादिति। किञ्चास्य श्रीकृष्णस्य रुक्मिण्येव भार्या भवितुमर्हति नापरे[२२३]ति। रुक्मिणीपदसमभिव्या[२२४]हृतैवकारेणान्यकान्तायोग-व्यवच्छेदः। यद्यपि सत्यभामादीना[२२५] योग्यतास्ति तथापि पौरजनानां भविष्य-ज्ञानाभावान्न तादृक् वितर्कः[२२६]।

पूर्वव्याख्याने तु अस्ये[२२७]ति पदसम[२२८]भिव्याहृतैवकारेणान्ययोगव्यव-च्छेदादार्थमवधारणमत्र तु शब्दमिति भेदः।

किञ्च रुक्मिणी अस्य भार्याभवितुं यद्वा अभार्या भार्या[२२९] तथा संपद्यमाना भवितुमिति च्विप्रत्यये[38] समस्तं पदम्। अर्ह[२३०]त्येवेति क्रियापद-

२१८. चै°।
२१९. °वे°।
२२०. °नी।
२२१. न्याये°।
२२२. °सं°।
२२३. °दे°।
२२४. °व्या°।
२२५. °नी।
२२६. °कर्त:।
२२७. °स्यै°।
२२८. समपद°।
२२९. या°।
२३०. °र्ह°।

समभिव्या[२३१]हृतैवकारेणयोग्यताया अत्यन्ताभावव्यवच्छेदात् योग्यतावधारणमिति त्रिधा व्याख्यानेन भैष्म्याः सकलगुणसंपन्नत्वं पूर्वार्द्धेन व्यज्यते। अथोत्तरार्द्ध-व्याख्या। अपिश्चार्थे च। परं अनवद्यात्मा स्तुत्यविग्रहः स्तुत्यस्वभावो वा।

आत्मा देहे धृतौ जीवे स्वभावे परमात्मनी (अमर० ३, ३, १०९ रामाश्रमीटीका) **त्यमरः**[२३२]। असावेव भैष्म्याः पतिर्वरः सम्यगुचितः समुचितः योग्योऽस्तीत्यर्थः। सकलगुणसंपन्नत्वेन स्पृहणीय[२३३]गुणत्वादित्यर्थः। उक्तञ्च–

कन्या वरयते रूपं माता वित्तं पिता श्रुतम्।
बान्धवाः कुलमिच्छन्ति मिष्टान्नमितरे जनाः॥

(सु.र.भा. श्लो० ४०१, पृ. ३८७)

इति। किञ्च भैष्म्या एव अनवद्यात्मासौ पतिः समुचितोऽस्ति[२३४] समीचीनसप्तवरगुणसंपन्नत्वाच्छस्त्रशास्त्रप्रवीणत्वाच्चेत्यर्थः। उक्तञ्च–

कुलं च शीलं च सनाथता च
विद्या च वित्तं[२३५] च वपुर्वयश्च।
एते गुणा यत्र वरे भवेयुः
समीक्ष्य देया जनकेन[२३६] पुत्रीति॥

(सुभाषितार्णवः ५, ६, पृ० २८५६)

अथ च-असौ भैष्म्याः पतिः समुचित एव नानुचितोऽस्ति। अत्रापि त्रिधा व्याख्याने एवकारेणान्ययोगव्यवच्छेदादवधारणत्रयं पूर्ववत् ज्ञेयम्। एवं च पूर्वार्द्धेऽवधारणत्रयं तथोत्तरार्द्धे त्रयमिति षडव[२३७]धारणानि इति।

ननु पूर्वार्द्धे[२३८] षष्ठ्यन्तपदेन प्रथमान्तपदेन च विवक्षितेऽर्थे सिद्धे

---

२३१. °व्या°।
२३२. °नित्परमः।
२३३. °णीगु°।
२३४. ति।
२३५. °त्ता।
२३६. जकेन।
२३७. °ड्व°।
२३८. °र्धे।

पुनर्विभक्तिव्यत्यासेणोत्तरार्द्धेऽपि तदेव कथनं पुनरुक्तिदो[२३९]षग्रस्तमिति चेत्।

पूर्वार्द्धे नास्ति आसमन्तात् परा उत्कृष्टेति व्याख्यानाद्रुक्मिण्युत्कर्ष-प्रतीतिः[२४०]। उत्तरार्द्धे तु अनवद्यात्मेति विशेषणात् श्रीकृष्णोत्कर्षाभिच्यक्तिरिति। इत्थं च परस्परगुणोत्कर्षाभिव्यक्तिर्वाक्यद्वयेनैवात्रास्तीति तस्मादनयोः परस्परं श्लाध्यसम्बन्धयोग्यतादृढीकरणार्थं वाक्यद्वयनिबन्धनमिति[२४१] दिक्।

एवकारस्य चादिगणा[39]न्तर्वर्तित्वेन निपात[40]त्वादस्य द्योतकत्वं वाचकत्वं वेति विचार्यते।

प्रादयो द्योतकाश्चादयो वाचका इति नैयायिकमतम्। यदागमे हि यो दृश्यते स तस्यार्थ इति न्यायान्निपातानां वाचकत्वमिति नैयायिकोक्तं नादरणीयम्। एतयोर्वैषम्ये मानाभावात्। तस्मान्निपातानां द्योतकत्वमेव समञ्जस-मिति वैयाकरणाः।

तार्किकमते तु निपातानां वाचकत्वे काव्यादा(वाक्यादा)वन्वयो न स्यादेव, वैयाकरणमते तु अन्वय एव नास्ति द्योतकत्वादिति न कश्चिद्दोषः।

'वागर्थाविव संपृक्तौ[२४२].............पार्वतीपरमेश्वरावहं वन्दे' इत्यत्र वागर्थयोर्वदिकर्मत्वाभावात्तदुत्तरद्वितीयाया अन्वयो न स्यादेव*। इवार्थस्य कर्मत्वान्वयबोधकासंभवश्चेति (वै० भू० सार० पृ० १४४) **स्पष्टं भूषणे**[41]।

यद्वा वेयाकरणानामालङ्कारिकाणां च द्योतकत्वपक्षे नाग्रहस्तेन[२४३]

स वाचको विशेषाणां संभवाद्द्योतकोऽपि वेति (वा० प० २, १८८) वाक्यपदीयवचनं[२४४] सङ्गतमेव।

निपाताश्चोपसर्गाश्च धातवश्चेति ते त्रयः।
अनेकार्थाः स्मृताः सर्वे पाठस्तेषां निदर्शनमिति वचनात्।

---

* अनन्वय : इति पाठः भूषणे।

२३९. दौ°।

२४०. °तेः।

२४१. °मिदि°।

२४२. °पत्तौ।

२४३. °हस्ते।

२४४. पदीयपदीयं वचनं।

निश्चयेन पतन्त्यनेकेष्वर्थेष्विति व्युत्पत्त्या[२४५] च निपातानामनेकार्थत्वादिति।

यत्तु भूषणे वागर्थयोर्वदिकर्मत्वाभावा[२४६]त्तदुत्तरद्वितीयाया अन्वयो न स्यादित्युक्तं न तत्समञ्जसम्। वदतोव्याघातात्। कर्मत्वाभावे द्वितीयाया अप्यभावात्केन[२४७] सूत्रेण द्वितीयाविधानमिति पूर्वपक्षः।

वस्तुतस्त्वत्र द्वितीयैव भवितुं[२४८] नार्हति किन्तु प्रथमै[२४९]वेति। तथा हि–

वागर्थाविवेत्यत्रेवशब्दस्य सादृश्यवाचकत्वं केन प्रकारेणात्र विवक्षित[२५०]-मिति चेदुच्यते।

वागर्थाविव वाग[२५१]र्थौ यथा नित्यसम्बन्धे[२५२]न संपृक्तौ संश्लेष्यैकीभूतौ। नित्यः शब्दार्थसम्बन्ध इति मीमांसकोक्तेः। तथा तेन प्रकारेण संपृक्तौ पार्वतीपरमेश्वरौ इत्यन्वयः। संपृचाते तौ[२५३] संपृक्ताविति[२५४] कर्तरि क्तप्रत्ययः[42]। कर्तुः कृता चोक्तत्वात् प्रथमैव न द्वितीयेति सुधिया[२५५] सूक्ष्मया दृशावधातव्य-मित्यालङ्कारिकाः।

किञ्च शब्दार्थयोर्बोध्यबोधकभावलक्षणः सम्बन्धो वृत्तिः। सा च शब्दनिष्ठा[२५६] अर्थविषया चेत्युभयधर्मा[२५७]। शक्तिलक्षणाव्यञ्जनाभेदात्त्रि[२५८]धा सेत्याहुः।

---

२४५. °त्या।

२४६. °कर्मत्वात्त°।

२४७. °क्तेन।

२४८. °यैभववितुं।

२४९. °मे°।

२५०. °ता°।

२५१. °गा°।

२५२. °ध°।

२५३. नौ।

२५४. °व्यति।

२५५. °ता।

२५६. °ष्ठा।

२५७. °र्मः।

२५८. त्रि।

तत्र चास्मात्पदादयमर्थो बोद्धव्य इति प्रवर्तकोपदेशः सङ्केतः। स एव शक्तिरिति तार्किकाः। तदतिरिक्ता तत्सहाया चेत्यालङ्कारिकाः। सर्वशब्दानां ग्राह्यत्वग्राहकत्वरूपे द्वे शक्ती। योगो इति वैयाकरणाः। वृत्तिविषयाभूता अर्थास्तथा च शब्दा अपि त्रिविधाः। तत्राद्यः शक्यो द्वितीयो लाक्षणिकस्तृतीयो व्यञ्जकश्चेति। वृत्तित्रयमध्ये सङ्केतसहकारिणी शक्तिः। सा च शक्तिस्त्रिधा। योगो रूढिर्यो[२५९] गरूढिश्चेति। जातिगुणक्रियायदृच्छेति तु प्रवृत्तिनिमित्ता[43]नि। एवं सति वागर्थाविवेति[२६०]प्रथमो यवया इवेति च द्वितीयस्त**योरिवेन विभक्त्यलोपः पूर्वपदप्रकृतिस्वरत्वं[44] चेति** (पा० अ० २, १, ४, वा० १) वक्तव्यमिति वार्त्ति[२६१]केन समासे सति या शक्तिः संपद्यते सा समस्तशब्दनिष्ठा योगशक्तिः।

ननु समासे खलु भिन्नैव शक्तिः पङ्कजशब्दवत्।

बहूनां वृत्तिधर्माणां वचनैरेव[२६२] साधने।
स्यान्महद्गौरवं तस्मादेकार्थीभाव[45] आश्रितः॥

(वै० सि० का० ३१)

इति सिद्धान्तादत्र अवयवविभागकल्पनाभावाद्योगशक्तिर्न स्यादिति वाच्यम्। जहत्स्वार्थावृत्तिपक्षे[46] विभागानङ्गीकारेऽपि अजहत्स्वा[२६३]र्थावृत्तिपक्षस्यापि व्यवहारोपयोगेन स्वीकारात्।

उद्बाहुरिवे (रघु० १, १३) त्यत्र तु इवशब्दस्य विशेष्यवामनपदेन सहान्वयस्य विवक्षा। (उ)द्बाहुशब्देन[२६४] साम[२६५]र्थ्या[47]भावान्न समासः।

ननु किमत्र समासप्रयोजनम्। सति समासेऽपि विशेषाभावादिति चेत्।

अभिन्नक्रमत्वं स्वरविपर्यासो नित्यसमासत्वं च समासप्रयोजनमिति हेतोरिति।

---

२५९. °र्या।

२६०. °र्थाविति।

२६१. °र्ति°।

२६२. °नेनैव।

२६३. °जहस्वा°।

२६४. °स्यन्विवक्षाशब्दाब्दाहुशब्देन।

२६५. °मा°।

किञ्च तार्किकाणां[२६६]म[२६७]ते तु शक्तं पदं चतुर्धा। रूढम्। यौगिकम्। योगरूढम्। यौगिकरूढम् चेति। गौः। पाच[२६८]कः। पङ्कजम्। उद्भिदि[२६९]ति। तत्र पाचक इति यौगिकोदाहरणे यत् शक्तं पदं पच अक इति न तद्यौगिकम्। समुदायस्तु यद्यपि यौगिकस्तथापि न शक्तइति। एवं च शक्तं पदं क्वचिद्यौगिकमित्यविचारिताभिधानम्। एवं रूढ्युदाहरणमप्यसङ्गतम्। गच्छतीति गौरिति व्युत्पत्तेरिति। अत्र समाधानं तु तदधीन[२७०]मित्यवधेयम्। किञ्च[२७१] सा[२७२]त्वतशब्दो[२७३]ऽपि द्विविधः। अकारान्तो हलन्तश्च। आद्यो डित्थादिवत्संज्ञा शब्दो यादवकुलजविशेषे रूढः।

'कञ्चि[२७४]त्सुखं सात्वतवृष्णि[२७५]भोजदाशार्हकाणामधिपः स आस्ते।' (श्री०भा०पु० ३, १, २९) इति। सात्वतादीनामधिपो राजा उग्रसेन इति श्रीमद्भागवते तथा वर्णनात्। द्वितीयस्तु पङ्कजादिशब्दवद्भक्तोपासक-विशेषेषु योगरूढः।

'नमो नमस्तेऽस्त्वृषभाय सात्वतामि' (श्री० भा० पु० २, ४, १४) त्यत्र सात्वतां ऋषभाय पालकायेत्यर्थः।

'अपि स्विदास्ते भगवान् सुखं वो यःसात्वतां कामदुधोऽनिरुद्ध' (श्री०भा०पु० ३, १, ३४) इत्यत्र सात्वतामुपासकानां भक्तानां वा कामान् दोग्धि पूरयतीति कामदुघो मनोरथपूरक इत्यर्थः। योगश्च। सत्त्व[२७६]स्य चित्ता[२७७]-

२६६. °णा।
२६७. मं°।
२६८. °व°।
२६९. °दादि°।
२७०. °धीममि°।
२७१. त।
२७२. शा°।
२७३. °ष्टो°।
२७४. °च्चि°।
२७५. °ष्टि°।
२७६. °त्व°।
२७७. °ता°।

हङ्कारबुद्धिमनोरूपस्य चतुर्विध[२७८]स्यान्तःकरण[२७९]स्य समूहः सात्वम्। तदधिष्ठानमस्त्ये[२८०]षामिति सात्वाः। क्रमेण वासुदेवसंकर्षणप्रद्युम्नानिरुद्धाख्याश्चत्वारः तदधिष्ठातृदेवास्तानतन्ति नित्यं ध्यानोपासनया प्राप्नुवन्तीति सात्वतः। **क्विपि शकन्ध्वादित्वात्पररूपं**[48] (पा०अ० ६, १, ९४ वा० ४) तेषां भक्तानामुपासकानां चेति तत्रैव व्याख्यातम्। अत्र योगस्यैव प्राबल्याद्योगरूढोऽयमिति तेनेदं शब्दद्वयं रूढियोगरूढ्योः पृथगुदाहरणं स्पष्टमेव। तथा च तुम्बुरुशब्दोऽपि गन्धर्वविशेषसंज्ञायां रूढः। तुम्बति सुशब्दं करोती[२८१]ति तुम्बुरुः। तुम्बधातोरुरुन्प्रत्य इति हेमकोशे देवजातिगन्धर्ववर्गप्रकारेण व्याख्याने तथा व्युत्पत्तिदर्शनात्[२८२]। तेन संज्ञारूढोऽयमेकार्थवाचकः शब्दस्तूकारत्रयविशिष्ट इत्यवधेयम्।

॥ अथ लक्षणा॥

शक्यसम्बन्धो लक्षणे (तर्कदीपिका वि० ५९) ति तार्किकाः।

सम्बन्धस्योभयनिष्ठ[२८३]त्वान्मुख्यशब्देऽपीयं प्रवर्तते। तस्माच्छक्यसम्बन्धेनाशक्यार्थप्रतिपादनीवृत्तिर्लक्षणेत्यालङ्कारिकाः। यथा केनचिद्बलवता धानुष्केण प्रेरितो बाणो वर्मच्छेदमुरो[२८४]भेदं प्राणाप[२८५]हरणं च करोति तथैकाभिधाख्य[२८६]व्यापारवतः शब्दस्य पदार्थोपस्थितिरिति लक्षणा च नाङ्गीकार्या स्याद्दीर्घाद्दीर्घाभिधाव्यापारेण तीरादिप्रसिद्धेरिति वैयाकरणाः। सा च लक्षणावृत्तिः **शब्दव्यापारत्वाच्छब्दनिष्ठा मुख्यार्थबाधे सति तत्सम्बन्धिनमर्थं विषयी[२८७]करोति** (त्रिवेणिका, प्र० २)। उक्तञ्च–

२७८. °धः।
२७९. °णे°।
२८०. °स्ते°।
२८१. °ती।
२८२. °न्।
२८३. °ष्ट°।
२८४. °दो°।
२८५. °णप्र°।
२८६. व्याख्य°।
२८७. °यीं।

मुख्यार्थबाधे तद्योगे रूढितोऽथ प्रयोजनात्।
अन्योऽर्थो लक्ष्यते यत्सा लक्षणारोपिता[२८८] क्रियेति[२८९]॥

(का० प्र० २, ९)

मुख्यार्थबाधे सति मुख्यार्थयोगे सति रूढेः प्रयोजनाद्वा यया वृत्त्या[२९०] अन्योऽर्थो लक्ष्यते सा लक्षणेत्यन्वयः।

प्रथमं तावल्लक्षणा त्रिविधा भवति-जहल्लक्षणा, अजहल्लक्षणा, जहदजहल्लक्षणा चेति। यत्र सति मुख्यार्थबाधे[२९१] शब्दः शक्यार्थं जहाति तत्र हि[२९२] जहल्लक्षणा। यत्र तमर्थं न जहाति तत्राजहल्लक्षणा। यत्र तदुभयं तत्र जहदजहल्लक्षणा।

पुनस्त्रिविधापीयं द्विविधा-निरूढा फलवती च। निरूढलक्षणा[२९३]याः शक्तितुल्यत्वात्को[२९४]शादिप्रसिद्धा। इयं तु शक्तितुल्यापि मुख्यार्थबाधे सति स्यात्तेन शक्तितोऽस्या विशेषः। अनादिलक्षणा चैषेत्याहुः। यत्र फलवती लक्षणा तत्र फलं तु व्यञ्जनाख्यव्या[२९५] पारगम्यमेव, न शक्तिलक्षणा[२९६]गम्यमिति व्यञ्जनावृत्तिनिरूपणे[२९७] स्फुटीकरिष्याम इति।

फलं तावत् कुत्रचित् गूढं कुत्रचिदगूढमिति द्विविधं भवति। गूढं फलं सुचतुरजनज्ञेयम्। अगूढं फलं तु सकलवेद्यमिति।

पुनरपि स[२९८]मानाधिकरणविषया व्यधिकरणविषया चेति द्विविधेयं लक्षणा। पुनरपीयं द्विविधा-गौणी शुद्धा चेति। व्यतिरेकलक्षणा प्रभेद एवेति

---

२८८. °ता।
२८९. °यते।
२९०. °त्या।
२९१. °ख्याबाधे।
२९२. ह।
२९३. °णी°।
२९४. कौ°।
२९५. °नाख्यापा°।
२९६. °ण°।
२९७. °पेण।
२९८. सा°।

विस्तरभिया संक्षेपतो निरूपणम्। विस्तरनिरूपणं त्वाशाधरभट्ट[49]कृतत्रिवेणिका[50]ग्रन्थे दृष्टव्यम्। निखिलभेदानां तत्र विशदतया निरूपणादिति।

इत्थं च जहल्लक्षणा। अजहल्लक्षणा। जहदजहल्लक्षणा। सारोपा साध्यवसाना। गौणी। शुद्धा चेति सप्तविधा फललक्षणा। क्रमेणोदाहरणानि। जहल्लक्षणा यथा–गङ्गाया[२९९] घोष इति। गङ्गाधिकरणको घोष इति शाब्दबोधः। गङ्गापदस्य प्रवाहे शक्तिः। सप्तम्यां अधिकरणरूपोऽर्थः। तत्र घोषासंभवान्मुख्यार्थबाधे सति तीरे लक्षणा। घोषपदं तात्पर्यग्राहकम्। वैय्याकरणास्तु– **आधारोऽधिकरणम्।**[51] (पा० अ० १, ४, ४५)। षड्विधमधि[३००]करणं औपश्लेषिकं सामीपिकमभिव्यापकं वैषयिकं नैमित्तिकमौपचारिकं चेति। तत्र वटे गावः सुशेरते इत्यत्रेव सामीपिकआधारः सप्तम्यर्थ इति शक्तिरेवात्र न लक्षणेत्याहुः। अत्र फलं तु शैत्यपावन[३०१]त्वद्योतनमेव। अजहल्लक्षणा यथा कुन्ताः प्रविशन्ति यष्टयः प्रविशन्तीत्यादि। अत्र कुन्ता[३०२]दीनामचेतनत्वेन स्वतः प्रवेशासंभवात्त[३०३]द्धारके पुरुषे लक्षणा[३०४]। अत्र फलं तु निः[३०५]शङ्कप्रहरणादिद्योतनमेव। अथ जहदजहल्लक्षणोदाहरण[३०६] यथा काकेभ्यो दधि रक्ष्यतामिति। अत्र शक्यकाकत्वपरित्यागेनाशक्यदध्युपघातकत्वपुरस्कारेण काकशब्दस्य दध्युपघातकत्व[३०७]मात्रे जहदजहल्लक्षणा। काकस्य दुष्टताप्रतीतिश्चात्र फलम्। यदा तु केनचिच्छिरसि धृतस्य दधिपात्रस्यान्यघातक[३०८]शङ्काया अ[३०९]भावात्ता[३१०]त्पर्योपपत्तिसत्त्वे[३११]न लक्षणा न भवति।

---

२९९. °या।
३००. °मधिमधि°।
३०१. °विन°।
३०२. °ता°।
३०३. °त°।
३०४. °क्षा°।
३०५. निश°।
३०६. °ण।
३०७. °घतकतक°।
३०८. °धातुकं°।
३०९. आ°।
३१०. °ता°।
३११. °त्वे°।

सर्वत्र **तात्पर्यानुपपत्तिर्लक्षणाबीज[52]मि** (तर्कदीपिका-तर्क संग्रह वि० ५९) ति सिद्धान्तात्। उदाहरणान्तरमाह-**न जातु ब्राह्मणं हन्यादि** (मनुस्मृति ८, ३८०) ति। अत्र शक्यब्राह्मणोत्तरद्वितीयैकवचन[३१२] परित्यागेनाशक्यद्वितीया-बहुवचनपुरस्कारेणैकवचनस्य बहुवचने लक्षणा। अन्यथा सर्वेषां ब्राह्मणानाम-वध्यत्वं न स्यात्। यत्तु त्रिवेणिकायां **न जातु ब्राह्मणं ह[३१३]न्यादित्यत्र व्यक्तिपरेण ब्राह्मणशब्देन तत्समवेता जातिर्लक्ष्यते** (त्रिवेणिका पृ० २०) इति प्राचीनमतानुसारेणोक्तं भविष्यति परन्तु न तत्समञ्जसं प्रतिभाति। तथाहि-अत्र लक्षणया व्यक्त्या जातिबोधाभ्युप[३१४]गमेऽपि जातेर्हननायोगान्पुनरपि व्यक्तौ लक्षणापेक्षा। यथा-**क्षत्रजाति[३१५]रुदि[३१६]याय भुजाभ्यां यस्तवेह सृ[३१७]जतोर्भुवनं प्रागि(या तवैव भुवनं सृजतः प्राक्।** नै.च. २१, ६३) त्यत्र जातिशब्देन तदाश्रयीभूता व्यक्तयो लक्ष्यन्ते। जातेरुत्पत्त्य[३१८]भावे मुख्यार्थबाधत्वात्। तद्वदिहापीति तद्दोषस्तावदवश्य[३१९]मेव। तस्मात् ब्राह्मणशब्दोत्तरद्वितीयैकवचनांशपरित्यागेना[३२०]शक्यद्वितीयाबहुवचन[३२१]स्वीकारेण लक्षणायाः प्रवृत्तिर्न तु जाताविति। इयमेव भागत्यागलक्षणेत्याहुः।

किञ्च[३२२] सोऽयं देवदत्तस्तत्त्व[३२३]मसीत्यादिवाक्ये(?) जहदजहल्लक्षणेति कैश्चिदुक्तं पूर्वाचार्यमतानुसारेण तथापि न त्वे[३२४]तत्समञ्जस[३२५] मुख्यार्थबाधाभावेन

---

३१२. °वचप°।
३१३. न°।
३१४. °पं°।
३१५. °दि°।
३१६. °द°।
३१७. स्न°।
३१८. °त्य°।
३१९. °तादवस्य°।
३२०. °नां°।
३२१. °चस्वी°।
३२२. किंश्च।
३२३. °त्व°।
३२४. °न्वै°।
३२५. °सा।

लक्षणाया अभावात्। यथा घटोऽनित्य इत्यत्र मुख्यप्रयोगे घटे घटत्वरूपां नित्यां जातिं विहाय घटपदस्यानित्यत्वेन सहान्वयः। किञ्च घटत्वं नित्यमिति मुख्यप्रयोगे घटानित्यत्वमपहाय घटत्वरूपायाः जातेर्नि[३२६]त्यपदेन सहान्वयस्तद्वदत्रापि विरु[३२७]द्धांशत्यागेनान्वयस्य संभवात्। एवं गेहे घटाः स्थिताः[३२८], शालागौर्बद्धास्तीत्यादिवा[३२९]क्येष्वपि दृष्टव्यम्। तत्त्व[३३०]मस्यादिवाक्ये आचार्याणां लक्षणोक्तिराग्रहवादेनेति वेदान्तपरिभाषायामप्युक्तमस्तीति तन्मतानुसारेणेदमाशङ्कितमित्य[३३१]वधेयम्।

किञ्च न जातु ब्राह्मणं हन्यादत्र विधिनियमः परिसंख्या वेति विचार्यते। प्रथम[३३२] तावद्विध्यादीनां विविच्य लक्षणमुच्यते–

विधिर[३३३]त्यन्तमप्राप्तौ नियमः पाक्षिके सति।
तत्र चान्यत्र च प्राप्तौ परिसंख्येति गीयते[३३४]॥

(तन्त्रवार्त्तिक ३, २, ४)

इति। अत्यन्ताप्राप्तप्रापणं विधिः। यथा स्वाध्यायोऽध्येतव्यः। अग्निहोत्रं जुहुयात् इति। पक्षेऽप्राप्तस्य प्रापणं[३३५] नियमः। यथा शुक्लपक्षे स्वाध्यायोऽध्येतव्यः। अत्र शुक्लपक्षे प्राशस्त्यं बोध्यते। समे यजेतेति यागः कर्तव्यतया विहितः। स च देशमपहाय कर्तुमशक्य इत्य[३३६]र्थाद्देशः प्राप्तः। स च देशः समो विषमश्चेति द्विविधः। यदा यजमानः स्वेच्छ[३३७]या स[३३८]मदेशे यज्ञं

३२६. नि°।
३२७. °स°।
३२८. °तः।
३२९. °त्यावा°।
३३०. °त्व°।
३३१. °त्यं°।
३३२. प्रमं°।
३३३. रं°।
३३४. परिसंख्यानिगद्यत।
३३५. पक्षेप्राप्तस्याप्राप्तपणं।
३३६. °त्या°।
३३७. °छ°।
३३८. य°।

करोति तदा तु इदं वचनं तथैवास्ते। स्वार्थस्य प्राप्तार्थत्वात्। यदा विष[३३९]मदेशे यजते तदा त्विदं वचनं स्वार्थं विधत्ते। स्वार्थस्य तदानीमप्रा[३४०]प्तार्थत्वात्। अन्यथा[३४१] अशास्त्रं यागोऽनुष्ठितः स्यात्। एवं प्राङ्मुखोऽन्नानि भुञ्जीतेति स्मार्तमुदाहरणं व्याख्यातम्। एकस्यानेक[३४२]त्रप्राप्तस्यान्यतो निवृत्त्य[३४३]र्थमेकत्र प्राप्त्यर्थं पुनर्वचनं परिसंख्या। तद्यथा ति[३४४]स्रो भार्या ब्राह्मणस्येति। अत्र विवाहविधिना चतुर्ष्वपि वर्णेषु संग्रहः प्राप्तः परिसंख्यया शूद्रानिषेधेन[३४५] बाध्यते। यथा वा–

इमामगृभ्णन् रशनामृतस्ये (यजुर्वेद २२, २) **त्यश्वाभिधानीमादत्त** इति मन्त्रः। स्वसामर्थ्याद[३४६]श्वाभिधान्या गर्द्दभा[३४७]भिधान्याश्च रशनाया ग्रहणे विनियुक्तः पुनरश्वाभिधानीमादत्त इति वचनेनाश्वाभिधान्यां विनियुज्यमानो गर्द्दभाभिधान्या[३४८] विनिवर्तते। इति। एवं **पञ्च पञ्चनखा भक्ष्या** (वा० रा० ४, १७, ३९)। अत्र हि यदृच्छ[३४९]या शशादिषु श्वादिषु च भक्षणं प्राप्तं पुनः शशादिषु श्रूयमाणं श्वादिभ्यो निवर्तत इति। इत्थं च किमत्र ब्राह्मणवधनिषेधवाक्यं विधिरूपं किं वा नियमरूपं परिसंख्यारूपं वा। अत्रोच्यते–न तावन्नियमविधिः। पक्षे प्राप्तस्याप्राप्तप्रापणाभावात्। नापि परिसंख्या। स्वार्थहानिः परार्थकल्पनाप्राप्त–बाधलक्षणदोषत्रयसमासत्तेः[३५०]। तस्मादपूर्वविधिरेवेत्याहुः। किञ्च शुक्लपक्षे स्वाध्यायोऽध्येतव्य इति नियमविध्युदाहरणे प्राशस्त्यमात्रं, न तु तदकरणे दोष इति। परिसंख्यायां तु शशादिभक्षणे न दोषप्राशस्त्यम्। श्वादिभक्षणे तु

---

३३९. °श°।

३४०. °प्र°।

३४१. °थाः।

३४२. °व°।

३४३. °त्य°।

३४४. त्रि°।

३४५. °ध।

३४६. °थ्यादि°।

३४७. °र्भर्द्द°।

३४८. °भाभिन्या।

३४९. °छ°।

३५०. °क्तेः।

दोषश्रवणेन प्रायश्चित्तविधानमिति[351] नियमविधेः सकाशात्परिसंख्याया भेदोऽवगन्तव्यः।

अथ शुद्धा सारोपा साध्यवसा[352]ना च। यथा आयुर्घृतम् आयुरेवेत्यादि। मुखचन्द्र इत्यादावारोपेऽपि न लक्षणा। समासोत्पन्नसमुदाय[53]शक्त्या[353] निर्वाहात्। सारोपलक्षणायां गुणमात्रस्य लक्षणा। गुणी तु शक्त्या परिगृह्यते। साध्यवसान-लक्षणायां तु विषयस्य स्वशब्देनानुपादानरूपनिगरणस्य सत्त्वादु्द्व[354]योरपीति। उक्तञ्च–

सारोपा सा मता यत्र विषयी विषयान्वितः।
ज्ञेया साध्यवसाना सा विषयी यत्र केवलः॥

(कोविदानन्द २, ११)

यथा द्रोणो व्रीहिरिति अत्र द्रोणरूपं यत्परिमाणं तत्परिच्छिन्नो[355] व्रीहिरित्यर्थः। प्रत्ययार्थे परिमाणे प्रकृत्यर्थोऽभेदेन संसर्गेण विशेषणम्। प्रत्ययार्थस्तु परिच्छे[356]द्यपरिच्छे[357]दकभावेन व्रीहौ विशेषणमिति। सिद्धान्ते तु प्रातिपदिकार्थेऽ[54]त्र प्रथमा न भवति किन्तु अर्थे प्रथमेत्येव सरसम्। अत्र अर्थशब्दो हि वृत्तिविषयपरः[358]। वृत्तिस्तु शक्तिर्लक्षणा चेति। एवं सति द्रोणो व्रीहिरित्यत्र द्रोणशब्दस्तत्परिमिते व्रीहावुपचारात्सिद्धः[359] गौर्वाहीकवत्।

अत्र केचिदाहुः–द्रोणादयः शब्दाः परिमीयन्तेऽनेनेति परिमाणं इति व्युत्पत्त्या लौहं दारुमयं वा परिमाणमेव। त[360]त्तु न व्यभिचरति परिमेयं तु व्यभिचरत्येव।

अतस्तस्य प्रातिपदिक[361]भावादप्राप्त[362]परिमाणग्रहणमिति।

---

३५१. °नमि।

३५२. °स°।

३५३. °समुदाशक्त्या।

३५४. सत्वाद्व°।

३५५. °छिन्नो।

३५६. °छे°।

३५७. °छे°।

३५८. °षपरः।

३५९. °द्धं।

३६०. त्त°।

३६१. °दिभा°।

३६२. °प्ते।

तन्न। गौणलाक्षणिकेषु सिंहो माणवकः, मञ्चाः क्रोशन्तीत्यादिष्व-व्याप्त्यापत्तेः। तत्र विशेष्यस्य माणवकादे[३६३]र्भेदेऽपि सिंहसदृशा इत्यर्थो गौण्यां नियतोपस्थितिक एवे[३६४]ति यदि, तर्हि व्रीह्यादेर्भेदेऽपि द्रोणपरिमितो नियत एवेति वैयाकरणाः। अत्रोच्यते–यथागौर्वाही[३६५]कः अग्निर्मा[३६६]णवकः, सिंहो देवदत्त इत्यादिषु सादृश्यसम्बन्धप्रतीतेर्गौण्यजहल्लक्षणा पूर्वार्थापरित्यागेन गुणरूपाधिकार्थग्रह[३६७]णात् तथा द्रोणे व्रीहिरित्यत्र सादृश्यसम्बन्धाभावान्न गौणी लक्षणा संभवति।

तस्मात्कथं मनोरमायां गौ[३६८]र्वाही[३६९]कवदित्युक्तं सङ्गच्छ[३७०]ते। आलङ्कारि-कमते त्वत्र शुद्धा फलवती जहल्लक्षणा।

तथा सति न किञ्चिद्दूषणमिति। यथा आयुर्घृतम्, आयुरेवेदमित्यत्र समानाधिकरणविषया सारोपा साध्यवसानी च लक्षणा शुद्धास्ति तद्वत् द्रोणो व्रीहिरित्यत्रापि द्रोणरूपमानपात्रेण परिच्छ[३७१]न्ने व्रीहौ द्रोणशब्दो लाक्षणिकः। **वस्तुतस्तु सामान्याकारेण परिमाणं शक्योऽर्थः। द्रोणरूपविशेषाकारेण लक्ष्यार्थ एवेति** (त्रिवेणिका पृ० १७) सिद्धान्त इति।

अथ साध्यवसानोदाहरणम्। यथा सिद्धान्तकौमुदीति शब्दकौस्तुभ[55] इति च। अत्र कौमुदीशब्देन कौस्तुभशब्देन च वृत्तौ साध्यवसाना लक्षणा। अन्यथा इवार्थे कन्विधानस्य दर्शनात् कौमुदी इव कौमुदिका, कौस्तुभ इव कौस्तुभक इति स्यात्। किञ्चात्र शब्दभूतः कौस्तुभः शब्दकौस्तुभ इति मध्यमपदलोपी समासः। शब्दरूपेण परिणतः इत्यर्थः। तेन परिणामालङ्कारः। शब्दत्वेन परिणतस्य कौस्तुभस्यार्थनिर्ण[३७२]यक्रियाहेतुत्वोक्तिसामञ्जस्यात्। न

३६३. °कार्भेदेपि।

३६४. °स्थितिकण्वे°।

३६५. °हि°।

३६६. °मा°।

३६७. °हा°।

३६८. गा°।

३६९. °हि°।

३७०. °छा।

३७१. °छि°।

३७२. °स्र्म°।

चोपमितसमासः। उद्ध[३७३]त इति साधारणधर्मप्रयोगात्। नापि मयूरव्यंसकादिसमासः[56]। तत्रोत्तरपदार्थस्य प्राधान्यात्। अत्र त्वर्थनिर्णयहेतुतया पूर्वपदार्थप्राधान्यावे[३७४]क्षणात्। अर्थनिर्णयो हि शब्दैरेव जायते न तु कौस्तुभे[३७५]न मणिनेति। न चोद्ध[३७६]त शब्दार्थानुरोधेनोत्तरपदार्थप्राधान्यं शक्यम् उद्ध[३७७]त इत्यस्योभयान्वयित्वात्। भाष्योद्ध[३७८]तानां शब्दानां निर्मलत्वद्योतनाय कौस्तुभपरिणामोक्तिरिति।

अत्रेदमवधेयम्–व्यस्तरूपकोदाहरणे सारोपा लक्षणा रूपकातिशयोक्त्युदाहरणे साध्यवसाना लक्षणेति। व्यतिरेकलक्षणा तु–

साधु दूति पुनः कर्त[३७९]व्यं किमतः परमि(कुवलयानन्द. उदा. ७१) त्यादिषु द्रष्टव्या। गौर्वाही[३८०]क इत्यादौ जाड्यमान्द्यादिगुणसाम्याद्गौणी लक्षणा। उक्तञ्च–

लक्ष्यमाणगुणैर्योगाद्वृत्तेरिष्टा तु गौणते।

(तन्त्रवार्त्तिक १, ४, १२, २२) सूत्रभाष्य)[57]ति।

शोणो धावतीत्यत्र शोणगुणविशिष्टे गुणिन्यश्वे लक्षणा। 'नखैर्युतं गर्भिणीनामधेयं', **'बाणैरश्वैश्च हायनै'** (त्रिवेणिका पृ० १६) रित्यादिषु च नखगतविंशतिसंख्यारूपे गुणे लक्षणा। नखादीनां विंशतिसंख्याकत्वेन बाहुल्याद्ब[३८१]हुवचनम्। भूचन्द्रादीनां तु **'विंशत्याद्याः सदैकत्वे'** (अमर० २, ९, ८३) इति कोशोक्तेर्मुख्यसंख्यावाचकत्वादेकवचनमेवेति। एवं बाणैरश्वैश्च हायनैरित्यत्रापि द्रष्टव्यम्। एवं च–नंपूभाभजपूरिजंजरिजपूघातास्तिथिर्मेषभादित्यादाववयवावयविसम्बन्धेन नंशब्देन नंदासंज्ञिकासु प्रतिपत्षष्ठ्येका–

३७३. °धृ°।
३७४. °पे°।
३७५. °भो°।
३७६. °धृ°।
३७७. °धृ°।
३७८. °धृ°।
३७९. °र्त्त°।
३८०. °र्हि°।
३८१. °ष°।

दशीतिथिषु लक्षणा। एवं (पू) शब्देन पूर्णा, भशब्देन भद्रा, जशब्देन जया, रिशब्देन रिक्तासंज्ञिकास्तिथयो लक्ष्यन्ते।

किञ्च–**'श्या[३८२]लः स्वस्त्रोरथाग्रहीदि'** (श्री. भा. पु. १०, ४, २३) त्यत्र तु स्वसा च (स्वसा च) स्वसारौ[३८३]। तयोरेकशेषे द्विवचनोपादान-स्यावश्यकत्वेनोपपत्तौ द्वितीयस्वसृशब्दस्यानुपपत्त्या[३८४] तत्स्वामिनि वसुदेवे लक्षणा। श्रीधरस्वामिनस्तु[३८५]लिङ्गसमवायेन प्राणभृत उपदधातीतिवत् स्वसृशब्देन द्विवचनानुपपत्त्या मिथुनगुणद्वारा मिथुनलक्षणया स्वसृतत्पत्योरभिधानमित्याहुः। एतदेव विवृणोति। तथा च पाणिनीयसूत्रम्–

तद्वानासामुपधानो मन्त्र इतीष्ट[३८६]कासु लुक् च मतो[58]रिति (पा० अ० ४, ४, १२५)।

अत्र प्राणभृत्[३८७] इति शब्दो यस्मिन्मन्त्रे स मन्त्रः प्राणभृद्वान्। तथा च प्रत्ययस्य सति लुकि[३८८] प्राणभृदिति हलन्तो मन्त्रवाचकः शब्दोऽभिधीयते। तेन मन्त्रवाचकेन प्राणभृत्शब्देन इष्ट[३८९]कासु लक्षणा। अन्यथा उपदधाति चिनोति इति चयनवाचकोपदधातीति क्रियापदानुपपत्त्या[३९०]मन्त्रस्य चयनासंभवात्। लिङ्गं चात्रोपदधातीति चयनवाचकं क्रियापदमेव। पूर्वत्र तु श्या[३९१]लपदं लिङ्गम्। अत्र वैयाकरणास्तु–यथा समानार्थानां विरूपाणामेकशेष[59] स्तथा भिन्नार्थाना[३९२]विरूपाणामप्येकशेषः। **प्रथमयोः पूर्वसवर्ण[60]** (पा०अ० ६, १,

---

३८२. °शा°।

३८३. स्वस्त्रौ।

३८४. °त्या।

३८५. °स्नस्तु।

३८६. °ष्टि°।

३८७. प्राभृत्।

३८८. लु°।

३८९. °ष्टि°।

३९०. °त्या।

३९१. शा°।

३९२. °ना।

१०२) इति ज्ञापकात्। तेन न लक्षणेत्याहुः। इत्थं च स्वसा च स्वसृपतिश्च स्वस्रौ। तयोरित्येकशेषः। ज्ञापके तु प्रथमा च द्वितीया च प्रथमे। तयोरिति फलितोऽर्थ इति संक्षेपः। विस्तरस्तु आशाधरगुरुकृतत्रिवेणिकायां द्रष्टव्यः।

अथ व्यञ्जना निरूप्यते।

श[३९३]क्यार्थलक्ष्यार्था[३९४]तिरिक्तप्रक[३९५]रणोपयोग्यन्यार्थबोधिका वृत्तिर्व्यञ्जना। उक्तं च काव्यप्रकाशे–

अनेकार्थस्य शब्दस्य वाचकत्वे नियन्त्रिते।
संयोगाद्यैरवाच्यार्थधीकृद्[३९६]व्यापृतिरञ्जनमिति॥

(का०प्र० २, १४)

नानाविधार्थस्य शब्दस्य वाचकत्वे संयोगाद्यैर्नियामकैर्नि[३९७]यन्त्रिते सति प्रकृतार्थोपयोग्यन्यार्थबोधजनको व्यापारो अञ्जन[३९८] व्यञ्जनाख्या वृत्तिरित्यर्थः। इयं च व्यञ्जना त्रिविधा। शब्दशक्तिमूला लक्षणामूला व्यञ्जनमूला चेति।

शब्दशक्तिमूला यथा–

तर्का[३९९] रदा यद्वदनस्य तर्क्या[४००]
वादे[४०१]ऽस्य शक्तिः क्व तथाऽन्यथा तैः[४०२]।
पत्रं क्व दातुं गुणशालिपूगं
क्व वादतः खण्डयितुं प्रभुत्वम्।

(नै० च० १०, ८३)

अत्र यद्वदनस्य सरस्वतीवदनस्य दा दन्तास्तर्कास्तर्कशास्त्ररूपास्तर्क्या

३९३. शश॰।
३९४. ॰र्थ॰।
३९५. ॰का॰।
३९६. ॰त्॰।
३९७. ॰नि॰।
३९८. ॰न॰।
३९९. ॰र्क्वा।
४००. ॰क्या।
४०१. वन्दे।
४०२. कथमन्यथातैः।

विचारणीयाः। अन्यथैवं नो चेदस्य वदनस्य वादे वादविषये शक्तिः सामर्थ्यं कथं स्यात्। न्यायशास्त्राध्ययनं विना वादं कर्तुं[४०३] न शक्यते इत्यर्थः। चतुर्विंशतिगुण[४०४]शालिनां पदार्थानां पूगः समूहो यस्मिन्नेतादृशं पत्रं दातुं च परं वादान् खण्डयितुं सामर्थ्यं कुत इति। वा इति द्वितीयाप्रकृतार्थे। नास्ति दन्ता यस्य स अदत्[४०५]। तस्य अदतः दन्तविहीनस्य तैर्दन्तैर्विना। वादे-वश्च दश्चानयोः समाहारो वादं, तस्मिन् वादे। वकारदकारोच्चारणे कुतः शक्तिः। व[४०६]कारस्य दन्त्यौ[४०७]ष्ठ्यत्वाद्दकारस्य दन्त्यत्वाच्चेत्यर्थः। किञ्चास्य गुणशालीपूगाः क्रमुको यस्मिन्नेतादृशं पत्रं नागवल्लीदलं ताम्बूलमिति यावत्। दन्तैर्विना दातुं खण्डनं कर्तु[४०८]म्। दोऽवखण्डने (दानखण्डने-धातुपाठ-११४)। क्व शक्तिः। हि यस्माद्दन्तरहितस्य पत्रमात्रमपि खण्डयितुं प्रभुत्वं क्व स्यात्। न कदापीत्यर्थः। अत्र प्रकृतसरस्वतीवदन[४०९] वर्णनेऽप्रकृतदन्तरहितपुरुषप्रतीतेरियं शब्दशक्तिमूला व्यञ्जना। **प्रकृताप्रकृतश्लेषे शब्दशक्तिमूला व्यञ्जनेति** (त्रिवेणिका-व्यञ्जनाप्रकरणम् पृ० २५) प्राचीनानां मतम्। लक्षणामूला यथा-

> **साहेंती सहि सुहअं खणेखणे दूम्मि[४१०]आसि मज्जकए[४११]।**
> **सब्भावणेहकरणिज्जसरिसअं दाव विरइअं तुमए[४१२]॥**
> **(साधयन्ती[४१३] सखि सुभगं क्षणे क्षणे दुना[४१४]सि मम कृते।**
> **सद्भावस्नेहकरणीयसदृशं तावद्विरचित[४१५]त्वया॥)**

(गाथासप्तशती ८६०)

---

४०३. °र्त्तुं।
४०४. °णा°।
४०५. °न्।
४०६. वं°।
४०७. °त्वो।
४०८. °र्त्तुं।
४०९. ने।
४१०. °मि।
४११. °ण्।
४१२. °ण्।
४१३. साधयं।
४१४. °नो°।
४१५. सदृशंद्विरचितं।

अत्र मत्कान्तं रमयन्त्या त्वया शत्रुत्वमुत्पादितमिति लक्ष्यते। ततो निजनायकविषयसापराधत्वप्रकाशनं व्यङ्ग्य[४१६] मिति लक्षणामूला व्यञ्जना। व्यञ्जनामूला यथा–

विपरीअरए[४१७] लच्छी बम्हं[४१८] दठ्ठू[४१९]ण णाहिकमलठ्ठं[४२०]।
हरिणो दाहिणणअणं रसाउला झत्ति ढक्केइ॥*

(का०प्र०उ० ५, उदा० १३७)

अत्र हरिपदेन दक्षिणनेत्रस्य सूर्या[४२१]त्मता व्यज्यते। तस्याच्छा[४२२]दनेन सूर्यास्तसमय[४२३]स्तेन कमलस्य संकोचस्तेन तत्स्थस्य ब्रह्मणोऽदर्शनं तेन लक्ष्मीनारायणयोर्निधुवनं निःशङ्कतयेति व्यज्यते। तेन व्यञ्जनामूला व्यञ्जना। इत्थं च–

वेदखाब्धि[४२४]वियच्चन्द्राः। १४४०४।[४२५]
शरेषुयुगखेन्दवः। १०४५५। इति (का०प्र० ४, ४४)

काव्यप्रकाशोक्ताः समुदायेन दशसहस्राणि चतुःशतानि पञ्चपञ्चाशद्[४२६]ध्वनिभेदाः कथ[४२७] व्यञ्जनावृत्तिं विना संभवन्ती[४२८]ति सावश्यमेवाङ्गी-

---

४१६. व्यग्यं।
४१७. विवरीअरण।
४१८. ब्रह्मं।
४१९. ठ्ठु°।
४२०. °ह्मं।
४२१. °या°।
४२२. °छा°।
४२३. °स्तमय°।
४२४. °ध्वि°।
४२५. १०६०६।
४२६. °शध्व°।
४२७. °थ°।
४२८. °भवती°।
* विपरीतरमणे लक्ष्मी ब्रह्माणं दृष्टवा नाभिकमलस्थम्।
हरेः दक्षिणनयंनं रसाकुला भूत्वा स्थगयति॥
(Sanskrit Version is not given in the text.)

कर्तव्या। किञ्च व्यञ्जनां विना फलवती लक्षणापि न स्यादेव। अस्यां फलप्रतीतिर्न शक्त्या। संके[४२९]ताभावात्। नापि लक्षणया। यया लक्षणया फलप्रतीतिस्तस्याः फलं कथं प्रतीयते? तदर्थमपि लक्षणा। सापि फलवतीत्येवं फललक्षणयोः परम्परायामनवस्था[61] स्यात्। उक्तञ्च काव्यप्रकाशे–

एवमप्यनवस्था स्याद्या मूलक्षयकारिणी (का०प्र० २, १७ अ) ति। न च तद्विशिष्टलक्षणा। विषयप्रयोजनयोर्युगपत्प्रतीत्यनभ्युपगमात्।

अपि च–काव्यनाटकादिभ्यो नवशृङ्गारादिरसाभिव्यक्तिर्निखिलसहृदय-सभ्यानुभवसिद्धा। अतोऽत्र का वा वृत्तिरङ्गीकार्या? न तावद्रसादिबोधनेऽभिधा। तत्र संकेताभावात्। विभावादिपदानां त्वत्रविभावादिमात्र शक्तत्वात् पदान्तरस्य चाभावात्। न हि विभावाद्यभिधानमे[४३०]व रसाद्यभिधानम्। रसस्य ताद्रूप्याभावात्। रसस्य स्वपदोपा[४३१]दाने रसदोषाङ्गीकाराच्च। तस्माद्रसादिप्रतीतौ व्यञ्जनावृत्तिरेवा-वश्यमभ्युपेया।

प्रसङ्गाद्रसस्वरूपमाह[४३२] काव्यप्रकाशकृत्–

कारणान्यथ कार्याणि सहकारीणि यानि च।
रत्यादेः स्थायिनो लोके तानि चेन्नाटय[४३३]काव्ययोः।
विभावा[४३४] अनुभावास्तत्कथ्यन्ते व्यभिचारिणः।
व्यक्तः स तैर्विभावाद्यैः स्थायिभावो रसः स्मृतः॥

(का०प्र० ४, २७, २८)

इति।

इत्थं च काव्योपनिबन्धमहिम्ना परिगृहीत[४३५] सीतात्वादिविशेषैः साधारण्येन प्रतीतैर्विभावादिभिर्व्यञ्जितं वर्ण[४३६]नीयसाधारण्येन गृहीतसामाजिकरत्याद्यव-

---

४२९. °क°।
४३०. °मै°।
४३१. °प°।
४३२. °हं।
४३३. °द्य°।
४३४. °भा°।
४३५. परिगृत°।
४३६. °र्स्म°।

च्छिन्नमानन्दांशे भग्नावरणमानन्दरूपतया प्रकाशमानं विभावादिसंभिन्नं चैतन्यं रस इति। यद्वा रत्याद्यवच्छिन्नं चैतन्यं रसः। यद्यपि–

शृङ्गारहास्यकरुणरौद्रवीरभयानकाः।
बीभत्साद्भुतशान्ता[४३७]ख्या नव नाटये रसाः स्मृताः॥

(भरत ना० शा० ६, १५)

अन्ये तु–

शान्तस्य शमसाध्यत्वान्नटे च तदसंभ[४३८]वात्।
अष्टावेव रसा नाटये[४३९] न शान्तस्तत्र युज्यते॥

(संगीतरत्नाकर० ७, १३१७ as quoted in र०गं० and र०वि०)

इत्याहुस्तन्न। नटे शमाभावादिति हेतुरसङ्गतः। नटे रसाभिव्यक्तेरस्वीकारात् सामाजिकानामेव रसास्वाद इति। तथा–

रतिर्हासश्च शोकश्च क्रोधोत्साहौ भयं तथा।
जु[४४०]गुप्सा विस्मयश्चैव निर्वेदश्चेति ते नवे॥

(भरत ना० शा० ६, १७)

ति स्थायिभावाः। तथा–

निर्वेदग्लानिशङ्काख्यास्तथासूयामदश्रमाः।
आलस्यं चैव दैन्यं च चिन्ता मोहः स्मृतिर्धृतिः॥
व्रीडा चपलता हर्ष आवेगो जडता तथा।
गर्वो विषाद औत्सुक्यं[४४१] निद्रापस्मार एव च॥
स्वप्नो विबोधोऽमर्षश्चाप्यवहित्थमथोग्रता।
मतिर्व्याधिस्तथोन्मादास्तथा[४४२] मरणमेव च॥

---

४३७. °ता°।

४३८. °भा°।

४३९. °द्ये।

४४०. ज°।

४४१. °ख्यं।

४४२. °श्चिन्ता।

त्रासश्चैव वितर्कश्च विज्ञेया व्यभिचारिणः।
त्रयस्त्रिंशदमी भावाः समाख्यातास्तु नामतः॥ इति।

(भरत ना० शा० ६, १८-२१)

शृङ्गारा[४४३]दिरसानामनेकत्वं तथापि ध्वनिभेदेष्वस[४४४] लक्ष्यक्रमरूपो रसध्वनिरेक एव स्वीकृत इत्यवधेयम्।

किञ्च रत्या[४४५]दीनामपूर्णत्वे स्थायित्वं संपूर्णपरिपुष्टत्वे रसत्वमिति रसस्थायिभावयोर्भेदः।

तथा च भरतसूत्रम्–

'विभावानुभावव्यभिचारिसंयोगाद्रसनिष्पत्ति'

(भरत ना०शा०, अ० ६) रिति।

सर्वत्र कार्यकारणसहकारिसंज्ञयैव व्यवहारसंभवे विभावादिसंज्ञान्तरकरणं रसस्यालौकिकत्वप्रतिपादनार्थमिति। विस्तरस्तु मत्कृते रसतरङ्गिणीव्याख्यान-रूपनूतनतरीयनाम्नि ग्रन्थे द्रष्टव्यः।

अपि च[४४६] व्यञ्जनावृत्त्य[४४७]स्वीकारे काव्यस्योत्तममध्यमाधमत्वव्यवस्थापि न स्यादेव। व्यङ्ग्याधिक्येनैवोत्तमत्वमिति।

उक्तञ्च–

'इदमु[४४८]त्तममतिशयिनि व्यङ्ग्ये[४४९] वाच्यात् ध्वनिर्बुधैः कथित' (का०प्र० १,४) इति। इदमिति काव्यम्। यथा वा–

कियत्त्यजन्नोदनमानयन् कियत्
करस्य पप्रच्छ गतागतेम याम्।

---

४४३. °र।
४४४. °स।
४४५. त्या°।
४४६. अ च।
४४७. °त्य°।
४४८. इदं उ°।
४४९. °गो।

अहं किमेष्यामि किमेष्यसीति वा
व्यधत्त नम्रं किल लज्जया मुखम्।।*

(नै०च० १६, ७९)

ओदनोऽस्त्री स[४५०] **दीदिविः** (अमर० २, ९, ४८) इत्यमरः। अत्रौदनं परिवेशयन्तीं तरुणीं प्रति कस्यचिन्नव[४५१] वरयात्रिकस्य पात्रपरिवेशितौदनं पुनः प्रसारणापकर्षणच्याजे न त्वया आगन्तव्यं[४५२] मया आगन्तव्यमिति पृ[४५३]च्छा व्यज्यते। ततस्तयापि तं प्रति लज्जाव्याजेन मुखनम्रीकरणचेष्टया त्वयैवागम्यतामित्युत्तरं दत्तमिति व्यज्यते। यथा वा–

निःशेषच्युतचन्दनं स्तनतटं निर्मृष्टरागोऽधरो
नेत्रे दूरमनञ्जने पुलकिता तन्वी तवेयं तनुः।
मिथ्यावादिनि दूति बान्धवजनस्याज्ञातपीडागमे
वापीं स्नातुमितो गतासि न पुन[४५४] **स्तस्याधमस्यान्तिकम्।।**

(अमरुशतकम् ६१)

अत्र अधमपदोपादानेन तदन्तिकं रन्तुमेव गतासीति वाच्या[४५५]पेक्षया व्यङ्ग्यार्थस्यातिशयो व्यज्यते तेनेदमुत्तमं काव्यमिति। मध्यमं यथा–

अतादृशि गुणीभूतव्यङ्ग्यं[४५६] **व्यङ्ग्ये**[४५७] **तु मध्यममिति।**

(का०प्र० १, ५)

अतादृशि वाच्यादनतिश[४५८]यिनि व्यङ्ग्ये सति गुणीभूतव्यङ्ग्य[४५९] मध्यमं काव्यमित्यर्थः।

---

४५०. च।

४५१. °ल°।

४५२. °गव्यं।

४५३. प्र°।

४५४. गतासिपुन°।

४५५. वावाच्या°।

४५६. व्यग्यं।

४५७. व्यग्ये।

४५८. °शा°।

४५९. °व्यग्यं°।

* लज्जयाऽननम् इति पाठः नैषधे।

यथा वा–

अम्मे गुडुदुअंम्मे उरमंरु वेअणा णत्थि ।
पुत्ती एहि सुहाओ जं पेख्ख[४६०]इ वेअणा तस्स ॥
(अम्ब[४६१] गडुद्वयं मे उरसि मध्ये* वेदना नास्ति ।
पुत्रि ह्येष स्वभावो यः प्रे[४६२]क्षते वेदना तस्य ॥)

(?)

अत्राज्ञातयौवनायास्तवाधुना तु वेदना नास्ति। सति यौवनानुभवे[४६३] भविष्यति इति व्यङ्ग्यापेक्षया यः प्रेक्षते तस्य वेदनास्तीति वाच्यार्थस्यासंग[४६४] त्यलङ्कारेण चमत्कृत्यु[४६५]त्कर्षाधायकत्वात् व्यङ्ग्यस्य गुणीभूतत्वं तेनेदं मध्यमं काव्यम्। अधमं यथा–

शब्दचित्रं वाच्यचित्रमव्यङ्ग्यं त्ववरं स्मृतमिति। (का०प्र० १, ५)

चित्रमिति गुणालङ्कारसहितम्। अव्यङ्ग्यमिति स्फुटप्रतीयमा[४६६] नार्थरहितम् अवरमधममित्यर्थः। यथा वा–

साटोपव्योमहट्टोषितरजनिवणिग्नायिकोन्मुक्ततारा
मुक्ताहारापहारात्तरलखगरवप्रोद्यताकीर्तिशान्त्यै।
कर्षन्नंभोजकुम्भोद[४६७]रकुहरबहिर्निस्सरत्षट्पदालि–
कालव्यालीं करेणाकलयतु दिनकृत् कल्मषोन्मूलनं वः॥

(सु०र०भा० २७, १३)

अत्र व्योमरूपहट्टोषिताया रजनिरूपाया व[४६८]णिग्नायिकाया हट्टस्थापित–

---

४६०. °रख°।

४६१. अबे।

४६२. प्र°।

४६३. °भे।

४६४. °सग°।

४६५. °त्यो°।

४६६. °तीमाना°।

४६७. °दा°।

४६८. वा°।

* Reading Doubtful.

तारारूपो मुक्ताहारस्तस्यापहारा[469]च्चौर्यात् तरला ये खगाः पक्षिणस्तेषामारवः शब्दस्तेनोक्ता[470] या अकीर्तिस्तस्याः शान्त्यर्थं कमलरूपकुम्भोदरमध्यान्निस्सरन्तीं भ्रमरपङ्क्तिरूपां कृष्णवर्णां सर्पिणीं करेण हस्तेन किरणेन। कर एव कर इति शिल[471]ष्टरूपकम्। कलयन्नाकर्षयन् दिनकृत्सूर्यः कल्मषोन्मूल[472]नं वो युष्माकं करोत्वित्यन्वयः। कस्मिंश्चिद्देशे तत्रत्यानामियं रीतिः। यस्य चौर्याद्यभिशापः प्राप्तस्तेन कुम्भमध्ये प्रवेशितसर्पस्य स्वहस्तेन निष्कासनं कर्तव्यम्। यदि तस्य सर्पो दशति तर्हि स एव चौरः, न दशति चेत् शुद्ध इति। अ[473]त्रौजोगुणेन शब्दार्थालङ्काराभ्यां च चित्रं ज्ञेयम्। यथा वा–

नयनरथचक्रमित्रं रूपाहारध्वजं सुवदनायाः।
वीक्ष्य पदाम्बरगात्रं हरिहरमदनाः कथं न विवदन्ते॥

सुष्ठु[474] वदनं यस्यास्सा तस्याः सुवदनायाः शुभाङ्ग्याः। अत्र वदनशब्देनाङ्गसामान्ये लक्षणा। प्रथमं मुखचन्द्रं वीक्ष्येत्यध्याहारेण योजना। अयं मुखचन्द्रे मदीयं नयनं वामनेत्रं इति हरे[475]र्विवादः।

निष्प्रत्यू[476]हमुपास्महे भगवतः कौमोदकीलक्ष्मणः
कोकप्रीतिचकोरपारणपटूज्योतिष्मती लोचने।
याभ्यामर्द्धविबोधमुग्धमधुरश्रीरर्धनिद्रायितो
नाभिपल्वलपुण्डरीकमुकुलः कम्बोः सपत्नीकृतः॥

(अनर्घराघवम् १, १)

इति मुरारिनाटके हरिवामनेत्रस्य चन्द्रात्मकतया वर्णनात्। अस्या अयं मुखचन्द्रो मदीयं रथाङ्गं चक्रम् इति हरस्य विवादः। **रथाङ्गे चन्द्रार्कौ**

---

४६९. °रो°।
४७०. °क्तां।
४७१. श्ले°।
४७२. °लं।
४७३. आ°।
४७४. °ष्टु।
४७५. °र°।
४७६. °त्य°।

रथचरणपाणिः शर (शिवमहिम्नः स्तोत्रम् १८) इति महिम्नः स्तोत्रे तथा वर्णनात्। अयं मुखेन्दुः कामो[४७७]द्दीपकत्वान्मदीयं मित्रमिति मदनस्य विवादः इति प्रथमं मुखं वीक्ष्य नयनरथचक्रमित्रमिति त्रयाणां योजना। अथास्याः नयनं वीक्ष्येत्यप्यध्याहारेण योजना। अस्या नयनं मीनसादृश्यान्मी[४७८]नरूपम्। तेन मे मत्स्या[४७९]वतारत्वान्मत्स्वरूपमेवेति हरेर्विवादः। एतस्या नयनमीनोऽयं ममाहारो भक्ष्यमिति हरविवादः। **त्यजति न मृगव्याधरभसः।** (शिवमहिम्नः स्तोत्रम् २२) इति वर्णनेन[४८०] शिवस्य व्याधरूपत्वात्। नयनमीनोऽयं मदीय-ध्वजरूप इति मदनविवादः। कामस्य मकरध्वजत्वे प्रसिद्धेः। सुवदनाया उदरं वीक्ष्येति योजना। उदरस्य गगनसाम्यादुदररूपं गगनं वीक्ष्य वा[४८१]मना-वताराक्रान्तमिदं मदीयं पदमिति हरेर्विवादः। इदं मदीयमम्बरं वसनं इति हरविवादः। शिवस्य दिगम्बरत्वात्। अनुदराया अस्या इदं अल्पोदरं मदीयं गात्रमिति मदनविवादः मदनस्यानङ्गत्वात्सूक्ष्माङ्गत्वादित्यर्थः। अत्र नञोऽल्पा[62]-र्थत्वमनुद[४८२]रा कन्येति वचनात्। **सदसत्संश**[४८३] **यगोचरोदरी**[४८४] (नै०च० २, ४०) ति नैषधे दमयन्त्यास्तथा वर्णनात्। अत्र मुखनयनोद[४८५]राणां त्रयाणामध्याहारेण योजनया झटित्यर्थबोधाभावेन व्यङ्ग्यर[४८६]हितत्वाच्चाधमत्वम्। इत्थं चोत्तममध्यमाधमेतित्रयाणामपि काव्यानां व्यवस्थाव्यञ्जनां वृत्तिं[४८७] विना न संभवतीत्यवश्यमेव साऽङ्गीकार्या। तथा चैषूदाहरणेषु सर्व[४८८]त्रार्थमात्रे व्यञ्जनेत्यभिधातो भिन्ना।

वाच्योऽर्थः शक्तिज्ञानवद्भिरवगम्यते व्यङ्ग्यस्तु सहृदयैरेवेति बोधभेदो

---

४७७. °मा°।

४७८. °त्मी°।

४७९. °त्सा°।

४८०. °ना।

४८१. मनाव°।

४८२. °दा°।

४८३. °स°।

४८४. °र्श°।

४८५. °दा°।

४८६. व्यंग्यहित°।

४८७. °र्तिं।

४८८. °व°।

व्यञ्जनायाम्। **'निःशेषच्युतचन्दनमि'**त्यत्र तदन्तिकं न गतासीति निषेधः शक्यार्थः। तदन्तिकं रन्तुं गतासीति विधिश्च व्यङ्ग्यः इत्यर्थस्वरूप-भेदोऽप्यभिधाव्यञ्जनयोः। किञ्च–'गतोऽस्तमर्क।' इत्यादौ शक्योऽर्थस्त्वेक एव प्रतीयते व्यङ्ग्यस्तु तत्र प्र[४८९]तिपात्रादिभेदेन नानैव भासते। तथा हि–आपणिकानां भृत्यान् प्रति विक्रेयवस्तूनि संह्रियतामिति। दूतीना[४९०]मभिसारिकां प्रति अभिसरणमुपक्रम्यतामिति शिष्यस्य गुरुं प्रति सान्ध्यो विधिरुपक्रम्यतामिति। नागतोऽद्य प्रेयानिति। दूरं मा गा इति प्राप्तप्रायस्ते प्रेयानिति निरवधिर्व्यङ्ग्योऽर्थः प्रकाशते। वाच्यस्त्वेक एवेत्यभिधाव्यञ्जन-योरर्थसंख्याभेदाद्भेदः। वाच्योऽर्थः शब्दोच्चारणमात्रादेव प्रतीयते। व्यङ्ग्यस्तु प्रतिभानैर्मल्यादिति निमित्तभेदः। वाच्योऽर्थस्त्वचमत्कारकारी व्यङ्ग्यस्तु प्रतीतिमात्रश्चमत्कारकारीति कार्यभेदः। वाच्यः केवलप्रतीतिको व्यङ्ग्यस्तु चमत्कारप्रतीतिक इति प्रतीतिभेदः। वाच्यः पूर्वं व्यङ्ग्यः पश्चात्प्रतीयते इति कालभेदः। अभिधा शब्दाश्रया व्यञ्जना तु पद-तदेकदेश-तदर्थ-वाक्याद्याश्रया इत्याश्रयभेदः।

कस्स वणहो[४९१]इ रोसो दठ्ठु[४९२]ण पिआए[४९३] सव्वणं अहरम्।
सभमरउपमग्धा[४९४]इणि[४९५] वारिअवामे सहुस एह्णिम्॥
(कस्य न वा स्यात् रोषो दृष्ट्वा प्रियायाः सव्रणम[४९६]धरम्।
सभ्रमरपदमाघ्रायिणि वारितवामे[४९७] सहस्वेदानीम्॥)

(quoted from ध्वन्यालोक १, ४, वृत्ति)

४८९. त्र°।
४९०. °नां°।
४९१. णवहो।
४९२. °ग्गुण°।
४९३. °ण।
४९४. °माद्धा°।
४९५. °इ°।
४९६. °दामधरम्।
४९७. वारितामया।

अत्र नेदं उपपति[४९८]कृतमधरदशनं किन्तु सभ्रमरपद्माघ्राणजनितमिति व्यङ्ग्यस्य कान्तो विषयः। अतः परं त्वया नै[४९९]तादृशं कर्म कर्त[५००]व्यमिदं तु मया यथाकथञ्चिदाच्छादितमिति व्यङ्ग्यस्य कान्ताविषयः प्रतिपाद्यते इति विषयभेदः। अपि च–

भम[५०१] धम्मिअ वीसत्थो सो सुणओ[५०२] अज्ज[५०३]मारिओदेण।
गोलाणईकच्छकुङ्गवासिणा दरिअसीहेण[५०४]॥
(भ्रम धार्मिक विस्रब्धः[५०५] स शुनकोऽद्य मारितस्तेन।
गोदानदीकच्छकुञ्जवासिना दृप्तसिंहेन॥)

(quoted from ध्वन्यालोक १, ४, वृत्ति)

अत्र ग्रहे श्वनिवृत्त्या[५०६]भ्रमणं विहितं गोदावरीतीरे सिंहोपलब्धे[५०७]-रभ्रमणमनुमापयति। यद्यद्भीरुभ्रमणं तत्तद्भयका[५०८]रणनिवृत्त्युपलब्धि[५०९]पूर्वकं भवति। व्यतिरेकव्या[५१०]प्तिमाह– गोदावरीतीरं भीरुभ्रमणायोग्यम्। सिंहवत्त्वा[५११]-त्। वनवत्। इत्यनुमित्यैव भ्रमणाभावः किं व्यञ्जनयेति[५१२] चेदुच्यते।

यद्यपि स्वयं भीरुस्तथापि गुरोः स्वामिनो राज्ञो निदेशेन प्रियानुरागेण

४९८. °त्ति°।
४९९. ने°।
५००. °त°।
५०१. भ्भम्म।
५०२. °हो।
५०३. °ज्जु।
५०४. दरिसिंहेण।
५०५. °श्रध्ब:।
५०६. °त्या।
५०७. °ध्व°।
५०८. °क°।
५०९. ध्बि°।
५१०. °कप्ति°।
५११. °त्वा°।
५१२. व्यंजनयेतिजनयेति।

वा सिंहोपलब्धि[513]सत्त्वेऽपि भ्रमतीत्यनैकान्तिको हेतुः। शुनो बिभ्यदपि शू[514]रत्वेन सिंहान्न बिभेतीति। तत्कथमेवंविधाद्धेतोः साध्यसिद्धिरिति[515]। इत्थं च निःशेषच्युतचन्दनमित्यत्र यानि चन्दनच्यवनादीन्युपात्ता[516]नि तानि स्नानतोऽपि भवन्तीत्यनैकान्तिको हेतुरिति। स्नानसाधारण्येन निबद्धानां विशेषणानामाभासत्वे[517]न ना[518] नुमापकत्वमपि त्वधमपदसाहचर्येण व्यञ्जकत्वमेव। तदन्तिके रन्तुं गतासीति[519] नानुमानम्। किञ्चानुमाने साध्यसाधननिर्देशो न चात्र तथा निर्दे[520]शः। साध्याद्यनुपादानात्। तस्माच्छक्तिलक्षणातिरिक्ता व्यञ्जनावृत्तिरवश्यमभ्युपेया।

इत्थं च व्यङ्ग्यं तावत् त्रिविधं भवति गूढमगूढं गूढागूढं चेति। तत्र गूढागूढं तावत् कामिनीकुचकलशवच्चमत्कारकारि भवति। उक्तञ्च–

नान्ध्रीपयोधर इवातितरां प्रकाशो
नो गुर्ज[521]रीस्तन इवातितरां निगूढः।
अर्थो गिरामपिहितः पिहितो विभाति
काव्येषु तत्र मरहट्ट[522]वधूकुचाभः॥

(सु०र०भा० ३९, ३९)

इति।

एषामुदाहरणानि विस्तरभिया नोक्तानि। अर्थनिष्ठा[523] व्यञ्जना तूक्ता काव्यप्रकाशकारैः–

---

५१३. °र्लब्धि°।

५१४. शु°।

५१५. °सिरिति।

५१६. °ता°।

५१७. °णानामासत्वेन।

५१८. मनाऽनुमाप°।

५१९. गतासीत्यस्येति।

५२०. °र्दे°।

५२१. °र्जु°।

५२२. °ग्ग°।

५२३. °ष्टा।

वक्तृ[५२४]बोद्धव्य[५२५] काकूनां वाक्यवाच्यान्यसन्निधे:।
प्रस्तावदेशकालादेर्वैशिष्ट्यात्प्रतिभाजुषाम्॥
योऽर्थस्यान्यार्थधीहेतुर्व्यापारो व्यक्तिरेव सेति॥

(का०प्र० ३, १-२)

बोद्धव्य: प्रतिपादनीयो जन[५२६]:। काकुर्ध्वनेर्विकार:। वाक्यवाच्याभ्यां सहितोऽन्यसन्निधि:। प्रस्ताव: प्रकरणम्। वक्त्रादीनां वैशिष्ट्यात् शक्तिलक्षणातिरक्तोऽर्थो व्यज्यतेऽनया सा व्यञ्जनेति व्युत्पत्ते:। इत्थं च शक्तिलक्षणातिरिक्तविवक्षितान्यार्थधीजनको व्यापारो व्यञ्जनेति सिद्धम्। दिङ्मात्रमुदाह्रियते। वक्तृ[५२७] वैशिष्ट्याद्यथा–

देव: पति[५२८]र्विदुषि नैषधराजगत्या[५२९]
निर्णीयते न किमु न व्रियते भवत्या।
नालं[५३०] नल: खलु तवातिमहानलाभो
यद्येनमुज्झ[५३१]सि वर: कतर: परस्ते॥

(नै०च० १३, ३३)

अत्र वक्त्र्या[५३२] सरस्वत्या दमयन्तीं प्रति कृते नलवर्णने श्लेषमहिम्नाखण्डलाग्नियमवरुणानां भैमीपरिणयनरूपकार्या[५३३]र्थं नलवेशधारिणां चतुर्णामपि संसूचनं व्यङ्ग्यमर्यादयैव कृतमस्तीत्यवधेयम्। अयं नलोऽस्त्येते नलवेशधारिणो देवा इति प्रकाशतया वर्णने तु सजातीयैर्देवै:। सहास्या: सरस्वत्या: शत्रुत्वं स्यादिति। अत्र विदुषीत्यनेन श्लोकोक्तिपरिज्ञानचातुर्यं दमयन्त्या[५३४] संपादितमस्तीति। अत्र वक्त्र्या:[५३५] सरस्वत्यास्तथा बोद्धव्यस्य प्रतिपादनीयस्येन्द्रादेस्तथा

५२४. °त्कृ°।
५२५. °ह्यव्यं°।
५२६. जना।
५२७. °त्कृ°।
५२८. °त°।
५२९. °त्वा।
५३०. °यं।
५३१. °ह्र°।
५३२. °त्र्या।
५३३. °र्यां।
५३४. °न्त्या:।
५३५. °त्र्या:।

त्वया किमु न निर्णीयते किमु न व्रियते इति काकोश्वेति त्रयाणामपि वैशिष्ट्यं ज्ञेयम्। यथा वा मम–

सत्यासक्तमना विभूषिततनुर्भूत्या गवामीश्वरः
सर्वज्ञो द्विजराजराजितवपुर्मायान्वितो वृत्तिवित्।
आनन्दीप्सि[५३६]तपूरकः सुमनसामानन्ददोऽनन्तदृक्
ब्रह्मोपासनतत्परः स भगवान् गंगाधरः पातु नः॥

अत्र श्लेषवशात् व्यञ्जनावृत्त्या[५३७] प्रतीयमानेषु[५३८]–

प्रथमं शिवपक्षे व्याख्यानमाह। धरतीति धरः। पचाद्यच्। गङ्गाया: धरो गङ्गाधरः शिवः। **गङ्गाधरोऽन्धकरिपु** (अमर० १, १, ३४) रित्यमरवचनात्। योगरूढोऽयं शब्दः। नः पात्वित्यन्वयः। स कीदृशः। सत्यां[५३९] दाक्षायि[५४०]–ण्यामासक्तमनाः। तथा भूत्या भस्मना। **भूतिर्भस्मनि संपदी** (अमर० ३, ३, ६९) त्यमरः[५४१]। विभूषिततनुः[५४२]। शोभितविग्रहः। तथा गवां सर्वविद्यानां ईश्वरः। **ईशानः सर्वविद्यानामि** (तै०आ० १०, ४७, १) ति श्रुतेः। यद्वा गवामिषूणामीश्वरो रक्षिता। दैत्यवधार्थमित्यर्थः। यद्वा गवां दिशां रक्षकः। गवां पञ्चमुखत्वेन पञ्चदशनेत्राणां[५४३] धारणे समर्थ[५४४] इति वा।

"गोर्नादित्ये बलीवर्दे क्रतुभेदर्षिभेदयोः।
स्त्री तु स्याद्दिशि भारत्यां भूमौ च सुरभावपि॥
नृस्त्रियोः स्वर्गवज्राम्बु[५४५]रश्मिदृग्बाणलोमस्वि"–

(अमर० ३, ३, २५ रामाश्रमीटीका)

---

५३६. °क्षि°।
५३७. °त्या।
५३८. प्रतीमानेषु।
५३९. °त्यायां।
५४०. °क्षि°।
५४१. संपत्यमरः।
५४२. विभूषितनुः।
५४३. °णा।
५४४. °थ।
५४५. °व्रजाबु°।

त्यभिधानात्। पुनः कीदृशः सर्वज्ञः सर्ववेत्ता। द्विजानां ब्राह्मणानां राजा इति द्विजराजश्चन्द्रः। **राजाहः सखिभ्यष्टच्**[63] (पा०अ० ५, ४, ९१)। **सोमोऽस्माकं ब्राह्मणानां राजे** (शु०यजु० १०, १८, ९, ४०)ति श्रुतेः। तेन राजितवपुः शोभितविग्रहः। तथा मायया योगमायया पार्वतीरूपया वा अन्वितो युक्तः। तथा वृत्तयः सर्वजनचित्तवृत्तयस्तावतीवृत्तिवित्। पुनश्च कीदृशः। आसमन्तात् स्ववाहनभूतो नन्दी वृषभस्तस्य यदीप्सितं तस्य पूरकः। सुमनसां देवाना-मानंदकर्ता।[५४६] अनन्तः। सर्प[५४७]विशेषस्तं पश्यतीति अनन्तदृक्। ब्रह्मण उपासने चिन्तने तत्परः इ[५४८]ति उक्तविशेषणविशिष्टः स भगवान् गङ्गाधरः शिवः नोऽस्माकं पातु। प्रार्थनाया[५४९] लोट्।

अथ विष्णुपक्षे। पादोदकीभूताया गङ्गाया धरो विष्णुः स जगत्प्रसिद्धः। भगवान् नानैश्वर्ययुक्तः। तथा सत्यायां सत्यभामायामासक्तमनाः। कृष्णस्तु भगवान् स्वयमित्युक्तेर्विष्णुकृष्णयोरभेद[५५०]वर्णनम्। पुनः कीदृशः। भूत्या संपत्त्या[५५१] भूषिततनुः। **भूतिर्भस्म[५५२]नि संपदी** (अमर० ३, ३, ६९) त्यमरः। गवां धेनूनां ईश्वरः पालको नियन्तेति यावत्। सर्वं जानातीति सर्वज्ञः। **यः सर्वज्ञः स सर्ववि** (मुण्डकोपनिषद्, १, ९) दितिश्रुतिद्वयदर्शनात्। द्विजराजेनेन्दुना शोभितशरीरः। वामनेत्रस्य चन्द्ररूपत्वात्। यद्वा रासोत्सवे–

स चर्षणीनामुदगाच्छुचो मृज[५५३]न्नि

(श्री०भा०पु० १०, २९, २अ) **ति**

चन्द्रोदयस्य सत्त्वा[५५४]त्तेन शोभितदेहः। तथा मायया योगमायया अन्वितः।

---

५४६. °र्त्ता।
५४७. °र्वं°।
५४८. इं°।
५४९. प्रार्थयां।
५५०. °न°।
५५१. °त्या।
५५२. °स्य°।
५५३. °द°।
५५४. °त्वा°।

योगमायामुपाश्रित[५५५] (श्री०भा०पु० १०, २९, १) इति भागवते तथा वर्णनात्। वृत्तिवित्। गोपिकानां याश्चित्तवृत्तयस्तासां वेत्ता। यद्वा षो[५५६]डशसहस्रराजकन्यानां युगपत्स्ववरणविषये याश्चित्तवृत्तयस्तासां ज्ञाता। तथा आनन्दी आनन्दवान्। आनन्दं ब्रह्मणो[५५७] रूपमिति श्रुतेः। भक्तजनानां गोपिकानां वा ईप्सितपूरकः। तथा सुमनसां[५५८] देवानामानन्ददः। शुद्धचित्तानां वा। अनन्तदृक् बहुनेत्रः। **सहस्राक्षः सहस्रपादि** (ऋग्वेद १०, ९०, १क) ति श्रुतेः। पुनः कीदृशः। ब्रह्मोपासने वेदाध्ययने तत्परः। यद्वा ब्रह्म उप समीपे यदासनं कमलं तदस्ति अस्येति ब्रह्मोपासनः पद्मनाभ इत्यर्थः। तत्परं प्रतिपाद्यं यस्येति विशेषणसमासः। अस्मिन्विष्णुपक्षे गङ्गाधरशब्दो यौ[५५९]गिकः।

अथ ब्रह्मपक्षे योजना। किञ्च-सत्ये सत्यलोके आसक्तमनाः। तथा भूत्या भस्मना भव्यमूर्तिः[५६०]। सर्वदा सन्ध्योपासनविधौ भ[५६१]स्मधारणस्य श्रुतिस्मृतिविहितत्वात्प्राशस्त्यं बोध्यम्। **त्र्यायुषमि** (शुक्लयजु० ३, ६२)ति श्रुतिः स्मृतिरपि–

धार्यं भस्म त्रिसन्ध्यं तु गृहिणा जलसंयुतम्।
वानप्रस्थयतीनां तु सायाह्ने जलवर्जितम्॥

(प्रयोगपारिजातः आह्निकसूत्रावलि)

इति। तथा गवां क्रतूनां ईश्वरः फलदाता। यद्यपि गोशब्दस्य क्रतुविशेषवाचित्वेनैकवचन[५६२]संभवस्तथापि क्रत्वङ्कर्मणामने[५६३]कत्वे बहुवचनम्। ब्रह्मणः क्रतूनां फलदातृत्वं चोक्तं भगवद्गीतायाम्–

---

५५५. योगमाययामुपाश्रित।
५५६. शो॰।
५५७. ब्रणो।
५५८. सुमसां।
५५९. यो॰।
५६०. ॰र्त्तिः।
५६१. भभस्म॰।
५६२. ॰नैकवनसंभव॰।
५६३. ॰जे॰।

सहयज्ञाः प्रजाः सृष्ट्वा पुरोवाच प्रजापतिः।
अनेन प्रसविष्यध्वमेष[५६४] **वोऽस्त्विष्टकामधुगिति॥**

(श्री०भ०गीता० ३, १०)

प्रसविष्यध्वमिति सार्वत्रिकः पाठस्तु[५६५] चिन्त्यः। स्यप्रत्यये लोटोऽसंभवात्। लङि अडागमस्य[५६६] दुर्वारत्वाच्च। यथा भागवते-**प्राचीनतूलेषु कुशेषु धीरः**[५६७]। (श्री०भा०पु० १, ११, १७) इति। प्राचीनयथार्थपाठे[५६८] तदर्थबोधान[५६९]वगमात् केनचिद्विदुषाभासेन प्राचीनमूलेष्विति कल्पितः पाठो[५७०] लेखकै[५७१]र्भ्रान्त्या परम्परया लिखितस्तद्वदयमपि। श्रीधरस्वामिना तु प्रागग्रेष्विति यथा स्थितः[५७२] एव पर्यायः कृतः। तूलस्यैवाग्रपर्यायः संभवति न तु मूलस्य। उक्तं च धर्मशास्त्रे-

अप्रसूता प्रसूताश्च कुशा हि द्विविधा मताः[५७३]**।**
अप्रसूतास्तर्पणादौ प्रसूतास्त्वासने स्मृताः॥ इति।

(?)

अप्रसूता ह्रस्वाः प्रादेशमात्रास्तर्पणपवित्रादिविधाने ग्राह्याः। प्रसूताः सतूला आसनविधौ ग्राह्याः। तूलं कुशा[५७४]ग्रमिति। अथ स्वाध्यायस्याध्ययनोपक्रमेऽन्ते वा त्रीन् कृच्छ्रां[५७५]श्चरित्वा पूतो भवत्यग्निं प्रतिष्ठाप्याग्न्य[५७६] भावे तूदगादित्यं

---

५६४. प्रसविष्यध्व एष।
५६५. पातस्तु।
५६६. अडागमणभस्य।
५६७. धीरत।
५६८. °वे°।
५६९. °नं°।
५७०. °तो।
५७१. लेखखकै°।
५७२. यथास्थिता।
५७३. अप्रसूताश्च कुशाहि द्विविधामताः।
५७४. °श°।
५७५. °च्छ्रा°।
५७६. °ग्न्या°।

वोपसमाधाय दर्भानुपस्तीर्य दर्भेष्वासीनः। प्राक्तूलेषु[५७७] उदक्तूलेषु[५७८] वेति श्रुतेः। दर्भेष्वासीनः प्राक्तूलेषु ब्रह्मवर्चस्कामः, उदक्तूलेषु पशुपुत्रकाम उभयेषूभयकामः पशुस्वस्त्ययनकामो व्रीहियवहोमं प्रयुञ्जीतेति। एवम्–

प्राक्तूले[५७९] बर्हिष्यासीनो गङ्गातीर उदङ्मुख* (श्री०भा०पु० १२, ६, १०) इति द्वादशस्क[५८०]न्धेऽपि बोध्यम्। अत्र तु प्राक्तूळे इति लेखकैः भ्रान्त्या लिखितमस्तीति।

यद्वा सरस्वतीरूपाणां गवां वेदानाम् ईश्वरः प्रवर्तकः। तथा सृष्ट्या[५८१]दिषु सर्वज्ञः। पुनः कीदृशः। ब्रह्मलोके ब्रह्मणामेव सत्त्वा[५८२]त्तैः कृत्वा शोभितविग्रहः। तथा सृष्टिकर्त्र्या[५८३] रजोगुणमय्या मा[५८४]यया अन्वितः। तथा वृत्तिर्जनानां व्यवहारस्तस्य वेत्ता। तथा आनन्दयुक्तः। तथा सुमनसां देवानामीप्सितपूरकः[५८५]। अत एवानन्ददः। तथा अनन्तानि ब्रह्माण्डानि पश्यतीत्य[५८६]नन्तदृक्। तथा सर्वदा प्राणायामपरत्वेन ब्रह्मणः परमात्मन उपासनैकनिष्ठः[५८७]। स इति सृष्टिकर्तृत्वेन प्रसिद्धः। भगवान् गङ्गाधरो ब्रह्मा नोऽस्मानवतु।

किञ्चायं गङ्गाधरशब्दो योगेन समुद्रवाचकस्तत्पक्षे योजना। सत्ये मर्यादापालने आसक्तचित्तः भूत्या रत्नमुक्तादिसंपत्त्या[५८८] भूषितवपुः। तथा

---

५७७. प्राक्तूषुलेषु।

५७८. उदक्तूबलेषु।

५७९. प्राक्तूळे।

५८०. °ख°।

५८१. °ष्टा°।

५८१. °त्वा°।

५८२. °त्र्या।

५८४. म°।

५८५. देवानांमीप्सीति°।

५८६. पश्यतीपश्यतीत्य°।

५८७. °ष्टः।

५८८. मुक्तादिसंपत्या।

* प्राक्कूले बर्हिव्यासीनो गङ्गाकूल उदङ्मुखः इति पाठः भगवतपुराणे।

गवां जलानामीश्वरोऽधिपतिः। डलयोरभेदाज्जडाधिपतिरपि। सर्वज्ञः नदीपर्वतादीनां द्वे द्वे मूर्ती। तज्ज्ञत्वात्[५८९]। द्विजराजेन सुपुत्रेण चन्द्रेण विराजित इत्यर्थः। पुनः कीदृशः। मां लक्ष्मीं याति प्राप्नोतीति मायो विष्णुस्तेनान्वितो युक्तः। तथा वृत्तिरीश्वरस्य चित्तवृत्तिस्तस्या वेत्ता ईश्वराज्ञापरिपालक इत्यर्थः। तथा आ[५९०]नन्दी चन्द्रोदये सतीत्यर्थः। पुनः किंलक्षणः। सुमनसां क्र[५९१]यविक्रये प्रशस्तचित्तानां नौयात्रिकाणां ईप्सितपूरकः। अत एवानन्दजनकः। अनन्तं शेषना[५९२]गं पश्यतीति अनन्तदृक्। विष्णोः पर्यङ्कतयास्य[५९३]। तस्य स्वस्मिन्[५९४] सर्वदा वर्तमानत्वात्। ब्रह्मणो विधेः उप समीपे आसनं रक्षणं तस्मिन् तत्पर उद्युक्तः। तथा स भगवान् नारायणसहित इति समुद्रपक्षे योजना।

अथ गङ्गाधरनामा शास्त्री द्विजस्तत्पक्षे योजना। यदृच्छाशब्दोऽयं पित्रादिकृतसंकेतत्वेन संज्ञात्वाद्द्विजविशेषे रूढः। सत्ये सत्यभाषणे आसक्तचित्तः। पुनः किंविशेषणविशिष्टः। भूत्या संपत्त्या[५९५] भस्मना वा भूषितविग्रहः। गवां वाचां ईश्वरोऽधिपतिः। साक्षाद्बृ[५९६] हस्पतिरेवायमित्यारोपः अर्थाद्गीष्पतिनिभ इत्यर्थः। अत एव सर्वज्ञः सर्ववेत्ता। यद्वा सर्वाणि शास्त्राणि सर्वलोकव्यवहारान्वा सकलवर्णाश्रमधर्माचारान्वा जानातीति तादृशः। पुनः कीदृशः। द्विजानां ब्राह्मणानां राजेति द्विजराजः। स चासौ राजितवपुश्चेति विशेषणसमासः। यद्वा द्विजाश्च राजानश्च तैः राजितवपुः। पुनश्च मा लक्ष्मीः

---

५८९. मूर्तास्तज्ज्ञत्वात्। (illegible reading)

५९०. अ°।

५९१. क्रि°।

५९२. °णा°।

५९३. पर्यंकतापं स्य।

५९४. स्वमिन्°।

५९५. °त्या।

५९६. °क्षात्बृ°।

अयः शुभावहो विधिः ताभ्यामन्वितो युक्तः। पुनश्च वृत्तिवित्। **कृत्तद्धित-समासैकशेषस**[५९७] **नाद्यन्तधातुरूपाः पञ्च**[५९८] **वृत्तयः** (ल०सि० कौ०पा० २, १, ४ वृत्ति)[64]। शक्तिलक्षणाव्यञ्जनारूपा वा तिस्रो वृत्तयस्तासां वेत्ता। तथा आनन्दी। सदानन्दयुक्तः। तथा सुमनसां विदुषामीप्सितपूरकोऽत एवानन्ददः हर्षजनकः। तथा दृश्यतेऽनेनेति दृक् ज्ञानम्। अनन्तं दृक् ज्ञानं यस्येति। यद्वा अनन्तं शब्दब्रह्म पश्यतीति। अनन्तो विष्णुस्तं पश्यतीति वा। अनन्तानि शास्त्राणीति[५९९] वा। पुनः कीदृशः। गायत्र्याख्यं परं ब्रह्म तस्योपासने तत्परः सदोद्युक्तः। तथा[६००] अत एव भगवान् भा[६०१]ग्यशाली सः सर्वत्र प्रसिद्ध इति गङ्गाधरशास्त्री[६०२]द्विजपरत्वे योजना बोध्या। अयं गङ्गाधरशब्दो योगशक्तया जह्नुनाम्नि ऋषिविशेषेऽपि प्रवर्तते। उक्तञ्च–

आदावादिपितामहस्य नियमव्यापारपात्रे जलं
पश्चात्पन्नगशायिनो भगवतः पादोदकं पावनम्।
भूयः शम्भुजटाविभूषणमणिर्जह्नोर्महर्षेरियं
कन्या कल्मषनाशिनी विजयते गङ्गा मनोहारिणीति॥

(महासुभाषितसंग्रह vol.III प० ११४३)

एतत्परत्वे योजना तु स्वयमूह्या अत्र। विवादचतुर्णामर्थानां प्रकृतत्वेऽपि समुद्ररूपार्थस्याप्रकृतत्वात्प्रकृताप्रकृतश्लेषस्तेन शब्दशक्तिमूलो ध्वनिरेवायमिति प्राचीनानां मतमित्यवधेयम्। किञ्च भगवानिति विशेषणोपादानादेतद्ग्रन्थकर्तुः कवेरपि नाम सूचितमस्ति। तेन मुद्रालङ्कारोऽपि व्यज्यते। **सूच्यार्थसूचनं**

---

५९७. सा॰।

५९८. ॰च॰।

५९९. ॰णिति।

६००. तथात।

६०१. भो॰।

६०२. ॰स्त्रि॰।

सा[६०३]**मुद्रे** (कुवलयानन्द० का० १३९) ति तल्लक्षणात्। यत्रोक्ति[६०४]विशेषे[६०५]ण चेष्टादिविशेषेण च गूढतया सुचतुरं प्रति यथान्यः सरलो जनो न जानाति तथार्थसंसूचनं क्रियते तत्र व्यञ्जनावृत्तिरेव। अथोक्तिविशेषेण गूढतया यथा–

इयं सुरतरङ्गिणी सपदि नात्र नौ सङ्गमो[६०६]
भ[६०७]**वेत्तरणिमज्जनं पथिक मा स्म**[६०८] **भीतिं व्रज।**
निधाय हृदि निर्भरं विपुलचारुकुम्भद्वयं
स्फुरद्[६०९]**घनघनागमे घनरसस्य पारं व्रजेति॥**

(सु०र०भा० ६, ८१० पृ० ३३४)

अत्र गङ्गातीरे जलानयनार्थमागताया नायिकायाः पथिकयुवानं प्रति ससूचनोक्तिरियम्– हे पथिकेयं सुरतरङ्गिणी गङ्गा वर्तते। महानदीत्यर्थः। स्वेन तरितुमशक्येत्यर्थः। सपदि नौकाया आगमनं न भविष्यति। तथा तर[६१०]णिमज्जने[६११] सूर्यास्तो भवेत्। अतो भयं मा गाः। दे[६१२]दीप्यमाननिबिडमेघ-प्रादुर्भा[६१३]वे सति हृदयमध्ये विशालं कुम्भद्वयं[६१४] गृहीत्वा घनरसस्य विपुलजलस्य पारं परतीरं गच्छेति प्रसिद्धोऽर्थः। व्यङ्ग्यो[६१५]ऽर्थस्तु हे

---

६०३. स।
६०४. °क्त°।
६०५. °ष°।
६०६. °मे।
६०७. भि°।
६०८. रा।
६०९. °त्°।
६१०. °रा°।
६११. °ज्ु°।
६१२. दै°।
६१३. भा°।
६१४. °य°।
६१५. °व्यंगो°।

पथिकेति सम्बुद्ध्या तवापि रसातिशयो भविष्यतीति व्यज्यते। [इमं लक्षणा।] (इयम् ललना।?) सुरते निधुवने रङ्गिणी प्रेमयुक्ता। सपदि अधुना दिवसे तु नौ आवयोः समागमो[६१६] न भविष्यति। किन्तु यदा तरणिमज्जनं सूर्यास्तो भविष्यति। भयं मा गाः। मम गृ[६१७]हे स्वाम्यादिभयन्नास्ति। एकाकिन्या स्थीयते। अस्मिन्वर्षाऋतौ हृदये उर[६१८]सि निर्भरं गाढं विशालपीनस्तनयुग्मं निधायारोप्य घनो निबिडो यो रसः[६१९] शृङ्गारादि[६२०]स्तस्यानुभवं कुरुष्वेति गूढतया सूचितमिति व्यञ्जना एव। चेष्टया यथा–

अयि अयि अपूर्वचरिअं काणामहिलेन जुं किजुअं कंमं।
दुअकरगहिऔ कण्णौ[६२१] अहरं परिहिअ चुंबिअं णअणं॥ (?)

अयिअयीति कोमलामन्त्रणेन[६२२] का[६२३] णकपुरुषभार्यया यत्कर्म कृतं[६२४] तदपूर्वमेव। अपूर्वता[६२५]मेव व्यनक्ति। द्विकराभ्यां कर्णौ गृहीतौ अधरं ओष्ठं[६२६] परिहृत्य नयनं[६२७] अविकृतनेत्रं चुम्बितमिति। अत्र स्वगृहे उपपतिना सह क्रीडन्त्या तया बहिर्गत्वा पुनः स्वगृहमागच्छन्तं स्वस्वामिनं प्रति मिथ्यारसाविर्भावं प्रकटीकृत्य क[६२८]राभ्यां कर्णद्वयपिधानेन बाधिर्यं[६२९] अविकृतनेत्र–

---

६१६. °मे।
६१७. ग्र°।
६१८. °दा°।
६१९. रोरसः।
६२०. °सस्त°।
६२१. °णौ।
६२२. कोमलामन्त्रेण।
६२३. कां°।
६२४. तत्त°।
६२५. °तो°।
६२६. °ष्टं।
६२७. नयनयनं।
६२८. का°।
६२९. बार्धियं।

चुम्बनेनान्ध्यं[६३०] च संपाद्य त्वया मद्गृहान्निर्भयतया[६३१] गम्यतामिति सूचितम्। विकृतनेत्रेण दर्शनाभावोऽस्ति। अविकृतनेत्रस्य तु चुम्बनेनान्ध्यमिति दर्शनाभावः। कर्णद्वयपिधानेन बाधिर्यादुपपतिपादसंचारज्ञानाभावश्च व्यज्यते इत्यवश्यमेव[६३२] शक्तिलक्षणातिरिक्ताव्यञ्जनावृत्तिरङ्गीकार्येत्यलम[६३३] तिविस्तरेणेति दिक्।

ग्रन्थो विचारदीपाख्यो रचितो विदुषां मुदे।
भगवद्विदुषा[६३४] चात्र नवं नैव प्रकल्पितम्।।१।।

यथा गेहे[६३५]गाढं तिमिरमपनीय प्रभवति
प्रदीपोऽयं लोके प्रकटयितुमर्थांस्तु निखिलान्।
तथायं सद्ग्रन्थो निखिलबुध[६३६]हृत्संशयतमो-
ऽपनीय प्रख्यातान् चरयतु पदार्थांस्तु सकलान्।।२।।

येऽलङ्कारविवेचनासु चतुराः सच्छास्त्रिणः सत्क्रिया-
निष्णाता रसकाव्यनाटकगुणग्राहैकतानान्विताः।
दंभेर्ष्याविमुखाः[६३७] स्वभावसरला ये वा गुण[६३८]ग्राहिणः
सुज्ञानां स[६३९]ततं मुदं वितनुतां तेषामियं मे कृतिः।।३।।

आनन्दरामविबुधा[६४०]त्मजतामुपेतः
शास्त्रार्थशोधनपरो भगवान् बुधोऽहम्।
याचे क्षमां विबुधवृन्दमथात्र मन्तौ
य[६४१]त्साध्वसाधुचरितं मयकानिबन्धे।।४।।

---

६३०. °नाध्यं।
६३१. मद्गृहान्निर्भयत्तगा।
६३२. व्यज्यतेत्यवश्यमेव।
६३३. °मि°।
६३४. भवद्विदुषा।
६३५. °है।
६३६. °द्ध°।
६३७. °ख्याः।
६३८. °णा°।
६३९. त°।
६४०. °द्धा°।
६४१. थ°।

लालीग्रामस्थितिजुषा नाम्ना भगवताधुना।
विप्रेणेदं विरचितं गङ्गाधरमुदेऽस्तु तत्।।५।।

संवदष्टादशे षष्टि[६४२]तमेऽब्दे मासि चाश्विने।
शुक्ले सोमे च पञ्चम्यां प्राप्तः[६४३] संपूर्णतामयम्।।६।।

इति[६४४] श्रीरैक्वज्ञातीयानन्दरामभट्टात्मजेन
भगवता रचितोऽयं ग्रन्थः
संपूर्णतामगमत्।
।। श्रीः श्रीः श्रीः श्रीः ।।

---

६४२. °ष्ठी°।
६४३. °तः।
६४४. °ती°।

CHAPTER - III

TRANSLATION

Salutation to *Śrīgaṇeśa*. Having bowed down at the pair of the feet of my reverend teacher, (and having bowed) to Lord Viṣṇu, to Śiva with Ambā, to the Sun and to Lord Gajānana (lit. one with the face of an elephant), I, Bhagavān, prepare a *Vādagrantha,* easy to comprehend, called Vicāradīpa, (lit. the lamp of thought) of the word *śāstra*.

The prose-order is like this: Having bowed down to the pair of feet of the four *gurus* mentioned in the *mantraśāstra* and to the five gods *Viṣṇu* etc. I, the poet, Bhagavān by name, compose a work called Vicāradīpa, an easily comprehensible work of detailed discussion of the term *śāstra*.

Here, if it is argued that as in the case of *praṇamya śitikaṇṭhāya* (having saluted to Blue-throat God) etc. so also in the case like *gurupādayugam* etc. there will be dative case and not the accusative,

(We reply) :

On the strength of the *paribhāṣā —upapadavibhakteḥ kārakavibhaktir' balīyasī "kāraka* case obstructs the dative *upapada* case" the accusative *kāraka* case obstructs the dative *upapada* case (here). In the cases like *praṇamya śitikaṇṭhāya* etc. there is dative case on the strength of the *sūtra.—kriyārho-papadasya ca karmaṇi sthāninaḥ* etc. i.e. in a sentence, when the purpose of an action is *upapada,* and that action is unexpressed, the object of that unexpressed verb takes dative case.

Only by the use of the qualifier *sāmba,* the qualified *śiva* shall be understood as accompanied by *śakti*. Only the qualifier is used for the comprehension of the qualified as in *sāgarāmbarā* etc.

Here the term *śāstra.* is mentioned without case-termination as in *rāmeti lokaramaṇāt* i.e. 'He is called Rāma as he pleases the people' because it is *anukaraṇa* like that in *bhū sattāyām.*

And it is said :

> "Only therefore, *go* is mentioned as in *bhūsattāyām*— '*bhū* in the sense of existence' it is neither *prāti-padika* nor *pada* and yet it is considered to be correct."

(*vicāradīpa* means) 'an enlightner of thoughts like a lamp kindler.' Here, by the word *dīpa* in the compound *sādhyavasānā lakṣaṇā* is established, because its definition is :

> "Where only *viṣayin* is expressed, it should be known as *sādhyavasānā lakṣaṇā.*"

Or else, the compound would have been *vicāradīpakam* as in *dīpakālaṅkāra*. There (in *dipaka* figure of speech) the termination kan is enjoined in the sense of *iva* on account of its similarity to a lamp which is placed on the street for the decoration of a palace, becoming beneficial to many.

> if it is argued : "but now here, the word *vicāra* possesses expectancy (of meaning) with the word *śāstra*.. On account of its uncompoundability according to the *vārttika-sākāṅkṣam asamarthavad vācyam,"*—word possessed of expectancy should be considered as uncompoundable," the *sūtra-samarthaḥ padavidhiḥ* will not apply and there is no other *sūtra*. enjoining a compound. Therefore, the compound (*vicāradīpa*) is not possible.

(We reply) —No.

Because, compounds can be formed everywhere on the strength of the statement of *bhaṣyavārttika-bhavati vai nityasāpekṣasya vṛttiḥ*-A compound is possible even of words which are ever-expectant.

> And it is said by Kaiyaṭa : "Every word which is related, is always used as a word possessed of an expectancy. As in a sentence, this expectancy is not rejected even in compoundation."

With the same import, Mallinātha also has said: "Even-when there is an expectancy, compound is possible due to comprehensibility." He has, therefore, explained-*rater'gṛhītā-nunayena kāmam*....etc., "who has accepted the urge of Rati," like *caitrasya śiṣyakulam and maitrasya gurukulam*. "The group of Chaitra's students" and "the house of Maitra's teacher."

And in this way having rejected the reading—*kṣatrasya-śabdo bhuvaneṣu ruḍhaḥ*—"The word of *kṣatra* is conventionally used in the worlds"....., the reading *kṣatre'ti sabdo bhuvaneṣu*... "the word *kṣatra* is conventionally used in the world.." should be accepted.

In *kurve*, 'I compose,' the first person 'I' should be understood by *adhyāhāra*. *adhyāhāra* means supplementing a part of the expected sense in the sentences. Expectancy belongs to the import only because construction always depends on the meaning. As in—*bhavānapīdam paravānavaiti* 'your honour, who is answerable to somebody knows this;' the meaning of the word (and not the word) *yuṣmad* is implied; or else, had the word been implied, there would not have been third person as here in the case of *avaiti* because the word *yuṣmad* itself would have been principal as the qualified, the word *bhavān*-your honour-would not haven been principal on account of its etymology from the root *bhā* 'to shine' and its acceptance as the qualifier. Because of this (reason), in *tattvam nivartasva vihāya lajjām gurorbhavān darśitaśiṣyabhaktiḥ*, "You, therefore , go back and don't feel ashamed, as your honour has already displayed a pupil's devotion for your teacher;"—there is no repetition. But in case like *bhavati bhikṣam dehi* "Your ladyship, give alms," etc. the word *yuṣmad* will have to be supplemented because only then, the word *bhavat* in the vocative sense will be meaningful. Or else, there would not have been the second person in *dehi'* give me.'

> If it is argued that when only meanings are construed, the supplementation of words is not proper,
>
> (We reply)—It is nor so.

According to the view that in the comprehension of a word, the word also shines, it is accepted that the construction of the meanings takes place only through the means of the words, thus, evenwhen one is thirsty for water only, it (water) is brought only by means of the pot.

Here, in the beginning, the word *śrī* has been employed to avoid the blemish of *niṣiddhagaṇa* etc.

At first then, he (the author), performs *maṅgala* in the form of salutation to observe the scholarly tradition and states the topic he intends to expound:

> "The Veda is the Lord incarnate. Grammar is His mouth. The statements of these two constitute the *śāstra*. The other branches of knowledge also reside within the two, therefore, they also possess *śāstratva-'śāstraic character'*."

By the Veda etc. he refutes those who prattle without traditional knowledge that the quality of *śāstra* is only in logic etc. numbered six as in–

"Two logics, two *Mīmāṁsās* and two *yogas,* as these six show the meaning of the Veda hence are called *darśanas* by the wise and not in other essays"

The purport is: The Veda is Lord Nārāyṇa incarnate. The mouth of that Lord is said to be grammar as confirmed in *śikṣā*. The sayings of these two are instruction or order. That meaning is to be denoted by the word *śāstra*. As it is said: 'Instruction is *śāstra* as it considers the statements of the ancient authorities.'

"Though it is explained in Manoramā in its *bhāṣyavṛtti,* that instruction is *śāstra* on the strength of its instrumental derivation as 'it is instructed by this' i.e. *śāstra,* yet, it is a bold statement only since the termination *ghañ (a)* is rare in the sense of instrument as it is obstructed by the termination *lyuṭ* (*an*)"

Yet, however, in the case of the word *śāstra* the derivation by instrumental only is justifiable, because of manifoldness in the affix *ṣṭran* from amongst *uṇādi* declensions applied to the root √*śās* on the strength of the rule *bāhulaka* under *pāṇinisūtra-uṇādayo bahulam.* As is explained in Amara: the word *śāstra* is used in the sense of *nideśa 'order'* and *grantha* 'a book.' *nideśa*= order. *śāstra* is that by which it is instructed. Kṣīras-wāmin has so established it by the termination *ṣṭran* used to convey the sense of instrument. Though the moderners have disregarded the ancients' view and refuted such derivation by instrumental, yet the *bāhulaka* suffixes are accepted only by helplessness therefore, on consideration, the view of the ancients appears appropriate only.

And thus when the *śāstraic* character of all the orders and works is established, it automatically evolves of *vyākaraṇa* as well as the *sūtras* within it.

In the parlance of the grammarians, while considering the aspects of a *śāstra,* it is said that which is well-stated is a *śāstra,* therefore, the question of *siddhatva or asiddhatva* arises of the *sūtras* only. Also it is said:

> "In fact, (in *śāstra*) the specific would be stronger than the general. Or mostly it is seen here that the former is subjugated by the latter."

Mādhava commenting on this also has said: "A rule is general and an appropriate statement or definition of it is *śāstra.*"

Thus it should be understood that as the Naiyāyikas have

definitions of Earth, Water, Light, Wind, and Ether, the Vaiyākaraṇas have their dicta.

> "The man who desires to speak in an assembly without studying grammar, the science of words, wishes to bind a strongly intoxicated elephant with the fibre of lotus in a forest."

In such verses and others, the word *śāstra* is employed for grammar, and it shoud not be said that there is no evidence to prove the *śāstraic* character of grammar, because even in the case of its not being *asiddha* as *śāstra* and in incidences like *sāmānyaśāstrato nūnam*.....etc. (as mentioned above) the only evidence of their *siddhatva* or *asiddhatva* will be the very sight of it. And, therefore, even their mutual actions are accomplished by *śāstra*. This is so even on the evidence of the statement "in this science the properties are non-distinctive' etc.

> Now, if it be argued that because of its being the mouth of the Vedas, if only *vyākaraṇa* is (accepted as) *śātra,* there will arise a contingency that the attainment of the *śāstraic* category in the case of Nyāya etc. will be hindered.

In the case of such a doubt it is replied: *tātsthyāt etc.* On account of the traditional authority (of Patañjali) *tātsthyāt-tāchchhabdyam* 'That which stays in it, can be called by that name.' That which stays in it is *tātstha. tātsthyam* is its abstraction. Therefore *pareṣu* i.e. in others, viz. in the sciences of Nyāya, Mīmāṁsā, Vedānta, eighteen Smṛtis, poetry, Alaṅkāra, Rasa, drama, music, Kāma, elephants etc, 'thatness' means the characteristic of being *śāstra* (science) is accepted by the learned. This is implied. The purport is that there is *śāstratva* in all the compositions an account of there being the existence of grammar in the form of the total structure as the outcome of the *sūtras* of *prakṛti* 'base', *pratyaya 'affix', utsarga* 'rule' and *apavāda* 'exception'. And thus:

> "Purāṇa, Nyāya, Mīmāṁsā, Dharmaśāstra and the

> Vedas alongwith their *aṅgas* are fourteen abodes of knowledge and religion."

In the Vedas and Purāṇa, Nyāya, Mīmāṁsā, Dharmaśāstra, Śikṣā, Kalpa, Vyākaraṇa, Nirukta, Chhandaḥ and Jyotiṣa being the fourteen abodes of knowledge described by Yājñavalkya, the *śāstraic* character is not objectionable.

Here it shoud be understood-just as in the human beings mouth (face) is all important among the limbs like hand, foot etc; so also in the case of the Vedas, *vyākaraṇa* is principal among the *vedāṅgas* like Sikṣā Kalpa etc. because in sacrificial rituals, grammarians are seen to be predominant. For example:

> "There, in the ritual applications, the ritualists expert in *ūha*, made appropriate changes in the *mantras* which were not obviously expressive in the Vedas with all the case and genders."

And so also, the poetry, too, is instructive and therefore, it is a *śāstra*. And its instructiveness is stated by the poeticians. To explain-

> "Poetry leads to fame, the acquisition of wealth, the knowledge of the ways of the world, the removal of inauspicious things, the instantaneous (attainment of the) highest bliss and the conveyance of advice in the manner of a beloved."

The definition of poetry is well-said in Rasavilāsa and Kāvyaprakāśa and thus, the essence of poetry in the form of Rasa is depicted in all its paraphernalia. Now, the definition of the essence of poetry which possesses the delimitorness i.e. which is the delimiter of the state of being defined which will describe the nature of that which is expressed by the word *kāvya* or poetry is being stated:

> "It (poetry) consists of word and sense which are free from defects, are possessed of excellences and again, are some times without figures of speech."

The word Kāvya conveys the meaning of word and sense characterised by the qualifications faultlessness etc. In *adoṣau* the negation has the sense of 'a little' as in *anudarā kanyā*-a maiden with slim belly because it is difficult to avoid blemishes completely. And, if it is to be totally free from blemish, it can not be said that a particular poem is defective (because a defective literary work cannot be called a poem at all.

If it is argued that poetry is not traditionally accepted as *śāstra,*

Then we reply that the same is the case with Purāṇa also. According to the statement-

'This Purāṇa named Bhāgavata is just like Brahma i.e. Veda; though Bhāgavata is very well-known as Purāṇa, the activity of this Bhāgavata *śāstra* is twofold, in brief and in detail-so is said by Śrītharaswāmin. The import is-a similar usage is seen in the case of the Purāṇa. Hence its *śāstraic* character.

Or else, among fourteen abodes of knowledge described by Yājñavalkya some might be called *śāstra* and some might not and there would arise the contingency of *ardhajaratīya* semiacceptibility.

And moreover, when Nyāya and other *darśanas* numbered six are accepted as *śāstra,* just as only *brahmins* have the previlege to study those scriptures and they are called *śāstrīs.* the controller of an elephant also would be called a *śāstrī* by studying the works on controlling elephants. Otherwise in-

> "The controller by virtue of his training, slowly brought under control the jumping child-elephant who had discarded the hook by appeasements and threats by turn. Where does *śāstra* not bring success to those who possess determined intelligence?"

etc., there would not be *arthāntaranyāsa* resulting from corroboration. Unless a treatise of controlling elelphants is considered to be a *śāstra,* its reader the controller would not be a *śāstrin* and there would not be any generalisation possible.

And when it is so-the general cannot be without the particular and the particular cannot exist merely by their mention-on this principle the particular is corroborated by the general; on account of the principle—"when a particular thing is to be described, and with it, another irrelevant general thing is suggested, or when the general is to be described and with it, another irrelevant meaning is suggested, the figure of speech will be *arthāntaranyāsa*-corroboration.

If fact, however, for treatises about the erotic science and the science of elephants, the word *śāstra* is used in secondary sense i.e. this *śāstra* is also like other sciences. it is to be understood that as a *śāstra* is fruitful to its students, in the same way, the works on sciences (said-above) are beneficial to those who study them. in this way, those who make a show of their arrogance either by pride or by jealousy in the company of fools saying "we are the very best *śāstra* experts, whereas these students of *purāṇas,* poetry, rhetorics aesthetics, drama etc. are only ordinary" are refuted. And moreover, wrong statements about that (literature) by recitation of which Śuka, Maitreya etc. and by hearing of which Parīkṣit, Vidura etc. attained to the state of Brahman, does incur blemish. it is also said:

> "A *śūdra* would become *cāṇḍāla,* if he drinks milk of a *kapilā* cow, if he enjoys sexual union with a brahmin woman, and if he recites the Veda-*mantras*. A *śūdra* therefore, should never listen to the Vedas knowingly. he should find their meaning in the Purāṇas explained by the sages."

And thus on the strength of this *smṛti-*

> "Those twice borns who earn their living by resorting to the *paurāṇika* profession, they also having penetrated through the orb of the Sun, reach the permanent *brahman;"*

just as the *paurāṇikas* by reciting *purāṇas* and just as the logicians by their knowledge of the entities, so also the grammarians by their knowledge of words and meaning attain emancipation.

And there is also such a *śruti:*

"A single word well-employed and properly-known becomes *kāmadhenu* i.e. fulfils one's desires in the heavenly world" as the words are of the nature of *brahman*.

And it is also said:

"Two *brahmans* are to be known, the *śabdabrahman* and that which is beyond. One who is well-versed in the *śabdabrahma* attains the *parabrahma.*"

This is a *smṛti* precept.

Incidentally, evidence for the existence of *sphoṭa* is shown here. According to the grammarians, sound is of two types: *sphoṭa* and *dhvani*. *Sphoṭa* is that owing to which the sense becomes manifest. That from which the *sphoṭa* becomes manifest is *dhvani,* which is the reminder of *sphoṭa* like script.

Now, if it is argued that meaning will become manifest by the last syllable accompanied by the impressions created by the utterance of each of the former syllables, what is the necessity of the concept of *sphoṭa?*

we reply—No. since both (the former and the final) syllables do not have *saṅketa,* 'convention' (to convey the sense), there would arise the contingency of partial acceptability, If there were no *sphoṭa* there would be no recognition that this is that same *mantra.* And it should not be said that this recognition is like a medicine depending upon similarity (i.e. a similar medicine).

Without *sphoṭa* there arise the fruitfulness of some different *mantra* like that of some another *mantra* of which *puraścaraṇa* is undertaken and there would arise the contingency of scopelessness (*nirviṣayatā*) of the *mantra* of which *puraścaraṇa* is performed.

And moreover, (without *sphoṭa)* there would arise the contingency of the mortality of gods. The concept of *sphoṭa,* therefore, is definitely appropriate. Now, if evenwhen the sound dies out, its impression is believed to convey sense, then(the corollary) that even after a pot is destroyed, the potentiality of impression arising out of its experience of its destruction to bring water will indeed be unavoidable.

And again. since the former impressions and the final syllable reside in different substrata, it is impossible that they bring about the one and the same result.

> Now, if it is argued that since sense cannot manifest itself in the absence of convention, the *varṇasphoṭa* cannot be established; then

(it should be said that) in *rāma* etc. and *bhavati* etc. by the alternative change of single letters, the perception being altered, the letters are proved to be expressive by *anvaya-vyatireka.* hence *varṇasphoṭa* is established. In words like *saraḥ, rasaḥ etc.* the conventions of the words are demarcated by the order of the syllables. Therefore, *padasphoṭa* is established. Isolated words cannot give rise to the transactions of activity or retirement. Hence *vākyasphoṭa* has to be accepted. Unless we accept the *varṇasphoṭa,* the potentiality of the *bījamantras* (syllables) to convey the sense of gods will not be established.

> Now,supposing on being asked, what thing this *sphoṭa* is, we define that *sphoṭa* is the absence of utter-destruction of syllables, then?

We reply—No, because it is not possible for a non-existence to bring about a positive effect. therefore, *sphoṭa* is a positive entity, *śabdabrahma* by name.

Eventhough eight varieties of *sphoṭa* are enumerated in theoretical treatises viz.

(1) *varṇavyaktisphoṭa, (2) sakhaṇḍapadavyaktisphoṭa, (3) akhaṇḍapadavyaktisphoṭa, (4) sakhaṇḍavākyavyaktisphoṭa, (5) akhaṇḍapadajātisphoṭa* and *(8) akhaṇḍavākyajātisphoṭa;* yet the purport lies in *vākyasphoṭa,* particularly in *jāti-*

sphoṭa.Thus the sound being suggestive, its being conveyer of the meaning by convention is the definition of *sphoṭa*.

Let us resume the subject in hand. Because the word *śāstra* is polysemic,. are all the meanings comprehended simultaneously by *yoga rūḍhi?* That is the controversy.

All the senses cannot be perceived simultaneously because of the maxim that a word uttered once can convey only one meaning. Just as a single arrow-shot once pierces only one target, similarly here also, that is meaning. Just as king having a number of horses cannot ride all of them simultaneoulsly but only by turns. Similarly here also.

The *ālaṅkārikās* believe thus: according to the maxim-a word uttered once conveys the meaning once only—considering the impermanence of this (polysemic word i.e. sound) from amongst its multiple meanings, wherever the import-conveyers like context etc. operate simultaneously, there, it will be a figure of speech called *śleṣa*. Where the imports are understood by turns, there, it is repetition. thus, everywhere, the context etc. are the conveyers of the import of (a polysemic word by turns.)

And it is said in Kāvyaprakāśā :

> "When the expressive power of a word which has more than one primary sense, is restricted to one sense by means of conjunction and the like, the process which produces the apprehension of a sense that is not expressed is suggestion."[1]

"conjunction, disjunction, association, antagonism. motive, context, special attribute, proximity of another word, power, propriety, place, time, gender, accent and others are the causes of recollection i.e. the apprehension of a particular meaning, when there is no determination regarding the meaning of a (homonymous) word."[2]

The meaning is : When there arises a doubt as to which sense of a homonymous word is intended in a context, the conjunction etc. are the (causes of recollection) of the sense specifically intended there. The examples of conjunction etc. are not described here for the fear of expansion.

Yet the instance of context is-*sarvaguṇavān sarvam jānāti devàḥ*-"Possessing all qualities, my lord knows everything." This is the statement of a messenger towards his king. The polysemicness of the word *deva* is on the evidence of the dictionary—*rājā bhaṭṭārako devaḥ. deva* means (i) king (ii) master.

> Now, if an objection is raised in the compound *sarvaguṇavān, the mat* suffix along with *karmadhāraya* is not appropriate because it is prohibited in cases where the meaning is conveyed by taking it as *bahuvrīhi,* and when the sense is accomplished by *bahuvrīhi* (resolution of the compound) as *sarve guṇāḥ yasya sarvaguṇaḥ,* why should one resort ot prolixity of employing two *vṛttis namely matup* suffix and *karmadhāraya?*
>
> To this we reply—

By the dictum : *varṇo varṇena* The compound *kṛṣṇasāraṅgḥ* can be explained either as *kṛṣṇena sāraṅgaḥ* the deer is colourful with the black colour, or *Kṛṣṇaḥ sāraṅgḥ,* the black deer. Now what is the difference between the two? On this occasion, when ambiguity between *bahuvrīhi* and *karmadhāraya* arose, the *bhāṣyakāra* has given his decision :

Here in the cases of appositional compound, it will be *bahuvrīhi* on account of *vipratiṣedha*—but sometimes it becomes *karmadhāraya* for the purpose of justifying compounds like *sarvadhana* (alongwith the *matvarthīya* suffix). Here, eventhough by *vipratiṣedha,* the *bahuvrīhi* is opportune for the purpose of avoiding prolixity of the duplication of employing *vṛttis*. The entire effort here is for this: when the stem (*prakṛti*) is a *karmadhāraya,* the *matvarthīya* suffixes are denied totally for the purpose of avoiding prolixity by the duplication of *vṛttis:* yet preceptors say (that sounds are effects) thinking that they are impermanent (like *ghaṭa* and *paṭa*) as they are *kārya (effect).*

And some distinction is certainly there between the two (i.e. *bahuvrīhi* and *karmadhāraya* with *matvarthīya* suffix): the seven specific senses like *bhūmanindā* etc. (profusion, censure etc.) indicated by *matvarthīya* suffixes are not conveyed by *bahuvrīhi*, Therefore, the prolixity for some specific purpose does not constitute a fault, and on that principle, even the duplication of *vṛttis* causing prolixity is accepted.

This being so, the *matvarthīya* suffix only will be justified for the purpose of conveying the specific sense of *bhūmanindā* etc. in usages like *sarvadhanī—one possessing all types of* wealth, *sarvabījī sarvakeśī, gāḍhānurāgī, ekadeśī, gaurakha-ravadaraṇyam, kṛṣṇasarpavān valmīkaḥ, lohitaśālimān-ghāmaḥ, nīlarūpavat sarojam, hansacihnadukūlavān* etc.

Then what can *bahuvrīhi* do (It will be useless.) Moreover, in the dictum: *vipratiṣedhe param* the word *para* denotes the sense of *iṣṭa* 'intended', owing to the explanation that whatever is later i.e. intended, is accepted, in *vipratiṣedha* i.e. in the opposition or confilict between two equally strong rules; and since there is absence of 'intendedness' here (in *sarvaguṇavān*) there will be not *bahuvrīhi*.

But on the strength of the indicatory statement i.e. the usage *kṛṣṇasarpavān valmīkaḥ* in Bhāṣya some say that (in *sarvaguṇvān* etc.) it is the *matvarthīya* suffix. Their opinion appears to be more acceptable.

In reality all usages cannot be justified by a single indicatory statement but only some exceptional (inexplicable) ones, due to the prohibition (by the rule) that everywhere the usage is not explained by an indicatory statement. In fact only exceptional usages are justified either by an indicatory statement or by a faulty employment and not all the usages.

And in this way–

The word *subhrū* in vocative cannot be short i.e. *subhru* because it (*subhrū*) cannot have *nadīsamjñā* according to the dictum नेयङुवङ्स्थानावस्त्री। (i.e. feminine words ending in ī and ū which admit the substitute *iyaṅ* and *uvaṅ* are not called *nadī* except the word स्त्री), and the dictum अम्बार्थनद्योर्ह्रस्वः (i.e. a short vowel is substituted in vocative singular for the *ā* of the feminine, in the sense of 'mother, mother dear'as well as for the long vowel of the feminines called *nadī*), does not apply in the case of *subhrū*. Therefore, the usage of short *u* in *subhru* (in voc. sing.) is faulty.

Therefore, it is not appropriate that some (critics) have justified the usage *subhru* as a faulty employment in हा पितः क्वासि हे सुभ्रु- 'O father! where are you? O *subhru!*' by Bhaṭṭi.

The word सुभ्रु is seen to be used with a short end (as सुभ्रु) in vocative singular everywhere, nowhere it is used with a long end (as *subhrū*.) sometimes even a faulty usage becomes universal. Its multiple usage is seen as in Naiṣadha-

> "Thou with eye-brows akin to the (flowery) bow of the flowerarrowed Cupid! like goldsmiths shall we burn that impudent, tawny gold which vies with the fair complexion of the body."[3] and in Rasavilāsa—"O lady with beautiful brows! since you are enraged, I have given up food and talking about other ladies (abandoned fragrant garlands and incense totally. O loving lady, give up your anger. forgive me who am bowing down to you. be pleased. Really, in your separation, all the directions are dark for me.)
>
> and also in Kāvyaprakāśa—
>
> "O lady with beautiful brows! we have taken resort into the sea as we are frightened by Kings (like Jarāsandha etc.)."
>
> in the same way in Śrīmadbhāgavatə—
>
> "O lady with beautiful brows! women who follow men like us, generally suffer agony."
>
> and the usage by Kālidāsa in Kumārasambhavam:
>
> "O lady with beautiful brows! how can there be humiliation in your father's house?" In this, someone

who creating a variant and effecting a word-change
as *subhrūḥ kutasāta gṛhe' vamānanā,*

thus rectifies (the text) is only a fool dear to the gods, because there will follow a contingency of the breach of the *ja* group *(jagaṇa)* in the beginning of the quarter of a *vaṁśasthavṛtta.* In Vṛttaratnākara the definition of the *vaṁśastha* metre is given as: the groups *jatajara* are called the metre *vaṁśastha.*

In fact the justification of the form *subhru* will be (as the following):

According to the *vārttika-aprāṇijāteścārajjvādīnām,* (i.e. the affix *ūṅ* comes after words ending in *ū,* not having *ya* as its penultimate letter, denoting non-animate *jāti* and except the words *rajju* etc.), the Bhāṣyakāra has illustrated the *ūṅ* suffix even from *ūkāra* as in अलाबूः, कर्कन्धूः etc. As Vāmana said: even from the words ending in *ū,* the *ūṅ* the declension takes place. Thus, the therefore, making the word *subhrū* to end in *ūṅ,* the word-change should be accomplished. Or, in dictum *ūṅ utaḥ* (i.e. *ūṅ* should be made from *ut*) application *ūṅ can* be separated (by *yogavibhāga*) and to it (i.e. *ūṅ*) the word *bahuvrīheḥ* should be brought for a definite purpose by continuity (*anuvṛtti*) and by frog-jump (*maṇḍūkapluti*). Thus the dictum-*kvacit bahuvrīheḥ ūṅ syāt.* (some times, in *bahuvrīhi,* there would be *ūṅ*) will be accomplished. Now, the word *subhrū* would have an ending in *ūṅ* termination, by word—change, it will obtain *nadīsaṁjñā* and have short *u* in vocative according to the dictum *ambārthanadyor hrasvaḥ.* Therefore, even the vocative *'he subhru'* is unobjectionable.

Even in the case of there being no continuity of = *'bahuvrīheḥ'*, the sense of 'sometimes,' is certainly obtained. therefore, the affix *ūṅ* even in the case of *alābū* (bottle-gourd) and *karkandhū* (jujube-tree) will be justified. By admitting *ūṅ* suffix even from the *ū* as in the case of these two examples, Bhāṣyakāra has, of course, indicated the *yogavibhāga* (division of a dictum). Either an absence of specific purpose in the making of a *pratyāhāra* with t in *utaḥ* be admitted? Or a non-continuity of the short *ukāra* in the *vārttika* अप्राणिजाते:......etc. be admitted? Or the letter *ca* having the sense of inclusion of unmentioned elements be admitted? (whatever it may be but)—

In short, therefore, on the stength of the *yogavibhāga* indicated by the examples ending in Long *ū,* the ending of *subhrū* in *ūṅ* termination is well-justified; and, therefore, by a word-change the word *subhrū* obtains *nadīsaṁjñā* and indeed becomes short *u* in the vocative.

Due to the occurrence of the words *bhavatyeva* (indeed becomes), the meaning of *eva* (indeed) is also explained. The meaning of *eva* is threefold. The first is connected with the verb, the second with the qualifier and the third with the substantive. If it is connected with the verb, it will mean the exclusion of total absence as in 'the blue lotus is definitely there, (not that it is not there.) If connected with the qualifier, it will mean exclusion of absence of any other thing as in the 'the conch is indeed white, (it cannot be of any other colour), and if connected with the substantive, it should mean the exclusion of everything else as in 'Pārtha only is the bow-wielder, (and noone else).

Therefore, it should be understood that *eva* has many meanings. It being so here in—

"Only Rukmiṇī and no other woman deserves to become only *his* wife; He also of a blameless form is a deserving husband of Bhaiṣmī" though having several meanings, the single *evakāra* has three restrictions of meaning in the first half-*asya eva* (his only), *rukmiṇīeva* (Rukmiṇī only) and *arhati eva* (deserves indeed); and in the latters half, the three restrictions are as *asau eva* (he only), *bhaiṣmyā eva* (of Bhaiṣmī only) *samucito bhavati eva* (is indeed deserving).

If you ask how six restrictions can simultaneously take place by construing with six items, (then) listen:

Here the intention of Śrīdharaswāmī is this: the *evakāra* associated with the word *asya* construes (with the other words) one after another and not simultaneously, because the tenet is : a word uttered once conveys the meaning once only, and construes (with other words) only once. The words *hari* etc. are homonyms but their expressive power is restricted (to one sense) by means of conjunction and the like. So they convey the various meanings by turns. In fact, a king possessing many horses does not ride all the horses simultaneously but (does so) only by turns. Similarly in the case of a single horse having three masters, all the three cannot ride him simultaneously.

And, thus, though *evakāra* every where conveys the three senses namely exclusion of absence, exclusion of everything else and exclusion of total absence. yet in the present case, there is only one *evakāra* namely exclusion of everything else construed with six different elements by turn in six ways. The simultaneous mention is indeed for suggesting the equivalence of different construing. The sense obtainable is that Rukmiṇī deserves to be the wife of this only i.e. of Kṛṣṇa only and of noone else. Therefore, by *evakāra,* the exclusion of all, like the lord of *cedya* etc. other than Śrīkṛṣṇa is to be understood.

In the expectancy of justification, he has said; *'nāparā'*. This (Rukmiṇī) in not any other woman, but on the strength of *purāṇa* statement: राघवत्वेऽभवत् सीता रुक्मिणी कृष्णजन्मनि। (She i.e. Lakṣmī became Sītā when Viṣṇu became Rāghava, and was Rukmiṇī in his birth as Kṛṣṇa.) Rukmiṇī is the same who was Sītā in the former birth and no one else, Such is the intention of the learned. or else, on account of her having heard the uncommon qualities of Śrīkṛṣṇa, for whom, there is none other than Śrīkṛṣṇa from the point of view of desirability. Or else, ā.i.e. in every way higher i.e. better than whom there is no other woman (as the wife of Śrīkṛṣṇa), Or else, only Rukmiṇī—none else deserves to be the wife of this i.e. Śrīkṛṣṇa.The *evakāra* associated with the word Rukmiṇī denotes the exclusion of all other wives (or beloveds). Though Satyabhāmā etc. (will) have (such) a capability, yet since the people do not have any knowledge of the future, there is no scope for such a conjecture.

In the former explanation, the *evakāra* mentioned with

the word *asya,* excludes the others, so the affirmation depends on the meaning, while here (in the latter explanation) the affirmation is dependent upon the word. Thus the two are distinct.

And again, one who is a non-wife, deserves to become a wife (=भार्याभवितुं) thus it will be a word compounded in *cvi* suffix. In *arhati eva* the *evakāra* associated with the verb determines here worthiness by excluding the total absence of her deservingness. Thus by threefold exposition, the first half suggests the daughter of Bhīṣma being endowed with all the virtues.

Now the exposition of the second half: *api* is in the sense of 'and'. And then *anavadyātmā* means having a praise-worthy body, or praise worthy nature. It is said in the Amarakośa: "The word *ātmā* gives the sense of 'body', 'patience', 'soul', 'nature' and 'god', It means that this (Kṛṣṇa) only is the self-chosen, suitable husband of Bhaiṣmī because he possesses all the virtues which are desirable. And it is said:

> "A maiden prefers handsomeness in the groom, her mother riches, her father knowledge, her relatives desire noble birth and the other people desire sweet-dishes (in a marriage)."

And again, this blameless Kṛṣṇa, on account of being endowed with seven appropriate groomly qualities and also on account of his expertise in arms and scriptures, is a worthy husband of Bhaiṣmī only. It is also said:

> "A father should give his daughter after proper investigation to a husband who has such virtues as noble birth, character, guardians, education, riches, handsome figure and youth."

And then—this (Kṛṣṇa) is indeed a worthy husband for Bhaiṣmī, and not unworthy. Here also, as before, the threefold determination should be understood from the *evakāra* by the exclusion of everyone else. And thus, there are three determinations in the first half and the three in the latter half-in all six determinations.

> If it is argued here that—when in the former half, the intended sense is established by one word in the possessive case (*asya*) and the other in the nominative case (*rukmiṇī*), then mentioning the same in the latter half also with the inversion of cases is marred by the fault of repetition.....

then we reply—in the former half, by the explanation 'there is no other woman better (in all ways) than Rukmiṇī,' the excellence of Rukmiṇī is suggested, while in the latter half, the qualifier *anavadyātmā* (one who has a praise-worthy form) expresses the excellence of Śrīkṛṣṇa. And in this way here, the excellence of their mutual qualities is expressed by two (independent) statements only. Therefore, to confirm the worthiness of their mutually admirable marriage, two statements are constructed. This is just an indication.

evakāra falls in the *cādi* group (*of nipātas*). *eva,* therefore, is a *nipāta*. Hence the discussion whether it is dyotaka—suggestive or *vacāka*—expressive.

The opinion of the *naiyāyikas* is that *pra etc.* (*upasargas*-prefixes) are suggestive and *ca* etc. (*nipātas*—particles) are expressive. In whichever *śāstra,* whatever is seen, is its meaning. On this maxim, the dictum of the *naiyāyikas* that the *nipātas* are expressive need not be accpepted, because there is no evidence showing the dissimilarity (between *nipātas* and *upasargas*). Therefore, the *vaiyākaraṇas* believe that only the suggestiveness of the *nipāta* is acceptable.

While in the view of the logicians the *nipātas* being expressive, there, will be no construction (word-order) in sentence etc; and according to the grammarians' view, (the *nipātas*) being suggestive, there will be no word-order at all. Therefore, (in either case) there is no fault.

It is clear in Bhūṣaṇa that in 'वागर्थाविव संपृक्तौ.......पार्वती-

परमेश्वरावहं वन्दे।'-I bow down to Pārvatī and Parameśwara closely related like word and sense-since '*vāk* and *artha*' are not object to the verb √*vad,* there will not be construction of the accusative case occurring in the later part of the word (*vāgartha+au*). Also the sense of *iva* cannot convey the sense of relatedness (to the verb √*vad*) as its object.

But otherwise, the vaiyākaraṇas and the ālaṅkārikas do not insist upon the suggestiveness (of the *nipātas*) therefore, the statement of the Vākyapadīya that "it (the *upasarga*) may be either expressive or suggestive because of the probability of the specific sense of the roots" is consistent because it is said that—

"The *nipātas*, the *upasargas* and the roots-all the three are said to be conveying several senses. The text is the evidence."

Also, on account of the polysemicness of the *nipātas* due to the etymology of (the word *nipāta*) as 'they definitely move into various meanings with certainty,' (the *nipātas* can be suggestive.)

The opposition disputes :

Again, the statement in Bhūṣaṇa, that there should be no relatedness of the accusative suffix occuring in the later part (of the word *vāgarthau)* because of the absence of its objectness to √वद्, is not consistent, because it is contradictory on the face of it. Also in the absence of the objectness, the accusative case also will be absent, then, on the strength of which *sūtra* is the accusative ordained?

In fact, there should not be accusative case here, it should be nominative instead. To explain—

In *vāgarthāviva*......how is the word iva intended to be expressive of likeness? If that is the dispute, we reply: In *vāgarthāviva*....etc. just as speech and sense are closely related, by the relation of invariable concommitance, united as one as the *mīmāṁsakas* have said that the relation between the word and sense is eternal, so also, i.e. in the same manner, Pārvatī and Parameśwara are closely related.That is construction. The two are closely related, therefore, they are *samprktau,* wherein the suffix *kta* is applied to denote the sense of doer, and by this *kṛt* suffix, the subject is indicated. So, here, there is the nominative case and not the accusative. The *ālaṅkārikas* believe that this should be understood by the intelligent people with a subtle insight.

And again, the *vṛtti* is the relation between the word and the sense characterised be signification. And this *vṛtti* resides in the word and in the sense, and thus has dual characteristic. It is of three kinds namely, *śakti* 'denotation', *lakṣaṇā* 'indication and *vyañjanā* 'suggestion' as they say.

And there—the instruction of an originator that a certain sense should be understood from a certain word is *saṅketa* 'convention'. The same is the *śakti* according to the logicians, but according to the *ālaṅkārikas* it (*saṅketa*) is different from it (*śakti*) and assisted by it; whereas the *vaiyākaraṇas* believe that all the words have two kinds of power namely *grāhyatva nad grāhakatva.* The first among these is *śakya* 'denotative', the second is *lākṣaṇika* 'indicative', and the third is *vyañjaka* 'suggestive'. Among these three *vṛttis, śakti* assists *saṅketa.* And this *śakti* also is of three types: *yoga* 'etymology', *rūḍhi* 'convention' and *yogaruḍhi* 'etymologico-convention'. The causes for the application of (the word) are genus, property, action and proper noun.

When it is so, there are two compounds, first—*vāgarthāv iva* and the second-*yavayā iva.* It should be stated that these two compounds are formed according to the *vārttika-ivena vibhakt yalopaḥ pūrvapadaprakṛtisvaratvam ca* 'a compound with *iva* takes non-elision of the case-termination and retaining of the original accent of the former member of the compound'. When a compound is formed by this *vārttika,* the power which is produced is called *yogaśakti* residing in the compounded word.

It is argued here that there is altogether a different power in a compound as in the word *paṅkaja*. "when a number of *vṛttis* are intended to be accomplished by their expression only, there will be fault of prolixity, therefore, *ekārthībhāva*, union of meanings has to be resorted to."

According to this principle it should be said that (in *paṅkaja*) there would not be *yogaśakti* because, there is no imagination of partial division. In *jahatsvārthāvṛtti* (where the constituent members give up their individual sense) the division in the sense is not accepted, yet, the aspect of the *ajahatsvārthāvṛtti* (where the constituent members do not give up their individual sense) is also accepted on account of its practical utility.

But in *udbāhuḥ iva* the word *iva* is intended to be connected with the word *vāmana,* the substantive. It does not form compound with the word *udbāhuḥ* on account of absence of *sāmarthya*.

If it be asked: what at all is the purpose of forming a compound here because evenif you form a compound, there is no difference?

(Reply:)

The purpose of forming a compound is (threefold): i.e. maintaining the order, change in the accent and indissolvability of the compound.

Then again, according to the logicians, the (potentially) denotative word is fourfold: *rūḍha* 'conventional', *yaugika* 'etymological', *yogarūḍh* 'etymologico-conventional' and *yaugikarūḍha* 'etymological/ conventional.[4] Here in the example of *yaugika* i.e. *pācaka,* the denotative word *paca aka* is not etymological. And though the totality is etymological, yet it is not denotative, And thus, the statement that the denotative word is sometimes etymological—is not properly thought out. Similarly, the example of convention is also inconsistent on account of the etymology 'that which goes (√गम्) is *gauḥ*.

Here it be noted that (responsibility of) justifying (these inconsistencies) lies on their part (i.e. of the logicians).

Further again, the word *sātvata* is also twofold: *akārānta* 'ending with a' and *halanta* 'ending with a consonant', The first is a proper noun like the word *dittha* etc. And it is conventionally used in the specific sense of 'born in the *yādava* dynasty' as in—

"Is that king of the *sātvatas,* the *vṛṣṇis*, the *bhojas,*
and the *dāśārhakas* happy?"

The king of the *sātvatas* and others was Ugrasena as it is described in the Śrīmad Bhāgavata. While the second (word *sātvat*) is etymologico-conventional and is used in the special sense of 'devotees, worshippers' like the word *paṅkaja* etc. For example—

"Salutation to you who are the best of the *sātvats.* ".

Here the meaning is 'to the best i.e. the guardian of the *sātvats* (i.e. worshippers)'. Here the meaning as well as etymology is like this: *kāmadughaḥ* 'one who fulfils the desires', i.e. fulfils or milks the wishes of *sātvats* i.e. worshippers or devotees. *Satva* means the fourfold internal organs-*citta, ahaṅkāra, buddhi* and *manas*; the group of these four is *sātva*. They are the seats of these four respectively of *vāsudeva, saṅkarṣaṇa, pradumna* and *aniruddha*. Hence *sātvas,* the four presiding deities. These they approach (√अत्) i.e. attain (प्र+√आप्) always by meditation and devotion. Hence they are *'sātvats';* according to the *vārttika kvipi śakandhvāditvāt pararūpam* etc. of them i.e. of the devotees and the worshippers; it is explained there only. Here in this example, the etymology is stronger and therefore, the word is *yogarūḍha* 'etymologico-conventional. Thus it is clear that these two words (*sātvata* and *sātvat*) are two separate examples of *rūḍhi* and *yogarūḍhi* respectively.

Similarly, the word *tumburu* also is established in the sense of a proper name of a particular *gandharva*. *tumbati* 'produces sweet sound' hence *tumburu*. In the Hemakośa, the word *tumburu* is derived from the root √तुम्ब् with the suffix *urun* and this derivation is observed in its explanation as a kind of a group of the *gandharvas* in the class of gods.

So it should be understood that this word characterised by three *ukāras* (i.e. *tumburu*) is established as a proper noun expressing the meaning of a single *gandharva*.

The *lakṣaṇā* 'Indication'

The logicians define *lakṣaṇā* 'Indication' as the "relation with the primary sense". The relation always resides in both, therefore, this Indication also is activated in the primary word. The poeticians, therefore, define *lakṣaṇā* as the *vṛtti* which brings out a non-primary sense through its relation—with the primary (meaning).

> The grammarians believe that just as an arrow shot by some strong archer pierces the armour, pierces the heart and removes life, similarly, (all the) meanings of a word (*pada*) are put forth a word (*śabda*) possessing the single power called *abhidhā;* therefore, on the strength of the longer and still longer function of the denotation on the analogy of an arrow etc. The *lakṣaṇā* should not be accepted.

And this power of Indication being a function of a word resides in the word, and when there is an incompatibility of the primary sense, it objectifies the meaning related to that (primary sense).

And it is said:

> "Indication is that process, which is superimposed on a word and by which another sense is indicated either through convention or on account of purpose when there is incompatibility of the primary sense as well as a connection with that (i.e. the primary sense).

The construction is like this: when there is incompatibility of the primary sense, either through convention or due to a purpose, by whichever power, another meaning is indicated, that is Indication.

In the first place, Indication is threefold namely, *jahal-lakṣaṇā ajahal-lakṣaṇā* and *jahad-ajahal-lakṣaṇā.*

Jahal-lakṣaṇā is where the word gives up the primary sense when it is incompatible. Where it does not give up the primary sense, it is *ajahal-lakṣaṇā*. Where there are both (i.e. giving up and not giving up of the primary sense), it is called *jahad-ajahal-lakṣaṇā.*

This threefold (indication), is also again twofold: *nirūḍhā* 'based on convention' and *phalavatī* 'based on purpose'. The meanings of *nirūḍhā lakṣaṇā* on account of their being almost similar to those of denotation, are found in *kośa* etc. But this *(lakṣaṇā)* though equal to denotation,happens only when the primary sense is incompatible and that is its distinction from denotation. They also call it beginningless *lakṣaṇā.*

Where the Indication is based on purpose, that purpose will be understood through the process called *vyañjanā* 'suggestion' only and not through either denotation or indication. We shall clarify this at the time of the treatment of 'suggestion.'

The fruit (i.e. the purpose) now is of two kinds: sometimes concealed, sometimes unconcealed. The concealed fruit is comprehensible to the very intelligent persons, unconcealed fruit is understood by everyone.

Again this Indication is twofold—*samānādhikaraṇaviṣayā* 'residing-in-the-same-substratum' and *vyadhikaraṇaviṣayā* 'residing-in-different substrata.'[5]

Vyatireka lakṣaṇā is a further sub-division only but due to the fear of increasing (bulk of the work, the topic) is briefly discussed. Detailed discussion should be seen in the work Triveṇika of Āśādhara bhaṭṭa because all the varieties (of Indication) are treated there clearly.

Thus the Indication based on purpose is sevenfold: *jahalla-kṣaṇā ajahal-lakṣaṇā, jahad-ajahal-lakṣaṇā, sāropā,* 'super imposition', *sādhyavasānā* 'introsusception,' *gaunī* 'qualitative' and *śuddhā* 'pure'.

Now their illustrations in order –

(1) *jahal-lakṣaṇā-e.g. gaṅgāyām ghoṣaḥ* 'a hamlet on the *gaṅgā*'. The denotative meaning will be 'the hamlet is situated on *gaṅgā*'. Hamlet being impossible there, there will be incompatibility of the primary sense and the indicative sense will be 'on the bank', The word *ghoṣa* 'hamlet' is the indicator of the purport. According to the grammarians –

Substratum is *adhikaraṇa* 'location'. and location is sixfold: *aupaśleṣika, sāmīpika, abhivyāpaka, vaiṣayika, naimittika* and *aupacārika,* Among these as in *vaṭe gāvaḥ suśerate* 'the cows sleep under the banyan tree, the *sāmīpika* 'nearing' substratum has the meaning of the locative case. Therefore, here (i.e. in the example *gaṅgāyām ghoṣaḥ*) only denotation operates and not Indication. Here the fruit is 'the suggestion of coolness and holiness'.

(2) *ajahal-lakṣaṇā*-e.g. *kuntāḥ praviśanti* 'lances enter', *yaṣṭayaḥ praviśanti* 'staffs enter' etc. here the lances etc. being inanimate, cannot enter by themselves. Therefore, the Indication is in the sense of 'their bearers', Whereas the fruit is the suggestion of their undoubted (potentiality) of striking (with the weapons).

(3) Then the example of *jahad-ahahal-lakṣaṇā : e.g. kākebhyo dadhi rakṣyatām.* 'let the curds be protected from the crows.' Here by abandoning the denotative sense 'crow' and by accepting, the non-primary sense 'one that harms the curds', the word 'crow' has indication of *jahadajahat* type only in the sense of 'the curds-harmer'. The fruit here is conviction of the crow's villainy. But when the vessel of curds is held on the head by somebody, and there is no fear of there being any other destroyer of the curds, then the purport being appropriately comprehensible, there is no Indication because everywhere,

the principle is, "the root-cause of Indication is failure in understanding of the purport".

(The author) states another example-*na jātu brāhmaṇam hanyāt* 'one should never kill a brahmin.' Here, the denotative singular coming after the word *brāhmaṇa* is given up, the accusative plural which is the non-primary sense is forwarded. The Indication of the singular is in plural. Otherwise inviolability of all the brahmins would not be (understood). What is said in Triveṇikā: "In (the example) 'one should never kill a brahmin', the word '*brāhmaṇa*' pertaining to an individual indicates the genus inherently connected with it," would be according to the views of the ancients. But this does not seem to be coherent. The reason is: here though by Indication, the individual is understood in the sense of genus, yet, because it is not possible to kill genus, the Indication will be expected to operate again in the individual. As in—

> "That *kṣatriya* race which had emerged from thine own arms, while thou wert creating the word in primordial times:"[6]

the word *jāti* indicates the individuals being the loci of *jāti*. Since the genus cannot be born, the primary sense (genus) is incompatible. Similar is the case in the example under discussion also.And that fault (necessity to employ *lakṣaṇā* twice) will certainly follow. therefore, the indicative power will operate by giving up the part of accusative singular coming after the word '*brāhmaṇa*' and by accepting the non-primary accusative plural but not into genus. They also call this itself as *bhāga-tyāga lakṣaṇā* 'Indication by partial abandonment'.

Moreover, some people have said that in sentences like *so' yam devadattaḥ* 'here is that Devadatta', *tattva masi* 'That thou art' etc. there is *jahad-ajahal-lakṣaṇā* following the ancient ācāryas, but that is not proper, as there is no incompatibility of the primary sense and therefore, Indication does not occur.

Just as in the example *ghaiṭaḥ anityaḥ* 'the pot is perishable,' when the principal purport is in the pot, the permanent genus in the form of 'potness' will be given up, and the word *ghaṭa* will be construed with the impermanence. And when the central purport is *'ghaṭatvam nityam* 'potness is permanent', the impermanence of the pot will be given up, and the genus in the form of 'potness'will be construed with the word 'permanent'. Similarly here also, construe will be possible by abandoning the contradictory parts. Thus, it should be seen in the sentences like *gehe ghaṭāh sthitāḥ* 'The pots are there in the house', *śālāgauḥ baddhā asti* 'the cow is tied in the cowshed'. It is to be understood that in Vedāntaparibhāṣā also it is said that the preceptors have shown *lakṣaṇā* in sentences like *tattvamasi* 'that thou art' by persistence, and this is apprehended in accordance with their opinion.

Now, it is to be considered whether there is *vidhi* 'injunction,' *niyama* 'specification' or *parisaṅkhyā* 'exclusion' in *na jātu brāhmaṇam hanyāt*. 'One should never kill a brahmin'.

First of all, the definition of *vidhi* etc. with their mutual distinction is being stated.

> "Injunction is that which enjoins something in a matter absolutely unavailable (i.e. enjoins something for the first-time). Specification is that which gives rules about partial application. And it will be called exclusion when something is available there and elsewhere (i.e. in both the contexts)."

Injunction is that which enjoins something which was completely unobtained, e.g. *svādhyāyaḥ adhyetavyaḥ,* 'The Vedas should be studied.' *agnihotram juhuyāt*. 'One should perform *agnihotra*. Specification is enjoining that which was not available in a part, like *śuklapakṣe svādhyāyaḥ adhyetavyaḥ*. 'The Vedas should be studied in the bright hald of a lunar month.' Here preeminence (of the activity) is understood. In the example *same yajeta* 'one should perform (a sacrifice) on a levelled ground', the sacrifice is enjoined as a duty and it is impossible to perform it without a place; so a place is implied.

That place may be of two kinds: levelled and unlevelled. When a sacrificer voluntarily performs that sacrificial rite on a levelled ground, this statement remains as it is, because the intended purpose is served automatically but when he performs it on an unlevelled ground then this statement enjoins its own meaning because then its meaning was unobtained. Otherwise, the sacrificial rite would not have been performed according to the scriptures. Similarly, the example from the *smṛti- prāṅmukho 'annāni bhuñjīta* 'One should partake of the food facing the east,' is explained.when one thing is found in many plaoes, the statement which is meant to exclude it from other places and to allow it in one place, it is called *parisaṅkhyā* 'exclusion'. To illustrate that *tisro bhāryā brāhmaṇasya* 'these three can be the wives of a brahmin.' here the acceptance (of a woman as wife) by marriage ritual in all the four classes is enjoined but by exclusion the prohibition of marriage with *śūdrā* restricts it. Or, as (in the *mantra)*-

> "They held this cord of the truth (restricted by the excluding *brāhmaṇic* statement) 'he holds the cord of a mare.'

(The *mantra)* which on its own strength is employed in the holding of the cord of a mare and a she-ass, when employed again in a mare on the strength of the statement *aśvābhidhānīm ādatte* 'he holds the cord of a mare'—reverts (i.e. excludes itself) from (its application to) the she-ass. Similarly, *pañca pañcanakhāḥ bhakṣyāḥ* 'five animals with five nails can be eaten'. Here the eating is freely enjoined in the case of hare etc. as well as the dog etc., but when again enjoined in hare etc. it (i.e. the injunction) receded (i.e. excludes itself) from dog etc.

And thus, therefore, is the statement about the prohibition of killing a brahmin, in the form of an injunction, or a specification or an exclusion?

To this, we reply—

It is not a statement of specification because there is no

injunction of the unenjoined in the case of that which is partially applied. Also, it is not exclusion, on account of a contingency of there arising three faults in the form of harm to its own import, imagining another meaning and incompatibility of the meaning obtained. Therefore, they call it an injunction only which is never mentioned before.

Also, in the example of specificatory statement *śukla-pakṣe svādhyāyo' dhyetavyaḥ* 'the Veda should be studied in bright lunar fortnight', it is only praise, but there is no fault in not doing it, whereas in exlussion, there is no mention of *doṣa* 'fault' in the case of eating rabbits etc. but in the eating of a dog etc. there is a mention of fault and an injunction of expiation. One should understand this distinction of 'exclusion' from 'specificatory statement.'

Now the types of *lakṣaṇā* 'Indication' viz. *śuddhā* 'pure', *sāropā* 'superimposed' and *sādhyavasānā* 'introsusceptive',[7] e.g. *āyurghṛtam* 'ghee is life', *āyureva* 'life itself' etc. In the examples like *mukhacandra* 'the facemoon' etc. there is superimposition but no Indication because the sense is (already) conveyed by the power of totality arising out of a compound. In the super-imposed variety the Indication is of the attribute only. The attribute-possessor is cognised by denotation only, while in introsusceptive variety, because there is swallowing up of the object in the form of verbal non-mention, there is swallowing up of the object in the form of verbal non-mention, there is Indication of both (i.e. the *guṇa* 'attribute' and the *guṇī* 'attribute-possessor'. And it is said:

> "That is called *sāropā* 'superimposed' where the object superimposed is associated with the object superimposed upon and that should be taken as *sādhyavasānā* 'introsusceptive' where only the object superimposed is mentioned."

The example is *droṇo vrīhiḥ* 'droṇaful rice.' Here the sense is: 'the rice measured by that measurement which is of the form of *droṇa*. 'When the measurement is of the form of the meaning of suffixes, the meaning of the orginal word will be a qualifier of (the substantive) by the relation of a connection of unity; but the meaning of the suffix itself will be a qualifier of the rice on the analogy of the measured and the meausrer. Theoretically here, the nominative is not in the sense of nounbase but it will be fine to take it as functional nominative. The word *artha* here pertains to the function; and the function is either denotation or indication. This being so, in the example 'a droṇaful rice' the word *droṇa* is established in the sense 'the rice measured by it' through *upacāra* 'secondary usage' as in the example *gaur vāhīkaḥ* 'the *vāhīka* is a bull'.

> Here some may argue: according to the derivation "*parimāṇam*—measurement' is that by which something is measured," the words *droṇa* etc. are the measurements only made either of iron or of wood. (That) measurement never varies but the measurable does vary and therefore, taking it as *prātipadika,* inclusion of measurement is not obtained. (To this we reply:) no. (If your argument is accepted, there will follow) a contingency of the examples of qualitative indications like *siṁho māṇavakaḥ,* 'the man is a lion', *mañcāḥ krośantī* 'cradles are crying' etc. being left out of the scope of *lakṣaṇā* (If we accept that) there, (i.e. in the cases mentioned above) inspite of there being distnction of the substantives *māṇavaka* etc. (from *siṁha etc.)* the meanings 'lion-like' etc. definitely stand forth in the qualitative (indication), then (we shall have to admit that) inspite of there being distinction of 'rice' etc. (from *droṇa* etc.) the (non-distinction) of the rice etc.) measured by the *droṇa* etc. will certainly have to be admitted, so propound grammarians.

Here we say—the *gauṇī ajahal-lakṣaṇā* occurs in the examples like *gaur vāhīkaḥ, agnirmāṇavakaḥ, siṁho devadattaḥ* etc. owing to the cognition of the relation of resemblance and acceptance of a further meaning in the form of an attribute without abandoning the original meaning but the *gauṇī lakṣa-ṇā* is not possible in a similar way in the example *droṇo vrīhiḥ* because there is no relation of resemblance.

> In that case, how is it justified as said in Manoramā that "This (i.e. droṇo vrīhiḥ) is like *gaur vāhīkaḥ* 'the vāhīka is a bull?" According to the Rhetoticians, this is the example of pure *jahal-lakṣaṇā* with purpose (and not *gauṇī)!*

Evenif it were so, there is no fault at all. Just as in the examples *āyur ghṛtam* 'ghee is life' and *āyur, evedam* 'this is life only,' etc. the indication residing in the same substratum and of the type of superimposition and introsusception is pure (respectively), similarly in *droṇo vrīhiḥ,* the word *droṇa* is indicative in the sense of 'the rice measured by the measuring cup in the form of a *droṇa.'* In fact, generally speaking the measurement itself is the denotative sense; in a specific form of a *droṇa,* it will be the indicative sense only. This is the final establishment.

Now, the examples of Introsusceptive:

e.g. *siddhāntakaumudī* and *śabdakaustubhaḥ*. Here the introsusceptive indication is in the compound made by the words *kaumudī* as well as *kaustubha*. Or else, on account of the observation of the application of *ivārthe kan* (i.e. *kan is* used in the sense of 'like that') the words would be formed as *kaumudikā* 'like *kaumudī'* and *kaustubhaka* 'like *kaustubha*,,. Actually, here, there is *madhyamapadalopī* compound as '*kaustubha* turned into a word'. it means—(the *kaustubha)* transferred into a word'. Therefore it is *pariṇāma* figure of speech, because the statment that '*kaustubha* transfered into a word' is appropriate for the purpose of the activity of deciding the meaning. Neither is it a compound of *mayūravyaṁsakādi* variety because in that variety, the meaning of the second member is prominent, whereas here, the prominence of the first member is seen, its purpose being the decision of meaning. The meanings are decided by words only and not by the jewel *kaustubha.* Nor is the prominence of the second member with consideration of the meaning of the word *uddhṛta* possible because the word *uddhṛta* is construed with both the first and the second member of the compound. The mention of transference of *Kaustubha* is for the purpose of suggesting the purity of the words quoted in the *bhāṣya.*

It should be noted here-in the example of *vyastarūpaka* 'uncompounded metaphor', there is *sāropā lakṣaṇā* 'Indication with superimposition'. In the example of *rūpaka atiśayokti* 'metaphorical exaggeration', there is *sādhyavasānā lakṣaṇā* 'Indication with introsusception'. The *vyatireka lakṣaṇā* 'contrastive Indication' should be seen in examples like—

"Well-done O female messenger, well-done! What more can be done than this?" etc. In *gaurvāhīkaḥ* 'the *vāhīka* is a bull' etc. there is *gauṇī* 'qualitative' Indication due to resemblance of qualities like dullness and stupidity. And it is said: "the process is, however, admitted to be qualitative on account of the connection (of the denotative sense viz. bull) with the qualities (of the entity viz. *vāhīka)* that is being indicated."

In *śoṇo dhāvati* 'the red is running' the indication conveys the sense of 'the horse distinguished by the quality of being reddish brown', And in *nakhaīryutam garbhiṇināmadheyam* and in *bāṇai' raśvaiśca hāyanaiḥ etc.* the Indication is in the attribute in the form of number 'twenty' associated with the nails. The nails etc. will be in plural on account of their plurality as they are twenty in number; but there will be singular for the earth, the moon etc. as they are naturally singular in number. This distinction is owing to their being indicatively denotative of the numbers; whereas (the figures themselves) *viṁśati* 'twenty' etc will be in singular only on the strength of the statement in the dictionary "twenty etc. are always in singularity" and due to their denoting the principal number. The same is the case with *bāṇai'* raśvaiśca *hāyanaiḥ* meaning 'in five and seven years'. In the same way in—*nampūbhābhaja-pūri jañjarijapūr ghātāstithir meṣabhāt* etc. by the part and whole relationship the word *nam* indicates the lunar dates *pratipadā* 'first', *ṣaṣṭhī* 'sixth' and *ekādaśī* 'eleventh'. Similarly, the word (i.e. the letter) *pū* indicates *pūrṇā* date, *bha* indicates *bhadrā, ja* indicates *jayā* and *ri* indicates the date called *riktā*.

And again, in *śyālaḥsvasroḥ athāgrahīt* 'the wife's brother fell at the feet of the sister and the sister ('s husband)', the sister and the sister' in the *ekaśeṣa* of these two, coherence requires taking of dual but since the second word 'sister' is incompatible, There will be the Indication in 'her husband i.e. Vasudeva'.

But Śrīdharaswāmin has said: dut to the inseparable relation of genders (and also) as in the case of (the Vedic Statement) *prāṇabhṛtaḥ upadathāti* 'he collects the *prāṇabhṛt* bricks', since the dual in the word *svasṛ* is incompatible, through the quality of being a pair (of the word *svasroḥ),* there will be indication in a couple, and it will denote 'the sister and her hubsand'. The author explains this itself:

And also there is a pāṇinian *sūtra: tadvāsāmupadhāno mantra itīṣṭakāsu luk ca matoḥ.*

"The affix यत् comes in the *chhandas* after a nominal stem, in the first case in construction, ending with the affix *matup, when the sense is* 'this is their *mantra* of putting up' provided that the things put up are bricks, and the affix *matup* is elided by *luk."*

Here, that *mantra* in which the word *prāṇabhṛt* occurs is *prāṇabhṛdvān* 'possessing the word *prāṇabhṛt'* and the affix (*matup*) being elided, the *mantra*-denoting word will be called *prāṇabhṛt* with a consonant ending. This *mantra*-denoting word *prāṇabhṛt* will have indication in 'the bricks', otherwise, the meaning of the verb *upadadhāti* being 'he collects' and since the collection of the *mantra* is impossible, the collection-denoting verb *upadadhāti* itself is the indicator. while in the previous example, the word *śyāla* is the indicator. Here the grammarian will, however, say: "Just as synonymous words with different forms are connected in an *ekaśeṣa* compound, words with different meanings as well as with different forms can also form an *ekaśeṣa* on the strength of the indicatory statement *prathamayoḥ pūrvasavarṇaḥ*. Therefore, this (i.e *śyālaḥ svasroḥ* etc.) will not be Indication. In this way, 'the sister and the sister's husband' are *svasārau*. Of them. This is *ekaśeṣa* (compound). In the indicatory statement 'the first and the second' will be *prathame* 'the first two'. of them.this in brief is the ultimate sense.

The details should be seen in the book Triveṇikā written by my teacher Āśādhara.

Now *vyañjanā* 'suggestion' is being treated.

The *vṛtti* 'function' which brings out the sense other than the denotative and the indicated sense and the sense which is suitable to the context, is *vyañjanā*. As is said in the Kāvyaprakāśa :

> "When the denotative power of a word which has more than one primary senses is restricted (to one sense) by means of conjunction etc. The process which produces the apprehension of a sense that is non-primary is suggestion."[8]

The meaning is: when the denotative power of a word with various senses is restricted by the restricting factors like conjunction etc., the process which produces apprehension of another sense suitable to the contextual matter is *añjana* or a function called *vyañjanā,* 'suggestion'. And this suggestion is threefold: *śabdaśaktimūlā* 'based on the denotative power of the word', *lakṣaṇāmūlā* 'based on indication' and *vyañjanāmūlā* 'based on suggestion'.

Based on denotative power—e.g.

> "The teeth of her mouth are to be considered arguments, otherwise, how could it argue with these and how could it,in disputes, cut asunder the leaf (of counter theses), and refute a host of meritorious (opponents)?"

(The implied meaning is, "Otherwise how could it

cut asunder a betel leaf (*patra*) and cut open a good betel nut (*pūga*)?"[9]

Here यद्वदनस्य-of the mouth of *sarasvatī*. रदाः-teeth, तर्काः-of the form of science of logic. तर्क्याः-considerable. अन्यथा-if it were not so. अस्य-of her mouth. वादे-in the subject of dispute. शक्तिः-power. How would it be? This means-without the study of the science of logic it is not possible to debate. That is—where would be the strength to cut (to give) a leaf (paper) in which is mentioned the *puga* 'the group' of objects possessed of twenty four qualities and then to refute the disputes? The word वा (suggests) another non-textual sense. अदत्-one who has no teeth. Of him. अदतः-of the toothless. Without those teeth. In the *vāda* (dispute, speaking). *vādam*-an aggregate of *va* and *da*. In this *vāda*. It means whence would he have power in pronouncing the letters *va* and *da* since *vakāra* is dentolabial and *dakāra* is dental? Where would he have the power without teeth to cut, i.e. to break into pieces (दा-in the sense of breaking.) the betel-leaf made from a leaf of a piper-betel in which there is a betel-nut of a good quality. *hi-because* how could a toothless person have the strength to cut even a leaf? It means never. Here there is suggestion based on denotation since in the contextual description of the mouth of Sarasvatī, there is perception of a non-contextual toothless person. The ancients believe that there is denotative suggestion when the contextual and the non-contextual senses are conveyed through pun. The Indicative suggestion e.g.

"O friend! subduing to the fortunate one (i.e. my lover) every moment, you are troubled for my sake. You have just done something which is worthy of good feeling and friendship."

Here, the sense indicated is that 'you have created enmity by flirting with my lover', the suggestion from this is the revellation of the guilt of her own hero. Thus indicative suggestion. The one based on suggestion as in—

"In the dalliance in reverse position, the amorously excited Lakṣmī, having seen Brahma sitting on the naval-lotus of Viṣṇu, quickly shuts his (Viṣṇu's) right eye,"

Here the sun is suggested to be the form of his right eye by the word *hari;* by its coverage, the time of sunset: by this , the contraction (shrinking up) of the lotus. So the disappearance of Brahmā sitting in it. Therefore, the dalliance of Lakṣmī and Nārāyṇa without restraint, is suggested. This, therefore, suggestion based on suggestion.

And thus-How can *veda*-four, *kha-zero, abdhi-four, viyat*-zero, *candra*-one=10404 and *śara*-five, *iṣu*-five] *yuga*-four, *kha*-zero *indu*-one=10455, in all ten thousand four hundred and fifty five types of *dhvani* as stated in Kāvyaprakāśa occur without *vyañjanā vṛtti* i.e. suggestive power? It must, therefore, be certainly accepted. And further the *phalavatī lakṣaṇā* i.e. Indication with purpose cannot occur without suggestion. The apprehension of the purpose. i.e. fruit is not obtained through denotation because there is no *saṅketa* (convention), nor by Indication. How can the fruit of that Indication which brings about that fruit(in the first place) be apprehended? For that also (another) *lakṣaṇā* (must be resorted to). This also would be fruitful. And thus, in the series of fruit and *lakṣaṇā,* there will result the fault of infinity. As is also said in Kāvyaprakāśa:

"Also in this way, there would be the absence of finality, which would cause the destruction of the very root (of the whole thing)."

Neither is there *viśiṣṭa lakṣaṇā* 'the Indication qualified by that purpose' because we cannot have the apprehension of both the object and the purpose i.e. fruit (of the knowledge) simultaneously.

And again—the manifestation of the nine *rasas śṛṅgāra* etc. from the poems and plays is established through the experience of all the connoisseur spectators. So here, which function should be admitted? There is no denotation in the perception of *rasa* etc. because there is no *saṅketa* 'convention.'

The words *vibhāvas* etc. in this context are expressive only of *vibhāvas* etc. Also because there is no other terminology and the mention of the *vibhāvas* etc. itself is not the mention of *rasa* etc. because *rasa* is not identical with them, and also because mention of *rasa* by its own terms is accepted as a blemish of *rasa,* therefore, in the apprehension of *rasa* etc. the function of suggestion must certainly be resorted to.

Incidentally, the author of the Kāvyaprakāśa has mentioned the nature of *rasa:*

> "Whatever are the causes, the effects and the associative emotions of the permanent emotions of *rati* etc. in the world, the same when they occur in drama or poem are called *vibhāvas, anubhāvas* and *vyabhicāris* and that permanent emotion manifested by these *vibhāvas* etc. is called *rasa.*".

And thus, the sentience, (1) which is suggested by the *vibhāvas* etc. (a) which have adopted specifications like Sītā etc. for the reason of their being employed in literary pieces, (b) yet are apprehended in a generalised form; (2) which is demarcated by the *rati* etc. of the connoisseurs involved (in the process) on account of the generalised nature of the describable (i.e.import) (3) which its veil (obstruction) in the aspect of bliss being broken shines forth in the form of bliss; and (4) which is variegated by the *vibhāvas* etc. is *rasa.* Or (in other words) the sentience demarcated by *rati* etc. is *rasa.*

Though—

> "In drama there are stated nine *rasas namely śṛṅgāra, hāsya, karuṇa, raudra, vīra, bhayānaka, bībhatsa, adbhuta* and *śānta,"*

others say that—

> "Because *śānta* is accomplished from *śama* and that *śama* is not possible to exist in an actor, there are only eight *rasas* in drama and *śānta* is not appropriate there."

Their (opinion) is not (justified); because the reason that

'*śama* (only) does not exist in an actor' is inconsistent. Manifestation of *rasa* is never accepted in an actor and the relish of *rasa* is with the connoisseurs only. Thus

> "*rati, hāsa, śoka, krodha, utsāha, bhaya, jugupsā, vismaya* and *nirveda*-these nine are" *sthāyibhāvas*. And "*nirveda, glāni, śaṅkā, asūyā, mada, śrama, ālasya, dainya, cintā, moha, smṛti, dhṛti, vrīdā, capalatā harṣa, āvega, jaḍatā, garva, viṣāda autsukya, nidrā, apasmāra, svapna, vibodha, amarṣa, avahittha, ugratā, mati, vyādhi, unmāda, maraṇa trāsa* and *vitarka* all these thirty three are *vyabhicāri bhāvas*".

It should be noted that though there are many *rasas* like *śṛṅgāra* etc., still among the types of *dhvani only one rasadhvani* namely *asaṅlakṣyakrama* is accepted.

And further, the distinction between *rasa* and *sthāyibhāva* is this: when the *rati* etc. are in premature stage, they have *sthāyitva* and when they are fully developed, they have *rasatva*. And again, the *bharatasūtra* is—"from the combination of the *vibhāvas, anubhāvas* and *vyabhicāris rasa arises.*" Though everywhere the routine communication is possible with the terms cause, effects, associative emotions etc. yet giving them a different terminology of *vibhāva* etc. is to establish the transcendental nature of *rasa*. The elaboration should be seen in the volume called Nūtanatarī written by me in the form of a commentary on Rasataraṅgiṇī.

And more than that, unless the *vyañjanā vṛtti*-'function called suggestion' is accepted, the scheme of the poetry being best, mediocre and low would not be possible, as the bestness of a poem is only by the superiority of the suggested sense.

And it is said: "when the suggested sense is more charming than the denotative one, in this (i.e.poetry) that is the best which is designated *dhvani* by the wise." Here 'this' means 'poem'. Or, for example—

> "A (guest) leaving some rice (on the dish), and drawing some towards him, asked a maid with this

> coming and going of the hand, 'shall I come, or wilt thou come?' At this, she bent her face in shame."[10]

Amara (kośa) says: "the words *odana* and *didivī* are used in masculine and neuter." Here the enquiry of some member of the bride-groom's group towards the young lady serving rice is suggested under the pretext of the spreading and collecting again and again of the rice served in his plate who is asking "will you come or should I come?" Then it is suggested that she also gave him the reply 'You only may come' by her gesture of lowering the face under the pretext of shyness. Or for example-

> "The slope of your breasts has its sandal completely fallen off. The lower lip has its red colour clean washed out. The eyes are void of collyrium at the far ends, (i.e. at the corner). This slender body of yours is horripilated. O you messenger, who are telling a lie! and who do not know the agony of your kinswoman! You had gone from here to the well to bathe but not to the vicinity of that wretch!"

Here the prominence of the suggested sense—

"You had gone to him only to dally" in comparison to the denotative sense is suggested by taking of the word 'wretch'. Hence this is the best type of poem. The *madhyama* mediocre (type) as-

> "But when the suggested sense is not of that kind (i.e. surpassing the denotative sense), the poem is of mediocre type, the suggested sense being subordinate."

'not of that kind' meaning 'not more charming than the denotative sense.' When such is the case, the suggested sense would be subordinate, and that would be a mediocre type of poem. As for example-

> "Mother, there are two bumps on my chest, but there is no pain in them." "Daughter, it is actually the nature. One who sees, feels pain."

It is a mediocre type of poetry because the suggested sense is subordinate as the denotative sense 'who sees feels pain' is more striking on account of the *asaṅgati* figure of speech in comparison to the suggested sense 'since you are unknown to youth, you do not feel pain now but you will, when you experience youth.' The lowest type of poetry as-

> "But that poem, which is striking in the word or striking in the denotative sense, is known as the lowest, i.e. *avarakāvya,* it is designated *avyaṅgya* i.e. void of the suggested sense."

The word *citra* means possessed of excellences and figures of speech. *avyaṅgya* means void of a distinct suggested sense. *avara* means the lowest. As for example—

> "May lord sun uproot your sins—that sun which pulls out with his rays-hands, the black serpent in the form of the series of bees emerging from the hollow of the pot of a lotus, to pacify the infamy sung loudly by the chirping of birds moved by the theft of a pearl-necklace of the stars put away by the merchant lady, the night, staying in the market-place of the clouded sky."

Here the pearl—necklace in the form of the stars is placed in the marketplace. (It is) of the merchant lady, in the form of night, staying in the market in the form of sky. By its removal i.e. theft, the birds have been moved. And their chirping (i.e. noise) pronounces the dishonour. To appease that (dishonour) the sun draws out with his rays i.e. hands (kara-' ray', kara-'hand'). *Kara* 'ray' itself is *kara* 'hand'. Thus para-nomastic metaphor. The female serpent of black colour in the form of the line of bees, coming out from the inside of the pot,. in the form of a lotus. *dinakṛt* 'the sun'. May this sun remove your sins. That is the construe. In some regions such was their practice: one who is accused of theft, should draw out the serpernt placed into a pot. If the serpent bites him, he is certainly the thief, if it doesn't he is guiltless. here it should be known as *citrakāvya* owing to the excellence of *ojas* and by the figures of speech of words and meanings. or another example—

> "Seeing the eye-like, chariot-wheel-like, and friend-like (face), (his) form-like prey-like and flag-like (eye) and (his) step like, garment-like and body-like (belly) of that beautiful-faced lady, how should Lord Viṣṇu, Lord Śiva and Lord Kāma not dispute among themselves?"

suvadanā 'one whose face is beautiful' i.e. whose limbs are beautiful. Of her. here the word *vadana* has an indication in the limbs generally. First the construe by supplying the ellipsis—'having seen the moon-like face.' 'This moon-face is my eye, my left eye'—this is the dispute of Viṣṇu, because Viṣṇu's left eye is described as the moon in the play of Murāri as-

> "Daily in the morning, we worship the two eyes of Lord (Viṣṇu), adorned with (the mace) *kaumodakī*-the eyes endowed with the light expert in pleasing the *carkravāka* (i.e. the sun) and in breaking the fast of *cakora* (i.e. the moon), by whom the bud of the lotus in (his) naval-pond half-bearing the soft sweet lustre of awakening and half asleep, is made the rival of (his) conch."

'The moon-face of her is the wheel of my chariot' disputes Lord Śiva, as it is so described in *(śiva)—mahimna-stotra*—'the sun and the moon are the limbs of his chariot and *cakrapāṇi* is his arrow'. 'This moon face is my friend because it excites desire of love,' thus disputes Kāmadeva. In this way, first of all having seen her face the three—the eye. the chariot wheel and the friend are construed. Again 'having seen her eyes' this construe is also by the supplement of ellipsis. On account of their similarity to the fish, her eyes are fish-like. Therefore, 'on account of my incarnation as a fish, they are my own form'—such is Viṣṇu's argument. The argument of Śiva is 'her eye-fish is my morsel, my food', on account of Śiva's form as a hunter as in the description 'even today (your arrow) does not release (Lord

Brahmā) from the anger of the deer-hunter.' 'This eye-fish is my flag, disputes Kāma since he is well-known as *makaradhvaja,* 'fish-flag'. Now, the construe—'having seen the belly of that beautiful lady'. On account of the belly's similarity with the sky, having seen the sky in the form of her belly, Lord Viṣṇu disputes—'this is my step walked upon in my Vāmana-incarnation'; Lord 'Śiva disputes 'this sky is my garment, since Śiva is *digambara* having only the directions for his clothing. 'Of her who is almost without belly, this slight belly is my limb', argues Lord Kāma, on account of his being without body-it means-having a very subtle body. here the negative is in the sense of 'little' on the strength of the statements like *anudarā kanyā* 'a girl with a slim belly'. Also on the strength of Damayantī's description in the Naiṣadhacaritam—"(She) possessed of a belly (waist) which is the subject of doubt whether it exists or not." Here the poem is of the lowest type because of the absence of a quick apprehension of the import, since all the three-the face, the eyes and the belly are elliptically employed and since the verse is void of a suggested sense. And thus, the scheme of the threefold poems, the best, the mediocre and the lowest is not possible without *vyañjanā vṛtti,* hence, it must be accepted. And again, in all these examples, *vyañjanā* 'suggestion' is in the meaning only, therefore, it is distinct from *abhidhā* 'denotation'

The denotative sense is comprehended by those who possess the knowledge of denotation, while the suggested sense (is understood) by the *sahṛdayas* i.e. connoisseurs only. Thus there is a distinction of apprehension. In *niḥśeṣacyutacandanam* etc. the denotative sense is negative—"you did not go to him", while the suggested sense is affirmative-"you did go to him for dalliance." Thus there is a distinction of nature between *abhidhā* and *vyañjanā*. Moreover, in 'the sun has set' etc. only one denotative sense is cognised, whereas the suggested sense appears to be varied as per the distinction in each of the characters etc. For example, the merchants to the servants (would mean) 'collect the commodities', the go-betweens to the *abhisārikā* (would mean) 'you may set out for the rendezvous', a pupil to his teacher (would mean) 'May start for the evening rites', or 'my dear did not arrive today','don't go far' or 'your love is almost to come' etc. thus unlimited suggested senses would shine forth; denotative, however, is one. Thus *abhidhā* and *vyañjanā* are distinct owing to the difference in numbers of their meanings. The denotative sense is realised only by the utterance of the word, the suggested sense is realised on account of the clearness of intellect, (thus there is) a distinction of cause. The denotative sense is non-striking whereas the suggested one is striking at the very moment of its cognition, such is their distinction of effect. The denotative sense gives (you) only cognition whereas the suggestive sense gives (you) striking cognition. i.e. the distinction of the cognition. The denotative is realised first, the suggested afterwords, which is their distinction of time. Denotation resorts to words whereas suggestion resorts to a *pada,* its part, its sense, the sentence etc., thus the distinction of resort.

> "Who is there that will not be enraged at the sight of his beloved's lip wounded? Thou didst smell the lotus with a bee inside, not heeding our warning forsooth; suffer now (for your obstinacy)!"[11]

Here, "the bruise on the lower lip is not made by the paramour, but has resulted from smelling the lotus with a bee within" this suggested meaning is for the husband. "Henceforth, you should not do such a thing, this time I have covered it somehow" this suggested sense is for the beloved herself. Thus there is the distinction of scope also.

And again—

> "Ramble freely, pious man! That dog tody is killed by the fierce lion that dwells in Godā river dells"[11].

If it is said:

> In this premise, 'moving on the banks of Godāvarī', prescribed by 'the dog being removed', actually causes one to infer 'non-moving on account of the

> existence of the lion there'. whichever is the wandering of a coward, is always resultant from the removal of the cause of fright. he then states the scope of logical discontinuance: "the bank of Godāvarī is not fit for the wandering of cowards. On account of its having a lion, like a forest." Thus by inference only, the absence of wandering is achieved. Why *vyañjanā* be resorted to?

We reply—Though coward himself, he may wander there inspite of the lion's presence due to either the order of his teacher or the master or the king or due to his love for the beloved. Thus the cause is *anaikāntika* 'multipronged', though fearing a dog, he may not be afraid of a lion due to his valour! Then from such causes, how can conclusion be established? And thus in *niḥśeṣacyutacandanam* etc. the signs like falling off of sandal etc. which are described, can result from bath also. The cause, thereofore, is multipronged. Even the adjectives construed commonly with bath are not grounds of inference since they are only apparent, but are suggestive owing to their association with the word *adhama*—'wretch'. (Thus), 'You went to him in order to dally' is not an inference. Again, there is no mention here of cause and conclusion as it would be in a regular inference since the conclusion etc. are not mentioned. Therefore. *vyañjanā vṛtti* 'the function of suggestion' other than *śakti* denotation and *lakṣaṇā* 'indication' must be accepted.

And thus the suggested sense is threefold: concealed, unconcealed and partially-concealed. Partially concealed among these is striking like pitcher-like breasts of a lady. As is said:

> "Not very obvious like the breasts of an Āndhra woman, not very concealed like the breasts of a woman from Gujarat, the meaning of words in the poems shines forth when partly covered and partly obvious like the breasts of a Marāthā woman."

The illustrations of all these are not given for fear of

expansion. The author of the Kāvyaprakāśa has described *arthaniṣṭhā vyañjanā* i.e. 'suggestion residing in sense' thus:

> "That operation of the (three-fold) sense, which owing to the speciality of the speaker, of import, the intonation, the sentence, the expressed sense, the proximity of something else, the occasion, the place, the time etc. becomes the cause of the apprehension of another sense in the case of persons possessing poetic genious is suggestion itself."[12]

boddhavya i.e. the person addressed. *kāku* i.e. intonation means modification of voice. *vākya-vācya-anyasannidhiḥ* means proximity of another person alongwith the sentence and the denotative sense. occasion means context. Owingto the speciality of the speaker etc. the sense other than the denotative and the indicated senses is suggested by this (function). Hence by that derivation it is called *vyañjanā.*

And thus it is established that the operation which produces the apprehension of the intended sense other than (the one conveyed by) denotation and indication is *vyañjanā* 'suggestion'. A few examples as direction. Owing to the speciality of the speaker—e.g.

> "Wise maid, why dost thou not conclude this divine being to be Nala? Nor choose him as thy consort? Certain it is he is not the real Nala. It would be an overwhelming loss to thee, if thou shouldst accept him not. Who else could be thy spouse?"[13]

It should be noted that in this description of Nala made by the speaker Sarasvatī towards Damayantī, the covert suggestion made on the strength of pun of all the four i.e. *indra, agni, yama* and v*aruṇa* who have adopted the guise of Nala for the purpose of marrying Damayantī is made within the boundaries of the suggested sense only. In explicitly describing—'this is Nala, and these are the gods in the guise of Nala', there would arise enmity of this Sarasvatī with the gods belonging to her own class. Here by the word *viduṣi* 'O wisemaid!' is established

Damayantī's cleverness to delve in the utterance of the verse. Here the speciality of all the three i.e. of the speaker Saraswati, of the object to be hinted at i.e. Indra etc. and of the intonation— i.e. "why do you neither decide nor choose?"—is to be understood. Or for example my own verse—

> "May that glorious Gaṅgādhara protect us— Gaṅgādhara whose mind is attached to Satī, whose body is adorned with ashes, the Lord of the senses, omniscient, whose body is adorned with the moon, who is endowed with Māyā, knower of the *vṛttis,* blissful, fulfiller of the wishes, giver of joy to good people, possessing innumerable eyes, and engrossed in the worship of *brahman."*

Here among the meanings realised due to *śleṣa* by the power of *vyañjanā,* the author explains first the meaning pertaining ot Śiva; One who bears is *dhara* (the affix *ac* is attached according to *pacādi ac.*)

One who holds the Gaṅgā is *gaṅgādhara* i.e. Śiva; as Amara says: "*gaṅgādhara* is *andhakaripu."* the enemy of *andhaka.* This word (i.e. *gaṅgādhara*) is *yogarūḍha* 'etymologicoconventional', May protect us such is the construe. How is he? Whose mind is attached to Satī i.e. the daughter of Dakṣa. With Bhūti i.e. ashes. "Bhūti means Bhasman i.e. 'ashes' as well as *sampad* i.e. riches," says Amara. *Vibhūṣitatanuḥ* i.e. whose body is adorned. Also Lord of *gavām* 'of all the *vidyās'*. On the strength of Vedic statement: 'He is the Lord of all *vidyās'*. Or *iśvara* 'protector' of *gavām* 'arrows', meant for the killing of demons. Or the protector of *gavām* 'all the directions'. or (*iśvara* meaning) strong enough to bear *gavām* 'the fifteen eyes' on account of his having five faces. because it is said :

> "The word *goḥ* in masculine is in the sense of sun, ox, a kind of sacrifice, a kind of sage; in feminine gender-direction, speech, earth, cow; in both masculine and feminine—heaven, *vajra,* water, rays, eyes, arrows and the hair on the body."

Again, how is he? *sarvajñaḥ* 'knower of all'. 'The king of brahmins' *dvijarājaḥ* 'the moon'. *rājāhaḥsakhibhyaṣṭac.* (i.e. The affix ṭac (a) is added to the words *rājan, ahan* and *sakhi* when standing at the end of a *tatpuruṣa* compound.) (thus *dvijarājaḥ*) on the strength of the Vedic statement "*soma* is the king of us, the brahmins." with him. *rājitavapuḥ* whose body is adorned. Again *anvitaḥ* joined with *māyā* i.e. *yoga māyā.* or in the form of *pārvatī.* Again *vṛṭṭayaḥ* mental states of all people. Knower of all such mental states. And again of what nature? *ā*-on all sides *nandī* 'the bull who has become his carrier,' whatever his desires, he is the fulfiller of that. *sumanasām*—'of gods.' Who gives joy to all gods. *anantaḥ* a particular serpent. he who sees him *anantadṛk.* Engrossed in *upāsanā* 'the meditation' of the highest *brahman.* Thus may that Lord Śiva, the bearer of Gaṇgā characterised by the above mentioned adjectives protect us.

Now the meaning pertaining to Viṣṇu :

That Viṣṇu who bears Gaṇgā who emerged as the water from his feet is well-known in the world. *bhagavān* means 'having a variety of affluences.' Again his mind is attached to *satyā* i.e. Satybhāmā. Kṛṣṇa and Viṣṇu are described as one on the strength of the statement 'Kṛṣṇa himself is the lord (Viṣṇu)'. Again, how is he? *bhūti*—'wealth'. Whose body is adorned with riches. Amara says: "*bhūti* means ashes and riches." *gavām* 'of the cows'. *iśvaraḥ* 'controller'. *sarvajñaḥ* 'one who knows everything', on the strength of the two vedic statements 'who is knower of all', 'he is omniscient'. Whose body is adorned by *dvija-rāja* 'the moon', because his left eye is the moon itself. Or in *rāsotsava* description it is said: "he (the moon) rose and removed the miseries of the living beings." His body looked charming on account of the moon rising at that time. Again, he was endowed with *māyā* i.e. *yogamāyā* since it is so described in the *Bhāgavata:* "he took recourse to *Yogamāyā.*" *Vṛttivit* 'the knower of the *vṛttis* i.e. the inner feelings of the cowherdesses. or else, the knower of the inner feelings of the sixteen thousand princesses at the time of his marrying them simultaneously. Again *ānandī* 'blissful' as the Vedic statement—"bliss is the nature of *brahman.*" Again, 'fulfiller of the desires of his devotees or of cowherdesses.' Similarly, 'the giver of Joy' to *sumanas* 'the gods', or to 'those with pure minds'. *anantadṛk* 'having many eyes', on the strength of the Vedic statement: "he has thousands of eyes and thousands of feet", Again how is he? engrossed in *brahmo-pāsana* 'the study of the Vedas'. Or, he has the lotus, the seat of Brahmā near him. Hence *brahmopāsanaḥ, padmanābha* means 'lotusnaval.' *tatparam* 'pertaining to Viṣṇu the word *gaṇgādhara* will be etymological.

Now, the meaning pertaining to Brahmā: whose mind is attached to *satya-'satyaloka'.* with a magnificent figure by *bhūti* 'ashes'. Applying ashes should be considered praiseworthy always in the ritual of *sandhyopāsanā* as it is prescribed by *śruti* and *smṛti*. *śruti* is 'thrice it should be' etc. Also (it is said) in *smṛti:*

> "The *gṛhastha* should apply ashes thrice in *sandhyā* ritual alongwith water, while the *vānaprasthas* and the *yatis* should do so in the evening without water".

Again *gavām* 'of the sacrifices. *iśvaraḥ* 'giver of fruits of (those sacrifices).' Though the word *go* conveying the sense of a particular type of sacrifice can possibly be in singular, yet plural is employed since the rituals secondary to the sacrifice are numerous. And it is said in the Bhagavadgitā that Brahmā gives the fruits of sacrifices—

> "Prajāpati-Brahmā created the people alongwith the sacrifices and said : 'May you all multiply by this (sacrifice) and may this fulfil your desires."

But the reading-*prasaviṣyadhvam* found everywhere is reconsiderble, because the imperative is impossible with the suffix *sya* (the second future *lṛt*) and in *laṅg* (imperfect past) *a* in the beginning is inevitable. This is also like the one in Bhāgavata where the ancient text *prācīnatūleṣu kuśeṣu dhīrah.* was correct but some so-called scholar, not understanding its meaning, imagined the reading—*prācīnamūleṣu* and it was written down by the scribes in the tradition. But *Śrīdharaswāmin* has given an appropriate synonym of it: *prāgagreṣu. agra* can be the meaning (lit. synonym) of *tūla* only and not *mūla.* As is said in the Dharmaśāstra :

> "The *kuśas* are known to be of two types: *aprasūta* 'soft' and *prasūta* 'brittle'. Soft are (employed in rites like) *tarpaṇa* 'offering of water etc' whereas the brittle are (used to make) seats."

aprasūta 'soft' are small, of the length of *prādeśa* (span between thumb and forefinger) and to be utilised in the rites of offering libations to manes and purification etc. *prasūta* 'brittle' are with tops, with a tuft of grass. They are used to prepare seats. *tula* means 'the sharp point of the blade of *kuśa* grass.'

Now, either at the begining or at the end of the study of the *vedas,* one performs three expiations and becomes pure, installs fire or in the absence of fire invokes the rising sun, spreading the *darbha* grass sits on them according to the Vedic statement: "on the grass with its tops eastward or northward" etc. and one performs the oblations of rice and barley sitting on *darbha* grass with tops eastward if one desires the lustre of *brahman,* with tops northward for the desire of cattle and sons and (with tops towards) both directions if desiring both i.e. cattle as well as general welfare. Thus even in the twelfth *skandha* (of Śrīmad Bhāgavata) it should be understood as "sitting on *barhiṣ* with tops eastward on the bank of the river Gaṅgā with his face northward, (Parīkṣit, a great *yogi* bereft of all attachments, with all his doubts cleared appeared as *brahma incarnate).*" But here, the reading *prāktūḷe* is written by the scribes due to mistake. or (Brahmā) *īśvaraḥ* 'the originator of *gavām* 'of the *Vedas* in the form of Sarasvatī. Again (he is) omniscient i.e. knows everything about the world etc. Again, how is he? Whose body is adorned with austerities since in *brahmaloka* there are only austerities. Again, he is associated with *māyā* composed of *rajoguṇa,* and creator of the universe. Again, the knower of *vṛtti,* the behaviour of the people. Also blissful. Again, the fulfiller of the desires of *sumanas* i.e. gods. hence giver of joy. Also *anantadṛk* i.e. 'one who observes the infinite universes.' Again, always engrossed in *prāṇāyāma*, in the meditation of the supreme *brahman*. He i.e. wellknown as the creator of the world, Lord Gaṅgādhara, i.e. *brahman* may protect us all.

Again, the word *gaṅgādhara* etymologically denotes 'ocean.' Hence construe in that sense: whose mind is engrossed in *satya* i.e. observing the boundaries, whose body is adorned with *bhūti* i.e. the wealth of jewels, pearls etc. Again, *īśvara* lord of *go,* 'waters', also the lord of *jaḍa* 'inanimates' owing to the non-difference between ḍa and *la*. Omniscient i.e. he knows the dual forms of (all) rivers and mountains. Shining with *dvijarāja* i.e. his own son, the moon. Again, how is he? *anvitaḥ* associated with *viṣṇu* as *māyaḥ* i.e. one who goes to (√*yā*) or obtains *mā* i.e. Godess Lakṣmī. Again *vṛtti* i.e. the attitudes of the lord, the knower of these means the obeyer of the orders of the Lord. Again, *ānandī* joyful i.e. at the rise of the moon. Again of what nature? fulfiller of the desires of sea-travellers whose minds are expert in selling and purchasing. Hence the giver of joy. *anantadṛk* 'one who sees the great serpent *śeṣa* also called *ananta,'* because he (*śeṣa*) has formed himself into the couch of Viṣṇu. And since he (i.e. *śeṣa*) always lives within himself (i.e. in the sea). Engaged in *āsana* i.e. sitting for protection near Brahmā i.e. the creater. Such will be the interpretation pertaining to *samudra* i.e. the sea.

Now, the explanation pertaining to a brahmin named Gaṅgādhara Śāstrī. This is a *yadṛchhā* word i.e. a proper noun, its *saṅketa* being decided by parents etc. Hence conventionally established in the sense of a particular brahmin. whose mind is devoted to *satya* i.e. speaking the truth. Again by what adjectives is he distinguished? Whose body is adorned with *bhūti* i.e. riches or ashes. the master of *gavām* i.e. speeches. The attribution that he is Bṛhaspati incarnate, meaning, he is like Bṛhaspati. Hence also omniscient. or such as he knows all the scriptures or all the ways of the world, or all the religious practices of castes and stages. Again, how is he? *dvijarājaḥ* i.e. the king of the brahmins, and also having a luminous body, or, whose body is adorned by brahmins and kings. Again *mā* i.e. *lakṣmī. ayaḥ* means an auspicious rite. endowed by both of these. And again *vṛttivit, i.e.* knower of five *vṛttis* namely *kṛt. taddhita, samāsa, ekaśeṣa* and *sanādyanta dhātu*. Or the knower of three *vṛttis* i.e. *śakti* 'denotation', *lakṣaṇā* 'indication' and *vyañjanā* 'suggestion'. Again *ānandī* always joyful. Also fulfiller of the desires of *sumanas* i.e. the learned, and hence the giver of joy. *anantadṛk*. That by which can be seen is dṛk. i.e. knowledge. 'one whose knowledge is endless.' Or he visualises the infinite *śabdabrahman*. Or he has seen *ananta* infinite i.e. Viṣṇu or endless scriptures. Again, how is he? Always engrossed in the meditation of the highest *brahman* called *gāyatrī*. Only therefore, *bhagavān* i.e. 'fortunate.' He is famous every-where. Such an interpretation should be understood in the sense of the brahmin named Gaṅgādhara Śāstrī.

The word *gaṅgādhara* also operates derivatively in the sense of a particular sage named Jahnu. It is also said:

> "She first stayed in the form of the water in the *kamaṇḍalu* of brahmā, the first grandfather, thereafter, she became the pious waters at the feet of Lord (*Viṣṇu*) lying on the serpent *(śeṣa),* then again, she became the crest-jewel in the matted hair of Lord Śaṅkara. That *Gaṅgā,* the beautiful daughter of the great sage Jahnu, the destroyer of the sins is victorious."

The interpretation applying to this (sage Jahnu) should be understood by one's own self. In this case, the views of the ancients should be understood as follows: though the meaning pertaining to four explanations are relevant (contextual), yet the meaning pertaining to the ocean is noncontextual. Therefore, this is paranomasia of relevant and non-relevant and therefore, suggestion based on words. And again, by taking the adjective *bhagavān,* the name of the author (i.e. Bhagavat Kavi) of this work is also suggested. Hence the *mudrā* figure of speech is also suggested because of its definition—'where the sense to be suggested is conveyed through a verse, it is a *mudrā alaṅkāra.* Where the specific sense is suggested covertly to a clever person with the help of a specific speech or a specific gesture in a way that a layman cannot understand it, that will be only *vyañjanā vṛtti* there.

Now, the example where the sense is suggested by a specific speech in a hidden way:

> "O traveller, this is (Gaṅgā) the river of gods. Now, you will not get any boat here. The sun will set soon. Don't be afraid Hold two, large, beautiful pots on your chest tightly and swim across these thick waters when the dark clouds are hovering (in the sky)."

This is a suggestive address made by a young lady who has come to bring water on the bank of the *Gaṅgā* to a young traveller:" O traveller, this is *Gaṅgā,* the river of gods," The sense is—'it is a large river'. (The suggested) sense is-'impossible to cross on one's own.' "No boat will arrive just now. And also, there will be drowning of the sun i.e. sunset. But don't be afraid". The explicit sense is this: "when the blazing dense clouds are arising, hold two large pots on your chest, and go across, i.e. to the other side of these thick waters." But by the address 'O traveller' it is suggested: "You also will enjoy, intense *rasa."* [This is *lakṣaṇā*](?) (This lady) is *raṅgiṇi* 'loving.' *surata,* 'dalliance, amorous sport'. "Our meeting is not possible *sapadi* ' now' in the daytime. but only when it is sundown, sunset. Don't be afraid. There is no fear of my husband etc. at home. I stay alone. In this rainy season, you keep, i.e. place the pair of large plump breasts intensely on your heart. Experience that dense sentiment of love" etc. This is covertly suggested, therefore, it is suggestion only.

Suggestion by gesture as in—

> "O dear! O dear! the wife of the one-eyed man did a wonderful thing today! She held his ears with both of her hands and then leaving his lips, kissed his other eye (which could see)."

The soft utterance *ayi, ayi* (conveys the sense) that the act performed by the wife of the one-eyed man was really wonderful; i.e. (one that was) never done before. It explains its uniqueness. Both the ears were held with both the hands. Avoiding the lower lip, the undamaged eye was kissed. Here she who was enjoying herself with her paramour in her own house. made a show of false love towards her husband who had gone out and had returned home. having created deafness by covering his two ears with both of her hands and blindness by kissing his undamaged eye. It was suggested (by her): "you may go out of my house withour fear." There is no seeing with the damaged eye and there was no seeing with the undamaged eye, on account of the blindness due to kissing. On account of deafness by covering his two ears even the absence of the knowledge of the movement of the paramour's feet, is suggested. Therefore, the power of *vyañjanā* different from the denotative and the indicative power must certainly be accepted. Enough of more details.

> This volume called Vicāradīpa is composed by the scholar Bhagavān for the joy of the learned and nothing new is depicted here. (1)
>
> Just as a lamp removes thick darkness in a house, and is able to illuminate all the objects in the world, similarly, may this worthy treatise remove the darkness of doubt from the hearts of all the scholars and may activate all the well known meanings of the words. (2)
>
> Those who are expert in literary criticism, are well-read in sciences, are experts in good deeds, who only have an eye for excellences of the *rasas,* the poems and dramas, who are averse to hypocrisy and jealousy, who are simple by nature-may this work of mine always bring joy to those connoisseurs. (3)
>
> The son of Ānandarāma, eager to make research into the meaning of sciences, I. the wise Bhagavān

request forgiveness of the group of scholars for whatever proper or improper might have been done by me in deliberations in my composition. (4)

May this, composed now, by the brahmin called Bhagavān situated in Lālīgrāma, be for the joy of Gaṅgādhara. (5)

This (work) was completed on Monday, the fifth day of the bright half in the month of Āśvina, in the (V.) *samvat* eighteen hundred and sixty. (6)

Thus ended this treatise composed by Bhagavān, the son of Bhaṭṭa Ānandarāma belonging to the Raikva *jñāti*.

śrī śrī śrī śrī.

FOOTNOTES

1. Tr. by Gajendragadkar. A. B.
2. Tr. by Gajendragadkar. A. B.
3. Tr. by Handiqui Krishna Kant.
4. As translated by K. Kunjunni Raja in 'Indian Theories of meaning', p.46.
5. With grammatical co-ordination and without grammatical corodination.
6. Tr. by Handiqui Krishna Kant.
7. Tr. by Gajendragadkar A. B.
8. Tr. mainly based on that by Gajendragadkar A. B.
9. Tr. by Handiqui Krishna Kant.
10. Tr. by Handiqui Krishna Kant.
11. Tr. by Dr. Krishnamoorthy K.
12. Tr. by Gajendragadkar. A. B.
13. Tr. by Handiqui Krishna Kant

CHAPTER - IV

DISCUSSION OF THE CONTENTS

As is clear by now, Vicāradīpa (VD) is a *vādagrantha* containing a number of discussions on various technical points requiring keen observations and scholarly acumen of a high order, Many of such discussions have points of references in grammar with a few in Mīmāṁsā and Nyāya also. The style of our traditional scholars has been highly allusive and would contain a number of covert and obvert references to the maxims of different *śāstras*. This fact renders the style of the author very compact, or rather terse, presupposing on the part of the reader a close acquaintance with various *śāstras* to which the author himself alludes. For a modern reader, therefore, such a traditional style requires an elaborate exposition of the arguments, discussions and conclusions included in the traditional text. VD of Bhagavatkavi Bhaṭṭa (BKB) also falls into this category of traditional scholastic works. It will, therefore not be out of place if an attempt is made here to present all the points discussed by the author in all its clear details so that the reader can have a clear grasp of the augthor's viewpoint on his points of discussion and an idea of the width and depth of the author's scholarship of various *śāstras*. An attempt is, therefore, made here to present the contents of the text VD in a clear and lucid exposition with all the arguments clarified from the viewpoints of the various *śāstras* involved in the discussion and with quotations from the original sources where necessary. It is hoped that this exposition of the contents of arguments presented by BKB in VD will render the text more graspable and make it easier for the reader to appreciate the scholarship of the author.

The manuscript starts with श्रीगणेशाय नमः।—This salutation could not be of the author but of the scribe.

IV. i *Maṅgala Śloka :*

The work proper begins with *maṅgala śloka:*

श्रीमद्गुरोः पादयुगं प्रणम्य श्रीशं च साम्बं तपनं गजास्यम्।
शास्त्रेति शब्दस्य विचारदीपं कुर्वे विवादं भगवान् सुबोधम्॥

Every treatise of Sanskrit *śāstras* commences with *maṅgala śloka.* This tradition is supported by the statement in the Mahābhāṣya: मङ्गलादीनि हि शास्त्राणि प्रथन्ते वीरपुरुषकाणि च भवन्त्यायुष्मत्पुरुषकाणि चाध्येतारश्च सिद्धार्था यथा स्युरिति।[1] 'Works marked with benedictory words at the beginning gain reputation and, people reading them, become valiant and longlived and are able to achieve all their goals'.

BKB follows this *śāstraic* tradition and opens his work with a salutation to his *guru* and other deities. His *guru* as we later learn is Āśādhara Bhaṭṭa (AB) who has taught him the Rasataraṅgiṇī as he has said in his commentary—Nūtanatarī on that treatise.[2] He also offers his salutations to the *pañcāyatana* gods namely *viṣṇu, śiva* with *ambā, sūrya* and *gajānana.* In Nūtanatarī he has paid homage to *gaurī* and *śambhu,* an indication of his *śaivite* family tradition.

In the second half of the *maṅgala śloka,* the author states the subject of this work. the title of the work is *Vicāradīpa* 'Lamp of thoughts (or views)'; and in his treatise, he proposes to depict the subject of *śabdaśāstra.* The nature of the work is also suggested in this statement itself. He uses the word वाद for his work. The word वाद is defined as: तत्त्वबुभुत्सुकथा वादः । (न्यायभाष्य) Discussions aimed at leading towards truth are *vāda.* The term is appropriately used as the work includes a number of detailed discussions on controversial or debatable points associated with *śabdaśāstra* namely,

(i) whether this work about *śabdaśakti* can be called a *śāstra*;

(ii) whether *nipātas* are *vācaka* (expressive, denotative) or *dyotaka* (suggestive);

(iii) whether certain grammatical formations are justified;

(iv) whether *sphoṭa* theory is acceptable and so on.

The author, of course, claims that his work is सुबोध 'easily comprehensive'. One may not easily agree with this statement of his as various technical *(śāstrīya)* discussions about grammatical formations are quite erudite.

Now, BKB explains each and every word of the *maṅgala śloka* in the style of an auto-commentary. He adopts the *bhāṣya* style; he presents the arguments of the *pūruvapakṣa* pretaining to the topic under discussion and then refutes those arguments with the support of various *śāstras*. This style gives this work the stature of a *śāstragrantha.*

The author proposes to prove that each and every word in the *maṅgala śloka* is perfectly formed from the grammatical point of view. Such is the drift of arguments. पादयुगं प्रणम्य........ about the construction पादयुगं प्रणम्य....., the *pūrvapakṣa* may argue against the usage as follows:

In प्रणम्य शितिकण्ठाय (कुमार० ६/८१), the dative case is used because the words conveying the person or the god to be saluted take the dative case. In the *śloka* here, गुरुपादयुगम्, श्रीशम्, साम्बम्, तपनम् and गजास्यम् take accusative case, though all the words convey the persons to be saluted. How is this to be explained?

Justification: The author takes support of a *paribhāṣā* "The *kāraka* case is stronger than the *upapada* case". This *paribhāṣā* states that there is greater force in a *kāraka* case than in an *upapada* case. In *kāraka vibhakti the case affix* is governed by a verb or a verbal derivative, in *upapada vibhakti* the affix is governed by a noun which does not possess any verbal activity. And the *paribhāṣā* quoted above states that the *kāraka vibhakti* has greater force. Therefore, the employment of a Kāraka case i.e. the accusative case in the present case in justified. The author also explains how in such case as प्रणम्य शितिकण्ठाय...the *pāṇinian* dictum क्रियार्थोपपदस्य च कर्मणि स्थानिनः। (II, iii, 14) enjoins the dative case. The *sūtra* says, the dative case-affix is to be employed to denote the object of that verb which is suppressed in a sentence, and which has in construction, therewith another verb, denoting an action performed for the sake of the future action. देवाः शितिकण्ठम् प्रसादयितुम् प्रणम्य.....'the gods having bowed down to *śitikaṇṭha* in order to please him-----', while in—गुरुपादयुगं प्रणम्य this *sūtra does* not apply. Hence the accusative case is perfectly justified. साम्बम्—The author then takes up the word साम्बम् in the *maṅgala śloka.* why is th*e* word साम्ब employed in the sense of *śiva?* The word is an adjective of *śiva* and it suggests that the author wants to offer his salutations to the *śiva* with *śakti,* both of them among the *pañcāyatana* gods. He supports his usage of the word with a dictum which says that the adjective **can** convey the sense of the substantive as the word सागराम्बरा is used in the sense of पृथ्वी 'the earth'.

It must be noted here that in the beginning of the work itself, the form and nature of the treatment of the topic are suggested. BKB virtually intends to compose a science-*śāstra* of the word and at every step, at every possible opportunity, he takes a halt to explain certain words and their grammatical formations. It is his intention and interest to elaborate the *śabdaśāstra* and not merely to depict the subject of *śabdaśakti,* the work which his teacher AB has already accomplished, in his two well-known works, Kovidānanda (KND) and Triveṇikā (TRN).

शास्त्रेति.......the word शास्त्र is used here purely in its प्रातिपदिक form without any case affix because it is the word uttered in अनुकरण 'imitation' of another word शब्दस्य—It is a word employed in an imitative manner like the word भू in भूसत्तायाम् or like the word राम in रामेति लोकरमणात्।

Someone may argue that the word शास्त्र is used here without any case-affix which is not justified, as it is ungrammatical according to the rule—अपदं न प्रयुञ्जीत। 'A word without any case-affix should not be used. The reply is: the *kārikā* cited by the *pūrvapakṣa* itself justifies the usage of the word शास्त्र in its *prātipadika* form. In गवित्याह and in भूसत्तायाम् the two words are अनुकार्य-अनुकरण, so evenif they are neither प्रातिपदिक nor पद their use without case-affixes is justifiable because अनुकरण words are not distinguished from अनुकार्य.

In the present case, the word शास्त्र is अनुकरण of the word शब्द (स्य) Hence it is grammatically justified.

Next, the compound विचारदीप is explained in greater detail as it is the title of the work. विचाराणाम् दीपः विचारदीपः। (षष्ठी तत्पुरुष) दीपः means 'illuminationg'. The word दीप 'lamp' is विषयिन् which only is mentioned. The word दीप 'illuminating' is विषय, which is understood i.e. not mentioned This treatise illuminates thoughts (about *śabdā*) as a lamp illuminates things. Though BKB does not explain, it will be a लुप्तोपमा-विचाराणां दीप इव दीपः।

Also, the title is not विचारदीपकम्, दीपकम् is a figure of speech explained by Mammaṭa as: सकृद्वृत्तिस्तु धर्मस्य प्रकृता-प्रकृतात्मनाम्। etc. (KP.X, 17) and the title is not to be confused with it. The author again resorts to grammar to explain this. The क in दीपकम् is इवार्थ in the sense of 'likeness' according to the *pāṇinian* dictum इवे प्रतिकृतौ कन्। (V,iii, 96)[3]. In विचारदीपः there is साध्यवसाना लक्षणा, The purport suggested from the title is this : the topic of *śabdaśakti* provoked certain thoughts in the author's mind. They are illuminated—expressed thoroughly and comprehensively in this work. As a lamp reveals objects, this book purports to explain clearly many queries about the science of words-the *śabdaśāstra,* grammar. To illustrate—(i) How is a discussion about words a *śāstra?* (ii) Is *adhyāhāra* of words or of senses? (iii) How is the word·*śāstra* derived? These and such other questions are discussed in detail in this work. At times, BKB even expresses his views at variance with his teacher. Such controversial points are also included in the course of discussion in the work with a clear expression of the differences of opinions. The title विचारदीप is, therefore, very amply justified.

IV. ii The title Vicāradīpa :

The author here forms opposition about the compound विचारदीप—experts in grammar may argue that the formation of the compound is ungrammatical. How? Thus : The word विचार 'thought' bears an expectancy with the word *śāstra* शास्त्र 'science' in the sentence. It is साकाङ्क्ष; and a साकाङ्क्ष word cannot enter into a compound; साकाङ्क्षं असमर्थवत् वाच्यम्।[4] The word which is more closely connected with another word in the sense, cannot enter into a compound with some other word. The word विचार is expectant of the word शास्त्र; hence it is असमर्थ 'unqualified' to enter into a compound here with word दीप—The dictum—समर्थः पदविधिः।[5] does not contenance such a formation.

The Reply :

The author quotes a dictum from भाष्यवार्त्तिक[6] which states that a compound can be formed by words which are ever-expectant. The formation of such a compound is also supported by Kaiyaṭa whose quote in the text form his Bhāṣyapradīpa says, "Every word which is related to some other word in sense, can be used as a word possessed of an expectancy. Such expectancy is not rejected in a compound as well as in a sentence".

Further, BKB also quotes in support Mallinātha commenting upon रतेर्गृहीतानुनयेन.....etc. (रघु० ६/२) Here गृहीतानुनय is a compound. The word अनुनय is expectant with रते: in the sentence and yet it forms a compound with the word गृहीत, because it conveys the meaning clearly: "One who has accepted the urge of Rati". Here though the word अनुनय is expectant, the compound गृहीतानुनय is justified. Mallinātha also comments upon the verse thus: रते कामप्रियायाः गृहीतानुनयेन स्वीकृतप्रार्थनेन गृहीतरत्यनुनयेनेत्यर्थः। सापेक्षत्वेऽपि गमकत्वात् समासः।[7] The same is the case with the compound विचारदीप. The word विचार is expectant with शास्त्र, yet the compound विचारदीप can be justified. The meaning, thus, of the title विचारदीप is "the work which illuminates the thoughts about *śabdaśāstra*. The author adduces some more examples of such compounds in चैत्रस्य शिष्यकुलम्। मैत्रस्य गुरुकुलम्। etc. The text at this point, however, seems to have lacunae hampering the flow of the argument in such a way that here it (the text) is beyond emendation. इत्थं च...The author here seems to reconnect the thread of argument to justify his usage of शास्त्रेति etc. Incidentally, he also offers a textual emendation in a verse of Raghuvaṁśa. The text which is traditionally handed down to us is: क्षत्रस्य शब्दो भुवनेषु रूढः.....। BKB suggests that the reading here should be क्षत्रेति in place of क्षत्रस्य as it is in शास्त्रेति शब्दस्य etc. in his *maṅgala śloka*. His grammar-oriented approach towards the acceptability of certain readings even in poetic expressions becomes obvious here.

Next, he takes up the verb कुर्वे from his *maṅgala śloka* for discussion and touches upon the topic of अध्याहार In कुर्वे the root कृ is used in the first person singular and the subject of the very\b i.e. "I" is to be understood, it is अध्याहार—The author incidentally, does not miss to define the word अध्याहार which means 'supplementing some expected part or element in a sentence'. This occasions the discussion whether अध्याहार

depends upon words or senses. The author treats the topic in some detail The question is how should an incomplete meaning in a sentence be supplemented when something is not uttered? Should we supplement some expected (necessory) word or should we understand the sense of that unuttered (अध्याहृत) word? For instance द्वारम्। In this statement, there in no verb uttered; now do we supplement the word पिधेहि or do we understand the sense 'close' without its utterance? The Mīmāṁsakas suggest that we directly apprehend the underlying sense instead of involving the intervention of the word. In the utterance द्वारम्। the word पिधेहि does not occur to the mind at all. We undetstand the sense itself straightaway. In an incomplete sentence, therefore, it is the अर्थ which is अध्याहृत and not the पद according to the Mīmāṁsakas. On the other hand, the Naiyā-yikas and the Vedāntins propound that an incomplete sentence can be completed in sense only by the supplementation of the missing word; and not by the apprehension of the sense directly. Only the comprehension of the missing word can eventually give the meaning fully and make the comprehension of the sentence possible.

BKB seems to accept both the views. he gives examples of both अर्थाध्याहार and पदाध्याहार and avers that as required by the context, both are acceptable.

The instance of अर्थाध्याहार is—भवानपीदं परवान् अवैति। (रघु० २/५६) 'you who are also dependent, know this'. In this sentence, the sense of युष्मद् is अध्याहार. If we supplement the word त्वम् (युष्मद्) here, the verb अवैति, which is third person singular, would not fit in. In that case, the word त्वम् (युष्मद्) 'you', would have to be taken as विशेष्य 'substantive' of भवान् and hence, as principal, the word भवान् itself being an adjective a subordinate, owing to its derivation as भाति इति भवान् one who shines out is (त्वम् i.e. you)'.

In understanding of अध्याहार in this sense, there would not be repetition in the classical usage of Kālidāsa in the verse- तत्त्वं निवर्तस्व विहाय लज्जां गुरोर्भवान् दर्शितशिष्यभक्तिः। (रघु० २/४०), where the two words त्वम् and भवान् conveying the same sense are used. Well, it has to be justified in this way: here there are two sentences: "you then return without feeling ashamed. and "you who shine out, have shown your devotion to your teacher." भवान् may be taken hefe as an adjective, meaning: "you, who have shone out showing devotion to your teacher, return without feeling ashamed."

In भवति, भिक्षां देहि। "O lady, give alms', however, there is अध्याहार of the word त्वम् (युष्मद्) because, in this sentence, भवति is in the vocative case and is an address, and therefore, it forms an independent sentence. Hence, भिक्षां देहि। will be an independent sentence and it has the अध्याहार of the word युष्मद् (=त्वम् 'you'). Otherwise, the form देहि imperative second person singular could not have been employed.

Now the *pūrvapakṣa* is presented from a different stand point: why should the शब्दाध्याहार at all be accepted if only the senses of the words are construed in a sentence?

The author justifies शब्दाध्याहार here, by replying to the argument: according to those (i.e. the *naiyāyikas* and the *vedāntins*) who believe that the sense is apprehended only by a word, and therefore, the word does occur to our mind as the senses are construed in a sentence through words only. The author gives an example: we understand 'thirst', when the word तोयम् 'water' is uttered, and we understand bringing when the word कलश–'the pot' is uttered. Thirst is satisfied by water and water is brought with a pot only. In the same way, words are necessary to convey sense. Senses are construed in a sentence through words only. Thus शब्दाध्याहार also is acceptable in some cases.

The author begins his work with the word श्री in order to avoid निषिद्धगणादि दोष-the defect of bringing prohibited letters in the beginning.

IV. iii Discussion of *śabda* 'the word' as a *śāstra*:-

Some people may argue that *śāstraicness* should be considered only in six philosophical systems namely *nyāya, vaiśeṣika, pūrvamīmāṁsā, uttaramīmāṁsā, sāṅkhya* and *yoga;* and grammar, the science of words cannot be a *śāstra; śabdaśakti* cannot be the subject to be discussed in the form of a *śāstra.*

In order to refute this argument, BKB states: वेदस्तु भगवान् साक्षात्........etc. and starts the discussion of *śabda* as a *śāstra.*

(1) Statement in Pāṇiniya *Śikṣa:*

शिक्षा घ्राणं तु वेदस्य मुखं व्याकरणं स्मृतम्। (VIII, 42) "*śikṣā* is the nose of the *veda* and grammar is its mouth." Now, the *veda* is God incarnate. So vedic statements are the statements of God. Grammar being his mouth, the *sūtras* in grammar are also *śāstra.* In fact, any kind of instruction can be called śāstra.

(2) Etymology of the word *śāstra* :

The author quotes from Manoramā : उपदिश्यते अनेन इति. ...ल्युटा बाधादित्युक्तम्। etc. शास्त्र is a tool for teaching or for instruction. So The word *śāstra* is used to denote 'instruction.' The word is thus explained in भाष्यवृत्ति, but according to Manoramā that is only a bold assertion, because the affix घञ् (कृत् affix अ) is not used in the sense of instrument. घञ् (अ) is subjugated by the affix ल्युट् (अन्) which is used in the sense of an instrument or an abode.

BKB does not accept this explanation. His etymology of the word शास्त्र is like this : √शास् 'to instruct' takes the affix ष्ट्रन् among the उणादि affixes;[8] which are similar to the कृत् affixes of Pāṇini. These affixes give derivation of such words as are not formed with the help of the *pāṇini sūtras.* As Pāṇini has stated in ताभ्याम् अन्यत्र उणादयः। (II, iv, 75), various *uṇādi* affixes are applied to various roots as prescribed in any *kāraka* sense except the sense of the संप्रदान and the उपादान—In other words, any one of the sense, agent object, instrument and abode is assigend to the *uṇādi* affix as suits the meaning of the word. Thus the root √शास् takes the affix ष्ट्रन् in the sense of instrument and the word शास्त्र is formed by बाहुलक.[9] Such etymology is acceptable to convey the sense 'instrument of instruction'. A book or something with which some principle or rule or subject is taught is शास्त्र—Thus grammar is a शास्त्र.

(3) Amarakośa statement :

Amarakośa states that the word *śāstra* is used in the sense of 'order' and 'book'. Kṣīraswāmin, the well-known grammarian has explained the word शास्त्र-शास्यते अनेन इति शास्त्रम् by करणार्थे ष्ट्रन्, i.e. with ष्ट्रन् in the sense of instrument.

BKB incidentally takes note the neo-grammarians do not accept this view of the ancients. Yet, बाहुलक being applicable wherever there is no other justification of a certain formation, it is justified to understand the word शास्त्र thus.

To conclude, all kinds of instructions and treatises can be called *śāstra.* Thus grammar and the rules therein are *śāstra.*

(4) The view of the grammarians :

It is said that *śāstra* is something well-said. So the question will be that of the सिद्धत्व or असिद्धत्व of grammatical dicta. The author quotes a verse सामान्यशास्त्रतो नूनं.......etc. which could not be traced out. The general statement is a rule, and an appropriate definition is *śāstra.* The gist of the whole discussion is this: As the *naiyāyikas',* definitions of the entities like earth, aquva, light, wind and ether, so are the *vaiyākaraṇās' sūtras,* both are *śāstra.*

(5) In the verses like शब्दशास्त्रमनधीत्य.......etc. where the grammar is admired, the word शास्त्र is employed for 'grammar' (शब्दशास्त्र).

(6) Somebody may raise an objection that if it is said that grammar is a *śāstra* for being the mouth of the *veda,* God incarnate, then it would be difficult to include *nyāya* etc. in *śāstra,* because they are not directly connected with the *veda.*

The author has given a logical justification for the argument in तात्स्थ्यात्........in the verse on the strength of the statement तात्स्थ्यात् ताच्छब्द्यम्।[10] in the Mahābhāṣya, the word (शब्द) शास्त्र can be used for न्याय, मीमांसा etc. beccause grammar is bound to reside in all these, in the form of प्रकृति, प्रत्यय, उत्सर्ग, अपवाद and सूत्र. Since grammar is a *śāstra,* the scriptures in which grammar resides, are also *śāstras*. Thus all the fourteen *vidyāsthānas,* abodes of knowledge described in the Yājña-valkyasmṛti are also *śāstra.*

(7) In sacrifical rites also, the prevalance of the grammarians is observed. when the vedic *mantras* are employed in sacrifices, the ritualists expert in *ūha* make change in cases, numbers, genders etc. as required. Such application of the *mantras* is possible for those who are expert in grammar. BKB quotes a verse from Śiśupālavadham in support. (नाञ्जसा निगदितम्.......etc.)

(8) Kāvya, poetry, is instructive and whatever is instructive is a *śāstra*. The three functions of a word, *śābdaśaktis* are connected with the poetic word. Therefore, BKB states the instructive nature of *kāvya* after Mammaṭa here: काव्यं यशसे... ....etc. here, again a problem of text editing intervenes. The text इदानीं....व्यवहारो न स्यात्। put in square brackets seems to be inconsistent in the context. The portion, however, is verbatim picked up from the Rasavilāsa[11]. The definition of poetry etc. is verbatim picked up from the Rasavilāsa. The definition of poetry

etc. is out of context here. This portion should be considered as interpolated. Had the editor availed another manuscript, the problem of confirming the correct text would have been solved. Is it written by scribe? Is it a case of false recollection on the part of the scribe? There is no evidence to come to conclusion.

To resume the discussion-it may be argued that poetry is not generally known as a *śāstra*. BKB replies that the same would be the case with *purāṇa* which is not known as *śāstra!* Śrīdharaswāmin has mentioned the Bhāgvata Purāṇa (BP) as a *śāstra,* and Yājñavalkya has included the *purāṇas* in *vidyā-sthānas*. If you consider some of them as *śāstra* and exclude some others, then there would arise *ardhajaratīyanyāya.*[12] Incidentally, BKB quotes a verse from the Śiśupālavadham, which established even the गजवशीकरणग्रन्थ, scripture on controlling elephants-as a *śāstra*. The author explains the *arthāntar-anyāsa* (corroboration) figure of speech in the verse. The specific incident—control on the boby elephant by the rider-is corroborated by a general proposition—*'śāstra* always succeeeds'. Unless गजवशीकरण is accepted as a *śāstra* here, the corroboration cannot occur. [The citation निर्विशेषं न सामान्यं. ......etc. is probably misquoted. The *śloka* in श्लोकवार्तिक runs as follows:

निर्विशेषं न सामान्यं भवेच्छशविषाणवत्।
सामान्यरहितत्वाच्च विशेपास्तद्वदेव हि॥

"As a horn of a rabbit is impossible, so a सामान्य (general) cannot exist without a (specific), on the other hand, the *viseṣas* without the *sāmānyas* are also like that (=शशविषाण) i.e. they cannot exist."

Of course, BKB clarifies that the word *śāstra*, actually used for such treatises as गजवशीकरण by गौणीवृत्ति i.e. in the secondary sense. As *śāstra* benefits its students, so such works benefit their readers.

Why such a lengthy, detailed, *śāstraic* discussion of *śāstra?*

Because, the author intends to reply those high-browed Vedic scholars, who look down upon the *paurāṇikas* and the students of poetics. We may read here, the reflection of contemporary brahmin society where study of the *purāṇas* and classical literature was looked down upon by the scholars of Vedic studies. The author extends the discussion upto the fruit (फल) of studying grammar being *mokṣa* salvation because it studies the *śabda* which is *brahman* itself. he has taken the clue of this discussion from KND.[13] The *śruti* द्वे ब्रह्मणी etc. is also quoted there.

In brief, grammar, the science of *śabdabrahma* is a *śāstra,* the knowledge of which leads to *mokṣa.* The aims, objectives and achievement (फल) of this *vādagrantha* are thus far discussed in the elaboration of the first two verses. What is more important is, it is discussed how grammar is a *śabdaśāstra* and how it is as important as other spiritual scripures. The author suggestively draws the reader's attention to the aims and objectives of this work. though his teacher AB has already written two books on the subject of *śabdaśakti,* his own approach to the topic is altogether different and it is grammar-oriented.

IV. iv The Theory of Sphoṭa :

In the natural course of discussion BKB brings in the *sphoṭa* theory, one of the most important contribution of the ancient Indian philology. AB has not included the treatment of *sphoṭavāda* both in KND and TRN, BKB fills the gap, and treats the topic in detail.

The term स्फोट is derived as (1) स्फुट्यते व्यज्यते शब्दैः वर्णैः वा। or (2) स्फुटयति प्रकाशयति अर्थम् or (3) स्फुटति प्रादुर्भवति अर्थः अस्मात्। (1) That which is manifested by words or letters, (2) That which brings out the meaning (3) that from which the meaning shines forth. The theory of *sphoṭa* was fully developed and systematised by the great grammarian Bhartṛhari in his Vākyapadīya. However, some of the ideas behind this theory can be found in earlier literature on grammar and philosophy. It is not clear whether Pāṇini knew anything about the theory, but Nāgeśa Bhaṭṭa ascribes the theory to sage Sphoṭāyana,[14] whom Pāṇini[15] mentions as an authority. The first mention of the term *sphoṭa* occurs in the Mahābhāṣya. Patañjali distinguishes between two aspects of शब्द (=sound): the *sphoṭa* and the *dhvani*. In Patañjali's opinion, *sphoṭa* is the permanent element in the word and it may be considered the essential word, *dhvani* is the actualized and ephemeral element and an attribute of the former: स्फोटश्शब्दः, ध्वनिश्शब्दगुणः।[16] *śphoṭa* as described by Patañjali may be a single letter *(varṇa)* or a fixed pattern of letters and is the norm, it remains constant and is not affected by the peculiarities of the individual speakers. Evenwhen spoken by different speakers with different tones, its Linguistic value remains the same. The absolute vowel-length and the individual peculiarities of the specific instances are of *dhvanis* and depend on the individuality of the speaker and the effort with which the words are uttered. *Sphoṭa* is permanent and unchanging and is manifested by the ephemeral *dhvanis,* uttered by the speaker and heard by the listener.

BKB refers to Patañjali's view when he states: वैयाकरणानां स्फोटो ध्वनिश्चेति द्विविधः शब्दः। In brief, the theory of *sphoṭa* maintains that a word or a sentence should be considered not as a concatenation made up of different sound units arranged in a particular order, but as a single meaningful linguistic sign. the word or the sentence thus considered as a single meaningful symbol is called *sphoṭa*. The articulated sounds used in a linguistic discourse are only the means by which this symbol is revealed. It is this symbol which is the meaning-bearer. This *sphoṭa* is indivisible and has no time-order. The articulated sounds with the timeorder are resorted to only as a means of revealing this symbol.

(1) The opposition-*pūrvapakṣa* against the theory:

BKB in his *śāstraic* style, presents the *mīmāṁsaka* and the *nyāya* view as the *pūrvapakṣa* against the theory of *sphoṭa* ननु पूर्वपर्व...... किं स्फोटकल्पनया इति चेत्। Let us put it in some detail. The Mīmāṁsakas and the *naiyāyikas* hold that *śabda* is a linguistic utterance and it is only a collection of sounds which are produced by the movements of the vocal organ of the speaker. The sounds vanish as soon as they are produced and are, therefore, ephemeral, Then how do we understand the meaning of a word or a sentence? They say that the meaning of a word is presented to the mind of the listener by the last sound aided by the memory impressions of the preceding sounds. Since the isolated sounds of a word cannot individually present its meaning, they must do so jointly. Since they come into the mind one after another, they are not perceived together as a whole. Each sound perceived leaves its impressions behind and the apprehension of the last sound aided by the accumulated impressions of the preceding sounds presents the meaning of the word. Thus, these philosophers do not find any need for postulating a spiritual entity like *sphoṭa* as causing the cognition of meaning.

(2) Reply to the opposition :

BKB strikes to the very root of the conceptions of the *mīmāṁsakas* and the *naiyāyikas*. तयोरुभयोरपि......प्रत्यभिज्ञापि न स्यात्।.......

(1) The *naiyāyikas* opine that the word is denoter शक्तं पदम्। The word denotes meaning by convention (*saṅketa)*. Now they say that this word consists of different sounds which have individual impressions, and which are accumulated, so they will have to admit that the first sound of the word does not have *saṅketa* but when it is aided by the last sound, both become शक्त, thus a part of a *pada* being अशक्त, non-denoter and the whole being शक्त denoter, there will arise अर्धजरतीयापत्ति—Their (i.e. of the *naiyāyikas)* basic conception would thus be harmed.

In short, you cannot cut the शक्तपद into different *varṇas,* as a lady cannot be half-young and half-old. Again, evenif we accept that the sense data are received as a series of atomic perceptions, we will have to assume that the memory impressions of the various sounds occur in the same order as they are uttered, otherwise, they will not be grasped simultaneously and could be the meaning-bearing word. And as our experience is, memory impressions never occur in the same order.

(2) The *mīmāṁsakas* believe in प्रत्यभिज्ञा-identification of the vedic *mantras.* A certain *mantra.* gives certain fruitful result after proper *puraścaraṇa of the mantra.* Now, unless you accept *sphoṭa* there would not be the recognition स एव अयं मंत्रः। This is the same *mantra* of which *puraścaraṇa* was performed and recognition is never resemblance, as it happens in medicine. Two medicines with similar formulae, can cure disease but this does not apply in *mantras.* A certain *mantra* can bring about a certain result or fruit which is its own. Actually, the *mantra* of which *puraścaraṇa* is performed, only can produce the fruit, and that is possible with the acceptance of *sphoṭa.* Unless you accept *sphoṭa* other *mantras* without *puraścaraṇa* will also be capable of producing desired fruits. Besides, the *mantras* are the deities incarnate, which are immortal. Unless the *sphoṭa* is accepted the god symbolised in a *mantra* would be mortal.

BKB, as if making fun of the *naiyāyikas* refutes their argument in a sweeping statement: if the sound can convey sense evenafter it dies away, then the memory impressions of a broken pot can also bring water! Again, acutally in the opinion of the *naiyāyikas* themselves, the seat of the memoy impressions, the mind (मनस्) and the seat of the last sound, vocal organ (कण्ठ) are different, and the causes located in different seats cannot produce a single effect i.e. the meaning.

It may be added here that one of the arguments adduced by the grammarians in favour of the *sphoṭa* theory is our experience in actual speech situations about the word or a sentence as a single entity. Nāgeśa Bhaṭṭa states that justification for the *sphoṭa* is the realization—'This is one word, one sentence'.[17] In the Sàrvadarśanasaṅgraha also it is stated that the acceptance of the *sphoṭa* is based on direct perception itself, since it is a conmon experience that a word like 'cow'is a unique entity, apart from the different letters we seem to here in it.[18] The same idea is emphasised in Sphoṭasiddhi[19] and Tottvabindu.[20]

(3) Classification of *sphoṭa* :

The later grammarians like Bhaṭṭoji Dīkṣita and Nāgeśa Bhaṭṭa enumerate eight varieties of *sphoṭa*. The basis of this classification is the meaning-bearing unit (*vācakatva*). Where the letter is meaning-bearing unit, there is the *varṇasphoṭa,* the word meaning-bearing unit, the *padasphoṭa,* the sentence meaning-bearing unit, the *vākyasphoṭa*. Again there is debate among the philosophers about the permance or the transience of the *śabda*. If we take the *naiyāyika* view, *śabda* is transient because it is produced at the time of utterance. Here, the letter, the word or the sentence would be considered as a class *(jāti)* denoting the class of object meant. By synthesizing the *sphoṭa* theory with the *naiyāyika* view about the *jāti,* we get three kinds of *sphoṭa-varṇajātisphoṭa, padajātisphoṭa* and *vākyajātisphoṭa*. On the other hand,if we take the *mīmāṁsaka* view that *śabda* is permanent (*nitya),* the word or sentence will have to be considered as a permanent pattern of the letters in a fixed order. Each example of its occurrence is only a case of revealing or manifesting the permanent sound-pattern. The semanitc unit is taken to be one and the same in all cases of its occurrence. Thus, if the *sphoṭa* theory is synthesized with the *mīmāṁsaka* view, we get three types of *sphoṭas: varṇavyakti-sphoṭa, padavyaktisphoṭa* and *vākyavyaktisphoṭa*. Again, the *pada sphoṭa,* and *vākyasphoṭa* taken as semantic units built of such smaller ones, which themselves have their own meaning, are different from *padasphoṭa* and *vākyasphoṭa,* considered as indivisible symbols denoting the sense of the whole without any reference to the parts. The former, smaller units are *sakhaṇḍasphoṭas* and the latter are *akhaṇḍasphoṭas*. This division cannot apply to the *varṇasphoṭa* as it can not be further split up. Thus eight subdivisions of *sphoṭa* are: *(1) varṇas-phoṭa (2) padasphoṭa (3) vākyasphoṭa (4) akhaṇḍapadasphoṭa (5) akhaṇḍavākya-sphoṭa (6) varṇajātisphoṭa (7) padajātisphoṭa (8) vākyajātis-phoṭa*. BKB enumerates these types as (1) *Varṇavyaktisphoṭa, (2) sakhaṇḍapadayakti sphoṭa, (3) akhaṇḍapadavyaktisphoṭa (4) akhaṇḍavākyavaktisphoṭa, (5) akhaṇḍavarṇajātisphoṭa (6) akhaṇḍapadajātisphoṭa (7) akhaṇḍavākyajātisphoṭa*. Here, due to some error of the scribe or some other reason, *sakhaṇḍavā-kyavyakti sphoṭa* seems to have been dropped. The author does not define the types of *sphoṭa* but substantiates *varṇasphoṭa, padasphoṭa* and *vākyasphoṭa*. Someone may argue against the acceptance of *varṇasphoṭa* that-when there is no *saṅketa* to denote the meaning in a *varṇa,* how can *varṇasphoṭa* be admitted? *varṇasphoṭa* is favoured by BKB with the support of indirect allusion from Nāgeśabhaṭṭa. If we utter the words राम or भवति by changing the letters' order, the sense also is changed, or reversed. Thus by *anvaya-vyatireka* the letter-syllables are proved to convey the sense. In the words like सर: रस: etc. the words demarcated by the specific order of the letters denote the sense by *saṅketa*. So *padasphoṭa* is also justified.[21] BKB adds one more argument in support of *varṇasphoṭa*: unless it is accepted, the *bīja* letters denoting definite deities would bc meaningless. In *mantraśāstra,* certain gods have certain *bījas*. Such an arrangement will be meaningless without the acceptance of *varṇasphoṭa*. No performance of any activity or even passivity is possible with the help of only words. Sentences are inevitable. The whole language behaviour of ours is based on sentences. hence *vākyasphoṭa*. Nāgeśa states :

एवं 'हरेऽव', 'विष्णोऽव' इत्यादौ प्रागुक्तरीत्या पदयोः स्पष्टमज्ञानेऽपि समुदायशक्त्या बोधात् समुदायस्यैव विशिष्टवाक्यार्थे शक्तिरिति वाक्यस्फोटः। (स्फोटवादः p.7)

Some may define *sphoṭa* as 'the non-existence of the letters' utter destruction' because the letters never perish.

But as BKB states it logically, the non-existence of something cannot produce something that is existent.

Sphoṭa named *śabdabrahma,* therefore, is an existent entity. BKB concludes the topic stating that of all the eight types of *sphoṭa,* it is the *akhaṇḍavākyasphoṭa*, which alone represent *sphoṭa* the rest being created for the purpose of enabling the student to comprehend the nature of *akhaṇḍavajyasphoṭa*. Though these seven divisions have no real value of their own, they carry some practical utility. The young bride who is supposed to have a look at *arundhati* (star), is asked to fix her gaze upon the bigger star *vasiṣṭha* (another star), and thereafter, she finds out the smaller star *arundhatī* twinkling by its side. Similarly, the grammarians maintain that the seven divisions of *sphoṭa* mentioned above enable the novice to understand the nature of the *akhaṇḍavākyasphoṭa*. The definition of *sphoṭa* given by BKB finally, is: 'the sound being suggestive, its being the conveyer of the meaning by convention is the nature of *sphoṭa'*.[22]

IV.v The word *śāstra*-a polysemic word :

BKB starts discussing one more debatable point. The word शास्त्र is polysemic (अनेकार्थ). In every language, there are words, which denote multiple senses, may be they have the same sound. The question is: can a polysemic word convey all the senses simultaneously by *yogarūḍhi*? Indian grammarians have discussed about the exact nature of such words. Is it the same word with different senses? Or they are different words having the same sound? Puṇyarāja has taken note of both the views, in his commentary on Vākyapadīya: अत्र एकशब्ददर्शनम् अनेकदर्शनम् चेति द्वौ पक्षौ।[23] The one word theory and the many words theory. Bhartṛhari refers to them as एकत्वपक्ष and नानात्वपक्ष, According to those who hold that a word can convey more than one meaning, the distinction between the primary and secondary senses of a word is based merely on the relative frequency of usage. That which is well-known through constant usage is called the primary and normal sense, while the sense which is used less frequently, is called secondary: प्रसिद्धिभेदाद् गौणत्वम् मुख्यत्वम् चोपजायते।[24] He states that the same word can convey more than one sense but consecutively, not simultaneously.[25] It is the context or the collocation of other words that determines the sense to be taken in a particular case.[26] On the other hand, those who hold that a word can have only one sense, consider that the word which conveys the primary sense and the word which conveys the secondary sense are actually different though they seem alike in sound.[27] Bhartṛhari refers to two theories about how various senses are conveyed in the case of polysemic words. According to the first one, it is the same word that gives various senses depending upon various contextual factors, according to second theory, there are different words having the same sound and the ambiguity about the sense is removed by contextual factors.[28]

BKB seems to follow the view of Bhartṛhari when he says that a polysemic word cannot convey more than one sense simultaneoulsy, because it is a rule that a word uttered once can convey ony one meaning. He follows into the footsteps of his *guru* AB who states:

सकृत् प्रयुक्तः शब्दोऽसौ सकृदेकार्थसाधकः।
बाणवल्लक्ष्यभेदे तु प्रयोगं पुनरर्हति।।[29]

BKB illustrates the principle after his *guru*. An arrow shot once can pierce only one aim, similarly a word can convey a single sense at a time. A king having a number of horses, can ride only one horse. He may ride them one after another and not simultaneoulsy. Mammaṭa seems to opine in this connection that in *śleṣa alaṅkāra,* there are two different words, similar in sound and are uttered simultaneously. The principle is: a word can convey only one sense when it is uttered. In *śleṣa,* therefore, it is to be considered that there are two different words having the same sound, which are uttered at a time.[30] Such a simultaneous utterance of two words (identical in sound) is called तन्त्र. The listener comprehends two different meanings which are intended by the speaker by repetition आवृत्ति. Nāgeśa states: बोद्धुरावृत्त्यैव बोधः। उच्चारणं तु तन्त्रमेव।[31] The words with the same sound (similar in form) may be uttered once, but the listener comprehends the sense by repetition. BKB refers to the same idea: आलङ्कारिकास्तु सकृदुच्चरितः.....प्रकरणादिकमेव। He also states that wherever these polysemic words are used, their varied senses are conveyed with the help of contextual factors.

(1) Factors restricting the sense of a polysemic word :

While dealing with the meaning of polysemic words, BKB quotes the definition of *abhidhāmūla vyañjanā* from KP. His intention is to enumerate the factors which cause restriction of a particular sense of a polysemic word to avoid ambiguity. Two *kārikās* quoted in this connetion are actually from *Vākyapadīya*. All these factors (संयोग, विप्रयोग etc.) have been discussed and illustrated in detail in KP. AB has also depicted the topic in KND.[32] BKB, therefore, does not spare much room for the discussion. Nevertheless, he gives an example of प्रकरण 'context' which gives him a chance for a grammatical discussion.

(2) The compound सर्वगुणवान्-*bhahuvrīhi* or a *karmadhāraya* with *matvarthīya* affix? :

BKB illustrates context (प्रकरण) by सर्वगुणवान् सर्वं जानाति देवः 'possessing all qualities, my lord knows everything.' The word देव is a polysemic word and it gives the sense of 'the king' here owing to the context though it has many senses like 'king', 'master', 'god' etc. And then BKB raises a question on behalf of the *pūrvapakṣa*-opposition:

The compound सर्वगुणवान् is not justifiably formed according to grammatical rules. सर्वे गुणाः यस्य सः सर्वगुणः। The *bahuvrīhi* compound formed thus conveys the sense 'one possessing all the virtues'. It is not necessary to add the मत्वर्थीय suffix वत् to the word सर्वगुण, being a *karmadhāraya* compound (सर्वे गुणाः सर्वगुणाः।) because in this formation, two *vṛttis* namely

समास and तद्धित (मत्वर्थीय suffix) are employed together which is a defect of duplicity. (कल्पनगौरव).

BKB replies to the question and justifies the formation of the compound सर्वगुणवान् with a strong support of Mahābhāṣya. Here are his arguments:

(1) The मत्वर्थीय suffixes convey seven specific senses भूमनिन्दाप्रशंसादि.[33] Such significations are not conveyed by a *bahuvrīhi* compound. In सर्वगुणवान् the speaker wishes to convey the praise of the king, which is signified by the मत्वर्थीय suffix. (2) Bhāṣyakāra has given an indicatory statement ज्ञापक in कृष्णसर्पवान् वल्मीकः।[34] the anthill having a black serpent' which justifies the compound सर्वगुणवान् because in कृष्णसर्पवान् also, कृष्णसर्प is a *karmadhāraya* compound and वत् is a *matvarthīya* suffix applied to signify the sense of censure. (3) फलमुखं गौरवं न दोषाय। cumbersomeness for some specific purpose is not a defect.

Hence the compound सर्वगुणवान् is justified.

(3) Acceptability of ज्ञापक 'an indicatory statemnt' and justifiability of the form सुभ्रु (vocative singular) :

BKB mentioned the techincal term ज्ञापक,[35] an indictory statement used in grammar. Now he begins the debate how far a ज्ञापक is acceptable. It should be applied in exceptional cases which are inexplicable otherwise, because ज्ञापकसिद्धं न सर्वत्र।[36] The indicatory statement does not justify each and every case of ungrammatical usage. He illustrates the statement with the justification of the form सुभ्रु which is found frequently in classical Sanskrit literature. The whole detailed discussion proves to be instructive and interesting for the student as it is abundant with a number of allusions not only from Sanskrit *mahākāvyas* and *purāṇa* texts but also from Aṣṭādhyāyī, Mahābhāṣya, Vṛttarātnākara, Kāvyālaṅkārasūtravṛtti and so on. The whole discussion is summarised here: The declension सुभ्रु (voc. sing.) is frequently found in classical Sanskrit Literature. The author lists out at least six such examples. He quotes from the reputed commentaries on the usage, gives citations from Pāṇini, Kātyāyana and Patañjali. He raises the opposition against the justifiability of the usage and finally gives his own explanation alongwith the one offered by Mallinātha. Let us put the problem precisely :

(1) On the strength of the *sūtra*-यू स्त्र्याख्यौ नदी,[37] words ending in ई *ī* and ऊ *ū* and being the names of females have नदीसंज्ञा.

(2) Again, the rule नेयङुवङ्स्थानावस्त्री।[38] offers an exception to the rule above. the feminine words ending in ई- ī and ऊ- ū which admit the substitute (आदेश) इयङ् and उवङ् respectively do not have नदीसंज्ञा except the word स्त्री.

(3) The feminine word भ्रू admits the substitute उवङ् on the strength of the rule अचिश्नुधातुभ्रुवांय्वोरियङुवङौ।[39] Thus ऊ in भ्रू is substituted by उवङ् e.g. भ्रुवम्। भ्रू therefore, does not fall under नदीसंज्ञा, due to the substitution, though it is with ending ऊ ū and is feminine.

(4) The *sūtra*—अम्बार्थनद्योर्ह्रस्वः।[40] does not work in the case of भ्रू or सुभ्रू as it is not नदी.[41] The meaning of अम्बार्थनद्योर्ह्रस्वः। is: "a short vowel is substituted in vocative singular for the आ of feminine, in the sense of 'mother' as well as for the long vowel of the feminines called नदी.......e.g. हे अम्ब! हे नदि! etc. This rule does not work out in the case of भ्रू or सुभ्रू since it is not नदी after substitution. The declension सुभ्रु in vocative singular, therefore, will be ungrammatical.

And yet, such usages as सुभ्रु (voc sing.) are not rare in Sanskrit literature. BKB quotes at least six:

(a) विमानना सुभ्रु कुतः पितुर्गृहे। (कुमार० V. 43)

(b) प्रसूननाराचशरासनस्य सहैकवंशप्रभवभ्रु बभ्रु। (नै०च० VIII, 99)

(c) सुभ्रु त्वं कुपितेत्यपास्तमशनं त्यक्ताः कथा योषिताम्। (चौरपञ्चाशिका, बिल्हणचरित-७६)

(d) हा पितः क्वासि हे सुभ्रु। (भट्टिकाव्यम्, VI, 2)

(e) राजभ्यो बिभ्रतः सुभ्रु समुद्रं शरणं गताः।[42] (श्री०भ०पु०, X, LX, 12)

(f) आस्थिताः पदवीं सुभ्रु प्रायः सीदन्ति योषितः। (श्री०भा०पु०, X, IX,13)

BKB argues that these many illustrations cannot be considered as प्रामादिक प्रयोग (faulty). Such प्रामादिक प्रयोगऽ are supposed to be a few and not frequent. Vallabhadeva in his commentary पञ्चिका on the Kumārasambhavam (KS) describes विमानना सुभ्रु.......as a faulty ungrammactical wordform,[43] while Mallinātha considers it to be justified following the preceding commentators:

अन्ये तु, 'अप्राणिजातेश्चारज्ज्वादीनामि' त्यत्र 'अलाबूः कर्कन्धूः' इत्यूकारान्तादप्यूङ्प्रत्ययमुदाजहार भाष्यकारः। एतस्मादेव ज्ञापकात् क्वचिदूकारान्तस्याप्यूङन्तत्वान्नदीत्वे ह्रस्वत्वमित्याहुः। अत एवाह वामनः 'ऊकारान्तादप्यूङ्प्रवृत्तेः' इति।[44] Mallinātha repeats the comments even in his commentary on Naiṣadha, VIII, 99 and on Bhaṭṭi-kāvyam, VI, II. What he means is this: The *sūtra* उङ् उतः। (P. IV, i, 66) prescribes feminine affix ऊङ् (=ऊ) after masculine nouns ending in उ and denoting a human being .e.g. कुरुः-कुरूः, a woman from the *kuru deśa*—पङ्गुः-पङ्गूः, a crippled woman etc. Naturally these nouns fall under नद्यादिगण after substitution accroding to the rule-यू स्त्र्याख्यौ नदी। Now, the *vārttika* on this rule is अप्राणिजातेश्चारज्ज्वादीनाम्। It permits that the affix ऊङ् (ऊ) comes under simlilar conditions after words denoting non-animate *jāti* except the word रज्जु and others. The Mahābhāṣya gives two examples in this connection—अलाबू 'bottleguard' and 'कर्कन्धू' The jujube tree' These two words end in ऊ and the *bhāṣyakāra* shows ऊङ् substitute for ऊ, supporting the *vārttika* (i.e. अलाबुवम्, कर्कन्धुवम). Vāmana states: ऊकारा-दप्यूङ्प्रवृत्तेः।[45] and then explains the quote 'सुभ्रु किं संभ्रमेण'..... ....etc. with the support of the two examples given by the *bhāṣ yakāra*. Thus Mallinātha with the support of even Vāmana explains that actually the word सुभ्रु has the substitution ऊङ् for ऊ, it falls into नद्यादिगण and takes the declension सुभ्रु in voc. sing. by the rule अम्बार्थनद्योर्ह्रस्वः।

BKB quotes this explanation without mentioning the name of Mallinātha, and moves a step further. he suggests *yogavibhāga*[46] in the rule ऊङ् उतः।[47] and then prescribes the *anuvṛtti* of the word बहुव्रीहेः। by *maṇḍūkapluti*[48] from the rule बहुव्रीहेश्चान्तोदात्तात्। (IV, i.52). The rule with this *anuvṛtti* will be बहुव्रीहेः ऊङ् (स्यात्)। Now सुभ्रू is a *bahuvrīhi* compound, so it will be ऊङ्प्रत्ययान्त by substitution, and शब्दान्तर will be resulted. (शब्दान्तर means the different wording resulting from modifications such as *āgama, ādeśa* or *lopa)*. Now, सुभ्रु is a word newly formed, it will have नदीसंज्ञा, the rule अम्बार्थनद्योर्ह्रस्वः। will work out in its case and the declension सुभ्रु, बभ्रु, एकवंशप्रभवभ्रु etc. in voc. sing. will be justified. Suppose, again, the *anuvṛtti* of the word बहुव्रीहेः is not considered, then, also, the two examples अलाबू, कर्कन्धू, offered by Patañjali will suffice as ज्ञापक for the योगविभाग in the rule because he himself has permitted ऊङ्प्रत्ययादेश from such ऊकारान्त words as include सुभ्रु also.

It is remarkable how BKB concludes this elaborate discussion with the use of grammatical terms in brief : तेन दीर्घोदाहरणज्ञापितेन योगविभागेनैवास्योङ्प्रत्ययान्तत्वं सुवचमिति शब्दान्तरत्वे नदीसंज्ञासद्भावात्सम्बुद्धौ ह्रस्वो भवत्येवेति सङ्क्षेपः।

This minute, detailed, systematic, technical analysis of the process through which a word-formation passes, indicates not only the erudition and sharp acumen, but also a scientific and logical aptitude of the author. He aims at justifying 'poetic word' used by the great poets and to serve the purpose, he takes a sound support of *pāṇinian* tradition of grammar. In this respect, therefore, it can be said, that he moves a step ahead of his great teacher AB who does quote relevant rules of Pāṇini but avoids their subtle complicated process of application. Nor does AB justify the illustration in such a detailed analytical fashion. On the other hand, such learned discussions offer a distinctive merit of a *śāstra* to the Vicāradīpa.

Incidentally, in the course of the discussion, BKB takes note of a different reading सुभ्रूः कुतस्तातगृहेऽवमानना। suggested by some commentator to correct the so-called faulty usage सुभ्रु He rejects it due to the contingency of occurring the breach of the metre by its acceptance. This verse is in वंशस्थ metre with the groups जतजर—if the reading सुभ्रूः is accepted, ज group in the beginning will be broken. BKB also quotes the definition of the said metre from Vṛttaratnākara. The confirmation of text on the basis of metres is quite usual in manuscriptology today.

To resume the topic, ज्ञापक is not applied in frequent usages like सुभ्रु etc.

(4) The multiple meaning of एव :

BKB used the word भवत्येव in the conclusion of the discussion on सुभ्रु. How can he skip over the problem which is debatable? He takes up one more elaborate discussion on the meaning of एव which falls into the class of indeclinable words. The meaning of such words as एव depends upon their relation to other word-units in a sentence. एव is either connected with the verb, or with a qualifier or with a substantive. Let this be explained in some detail.

(1) When एव is connected with the verb, it will mean the exclusion of total absence. e.g. नीलं सरोजं भवति एव। The blue lotus definitely exists. (Not that it is not there)

(2) When एव is connected with a qualifier, it will mean the exclusion of the thing's connection with any other qualifier. e.g. शङ्खः पाण्डुरः एव। The conch is white only (i.e. it is not of any other colour.)

(3) When एव is connected with a substantive, it will mean exclusion of all others. e.g. पार्थ एव धनुर्धरः। Pārtha only is the bow-wielder (i.e. no one else can be a bow-wielder like Pārtha.

Thus एव is a polysemic (नानार्थ or अनेकार्थ) word.

(5) अस्यैव भार्या........the example to illustrate एवकारार्थ and its explanation :

BKB quotes a verse from BP and explains elaborately how the polysemic word एव construes with other word-units and conveys varied senses. The discussion about नानार्थ words is slightly repeated here.[49] Owing to the rule सकृदुच्चरितः शब्द.... .etc. a word uttered once can convey only one sense and be construed once in a sentence. Thus एव cannot be construed with all the words simultaneously. It conveys the meaning in the said verse thus:

(1) Rukmiṇī deserves to be the wife of Kṛṣṇa only and not of any other man. Thus Cedirāja Śiśupāla etc. are excluded by एव. (2) No other woman except Rukmiṇī deserves to be the wife of Kṛṣṇa. Thus other maidens are excluded. (3) Rukmiṇī deserves definitely, not that she does not deserve to be the wife of Kṛṣṇa, because she is possessed of all the virtues expected in a wife. (4) Only Kṛṣṇa is a suitable husband for Rukmiṇī, since only he possesses all the desirable qualities expected in a husband. (5) Kṛṣṇa is definitely a suitable husband. (not that

he is undeserving.) (6) Kṛṣṇa deserves to be the husband of Rukmiṇī only and no other woman.

Thus the imperishable word एव *(nipāta)* is construed with other words in the sentence and consecutively conveys sixfold senses.

BKB has rendered such interpretation on the basis of Śrīdharaswāmin's commentary on the verse: अस्यैव। रुक्मिण्येवार्हत्येव असावेव भैष्म्या एव समुचित एवेति षडवधारणानि। तत्रैकस्मिन् व्यतिरेकप्रदर्शनमुपलक्षणार्थम्। नापरेति। न च वाक्यभेददोषः। अनुवाद्यविधेयभेदेन विभिन्नानामेव वाक्यानां सहप्रयोगात्। ग्रहं प्रमार्ष्टि इत्यादिवत्।[50] एव in this verse is construed with six *padas* in the sentence like this: अस्य (कृष्णस्य) एव। रुक्मिणी एव (न अपरा), अर्हति एव (न नार्हतीति), असौ (कृष्णः) एव, भैष्म्याः (न कस्या अपि अपरायाः) एव, समुचितः एव (न किमपि अनुचितः) पतिः। etc. BKB also quotes from *purāṇa* and *subhāṣitasaṅgrahas* to support his interpretation, as is his practice.

Somebody may raise an objection as to why this kind of repetition when the meaning intended is clear from the first half in the verse with the inversion of cases!

BKB states in justification that in the former half, the poet convinces us of Rukmiṇī's eminence, while in the latter half, the eminence of Kṛṣṇa is expressed. The speaker wants here to confirm the desirablility of their marriage.

(6) *vācaktva* or *dyotakatva* of the *nipātas* :

The polysemic word एव falls into चादिगण, a class of words headed by *ca* which are termed निपात by Pāṇini, Now, there is a debate whether *nipātas* are suggestive or expressive. BKB plunges into this debate which has, perhaps, no direct connection with the subject in hand. He mentions the views of the *naiyāyikas* and the *vaiyākraṇas*. The *naiyāyikas* see a distinction between the प्रादयः (i.e. उपसर्गs) which are suggestive and the चादयः (i.e. *nipātas)* which are expressive, but BKB disagrees with them stating that there is no evidence proving their dissimilarity. Considering the *nipātas* to be *vācaka* expressive) after the *naiyāyikas,* their construe in sentences will be impossible. As the *vaiyākaraṇas* take them to be suggestive, the question of their construe does not arise. BKB quotes a discussion from Vaiyākaraṇa-bhūṣaṇa to support the suggestiveness of the *nipātas:*

In वागर्थाविव संपृक्तौ....पार्वतीपरमेश्वरौ अहं बन्दे।.....वागर्थौ is not the object of the verb वन्दे, the affix औ after वागर्थ conveys the sense of accusative case and it is related to पार्वतीपरमेश्वरौ..... ...If इव here, is taken in the sense of 'resemblance', it will not be connected with the object. In fact, with the suggestive power of the word इव, वागर्थौ indicates the sense of likeness by *lakṣaṇā*. Thus the meaning of the sentence is "Parvatī and Parameśvara are eternally related to eachother like the word and the sense." They are the object of the action of bowing down, the doer of which is 'I'. In fact वागर्थौ though taking accusative case, is not the object of वन्दे as वागर्थौ is not connected with that action, इव connects by suggestion 'वागर्थौ' with 'पावतीपरमेश्वरौ'.

However, the *vaiyākaraṇas* or the *ālaṅkārikas* do not insist upon the suggestiveness of the *upasargas*. The author quotes from Vākyapadīya that the *upasarga* may be expressive or suggestive as per the specific sense of the roots to which it is prefixed. To support this he brings in another quotation which cannot be traced out: "The *nipātas,* the *upasargas* and the *dhātus* (roots) all convey several senses, the *pāṭha* i.e. *gaṇapāṭha* and *dhātupāṭha*-is the illustration of it". The etymology of the word निपात is given as 'निश्चयेन पतन्ति अनेकेषु अर्थेषु।'—They (i.e.निपात) definitely move into various meanings, so they are polysemic (अनेकार्थ), hence suggestive.

Here again, the author states the elaboration of वागर्थाविव. ....etc. by Bhūṣaṇa as the *pūrvapakṣa* and expresses his disagreement to it. it is said in Bhūṣaṇa that 'वागर्थौ' is not the object to the verb 'वन्दे', so the accusative case in the word will not construe in the sentence. According to BKB, this is not justified because as per rule, there can be no accusative case in the absence of objectness. Then the problem is—which *sūtra* confirms accusative case in वागर्थौ.

It is surprising to note here that BKB recommends to take nominative case in वागर्थौ. Then how does the word इव convey the sense of 'resemblance' in वागर्थाविव? The author replies: The *mīmāṁsakas* state that the relation between the word and the sense is permanent. इव conveys this permanent relation by its word-power. As the word and the meaning are permanently related, similarly, Pārvatī and Parameśvara are related to each other permanently. The word संपृक्तौ here is in nominative case, संपृचाते तौ संपृक्तौ, 'those two who are related.' The कृत् suffix क्त denotes the doer, the subject. Such is the opinion of the *ālaṅkārikas*.

Hitherto, are depicted the clumsy, elaborate discussions emerging from the topic of polysemic words. Most of these are connected with the grammatical usages. It seems to be the prime interest of BKB to plunge into such discussions in order to make his work a *vādagrantha* and to give it the *śāstraic* stature. Some of these may seem to be inconsistent so far as the theme of the work is concerned, but they are definitely justifiable so far his objective in writing this book is concerned.

IV.vi. *vṛtti*—the definition, threefold function of the word:-

Most of the well-known treatises on the *śabdaśakti* viz. Abhidhāvṛttimātṛkā (Abhm.), Vṛttivārttika (Vṛ), Kovidānanda (KND) and Triveṇikā (TRN) commence with the direct depiction of the topic after either *maṅgalaśloka* or *iṣṭastuti*. In Abhm. Mukula Bhaṭṭa introduces the subject thus: The *padārthas* are means to enjoyment-*bhoga* and emancipation-*mokṣa*. The knowledge of these objects (i.e. *padārthas)* can bring enjoyment as well as emancipation. This knowledge is acquired through *pramāṇa.* The subject of knowledge is *padārtha.*This object can be known through the knowledge of the meaning of the word. The meaning of the word is cognised through *abhidhā* and *lakṣaṇā,* the functions of the word.[51] Vṛ opens with *sarsasvatīstuti* and the direct statement of subject thereafter. "The writers of treatises on *alaṅkāra,* depicted the three functions of the word, namely *abhidhā, lakṣaṇā* and *vyakti* (i.e. *vyañjanā).* Vṛttivārttika is composed to depict those topics which have not been clarified by the elders".[52] Then the work directly starts with the definition of the *abhidhā.* In KND, AB offers a salutation to Śaṅkara, brings out the importance of the knowledge of *śabdārtha* in a few verses, as a means to absolute knowledge of reality. Then he starts discussion of various views on *saṅketa* directly. This applies to TRN also. What is meant to be stated here is, all the *prakaraṇagranthas* on *śabdaśakti* plunge into the subject at once, whereas BKB does not follow the tradition. He intends to spin all the controversies involved in the subject, starting from the etymology of the word *śāstra* to the polysemic words. *Śabda* and its functions are the subject of the work, yet, a detailed commentary on various terms used in the *pratijñāśloka* occupies more than half of the room in the work, which justifies the nomenclature *vādagrantha* for this work. Thus the topic *vṛtti* falls almost in the midlle of the work.

The term *vṛtti* has been used in the sense of 'function' or 'power' of the word. AB derives the word as—प्रवर्त्तते अनया इति वृत्तिः। 'that by which the word gives the meaning'. वृत्तिः व्यापार क्रिया चेति पर्यायशब्दाः।[53] In KND he has used the term शब्दव्यापार-निर्णयम्.[54] BKB eloborates a little: शब्दार्थयोर्बोध्यबोधकभावलक्षणः सम्बन्धो वृत्तिः। *Vṛtti* is the relation between the word and the meaning. This relation is that of the indicator and the indicated. To include *vyañjanā* in *Vṛtti,* he adds that this *vṛtti* resides in both the word and the sense, and thus it is of dual character. They are namely *abhidhā,* lakṣaṇā *and vyañjanā.* Viśvanātha employs the word *śakti* for *vṛtti* as AB records.[55] Mukula Bhaṭṭa used the word *vyāpāra.*[56] Mammaṭa also used the same word.[57] AB uses the word व्यापार, in KND while in TRN he employs the word Vṛtti as it is already noted. To denote *abhidhā* AB uses word शक्ति, so does BKB in VD.

Incidentally, it may be noted, here, that AB has mentioned the *tātparyavṛtti in* KND[58] after Mammaṭa, whereas BKB does not.

IV.vii *Śakti* (*abhidhā*) :

BKB begins to depict *śakti* with a well-known definition of *saṅketa* 'convention'. He quotes different views about *śakti* and *śaṅketa.* The *naiyāyikas* do not see any distinction between *saṅketa* and *śakti :* शक्तिश्च पदेन सह पदार्थस्य सम्बन्धः। सा चाऽस्माच्छब्दादयमर्थो बोद्धव्य इतीश्वरेच्छारूपः।[59] In the opinion of the *ālaṅkārikas śakti* is different from *saṅketa* being a power which helps *śakti* in conveying the sense: इहागृहीतसंकेतस्य शब्दादर्थ विशेषप्रतिपत्तेरभावात् संकेतसहाय एव शब्दोऽर्थविशेषं प्रतिपादयति।[60] The *vaiyākaraṇas* propound that all the words possess twofold power viz—*grāhyatva* and *grāhakatva.*

ग्राह्यत्वं ग्राहकत्वं च द्वे शक्ती तेजसो यथा।
तथैव सर्वशब्दानामेते पृथगवस्थिते।[61]

"As light contains twohold power to lighten and to be lightened, all the words have twofold power to convey sense and to be conveyed itself". Light shows things like *ghatādi,* at the same time it shines itself. Similarly, word is manifested and it expresses the sense.

Unlike his predecessors Mammaṭa and AB, BKB does not give elaborate exposition of various theories about *saṅketa.* AB has discussed them i.e. *jātivāda, vyaktivāda, jātyādivāda, jātiviśiṣṭavyktivāda* and *apohavāda* in KND[62]. He also has enumerated *saṅketa-grahaṇa-hetu-s* i.e. factors which cause acquirement of *saṅketa*, namely grammar, lexicon, *nirukta, āpta-vāklya, vyākhyāna.* context, association with the known word, *upamānapramāṇa,* and tradition, He illustrates all of them, in detail.[63] BKB avoids the repetition on that score. He states three kinds of words and senses (1) *śakya—(vācaka)* denotative (2) *lākṣaṇika* indicative (3) *vyañjaka-suggestive.* All these are the object of the *vṛtti*. In other words. *Vṛtti* conveys these sense, as per context. Among these, *śakti* assists *saṅketa* to denote the denotative (=expressive) sense. So far as the treatment of *śakti* is concerned, there is hardly any difference between that of AB and that of BKB.

TRN	VD
संकेतस्तु अस्मात् पदादयमर्थो बोध्य इति प्रवर्तकोपदेशः। स च शब्दे स्थितो ज्ञातः सन् अर्थान् विषयीकरोति। सा (शक्तिः) त्रिविधा योगो, रूढिः योगरूढिश्चेति।	तत्र चास्मात्पदादयमर्थो बोद्धव्य इति प्रवर्तकोपदेशः सङ्केतः। सा च शक्ति-स्त्रिधा। योगो रूढिर्योगरूढिश्चेति।

Of course, there is no point in changing even words because this is purely a technical point.

(a) Threefold *śakti*:

As noted above, BKB following tradition, states three kinds of *śakti*: योग, रूढि and योगरूढि; but does not define any of them. AB has done the job both in KND and TRN. He states in KND : अखण्डशब्दे सा रूढिर्योगः खण्डनकल्पिते।[64] The words in which the constituent parts cannot be separated as *prakṛti* (stem), *pratyaya* (affix) etc., are रूढ words. The words which can be separated into derivative parts, are *yaugika* words. In TRN, AB presents the definition in more comprehensive form: तत्रावयवयोगप्रधाना योगशक्तिः तत्र सुप्तिङन्तयोः 'कृष्णो भवती' त्यादौ प्रकृतिप्रत्ययजन्या योगशक्तिः।[65] where अवयवयोग 'combination of parts' prevails is called *yogaśakti*. *subanta*- 'affixes applied to nouns' and *tiṅanta*—'affixes applied to roots' produce *yoga-śakti*. In words like कृष्णः and भवति the *yogaśakti* is produced by *prakṛtipratyaya* combination. AB explains रूढि in these words: अथ रूढिः–गच्छतीति गौः, पातीति पिता, गच्छतीति गङ्गा, पातीति पुमान्-इत्यादौ व्युत्पत्तिकल्पनेऽपि रूढिरेव। अर्थबोधे व्युत्पत्तेरनुपयोगात्।[66] In words like गौः, पिता, गङ्गा, पुमान्, devision of parts is possible by etymology yet, this etymology does not employ in conveying their sense. Hence they are रूढ words. In योगरूढि there is combination of योग and रूढि. AB states : अथ योगरूढिः-युधिष्ठिरः, युधि स्थिरः इति योगः, ज्येष्ठपाण्डवे रूढिः।[67]

(b) योगशक्ति in compounds—a view :

BKB brings in grammatical discussion about योगशक्ति. In is however, not clear whether he himself accepts योगशक्ति in compounds. The point is this: The compounds like व्रागर्थाविव and यवया इव are formed on the strength of the *vārttika*—इवेन विभक्त्यलोप...च। and when thus, words are compounded, the power produced within the compound to convey the sense is called *yogaśakti,* and it resides in the compounded word.

Now, the grammarians believe that there is altogether a different power in compound-words like पङ्कज etc. The principle behind this is: If a number of *vṛttis* (viz. कृत्, तद्धित etc.) are considered to be expressive, there will arise a great prolixity, therefore एकार्थीभाव is to be resorted to. When the compounds are formed, as the grammarians state, एकार्थीभाव is resorted to, i.e. two words with different senses are compounded and they are supposed to convey a single sense. e.g. in राजपुरुषः the word राजन् denotes the sense of a king and the word पुरुष denotes the sense of a man. Now, there is एकार्थीभाव (singularisation?) of both these words in the compound. The word राजन् and the word पुरुष both convey the sense of 'a man' only. The word राजन् (by जहत्स्वार्थावृत्ति) conveys the sense of qualifier and then denotes the sense 'man'. Thus both the words denote a single sense. We may say that (by जहत्स्वार्थावृत्ति) the senses of these two words though different are merged in समुदायार्थ

(meaning of totality), their individual occurrence is not there, we cannot separate the sense of the constituent parts. They merge in a whole by पांसूदकन्याय—This inseparable existence of the senses of two words joined in a compound is called एकार्थीभाव. Thus in compounds like पङ्कज the constituent parts of the word do not convey the sense separately, therefore, we cannot accept *yogaśakti* in compounds.

It is quite unrequired, but BKB states that in उद्बाहुरिव the word इव does not form a compound with the word उद्बाहु because it is intentionally connected with the word वामन in meaning, and the word वामन is the substantive of the qualifier उद्बाहु—hus there is no सामर्थ्य, i.e. इव is not connected with उद्बाहु by way of sense. 'उद्बाहुः इव' cannot convey the sense without being connected with the word वामन—In other words इव bears expectancy with the word वामन being उपमान—So it cannot form a compound with the word उद्बाहुः.

Incidentally, BKB states the purpose behind the formation of a compound. Evenif there is distinction in meaning between a compound and a sentence, there is a difference of process. (a) अभिन्नक्रमत्वम् -In compounds, the order of the constituent words is definite, while in a sentence, words can be construed voluntarily., We may say either राज्ञः पुरुषः। or पुरुषः राज्ञः। (b) स्वरविपर्यासः- So far as Vedic Language is concerned, we have definite accents. IN vedic compounds there is a different accent system from that in a sentence. (c) नित्यसमासत्वम्- In a sentence, the case affixes are not dropped, while in a compound, they are generally dropped. In a sentence we can add a word between the two words related by way of sense e.g. राज्ञः ऋद्धस्य पुरुषः। whereas in a compound, it is not allowed.[68]

The point is, however, not directly related to the topic under discussion.

BKB resumes the topic of *śakti* and mentions the view of the *naiyāyikas* about the types of *śakti*. They propound that a word is denotative (शक्त) and it is fourfold viz. रूढ, यौगिक, योगरूढ and यौगिकरूढ[69] All the words are defined thus: तथाहि यत्रावयवार्थ एव बुद्ध्यते तद्यौगिकम्। यथा पाचकादिपदम्। यत्रावयवशक्ति-नैरपेक्ष्येण समुदायशक्तिमात्रेण बुद्ध्यते तद्रूढम्। यथा गोमण्डला(पा) दिपदम् यत्र तु अवयवशक्तिर्विषये समुदायशक्तिरप्यस्ति तद्योगरूढम्। तथा पङ्कजा-दिपदम्। यथा हि-पङ्कजपदमवयवशक्त्या पङ्कजनिकर्तृत्वरूपमर्थं बोधयति, समुदायशक्त्या च पद्मत्वेन रूपेण पद्मं बोधयति। न च केवल- याऽवयव. शक्त्या कुमुदे प्रयोगः स्यादिति वाच्यम्। रूढिज्ञानस्य केवल- यौगिकार्थज्ञान-प्रतिबन्धकत्वादिति प्राञ्चः।......यत्र तु यौगिकार्थरूढ्यर्थयोः स्वातन्त्र्येण बोधः तद्यौगिकरूढम्। यथोद्भिदादिपदम्। तत्र हि उद्भेदनकर्ता तरुगुल्मादिरपि बुद्ध्यते। यागविशेषोऽपीति।[70] The definitions of यौगिक, रूढ and योगरूढ words are here analogous to those given by AB, but the *naiyāyikas* add one more यौगिकरूढ type word in the classification of the *ālaṅkārikas*. BKB does not accept the word पाचक as an example of यौगिक word and the word गौः as that of रूढ word, because गौः can be etymologically explained as गच्छति इति गौः। It should be noted here that AB considers the word गौः as an instance of रूढि. BKB leaves the justification of the problem to the *naiyāyikas*.

(c) The two words सात्वत and सात्वत् two examples of रूढ and योगरूढ words respectively :

BKB, as is his practice, renders a detailed elaborate explanation of both the words. सात्वत is a word ending in अ, a vowel-ending word, while सात्वत् is a consonant-ending word. सात्वत् is a proper noun like the संज्ञा-डित्थ. It is traditionally used for a person born in *yādava* dynasty. In BP it is used in this specific sense as in—

कच्चित्सुखं सात्वतवृष्णिभोज-
दाशार्हकाणामधिपः स आस्ते। (BP III, i, 29)

The reference is to Ugrasena, the king of the *yādavas*. Hence सात्वत traditionally denotes 'a specific person'. The consonant-ending word सात्वत् is योगरूढ used in the sense of 'devotee, worshipper'. Like the word पङ्कज, so far as the nature of the word योगरूढ is concerned, the author seems to agree with the *naiyāyikas*. The word which conveys the sense by both अवयवशक्ति and समुदायशक्ति, is योगरूढ. It combines the etymological as well as the conventional sense. The word पङ्कज, by the power of its constituent members, denotes the sense 'born in mud' (पङ्के जायते इति।), and totally it denotes the sense 'lotus' only. It cannot be used in the sense of 'Lily' or 'anything born in mud' by अवयवशक्ति because the understanding by convention is stronger than that by etymology. The word सात्वत् is योगरूढ meaning 'a devotee'. It is used in this sense in BP. The author quotes two lines which indicate his inclination to BP: नमो नमस्तेऽस्त्वृषभाय सात्वताम्। (II, iv. 14) and अपि स्विदास्ते भगवान् सुखो वो यः सात्वतां कामदुधोऽनिरुद्धः। (III, i, 34). In both the cases, the word सात्वताम् (possessive plural) is used in the sense of 'worshippers' by convention. BKB explains its etymology fully :

सत्व-fourfold अन्तःकरण namely चित्त, अहङ्कार, बुद्धि and मनस्. The group of all these is सात्वम्. The seat of these four-सात्वाः namely वासुदेव, संकर्षण, प्रद्युम्न and अनिरुद्ध respectively, are their अधिष्ठातृ gods. Those devotees who ever make an attempt to attain these gods by meditation and worship are सात्वत्ऽ. It is not that this explanation is imaginative. It has a sound base of Śrīdharī on BP which runs: सात्वतामुपासकानां कामान् दोग्धि पूरयतीति कामदुधः। भगवत्त्वे हेतुः। यं शब्दस्य शास्त्रस्य योनिं कारणमानन्ति वेदाः। कुतः मनोमयं मनसः प्रवर्तकम्। तत्कुतः। सत्वस्यान्तःकरणस्य चतुर्विधस्य नुरीयं तत्त्वं चतुर्थमधिदैवम्। चित्ताहङ्कारबुद्धिमनसामन्तःकरणभेदानां क्रमेण

वासुदेवसंकर्षणप्रद्युम्नानिरुद्धाः ह्यधिष्ठातारः मनसश्च शब्दयोनित्वं प्रसिद्धम्।[71] BKB also describes the process through which the declension सात्वत् is formed. There is a *vārttika* on P, VI, i, 94-शकन्ध्वादिषु पररूपम् वक्तव्यम्।[72] On the strength of this *vārttika,* the word सात्वत् iz formed: सात्वान् अतन्ति इति सात्वतः। सात्व+अत्=सात्वत् according to the *vārttika* above-stated. In this grammatical formation, etymology is employed and the sense of √अत् 'to attain' is gained by tradition, convention or रूढि़ Thus the सात्वत् is an example of the combination of etymology and convention, hence a योगरूढ word. तुम्बुरु- the specific name of a *gandharva* is an example of रूढि—The word is conventionally established in that sense, however, in Hemakośa its etymology is given as तुम्बति सुशब्दं करोति इति तुम्बुरुः।—But BKB states that this word is रूढ as a संज्ञा, a specific name and denotes a single sense of a *gandharava,* and the word is qualified by three उकारs; which should be noted.

To conclude, in the treatment of *śakti* i.e. *abhidhā* BKB follows into the footsteps of his predecessors like Mammaṭa and AB.He states necessary details about the topic but carefully avoids unnecessary repetitions. He seems to fill the gaps with elaborate grammatical discussions and explanations: yet, where he himself differs from the previous scholars, he definitely discusses the point alongwith a due suport, The discussion of समुदायशक्ति in compounds is one such example. He has added the treatment of the *sphoṭa* theory intentionally to provide his work the status of a *śāstra:* which is quite important so far as the evaluation of his contribution is concerned. He carefully moves further step by step making his work a *vādagrantha* in the real sense of the term.

IV. viii *Lakṣaṇā* :

(a) Definition and nature of *lakṣaṇā* :

In the treatment of *lakṣaṇā* 'indication', BKB follows

Āśādhara Bhaṭṭa (AB) almost verbatim. He quotes either from KND or from TRN. BKB unfolds the topic of *lakṣaṇā* with various opinions of the ancients pertaining to *lakṣaṇā*. He quotes the definition of the *naiyāikas* from Tarkadīpikā, the auto-commentary on Tarkasaṅgraha by Annam Bhaṭṭa: शक्यसम्बन्धो लक्षणेति तार्किकाः। *lakṣaṇā* is the relation of the secondary sense to the denotative sense, which arises when the purport of the speaker is not comprehended properly.[73] Now logically, the relation can exist between two things only. Thus *lakṣaṇā* can be believed to function with the expressive word also. Appaya Dīkṣita defines *lakṣaṇā* as: सा (लक्षणा) च मुख्यार्थसम्बन्धेन शब्दस्य प्रतिपादकत्वम्।[74] 'when a word conveys some secondary sense resorting to its relation to the denotative sense, the power of the word that conveys that particular sense is called *lakṣaṇā*'.

The definition of the logicians is not acceptable according to AB who states in KND:

शक्यलक्ष्यार्थसम्बन्धं लक्षणां तार्किकाः विदुः।
अन्यैः शक्यान्यसम्बन्धे प्रोक्ता भक्तेः सहायता।।[75]

"The logicians say that the relation between the denotative and the indicative sense is *lakṣaṇā* but, that is not proper because *lakṣaṇā* being a function (व्यापार), it cannot be a relation, so the *ālaṅkārikas* use the word भक्ति, which is derived as: शक्यार्थस्य सम्बन्धे भज्यते अनया द्वितीयोऽर्थः सा भक्तिः। A Relation is something different from a function; it (relation) can abide in the sense only. भक्ति is a process by means of which a secondary sense is conveyed from a word, on the basis of its relation with the denotative sense of that word. In TRN, AB elaborates the issue: शक्यसम्बन्धसहकारिणी वृत्तिर्लक्षणा। सा च शब्दव्यापारत्वाच्छब्दनिष्ठा मुख्यार्थबाधे सति तत्सम्बधिनमर्थं विषयीकरोति। सम्बन्धश्च मुख्यार्थे प्राधान्येन वर्तमानोऽपि लक्ष्यार्थमाश्रयति। शक्यसम्बन्धो यद्यपि शब्देऽपि वर्त्तते तथापि लक्षणायामप्रयोजकः। *lakṣaṇā* indicates the sense which is related to the primary sense, therefore, it functions only with the support of the relation with the primary sense. *lakṣaṇā* does abide in the word as it is the function of the word, but only when the primary sense is incompatible, it objectifies the meaning which is in someway related to that primary sense. The relation is principally located in the primary sense i.e. the primary sense is directly related to the word, but that relation takes resort to the secondary sense. In other words, the relation with the primary sense is definitely there in the denotative word, but that does not employ in *lakṣaṇā*. It is the relation between the primary-denotative and the secondary sense that employs in *lakṣaṇā*.

The *ālaṅkārikas* explain *lakṣaṇā* as a process (*vṛtti)* which conveys the sense other than the denotative sense through its relation to the primary sense. In other words,, *lakṣaṇā* functions when *abhidhā* fails to convey the intended sense, or when the primary sense is incompatible to the purport of the speaker, but *lakṣaṇā* can only indicate the sense which is in some way related to the primary sense, otherwise it would be possible to understand any sense from any word.

(2) *dīrgha-dīrgha-taravyāpāra-vāda* :

BKB mentions the opinion of the grammarians who do not admit *lakṣaṇā* as an independent functiton of the word:

When a strong archer shoots an arrow, he pierces through the armour, the heart and takes away the life of an enemy. Similarly, a single function called *abhidhā* 'denotation' conveys all the senses of the word.So *lakṣaṇā* need not be accepted.

BKB quite surprisingly, does not render any reply to the grammarians' argument against *lakṣaṇā*. He quotes first from TRN and then from KP to define *lakṣaṇā*. The definition quoted from KP emphasises three conditions or *hetus* of *lakṣaṇā* : First if the primary sense does not fit in the context, i.e. with the sense of other words used in the sentence or cannot convey the purport of the speaker (i.e. मुख्यार्थबाध);

Second this secondary sense conveyed through *lakṣaṇā*

must be related to the denotative sense in some way or the other (i.e. तद्योग); and third, there should be some tradition or some purpose for using that word in that particular meaning (i.e. रूढि-प्रयोजन).

(c) Comparison of *lakṣaṇā* as depicted in TRN and in VD :

As it is stated already. BKB almost verbally follows his *guru* AB in the treatment of *lakṣaṇā*. BKB however, clearly announces his indebtedness towards his teacher : विस्तरनिरूपणं त्वाशाधरभट्टकृतत्रिवेणिकाग्रन्थे द्रष्टव्यम्। निखिलभेदानां तत्र विशदतया निरूपणादिति।

The following table will bring out the similarity at a glance.

Treatment of *lakṣaṇā* in TRN and in VD.

TRN

(१) शक्यसम्बन्धकारिणीवृत्तिर्लक्षणा। सा च शब्दव्यापारतवाच्छब्दनिष्ठा मुख्यार्थबाधे सति तत्सम्बंधिनमर्थं विषयीकरोति।

(२) सा च त्रिविधा-जहल्लक्षणा, अजहल्लक्षणा, जहदजहल्लक्षणा च यत् सत्त्वे शब्दः शक्यार्थं जहाति सा जहल्लक्षणा, न जहाति चेदजहल्लक्षणा तदुभययुक्ता जहदजहल्लक्षणा।

(३) त्रिविधापि पुनर्द्विविधा-निरूढा फलवती च। शक्तिवत कोशादौ प्रसिद्धा निरूढा। इयं च मुख्यार्थबाधे प्रवर्तते इति शक्तितो विशेषः। एषाऽनादिलक्षणेत्याहुः।

(४) अस्याः (फलवतीलक्षणायाः) फलं तु व्यङ्ग्यार्थप्रतीतिः। तत् क्वचिद्गूढं क्वचिदगूढं चेति द्विविधम्। गूढं सहृदयमात्रसंवेद्यम्। अगूढं तु सर्वजनवेद्यम्।

(५) पुनरपि लक्षणा द्विविधा-व्यधिकरणविषया समानाधिकरणविषया चेति।

(६) पुनरपि गौणी शुद्धा चेत्येषा द्विविधा।[76]

VD

(१) सा च लक्षणा वृत्तिः शब्दव्यापारत्वाच्छब्दनिष्ठा मुख्यार्थबाधे सति तत्सम्बंधिनमर्थं विषयीकरोति।

(२) प्रथमं तावल्लक्षणा त्रिविधा भवति-जहल्लक्षणा, अजहल्लखणा, जहदजहल्लक्षणा चेति। यत्र सति मुख्यार्थबाधे शब्दः शक्यार्थं जहाति तत्र जहल्लक्षणा, यत्र तमर्थं न जहाति तत्राजहल्लक्षणा। यत्र तदुभयं तत्र जहदजहल्लक्षणा।

(३) पुनस्त्रिविधापीयं द्विविधा-निरूढा फलवती च। निरूढा लक्षणा शक्तितुल्यत्वात् कोशादि-प्रसिद्धा। इयं तु शक्तितुल्यापि मुख्यार्थबाधे सति स्यात्तेन शक्तितोऽस्याः विशेषः। अनादिलक्षणा चैषेत्याहुः।

(४) यत्र फलवती लक्षणा तत्र फलं तु व्यञ्जनाव्यापारगम्यमेव, न शक्तिलक्षण्सणागम्यमिति.....फलं तावत् कुत्रचित् गूढं कुत्रचिदगूढमिति द्विविधं भवति। गूढं फलं तु चतुरजनज्ञेयम्। अगूढं फलं तु सकलवेद्यमिति।

(५) पुनरपि समानाधिकरणविषया व्यधिकरणविषया चेति द्विविधेयं लक्षणा।

(६) पुनरपीयं द्विविधा गौणी शुद्धा चेति।[77]

It can be obviously seen how BKB follows into the footsteps of his *guru,* in treating the topic of *lakṣaṇā*. In KND, AB has given the names जहती, अजहती and उभयी for जहल्लक्षणा, अज-हल्लक्षणा and जहदजहल्लक्षणा respectively. Incidentally, it should be noted here that BKB does not follow Mammaṭa so far as the terms used for classification of *lakṣaṇā* are concerned. The classification of Mammaṭa is too well-known to be repeated here.

(d) BKB's classification of *lakṣaṇā* :

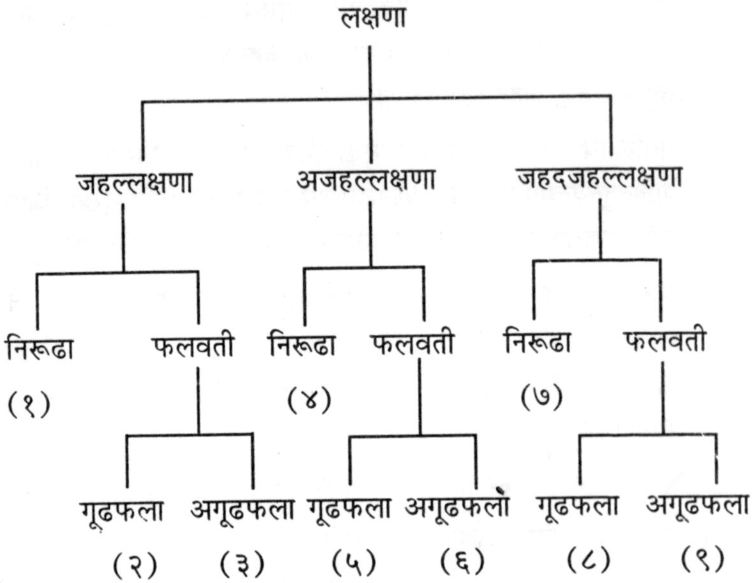

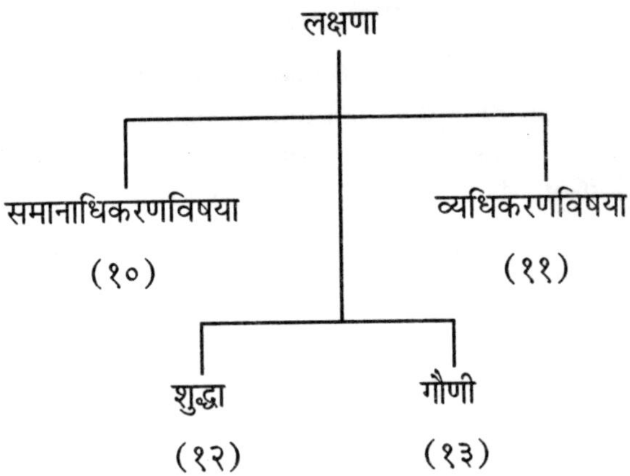

(e) Elaboration of the classification of *lakṣaṇā* :

It is obvious that BKB completely follows his *guru* in the classification of *lakṣaṇā*. At first there are three types of *lakṣaṇā* in view of the compatibility of the denotative sense: (1) जहल्लक्षणा–when the primary sense is totally unsuitable and it is to be given up and the secondary indicative sense is taken, there is जहल्लक्षणा—The well-known example of it is गङ्गायाम् घोषः। The घोष–hamlet is located on the *gaṅga*. Now, the word गङ्गा conveys the primary sense 'flow' by *abhidhā-śakti*. The locative case gives the sense of 'locus' and the hamlet cannot be located in 'the flow'. Hence the primary sense incompatible. Now, the word गङ्गा indicates the sense 'bank' (by *lakṣaṇā*). The relation between the denotative meaning of the word and the actual (indicative) meaning is one of proximity. The word घोष 'hamlet' becomes तात्पर्यग्राहक, 'a factor enabling the word गङ्गा to convey the intent'.

The view of the grammarians, however, in this example is different. According to the *pāṇinisūtra*—आधारोऽधिकरणम्। (I, iv, 45), "that which is related to the action as the site where it is performed is-आधार 'locus' and it is called अधिकरण; the location." The अधिकरण takes the locative-seventh-case. e.g. वटे गावः सुशेरते। 'cows sleep under the banyan tree'. The अधिकरण is sixfold in the grammarians' opinion, namely औपश्लेषिक, 'resulting from immediate contact', सामीपिक resulting from nearness', अभिव्यापक 'including', वैषयिक 'topical', नैमित्तिक 'pertaining to the effect' and औपचारिक 'resulting from उपचार', 'metonymical'. In वटे गावः सुशेरते। the location is सामीपिक, it indicates the site of action—'near the banyan tree.' वट is the सामीपिक आधार of the action of sleeping; and the locative case (वटे) conveys the sense of this सामीपिक आधार by *abhidhā śakti*-denotation, and therefore, *lakṣaṇā*-indication need not be employed here. BKB, however, does not here take a halt to enter into a detailed discussion.

To resume the topic of the discussion, i.e. जहल्लक्षणा in गङ्गायाम् घोष:।, it is फलवती–'having a purpose' where शैत्यपावनत्व-प्रतीति the indication of coolness and sancity is the fruit (motive). Mammaṭa has described this type of *lakṣaṇā* under the name लक्षणलक्षणा.[78] अजहल्लक्षणा is that in which the denotative sense is not discarded. The secondary sense is added to the primary sense in order to make it compatible in the context. e.g. कुन्ता: प्रविशन्ति। 'the lances enter' or यष्टय: प्रविशन्ति। 'the staffs enter'. The lances and the staffs being inanimate cannot enter on their own. The words कुन्ता: and यष्टय: therefore, convey the secondary senses 'men with lances' and 'men with staffs' respectively. The secondary sense here includes the denotative sense. The motive, फल, intention, here, is to suggest their unfailing power of thrashing. Mammaṭa terms this as उपादान-लक्षणा.[79] Again, जहदजहल्लक्षणा occurs when the primary sense is neither completely given up nor completely accepted. It is partly given up and partly accepted. The example thereof (i.e. of जहदजहल्लक्षणा) is—काकेभ्यो दधि रक्ष्यताम्। 'Save the curds from the crows'. In this example, the denotative sense of the word काकेभ्य: is 'from the crows'. It is not totally given up, but extended to the secondary sense 'all the creatures harmful to the curds'. Thus the word काक conveys the sense 'harmful to curds' by *lakṣaṇā* 'indication'. The motive (intention) here is to suggest the villainy of a crow. It is the fruit of *lakṣaṇā*. BKB incidentally points out the importance of context: When somebody is passing with the pot of curds put on his head, the word काक denotes the sense 'crow' only because there is no possibility of any other harmful creatures than the crow.The intended sense is conveyed by *abhidhā-śakti* itself. So no *lakṣaṇā* occurs in that case. The reason is that in all the cases of *lakṣaṇā* the root cause of indication is the failure in grasping the meaning intended. BKB quotes from Tarkadīpikā on Tarkasaṅgraha.[80] We are also reminded of Bhāṣāparichheda here.[81]

Another example of जहदजहल्लक्षणा :

AB has given another example of जहदजहल्लक्षणा from Manusmṛti: न जातु ब्राह्मणं हन्यात्। (VII, 380). BKB also quotes it but with a different explanation. He elaborates: In न जातु ब्राह्मणं हन्यात्। 'one should never kill a brahmin;' the word ब्राह्मण takes accusative singular, meaning 'one brahmin' but the sense of singular is discarded and the sense of plural is understood by *lakṣaṇā*, meaning '(all the) brahmins'. The singular will not be applicable as the purport of the statement is—'one should never kill brahmins (in general)'. Unless we understand plural here by *lakṣaṇā*, the statement will not apply in the case of all the brahmins in general and the primary sense 'a brahmin' will be thus incompatible.

BKB records the interpretation of AB with his disagreement thus : यत्तु त्रिवेणिकायां न जातु ब्राह्मणं हन्यादित्यत्र व्यक्तिपरेण ब्राह्मणशब्देन तत्समवेता जातिर्लक्ष्यते इति प्राचीनमतानुसारेणोक्तं भविष्यति। परं तु न तत्समञ्जसं प्रतिभाति। AB has explained the example while discussing various relations between शक्यार्थ denotative and लक्ष्यार्थ, indicative sense upon which *lakṣaṇā* is based. One of such relation is *samavāya* 'inherent' relation i.e. जातिव्यक्तिभाव 'relation between genus and individual' AB states; जातिव्यक्ति-भावश्च सम्बन्धः। 'न जातु ब्राह्मणं हन्यात्' इह व्यक्तिपरेण ब्राह्मणशब्देन तत्समवेता जातिर्लक्ष्यते। अन्यथा सर्वेषामवध्यत्वं न स्यात्।[82] According to AB, in this example, the word ब्राह्मण denotes the sense of 'an individual brahmin'. Since the *jāti* 'genus', universal, is inherently related to it, this jāti is indicated (by *lakṣaṇā*). BKB does not agree to this interpretation of his *guru,* who has probably followed the traditional explanation. BKB substantiates his own interpretation thus: we may admit that *lakṣaṇā* conveys *Jāti* (universal, the class) through *vyakti* (individual) but *jāti*

(ब्राह्मणत्व) is again incompatible to the context as *jāti* cannot be killed (*jāti* being नित्य eternal). So again, we will have to resort to *lakṣaṇā* to understand the sense of indiviuals. BKB supports his view with an illustration from Naiṣadha Mahākāvya (which is described as a *śāstra-kāvya* in the tradition of classical Sanskrit literature):

क्षत्रजातिरुदियाय भुजाभ्यां या तवैव भुवनं सृजतः प्राक्। (नै० च० २१-६३) "that *kṣtriya* race which had emerged from your own arms while you were creating the world." Here the word *jāti* indicates individuals which are the substratum-loci of it. *Jāti,* genus being eternal cannot be born, so the denotative sense of (क्षत्र) जाति, is incompatible here, hence *lakṣaṇā* is resorted to. Similar is the case in the example—न जातु ब्राह्मणं हन्यात्। Killing of ब्राह्मणत्व-जाति is impossible so we shall have to take resort to *lakṣaṇā* to understand ब्राह्मणव्यक्ति, which would bring about the contingency of repetition. BKB explains *lakṣaṇā* in this example thus: the part of accusative singular coming after the word ब्राह्मण as the denotative sense should be given up here, and the non-primary (secondary) sense accusative plural should be accepted, by *lakṣaṇā*. Thus the statement will be applicable to all the brahmins, and not to an individual brahmin only. This जहदजहल्लक्षणा is also called भागत्यागलक्षणा, indication by partial abandonment.

(f) The problem of the Reading—क्षत्रजातिरुदियाय.......प्राक्। (नै०च० २१.६३) :

The reading of this verse in the ms. is क्षत्रजातिदुदियाय भुजाभ्यां यस्तवेह सृजतोर्भुवनं प्राक्। whereas the text in the printed editions of the Naiṣadhacaritam has the reading—

क्षत्रजाति......या तवैव भुवनं सृजतः प्राक्। The context shows that in order to make the text grammatically correct, one must make two emendations in the text, यः should be made into या and सृजतोः should be either सृजतो or सृजतः Evenafter these two emendations, the order of the words in the ms, does not confirm to that in the printed text; which from the point of view of diction is better and more poetic. In a normal case of editing, the editor should adhere to the text with minimum possible emendations. If we accept and adopt this principle, the text in this case should be या तवेह सृजतो भुवनं प्राक्। However, evenafter two emendations, the emended text would still involve inversion of two words and a less poetic reading. We have for once diverted from the normal practice of editing and quoted the text from the printed versions only rather than reconstructing it from the ms. Both the readings are given in the running (the printed reading is given in brackets). The justification for diverting from the normal practice of emending the manuscri-ptural text is this: (1) the author is barely two hundred years old, and obviously, he may be quoting from memory; (2) on the other hand, the printed text has a strong support of numerous mss. much older than the date of our author and moreover, it has the support of the stalwart ancient commen-tators like Mallinātha; (3) We must also keep in mind that this is only a *single codex* manuscript and we have no other manuscriptural source to verify whether our author's memory is slipping him. We have, therefore, some justification in setting aside for once, the normal *princepts editio* and adopting a correct text from outside the manuscriptural source.

(g) *Lakṣaṇā* in the examples:—सोऽयं देवदत्तः। तत्त्वमसि। etc.:

BKB does not accept *lakṣaṇā* in the examples like-सोऽयं देवदत्तः। 'Here is that Devadatta' or तत्त्वमसि 'that thou art'. He has refuted the opinion of his *guru* AB who has stated these two as the examples of निरूढा जहदजहल्लक्षणा। he states: अथ निरूढा जहदजहल्लक्षणा। 'गृहं सम्मार्ष्टि', अत्र गृहशब्देन तदेकदेशे निरूढा जहदजहल्लक्षणा। एवं 'कुसुमितद्रुमम्' इत्यादावपि। अथ 'सोऽयं

देवदत्तः' अत्र पूर्वकालोत्तरकालवर्त्तित्वपरित्यागेन देवदत्तमात्रं लक्ष्यते। एवं 'शिवोऽहम्' 'सोऽहम्', 'तत्त्वमसि' इत्यादावपि।[83]

In AB's opinion, सोऽयं देवदत्तः। is an example of निरूढा जहदजहल्लक्षणा. The primary senses of सः—'the Devadatta belonging to the former time' and अयम्—'The Devadatta at this time' are given up. The general sense of Devadatta is conveyed by निरूढा जहदजहल्लक्षणा—BKB disagrees to this. The reason he gives is this: the very first condition of *lakṣaṇā* मुख्यार्थबाध incompatibility of the denotative sense-is not fulfilled here. He gives some more examples of such language behaviour like घटः अनित्यः।, गेहे घटाः स्थिताः।, शालागौः बद्धा अस्ति। etc. He explains the first one घटः अनित्यः। 'The jar is transitory'. In this sentence, the word घट signifies 'an individual jar'. It is possible to connect the word घट with transitoriness leaving the eternal generic attribute (जाति) घटत्व, aside; while in the sentence घटत्वं नित्यम्। Jarness is imperishable, the word घटत्व signifies the eternal generic attribute (जाति), so it is possible to connect the word घटत्व with eternity (नित्यत्व) leaving aside the transitoriness of a jar. Similar are the cases like सोऽयं देवदत्तः।, तत्त्वमसि।, गेहे घटाः स्थिताः।, शालागौः बद्धा अस्ति etc. Such sentences are usually seen to be used in language behaviour, and incompatibility of the denotative sense does not seem to occur, therefore, there is no need to consider *lakṣaṇā* in such cases.

The Vedāntins have accepted *lakṣaṇā* in the sentence like तत्त्वमसि by persistence to follow Śaṅkarācārya, BKB alludes to Vedāntaparibhāṣā where it is said: तस्मात् 'तत्त्वमसि' इत्यादिवाक्येषु आचार्याणां लक्षणोक्तिरभ्युपगमवादेन बोध्या।[84] The whole discussion is based on that which has been clearly taken up in Vedānta-paribhāṣā. It would not be, therefore, out of place to quote from the same:

यथा वा 'तत्त्वमसि' इत्यादौ 'तत्' पदवाच्यस्य सर्वज्ञत्वादिविशिष्टस्य 'त्वं' पदवाच्येनान्तःकरणविशिष्टेनैक्यायोगात् ऐक्यसिद्ध्यर्थं स्वरूपे लक्षणेति, साम्प्रदायिकाः। वयन्तु ब्रूमः-'सोऽयं देवदत्तः,' 'तत्त्वमसि' इत्यादौ विशिष्ट-वाचकपदानामेकदेशपरत्वेऽपि न लक्षणा, शक्त्युपस्थितविशिष्टयोः अभेदान्वया-नुपपत्तौ विशेष्ययोः शक्त्युपस्थितयोरेव अभेदान्वयाविरोधात्। यथा 'घटोऽनित्य' इत्यत्र 'घट' पदवाच्यैकदेशघटत्वायोग्यत्वेऽपि योग्यघटव्यक्त्या सहानित्य-त्वान्वयः। यत्र पदार्थैकदेशस्य विशेषणतयोपस्थितिः, तत्रैव स्वातन्त्र्येण उपस्थितये लक्षणाभ्युपगमः। यथा 'नित्यो घटः' इत्यत्र 'घट'पदात् घटत्वस्य शक्त्या स्वातन्त्र्येणानुपस्थित्या तादृशोपस्थित्यर्थं 'घट'पदस्य घटत्वे लक्षणा। एवमेव 'तत्त्वमसि' इत्यादिवाक्येऽपि न लक्षणा, शक्त्या स्वातन्त्र्येणोपस्थितयोः 'तत्त्व' पदार्थयोरभेदान्वये बाधकाभावात्। अन्यथा 'गेहे घटः,' 'घटे रूपम्,' 'घटमानय' इत्यादौ घटत्वगेहत्वादेरभिमतान्वयबोधायोग्यतया तत्रापि 'घट-आदिपदानां विशेष्यमात्रपरत्वं लक्षणयैव स्यात्। तस्मात् 'तत्त्वमसि' इत्यादिवाक्येषु आचार्याणां लक्षणोक्तिरभ्युपगमवादेन बोध्य।[85]

"Or as according to the traditional interpreters of Vedānta, in a sentence like 'That thou art' (Chhā. VI, Viii, 7) since the entity meant by the word 'that' viz. God as possessed of omniscience etc, cannot be identical with what is meant by the word 'thou' viz. the individual self endowed with a mind, Therefore, in order to make their identity possible, the words refer by indication (लक्षणा) to their essential nature. We, however, maintain that in sentences like 'That is this Devadatta' and 'That thou art', although words signifying qualified entities refer only to one portion of their meaning, yet, there is no indication; for, notwithstanding the fact that two qualified entities presented to the mind) by significance (denotation) cannot be (logically) connected with each other to convey an identical meaning, there is no contradiction in connecting two substantives also presented by denotation so as to yield an identity of meaning. As in the sentence 'The jar is transitory' although it is inconsistent to connect with transitoriness, only one part of what is meant by the word 'jar, viz. jarhood, yet, it is, all right with regard to an individual jar, which is capable of being so connected, Indication is admitted there only, where one part of the meaning of a word is presented as a qualifying attribute (विशेषण), so that the meaning may be presented independentiy. As, in the sentence घटो नित्यः 'The jar is eternal', since jarhood is not independently presented by the denotation of the word 'jar', the latter indicates 'jarhood' in order to effect such cognition. Similarly in sentences like 'That thou art' also, there is no indication because the meanings of the words 'that' and 'thou' are presented independently by denotation (of these two words) and there is no obstacle to their being logically connected so as to mean an identical thing. Otherwise, in sentences like 'There is a jar in the house'. 'There is colour in the jar' and 'Bring the jar', since jarhood, household etc. are incapable of leading to the desired comprehension of the logical connection, the words such as 'jar' etc. would convey mere substantives just by indication. Therefore, the statement about indication by the traditional teachers in sentences like 'That thou art' should be understood as mere tentative admission."

It is clear from the whole detailed discussion that BKB differs from his *guru* AB on the point but be has some solid *śāstraic* ground for the difference of opinion.

(h) विधि-नियम-परिसंख्या and the statement—न जातु.....हन्यात्।:

Here, there is a digression in the course of discussion about *lakṣaṇā*. Instead of talking about other types of *lakṣaṇā* as the course of discussion demands, BkB diverts the discussion to decide whether the *smṛti* statement न जातु ब्राह्मणं हन्यात्। is *vidhi, niyama* or *parisaṅkhyā*. He brings in the subtle technicalities of Mimāṁsā system by citations he quotes from the famous Mimāṁsā works. The discussion is not, however, required so far as the treatment of the topic in hand is concerned.

It is perhaps included in this *vādagrantha* to provide the work the stature of *śāstra*. Arthasaṅgraha gives definition of *vidhi* 'injunction' thus : प्रमाणान्तरेणाप्राप्तस्य प्रापको विधिः अपूर्वविधिः। यथा यजेत स्वर्गकामः। स्वर्गार्थकयागस्य प्रमाणान्तरेणाप्राप्तस्यानेन विधानात्।[86] Injunction is that which enjoins something in a matter absolutely unavailble by other evidences. e.g. यजेत स्वर्गकामः। A person desirous of heaven should perform a sacrificial rite. The sacrificial rite required to fulfil the desire for heaven and not availed by other evidences is enjoined here. Hence it is a *vidhi* statement. The example of *vidhi* given by BKB is स्वाध्यायः अध्येतव्यः। 'The *vedas* should be studied.' *niyama* is thus defined in Arthasaṅgraha: नानासाधनसाध्यक्रियायामेकसाधनप्राप्तावप्राप्तस्यापर-साधनस्य प्रापको विधिर्नियमविधिः।[87] Specification is enjoning some optional means which has not been stated as a means to achieve a purposeful activity. *Niyama* is partially applicable. e.g. शुक्लपक्षे स्वाध्यायोऽध्येतव्यः। The vedas should be studied in the bright half of the lunar month. This statement implies admirability of the studies of the Vedas particularly in शुक्लपक्ष. There won't be any harm. however, if a brahmin studies the Vedas in कृष्णपक्ष. BKB gives another example of *niyama* in समे यजेत। which is clearly explained in the text itself. Such an example of *niyama* from the *smṛti* is प्राङ्मुखः अन्नानि भुञ्जीत। 'One should partake the food facing the east'. Again, to define *parisaṅkhyā* it is stated: उभयोश्च युगपत्प्राप्तावितरव्यावृत्तिपरो विधिः परिसंख्याविधिः। यथा पञ्च पञ्चनखा भक्ष्याः। When two things are found simultaneously in many places, the statement which is meant to exclude it from other place and to allow iot in one place, it is called *Parisaṅkhyā* exclusion'. e.g. Five animals with five nails are eatable.Thus statement permits that either rabbits or dogs can be taken as food; but when it is specifically stated that rabbits should be taken as food, then the dogs are excluded. Now the question is-whether the statement न जातु ब्राह्मणं हन्यात्। is a *vidhi, a niya-mavidhi* or a *parisaṅkhyā*. BKB explains that it is not a *niyama vidhi* as it does not contain specification of options. Neither can it be considered a *parisaṅkhyā* which would cause the contingency of three defects, namely श्रुतहानि harm to the import of the Vedic statement, परार्थकल्पना imagination of some other (than being stated) and प्राप्तबाध—incompatibility of the sense conveyed. Thus the statement न जातु ब्राह्मणं हन्यात्। is an *apūrvavidhi* 'injunction'. The meaning thereby—one should (in no case) kill a brahmin otherwise it will definitely bring दोष, 'blemish.'

BKB incidentally points out the difference between *niyamavidhi* and *parisaṅkhyāvidhi*: In *niyamavidhi* the option specifically stated, implies the prieminence thereof. If that act is not performed, no harm e.g studying the Vedas in the शुक्लपक्ष is prieminent or praiseworthy but if someone studies the Vedas in कृष्णपक्ष also, it won't bring any harm to the student; whereas in *parisaṅkhyā,* what is excluded, must not be done, or else, it will cause दोष, blemish or sin and expiation to atone for that sin would be inevitable.

A peculiarity of the author's style which bears the finger-prints of his *gujaratiness* should be noted here: नियमविधेः **सकाशात्** परिसंख्यायाः भेदोऽवगन्तव्यः The word सकाशात् suggests the impact of Gujarati language.

To resume the topic under consideration, the author mentions two subtypes of शुद्धा लक्षणा namely सारोपा superimposed and साध्यवसाना introsusceptive. BKB does not find any need to explain the difference between शुद्धा and गौणीलक्षणा as it is quite well-known, from KP, KND and TRN. We may take note that when the secondary-metaphorical use of a word is based on the relation of similarity (सादृश्य), it is गौणीलक्षणा and when it is based on some other relation than similarity between the denotative and secondary sense, it is शुद्धालक्षणा. The examples of शुद्धा सारोपा and शुद्धा साध्यवसाना are आयुर्धृतम् 'ghee is life' and आयुरेव life itself' respectively. The examples are the same as given by Mammaṭa in KP. The relation causing indication here is कार्यकारणभाव 'cause and effect relation', which is other than similarity. The author here noticieably explains the difference between the compound मुखचन्द्र and सारोपा लक्षणा. In compounds like मुखचन्द्र, though चन्द्र, the object is imposed upon मुख, the similarity between the two is conveyed by the power of totality produced from the compounded words. Therefore, *lakṣaṇā* is not required. Here again, BKB follows AB almost verbatim. AB states in TRN: 'मुखचन्द्र' इत्यादौ समस्त-रूपके त्वारोपसत्त्वे तस्य समासोत्पन्नसमुदायशक्त्या निर्वाहाल्लक्षणा- भावः। अत एव व्यस्तोदाहरणानि प्राचीनैर्दर्शितानि।[88] In मुखचन्द्र etc. there is metaphor in the compound. उपमान is imposed upon उपमेय—Yet there is no *lakṣaṇā* because the sense of similarity is indicated by the समुदायशक्ति 'the power of the words joined in the compound'. It is for this reason that the ancients have given such examples of *lakṣaṇā* as are not compound-words. Both AB and BKB bring out the difference between सारोपा and साध्यवसाना लक्षणा almost in the same words. Vide :

TRN	**VD**
सारोपायां गुणमात्रे लक्षणा।	सारोपलक्षणायां गुणमात्रस्य लक्षणा।
गुणी तु शक्त्या गृह्यते।	गुणी तु शक्त्या परिगृह्यते।
साध्यवसानायां तु द्वयोरपि तत्र	साध्यवसानालक्षणायां तु विषयस्य
विषयस्य निगरणात्।[89]	स्वशब्देनानुपादानरूपनिगरणस्य
	सत्त्वाद् द्वयोरपीति।[90]

In सारोपालक्षणा, only the attributes are indicated through *lakṣaṇā,* the sense of गुणिन् the attribute-possessor is cognised by denotation only while in साध्यवसाना, both the attributes and the attribute-possessor are cognised by indication because the object super imposed upon (विषय) is not mentioned by its denoter (the expressive word). It is swallowed up by the object super-imposed (विषयिन्). BKB quotes the definitions of सारोपा and साध्यवसाना लक्षणा from KND.

(i) शुद्धा सारोपा लक्षणा in द्रोणो व्रीहिः। :

द्रोणो व्रीहिः। is an example of शुद्धा सारोपा लक्षणा. BKB elaborates the example in some more details than those given by AB in TRN. He adds the *pūrvapakṣa* of the grammarians who do not accept *lakṣaṇā* in द्रोणो व्रीहिः। 'the droṇaful rice'. The sense is 'the rice measured by that measurement which is of the form of *droṇa*.' In fact, *droṇa* is a cup for measuring rice. It cannot be the rice itself. Hence मुख्यार्थबाध i.e. the denotative sense is imcompatible. Now both the *droṇa* 'cup' and the rice meausred by it are related by परिच्छेद्य-परिच्छेदकभाव, the analogy of the measured and the measurer. So the word *droṇa* can convey the sense 'the rice as much as contained in a *droṇa*', by indication.

The grammarians do not accept *lakṣaṇā* in द्रोणो व्रीहिः।—In their opinion, the case—suffix denotes the sense of measure, the quantity and when it is applied to the stem (प्रकृति), it gives a specific sense. The suffix thus becomes qualifier of व्रीहि by a connection of unity (अभेदसंसर्ग)—Otherwise द्रोण would not have taken the nominative case. The word द्रोणः used in the nominative case singular (with व्रीहिः) conveys the sense of qualifier, hence we need not resort to *lakṣaṇā*.

But Both AB and BKB, state almost in the same words that the measure in general is denoted by the case-suffix whereas, meausre, in a specific sense is indicated by *lakṣaṇā* only.

Again, the grammarians may argue thus: the word परिमाण is derived as—'that by which something is measured is परिमाण-measurement'. Now, the words द्रोण etc. are परिमाण measurement only, may be the cups are made of iron or wood. That measurement does not vary, but the thing to be measured varies, the word that denotes the thing measured is always in प्रातिपदिक form and when the case—suffixes are applied to that word, the measurement is cognised thereby. Then why *lakṣaṇā* to be employed?

The author replies to their argument in these words: the argument they (the grammarians) have put forth would not work in the examples of *gauṇī lakṣaṇā* viz. सिंहो माणवकः, 'The man is a lion', मञ्चाः क्रोशन्ति 'the cradles are crying' because there is no परिच्छेद्यपरिच्छेदक भाव 'analogy of being measurable and measurer' between the denotative and indicative senses in these examples. Such cases would remain out of the scope of the explanation they have given for not accepting *lakṣaṇā* and there would arise the contingencey of अव्याप्तिदोष—How will they explain those cases then?

The *pūrvapakṣa*-the grammarians may again say that in examples of *gauṇī* like सिंहो माणवकः। etc. the substantives माणवकः etc. may change or vary but they are 'like the lion' only. Such a meaning is always present there definitely. Similarly in द्रोणो व्रीहिः। etc. the *vrīhi* etc. may vary but they are measured by *droṇa* only. This is definite. So this definiteness of sense applies to both शुद्धा and गौणी of yours. Then why *lakṣaṇā?*

BKB states the difference between शुद्धा and गौणी लक्षणा in conclusion: In sentences like गौर्वाहीकः, अग्निर्माणवकः, सिंहो देवदत्तः etc. there is गौणी अजहल्लक्षणा because (1) the relation of resemblance due to similar attributes between the denotative sense and the indicative (secondary) sense is cognised, (2) the original meaning is not totally abandoned, (3) additional meaning of the attributes is accepted. But in द्रोणो व्रीहिः there cannot be गौणी लक्षणा because there is no relation of resemblance between the primary and the secondary sense. Thus the difference of relation between शक्यार्थ (denotative, primary sense) and लक्ष्यार्थ (indicative, secondary sense) results into two different kinds of *lakṣaṇā* namely गौणी qualitative and शुद्धा 'pure'.

The question may here arise : why then is it said in Manoramā—गौर्वाहीकवत् 'like that in गौर्वाहीक:' in the discussion about द्रोणो व्रीहि:। when the *ālaṅkārikas* consider द्रोणो व्रीहि:। as an example of शुद्धा फलवती जहल्लक्षणा?

BKB explains : There is nothing wrong evenif it is so said in Manorama. In the examples like आयुर्घृतम्, आयुरेवेदम् etc. there is समानाधिकरण विषया लक्षणा, indication residing in the same substratum and it is of the type of superimposition (सारोपा) and introsusception (साध्यवसाना) respectively because the relation as the base of indication here is cause—effect relation, hence शुद्धा pure *lakṣaṇā,* the विषयिन्-the object-superimposed, and the विषय-the object super-imposed upon, both are in समानाधिकरण, i.e. they are words which have got the same individual object (द्रव्य) referred to by means of their own sense and which are put in the same case. Similarly, in द्रोणो व्रीहि:, the word द्रोण is लाक्षणिक 'indicative' of व्रीहि measured by the measuring cup द्रोण. In fact, the sense of 'measurement in general' is denotative, while the sense 'in the specific form of a *droṅa* is indicative only. Thus the similarity between द्रोणो व्रीहि:। and गौर्वाहीक:। is limited to आरोप the superimposition and समानाधिकरण 'same substratum' only. BKB had not defined समानाधिकरण and व्यधिकरणविषया लक्षणा, as AB has given their definitions in TRN : यत्र व्यधिकरणपदं तात्पर्यग्राहकं सा व्यधिकरणविषया यत्र च समानाधिकरणपदं तात्पर्यग्राहकं सा समानाधिकरणविषया। मुख्यार्थ-बाधकं तात्पर्यग्राहकं तदेव लक्षणाग्राहकमित्युच्यते।[91]

The sentences in which words characterised by different case-relations cause incompatibility of the denotative sense, have व्यधिकरणविषया लक्षणा, and the sentences wherein the words referring to the same individual object by means of their own sense and put in the same case, cause incompatibility of the denotative sense have समानाधिकरणविषया लक्षणा।

(j) Examples of गौणी साध्यवसाना लक्षणा :

BKB takes up two well-known words as examples of गौणी साध्यवसाना लक्षणा: सिद्धान्तकौमुदी and शब्दकौस्तुभ, both being compound-words. कौमुदी and कौस्तुभ are respectively the words by which लक्षणा is employed in the compounds. शब्दकौस्तुभ is मध्यमपदलोपी compound: शब्दभूतः कौस्तुभः शब्दकौस्तुभः। The sense is: '*Kaustubha* transformed into a word'. The figure of speech here is परिणाम—Candrāloka defines and illustrates it thus:

परिणामः क्रियार्थश्चेद्विषयी विषयात्मना।
प्रसन्नेन दृगब्जेन वीक्षते मदिरेक्षणा।।[92]

Pariṇāma is a figure of speech allied to *rūpaka,* by which the properties of any object are transferred to that with which it is compared. The property (उद्धृत) of कौस्तुभ is transferred to शब्द. शब्दकौस्तुभ is not an *upamita samāsa* because the common property—उद्धृत is employed here,. As the *kaustubha* was brought out, so the word is drawn out. In *upamita* compound, common property is not employed. It is neither the compound belonging to मयूरव्यंसकादि variety,[93] In मयूर-व्यंसकादिसमास, the meaning of the second member is predominant whereas here (i.e. in शब्दकौस्तुभ), the first member is predominant because the meanings are decided by words and not by the jewel *kaustubha.* Again the second member is not predominant also considering the sense of the word उद्धृत because the word उद्धृत is construed with both the first and the second member of the compound. The purpose-motive of employing *lakṣaṇā* here is to suggest the purity of the words quoted in the *bhāṣya.*

BKB relates two figures of speech with two types of *lakṣaṇā :* when there is *rūpaka* 'metaphor' in uncompounded words, it is सारोपा लक्षणा; and in all the examples, of *rūpaka-atiśayokti* i.e. निगीर्णाध्यवसाना अतिशयोक्ति, it is साध्यवसाना लक्षणा.

(k) व्यतिरेकलक्षणा :

BKB does not define व्यतिरेकलक्षणा—he only gives its example. AB briefly mentions its nature in KND:

विरुद्धा व्यतिरेके च लक्षणोक्ता मनीषिभिः।
इह साधुकृतं तेन शम्भुर्येन न पूजितः॥

and the further comments thereon : विरुद्धेति। व्यतिरेके वैपरीत्ये साधुकृतं साधुशब्देन तद्विपरीतेन लक्षणा, व्यतिरेकलक्षणामपीमां वदन्ति। फलवती चेयं न निरूढा।[94]

The learned also admit विपरीतलक्षणा by contrariety relation. e.g. 'He who has not worshipped *śambhu,* has done good'. In the statement, the word साधु indicates the sense of असाधु—This is also called व्यतिरेकलक्षणा Indication in contrariety. BKB has given the illustration of this type from Kuvalayānada: "O messenger-maid! well-done, well-done, what more can be done than this?" The heroine in fact, desires to take her messenger-friend to task that she should not have kept amorous relations with the heroine's lover, the words spoken by her, however, are just reverse. hence व्यतिरेकलक्षणा.

(l) गौणीलक्षणा and गौणीवृत्ति :

When the indication is based on the relation of resemblance due to common attributes, it is called *gauṇi lakṣaṇā.* e.g. गौर्वाहीकः। Here the attributes of dullness and stupidity are common in गौः 'the bull' and the *vāhika.* As Mammaṭa has done in KP, BKB quotes a *kārikā* from Kumārila Bhaṭṭa defining *gauṇī vṛtti:* लक्ष्यमाणगुणैर्योगाद्वृत्तेरिष्टा तु गौणता। According to Kumārila, the process is to be called qualitative on account of the connection of the denotative sense i.e. the bull, with the qualities (of *vāhika)* which are being indicated. This *gauṇī vṛtti* is the same as *gauṇī* termed by Mammaṭa, AB and BKB.

A small point to be noted here is that in the interpretation of शोणो धावति, an example of *gauṇī lakṣaṇā,* BKB differs slightly from his *guru* AB, BKB states that in this sentence the word शोण indicates शोणगुणविशिष्टः अश्वः, i.e. गुणिन् 'a horse qualified by red colour', whereas AB. considers शोणो धावति। to be an ambiguous sentence: शोणो धावतीति प्रसिद्धोदाहरणं तून्नेयप्रकरणत्वेना-स्पष्टम्।[95] शोणो धावति is a famous example (of *lakṣaṇā)* but in various contexts, the word शोण may indicate more than one meanings so it is ambiguous. AB himself gives another example: ॐकारलिङ्गं रेवायां शोणैरर्च्यं दिनोदये। 'Early in the morning, the *liṅga* of Śaṅkara should be worshipped on the Reva with red'. Here शौणैः can mean 'red flowers' etc. as only they are used in worship.

While AB describes and illustrates various relationships between denotative and secondary sense on which *lakṣaṇā* is based both in KND and TRN in detail,[96] BKB mentions only one or two relations namely *guṇa-guṇi-bhāva* and avayava-*avayavī—bhāva*, illustrates them in brief and then skips over to the next topic without entering into details. In fact, he does not want to duplicate upon his teacher. He exemplifies how the words like नख, बाण, अश्व etc. indicate the guṇa 'attribute' in the form of *saṅkhyā* number. Thus नख meaning twenty, बाण five, अश्व–seven and so on. As an illustration of अवयव-अवयवी-सम्बन्ध 'part and whole relation' he has stated the line:

नंपूभाभजपूरिजंजरिजपूघातास्तिथिर्मेषभात्। which seems to be from some *jyotiṣa grantha.* The citation, however, cannot be traced out, but—नं means नन्दा i.e. प्रतिपदा, षष्ठी, एकादशी तिथि, पू-पूर्णा, भ-भद्रा i.e. द्वितीया, सप्तमी, द्वादशी; ज-जया i.e. तृतीया, पञ्चमी, अष्टमी and रि-रिक्ता i.e. चतुर्थी, नवमी, चतुर्दशी—Here occurrence of a part of the word indicates the complete word itself. Hence *lakṣaṇā* 'indication' by अवयव-अवयवीभाव.

(m) *lakṣaṇā* 'indication' in श्यालः स्वस्त्रोरथाग्रहीत्। (श्री०भा०पु० X, iv, 23) :

This line is quoted from Bhāgavata Purāṇa (BP), only after AB who has quoted it in TRN, as an example of साहचर्य, concommitance between the denotative and the indicative sense,. vide:

साहचर्यं च सम्बन्धः। 'श्यालः स्वस्त्रोरथाग्रहीत्' इत्यत्र स्वसा च स्वसा च स्वसारौ तयोः। अत्र द्वितीयस्वसृशब्देन तत्पतिर्लक्ष्यते यज्ञादिषु साहचर्यात्। एवं 'प्रथमयोः पूर्वसवर्णः' अत्र अपरेण प्रथमाशब्देन द्वितीया लक्ष्यते साहचर्यात्, शब्दस्य द्रव्यत्वाच्च।[97] BKB adds a detailed explanation how *lakṣaṇā* operates in the example; he also alludes from the commentary of Śrīdharaswāmin on the sentence, and elaborates the issue with a detailed explanation of the *pāṇinian sūtra* quoted by Śrīdharaswāmin. *Lakṣaṇā* employs thus in the word स्वस्त्रोः। It is a compound word; स्वसा च स्वसा च स्वसारौ। तयोः स्वस्त्रोः। This is an *ekaśeṣa* compound. Dual number is necessary in *ekaśeṣa*[98] compound; but the second word स्वसा is incompatible in the context. Kansa fell at the feet of his sister and the sister Devakī is only one. So the second word स्वसृ has to be taken in the sense of 'स्वसृपति', 'sister's husband' The relation between स्वसा the शक्यार्थ, 'denotative' and स्वसृपति the लक्ष्यार्थ the secondary sense is साहचर्य- 'constant association' between husband and wife. Thus the second word स्वसा would give the sense of Vasudeva by *lakṣaṇā*. It will not be out of place here to take note of Śrīdharaswāmi's commentary.

श्यालः कंसः। स्वस्त्रोरिति। स्वसृशब्देन द्विवचनानुपपत्त्या मिथुनगणनद्वारा मिथुनीलक्षणया स्वसृतत्पत्योरभिधानम्। लिङ्गसमवायन्यायेन प्राणभृतः उपदधातीतिवद्देवकीवसुदेवयोः प्रत्येकं पादमग्रहीदित्यर्थः। श्यालशब्देन वा कथंचिद्वसुदेवाभिधानम्।[99]

श्याल means the brother-in-low i.e. Kansa. In स्वस्त्रोः the word स्वसृ in dual number is incompatible as there is only one sister Devaki. This dual number indicates 'the sister and her husband', because in sacrificial rites etc. both are bound to be together. The meaning of the whole sentence is—'he (i.e. Kansa) held each foot of Devakī and Vasudeva as in प्राणभृत: उपदधाति' the sense is understood by *liṅgasamavāya*. The word श्याल helps to understand the sense of Vasudeva.

BKB elaborates the discussion further as he feels the need to clarify the matter with a detailed explanation of the *pāṇinian sūtra*. There is a *pāṇinian* dictum-तद्वानासामुपधानो मन्त्र इतीष्टकासु लुक् च मतोः। (P.iv,vi, 125) It is thus explained:

The affix यत् (य) comes in the *chhandas* (i.e. Vedic *mantras*) after a nominal stem, in the first case (i.e. nominative) in construction, ending with the affix मतुप् (मत्, वत् etc.), when the sense is—"This is their *mantra* of putting up," provided the things put up are bricks; and the affix मतुप् is elided by लुक्. Now in प्राणभृत उपदधाति। the present *sūtra* applies thus- The *mantra* with the word प्राणभृत्, is प्राणभृद्वान्, then the मतुप् is elided so it becomes प्राणभृत्, it is हलन्त–'consonant-ending' and it expresses the sense of *mantra* by अभिधा, the same word प्राणभृत्–denotative (वाचक) of 'a *mantra*' conveys the sense 'bricks' by *lakṣaṇā* 'indication'. The word उपदघाति means चिनोति 'collects'. It is not compatible with प्राणभृत् (=मन्त्र) because a *mantra* cannot be collected, but उपदधाति (meaning 'collects') becomes a लिङ्ग–an indicative sign for indication (=लक्षणा). And the sense of the sentence—'प्राणभृत: उपदधाति। will be 'he collects bricks (put up for sacrificial rites)'. Similarly, in 'श्याल: स्वस्रोरथा-ग्रहीत्।', the word श्याल acts as लिङ्ग 'indicator' and enables the word स्वस्रोः to indicate the sense—'the sister and her husband', by *lakṣaṇā*.

The grammarians do not accept indication in such cases as they consider them to be those of *ekaśeṣa* compound. It is stated: विरूपाणामपि समानार्थानाम्।[100] in continuation of the *sūtra*— सरूपाणामेकशेषे एकविभक्तौ।[101]; meaning thereby-the words with similar sense and with diverse forms are compounded in *ekaśeṣa* compound. On the strength of the *vārttika* विरूपाणामपि समानार्थानाम्। the words with different sense and with diverse forms also can form *ekaśeṣa* compound. The indicatory statement (ज्ञापक) for this is प्रथमयोः पूर्वसवर्णः।[102] Here प्रथमयोः-प्रथमा च द्वितीया च प्रथमे। तयोः। The latter word प्रथमा denotes the sense of द्वितीया by *ekaśeṣa*. Similarly, according to the grammarians, स्वस्रोः also is an *ekaśeṣa* compound: स्वसा च स्वसृपतिश्च स्वसारौ। तयोः स्वस्रोः। Therefore, as the grammarians say, indication is not required in श्यालः स्वस्रोरथाग्रहीत्।

BKB surprisingly, seems to be satisfied here merely with the mention of the grammarians' opinion. He avoids dispute. Nor does he give examples of each and every small type of *lakṣaṇā*. He avoids the duplication of such details upon his *guru* AB, who has already treated the subject in minute details in KND[103] and TRN[104] and has done full justice to the subject. It should, again be stated here despite the risk of repetition, that the prime interest of BKB lies in such subtle, elaborate explanations of the illustrations from grammatical point of view. He has, here, again, filled up a gap for *śāstraic* discussion, kept by his predecessors.

IV. ix *vyañjanā* 'Suggestion' :

(1) Definition :

Most of the poeticians accept *vyañjanā* as an independent function of the poetic word since it was elaborately established by Ānandavardhana and was strongly approved of by Abhinavagupta in his commentary Locana on Dhvanyāloka. Mammaṭa, a faithful disciple of Ānandavardhana, does not give us a general definition of *vyañjanā* applicable to both *lakṣaṇā-mūlā* and *abhidhāmūlā* but commences his treatment of it with *lakṣaṇā-mūlā vyañjanā*. cf:

यस्य प्रतीतिमाधातुं लक्षणा समुपास्यते।
फले शब्दैकगम्येऽत्र व्यञ्जनान्नापरा क्रिया॥[105]

"With reference to this fruit, for conveying the apprehension of which *lakṣaṇā* is resorted to, and which is understood from the word alone there is no other process than suggestion." But Āśādhara does the job both in KND and TRN:

cf : सङ्केतशक्यसम्बन्धविभिन्नसहकारिणी।
वाच्यलक्ष्यातिरिक्तार्थधीहेतुर्वृत्तिरञ्जना॥[106]

and this is simplified in TRN vide:

शक्यलक्ष्यातिरिक्तार्थबोधिकावृत्तिर्व्यञ्जना।[107]

Thus according to AB, the function by which a sense other than the denotative and the indicative is conveyed, is called *vyañjanā*. BKB almost repeats the definition of his *guru* with a slight modification: शक्यार्थालक्ष्यार्थातिरिक्तप्रकरणोपयोग्यन्यार्थबोधिका-वृत्तिर्व्यञ्जना। suggestion is such a function of the word, which conveys a sense other than the primary (denotative) and the secondary (indicative) ones, the sense, that is suitable to the context. He seems to emphasise that the suggestive sense (व्यङ्ग्यार्थ) is bound to occur in a specific context. The apparatuses employed in this process are different from those employed in *abhidhā* and *lakṣaṇā*.

BKB naturally does not see any requirement to elaborate upon the definition as volumes have been said thereon in Dhvanyāloka, KP, KND and TRN. He at once quotes Mammaṭa to define *abhidhāmūla vyañjanā* which is quite surprising. He had already quoted this definition during the discussion of polysemic words (अनेकार्थशब्द) and the process how they convey different senses. The author seems to be in search of some general definition of *vyañjanā* in support of his own view; and Mammaṭa's definition specifically applies to *abhidhāmūlā vyañjanā* alone! Is it a slip of pen on the part of the author? We have some ground to think so, because immediately after the quotation and its explanation follows the statement of threefold *vyañjanā!* and then again the author illustrates *śabdaśaktimūlā vyañjanā*.

It should be noted that unlike Mammaṭa, BKB starts with *śabdaśaktimūlā vyañjanā* which is based on *abhidhā*. Again, Mammaṭa expleins determinants of *abhidhā* in polysemic words (i.e. संयोग etc.) during the discussion of *abhidhāmūla-vyañjanā,*[108] whereas BKB, took up the topic while discussing the polysemicness (अनेकार्थत्व) of the word शास्त्र and had quite a long discursion, to plunge into detailed grammatical elaborations.

(2) Classification of *vyañjanā* :

vyañjanā is threefold: शब्दशक्तिमूला 'based on suggestion'.

In this classification also BKB follows AB verbatim. AB has classified *vyañjanā* thus in KND:

वाच्यमूला व्यञ्जनैषा लक्ष्यगा प्राक्प्रदर्शिता।
उदाहृतेषु दूरार्थभाने व्यङ्ग्यगतोप्यसौ।।[109]

"In the preceding examples *vācyārthamūlā vyañjanā* and *lakṣyārthamūlā vyañjanā* have been discussed. In such examples, where more than one sense are suggested, evenafter one suggested sense is conveyed, the *vyañjanā* is called *vyañjanāmūlā* or based on suggestion." In TRN AB states: तेन शक्तिमूला लक्षणामूला चेत्याहुः। दूरार्थबोधे व्यञ्जनामूलापि व्यञ्जना भवति।[110]

AB has also brought out the difference between *vyañjanā* and other two ıunctions viz. *abhidhā* and *lakṣaṇā:*

अस्त्रमन्त्रितबाणस्य वृत्तिवद्विविधार्थकृत्।
एषा शब्दगतैवार्थानाश्रित्यापि प्रवर्तते।।[111]

"As arrows empowered by *vāyavyāstra* etc. pierce various aims, the Word empowered by *vyañjanā* conveys a series of senses. It is basically the function of the word but it also employs resorting to the (denotative and indicative) senses". In other words *vyañjanā* can be either शाब्दी or आर्थी, while other functions resort to the word only. Mammaṭa's statement in KP: सर्वेषां प्रायशोऽर्थानां व्यञ्जकत्वमपीष्यते।[112] "All the threefold senses *vācya, lakṣya* and vyañgya are also suggestive." BKB does not define these three types of *vyañjanā* neither does he explain the difference between आर्थी and शाब्दी, to avoid duplication and unnecessary repetition. However, he illustrates all these types of *vyañjanā* and explains the illustrative verses at length.

(a) शब्दशक्तिमूला or अभिधामूला—Suggestion based on denotation. The definiton, as said above is quoted from KP.[113]

अनेकार्थस्य शब्दस्य वाचकत्वे नियन्त्रिते।
संयोगाद्यैरवाच्यार्थधीकृद्व्यापृतिरञ्जनम्॥

"When the expressive power of a word, which has more than one primary sense, is restricted to (one sense) by means of conjunction etc. the process which produces the apprehension of a sense that is not denoted, is suggestion."

Words like कर (hand, elephant's trunk, tax). वंश (family, bamboo) and सैन्धव (salt, horse) can denote more than one sense. They are polysemic (अनेकार्थ) words. When such a word is used in literature, circumstances like, conjunction (संयोग) restrict its sense to only one of the multi-senses it can express. Thus it can convey only this (one) sense by *abhidha*. But it often happens that evenafter this denotative *(abhidheya, vācya)* sense has been conveyed, apprehension of some other sense (which is only primary) of the same word occurs. This another sense, though ordinarily a *vācyārtha* of the word in question cannot is this specific context be regarded as denotative (i.e. conveyed by *abhidhā)* because *abhidhā* has been already controlled, so as to denote *vācyārtha* due to factors like conjunction and, *abhidhā* can be employed only once. Yet, another, different sense is definitely conveyed, by a particular context. This another sense cannot be considered to have been conveyed by *lakṣaṇā* because the three conditions मुख्यार्थबाध incompa-tibility of the primary sense etc. are not satisfied. It must be acknowledged, therefore, that the function which causes the apprehension of that other sense is *vyañjanā.* This sense is though really *vācyārtha,* not *vācyārtha* in the present context. This process is named *abhidhāmūlavyañjanā,* for, it does not occur unless *abhidhā* in the first place conveys the primary sense, and, moreover, the sense conveyed in the second stage is also based on *abhidhā.* AB defines शब्दशक्तिमूला व्यञ्जना afte tradition: प्रकृताप्रकृतश्लेषे शब्दशक्तिमूला व्यञ्जनेति प्राञ्चः।[114] When there are more than one sense, one being contextual and the other non-contextual and these are coveyed solely by the suggestive power of the word that is called *śabdaśaktimūlā vyañjanā* e.g.

आशाधरसमुत्पन्ना विमला बुद्धिशुद्धिदा।
कोविदानन्दसहजाऽनुग्राह्यैषा त्रिवेणिका।।[115]

This verse can be interpreted in three ways; It can be applied to the work Triveṇikā, to the girl named Triveṇikā and to the holy place Triveṇikā. The contextual sense is pertaining to the work Triveṇikā which has been created alongwith Kovidānand, from the pure heart of Āśādhara. It is faultless and will purify the intellect of the reader. Hence acceptable. The non-contextual sense is pertaining to Triveṇikā the daughter of Āśādhara, she is the sister of Kovidānand, she is innocent, pleasing and should be looked upon with favour. Here the resemblance between the book and the holy place Triveṇikā (Prayāga) is also suggested. The identification between the two is suggested by the power of the words. BKB's example of शब्दशक्तिमूला व्यञ्जना-तर्का रदा.....is quoted from Naiṣadhacaritam, known as a *śāstrakāvya.* The author explains both the meanings in detail.The contextual (प्रकृत) sense applies to Sarasvatī. The teeth in the mouth of Sarasvatī should be thought of as logical arguments, because without them, she cannot refute counter-arguments, and without them she would not be able to present the paper containing seven categories of the entities viz. सामान्य,

विशेष etc. with twentyfour attributes namely शब्द, रूप, रस, गन्ध, etc. The non-contextual (अप्रकृत) sense is pertaining to a person without teeth: One who is tooth-less will not be able to utter two letters *va* and *da* because *va* is dentolabial and *da* is dental. He cannot cut asunder a betel leaf and cut open a good betel nut. In this verse the teeth are fancied as arguments with which the mouth refutes counter-arguments just as, it, with those very teeth, chews betel leaf and cracks betel nuts. Both of these meanings depend upon the double meaning of the words वाद (=dispute, *va* and *da*) and पूगपत्र (a paper containing the list of entities, a piper betel with betel nut). The first meaning is restricted by the context, it is denotative. The second non-contextual sense is suggested by *vyañjanā* due to the power of words. Hence शब्दशक्तिमूला व्यञ्जना.

(b) लक्षणामूला व्यञ्जना–Suggestion based on indication.

Lakṣaṇāmūlā vyañjanā, suggestion based on indication is related to फलवती (=प्रयोजनवती) लक्षणा, 'indication with motive', wherein motive (फल) is suggested by *vyañjanā*. Both Āśādhara and BKB do not define *lakṣaṇāmūlā vyañjanā*. Mammaṭa's definiton and elaboration of *lakṣaṇāmūlā vyañjanā* is so well-known. Here the primary sense (वाच्यार्थ) is either given up or partially accepted. The secondary sense is accepted to suggest a specific purpose, which is more important. BKB's example of लक्षणामूला व्यञ्जना is quoted from KP and it is in *prākṛta*. The secondary (indicative) sense is understood by काकु 'intonation', 'tone' and श्रोतृवैशिष्ट्य the speciality of the listener. The direct-denotative sense of the sentence is not compatible to the context, because the heroine is offended by her friend's behaviour. The sense she intends to indicate by *lakṣaṇā* is "you have exerted enmity by flirting with my lover". Through this indicated sense she wants to suggest the serious guilt committed by the lover. Suggestion is based on indication here. Hence *lakṣaṇāmūlā vyañjanā*

(c) व्यञ्जनामूला व्यञ्जना– Suggestion based on suggestion.

When the suggested sense further becomes suggestive of another sense, i.e. *vyañjanā* conveys a number of senses in various contexts, due to varied causes, it is named as *vyañjanā-mūlā vyañjanā*. Mammaṭa calls it व्यङ्ग्यस्य व्यञ्जकत्वम्।[116] Again, it is defined neither by AB nor by BKB.

BKB again quotes the illustration *vyañjanāmūlā vyañjanā* from KP, which is in *prākṛta* the Sanskrit equivalent of which is not given in the text: it is given from KP :

विपरीतरमणे लक्ष्मी...........etc.

"In the alliance in reverse position, the amorously excited Lakṣmī. having seen Brahmā siting on the naval lotus of Viṣṇu, quickly shuts his (Viṣṇu's) right eye".

In this verse; the word Hari suggests that the sun is his right eye. When it is covered, there is sunset, hence, the lotus contracted. Consequently, Brahmā staying in that lotus, cannot see the sport of Lakṣmī and Hari and their free enjoyment of the sport is thus suggested. The suggestive sense is conveyed here step by step. hence व्यञ्जनामूला व्यञ्जना.

(3) Arguments in support of *vyañjanāvṛtti* :

Ānandavardhana who has established *dhvani* on solid grounds has logically refuted the arguments of the opposition (viz. the *mīmāṁsakas* and the *naiyāyikas)* who do not accept *dhvani-vyañjanā* as an independent function of the poetic word.[117]. Mammaṭa has referred to at least two different views of the *mīmāṁsakas,* and presented the arguments in support of *vyañjanā.*[118] AB states this *pūrvapakṣa* against *vyañjanāvṛtti* and also gives the refutation thereof both in KND and TRN. In KND, AB states:

अथाभिधा लक्षणा च वृत्तिरस्तु द्विधैव यत्।
आद्यायां वा द्वितीयायां व्यञ्जनान्तर्भविष्यति।।[119]

The *naiyāyikas* propound that only two functions of the

word, *abhidhā* and *lakṣaṇā* should be accepted because *vyañjanā* is included in either of the two.

> दीर्घादीधाभिधा व्यङ्ग्यानर्थान् बोधयितुं क्षमा।
> यत्परन्यायमाश्रित्य व्यङ्ग्यार्थस्यापि वाच्यता॥[120]

They say that just as an arrow extends its function to cutting armour, body and then takes away life, the word conveys all the senses including *vyaṅgyārtha* by *dīrgha-dīrghatara-abhidhā-vyāpāra*. These scholars follow the rule—यत्परः शब्दः सः शब्दार्थः। Whatever sense is intended to be conveyed by a word, that sense, is the meaning of that word. Thus the suggested sense (व्यङ्ग्यार्थ) is also *abhidhā-vyāpāra-vācya* i.e. conveyed by denotation only. Thus *vyañjanā* should be included in *abhidhā*. It may be included in *lakṣasṇā* either:

> अथवा लक्षणा व्यङ्ग्यं प्रत्याययतु केवला।
> उभे वा स्वस्वविषये न शक्यं कोविदैरिदम्॥[121]

These scholars even say that if *abhidhā* is not capable of conveying this *vyaṅgyārtha, lakṣaṇā* can be resorted to. Sometimes both these functions collectively serve the purpose, i.e. convey the intended meaning. Hence *vyañjanā* is not to be postulated.

AB presents the refutation of these arguments and the justification of *vyañjanā* both in KND and TRN:

(1) There is a universal rule: सकृदुच्चरितः शब्दः सकृदर्थं गमयति। A word uttered once conveys only one meaning, because word, intellect and action never function again once having taken a pause. (शब्दबुद्धिकर्मणां विरम्य व्यापाराभावात्।) According to this rule, *abhidhā* stops functioning having once denoted the *vācyārtha,* the denotative sense. It cannot function any further to convey the *vyaṅgyārtha,* the suggestive sense.

(2) A word cannot convey infinite sense. Eventhough we

believe that the intended meaning itself is the real sense of the word, it is not proved that only *vācyārtha* is intended. The purport of the speaker may be the suggestive sense. The actual meaning of the Mīmāṁsaka statement यत्पर: शब्द: स: शब्दार्थ:। is this: Any *vidhivākya,* statement of injunction, conveys only that sense which is not denoted by the former statements so *vidhi* statements must be understood only in that meaning, which is intended in the utterance of those statements. Otherwise, there will be पुनरुक्तिदोष (fault of repetition) in most of the cases of *vidhi* statements.

(3) There is an order between the denotative and the suggestive sense. At first, *abhidhā* denotes the *vācyārtha,* then, if it is incompatible, *lakṣaṇā* indicates the *lakṣyārtha,* the *vyanjanā* functions in the last stage. Thus, there is a consecutive order in the apprehension of all the three meanings. Therefore, it is not possible to include *vyañjanā* in the former functions of the word.

(4) Both *abhidhā* and *vyañjanā* are quite distinct from each other because—

(a) *abhidhā* conveys a non-striking sense while *vyañjanā* produces striking cognition of sense; (b) *abhidhā* depends on words only, while *vyañjanā* conveys the mea-ning through *pada, padāṁśa,* affixes, letters, sentences, the sense of word-may it be denotative or indicative or suggestive, etc.; (c) *abhidhā* conveys only one meaning while *vyañjanā* brings out a multitude of meaning: (d) The denotative sense is realised by all, while the suggestive sense is understood only by those connoisseurs who have clear intellect (प्रतिभान).

(5) *vyañjanā* cannot be included in *lakṣaṇā* either, as *lakṣaṇā* indicates only one meaning necessarily connected with the denotative sense, whereas *vyañjanā* suggests multiple meanings, and all together.

(6) *vyañjanā* cannot be included in inference as Mahīma Bhaṭṭa propounds. The reason is this : inference employs only in such cases where there is *vyāptisambandha*-inherent relation between *hetu* 'cause' and *sādhya,* 'the major term' (thing to be proved). There is no inherent relation between the denotative word (*vacāka śabda*) and the suggestive meaning *(vyaṅgyārtha)*. Thus *vyañjanā* is completely a different and independent function of the word.[122]

BKB simply summarises the whole discussion with a few additional arguments. Here are the arguments added by BKB, of course, after Ānandavardhana and Mammaṭa.

(1) Mammaṭa has enumerated ten thousand four hundered and fiftyfive types of *dhvani*. These many types cannot occur unless *vyañjanāvṛtti* is postulated.

(2) फलवती लक्षणा–indication with purpose will not be admissible without *vyañjanā* as the congnition of the purpose is not obtained without *vyañjanā*. This फल-purpose is not cognised through *abhidhā* owing to the lack of *saṅketa* 'convention'. It cannot be conveyed through *lakṣaṇā* because all the three conditions of *lakṣaṇā* are not fulfilled and there will occur the contingency of अनवस्था infinity of फल 'fruit' and *lakṣaṇā* both in understanding it through *lakṣaṇā*. Even विशिष्टलक्षणा, indication qualified by that purpose, does not function to convey this फल because the purposc and the object—the content of the cognition cannot be cognised simultaneously. All this is discussed in detail in KP[123].

(3) The manifestation of *rasa* is proved by the experience of the connoisseurs, from poetry, drama and other literary works. Which function of the poetic word conveys this *rasa?* It is not *abhidhā* as there is absence of *saṅketa*. The words *vibhāvādi* denote only the primary sense of the word. Besides, the expression of *vibhāvādi* is not the expression of *rasas,* as *rasa* is altogether different from *vibhāvādi*. If we postulate that *rasa* is denoted, expressed

by the expressive words *rasādi,* then there would occur *rasadoṣa, a blemish of rasa,* vide:

व्यभिचारिरसस्थायिभावानां शब्दवाच्यता।
अनङ्गस्याभिधानं च रसे दोषास्युरीदृशाः॥[124]

Thus, for the cognition of *rasa* etc. the *vyañjanā* must be accepted.

(4) Again, the scheme of threefold poetry, being best (उत्तम), mediocre (मध्यम) and low (अधम) will not be possible because the superiority of the suggested sense (i.e. व्यङ्ग्यार्थ) is the base of such scheme and the suggested sense is conveyed through *vyañjanā* only.[125]

(5) BKB elaborates how *vyañjanā* cannot be included in inference in some more detail while explaining the illustrative verse—निःशेषच्युतचन्दनम्.....etc. The process of inference invariably requires ऐकान्तिक हेतु, exclusive cause which is inherently connected with साध्य, the major term. For example धूमवत्त्व is invariably related to अग्निमत्त्व. In the premise, निःशेषच्युतः..........etc. the causes चन्दनच्यवन etc. also are not exclusively connected with dalliance only, they may occur due to bath etc. They are अनैकान्तिक multi-pronged, which cannot, lead to correct inference. We cannot, therefore, accept inference in such cases as निःशेषच्युत..........etc. The discussion on the verse is taken almost verbatim from Rasavilāsa. cf. निःशेषच्युतचन्दनमित्यत्र स्नानसाधारण्येन निबद्धानाम् विशेषणानामाभासत्वेन नानुमापकत्वम्। अपि तु व्यञ्जकत्वमेव। तदन्तिके रन्तुं गतासीति नानुमानम्, किञ्चानुमाने परार्थमेव स्यात्, शब्दरूपत्वात्। तत्र च साध्यसाधननिर्देशः। न चात्र तथा, साध्याद्यनुपादानात्।[126] BKB also explains how inference cannot be accepted in भ्रम धार्मिक......etc. The cause for *vyāpti,* invariable concomitance of the middle term (हेतु) with the major (साध्य), must not be faulty. Though the

sage (in the present verse) is a coward, he may wander in the forest on the river-bank by the order of his *guru*. or the king, or the master, or due to his strong love for his beloved. It is also possible that one may not be afraid of a lion due to his valour though he is frightened by a dog! So, सिंहवत्त्व, the lion being there, a faulty cause, a दुष्टहेतु, cannot lead to the inference of भ्रमणाभाव, non-wandering cannot be cognised by inference, *vyañjanā* must be resorted to for such cognition. Suggestion, as an independent function of a word, must be accepted thus.

(4) Distinction between the *vācyārtha* and the *vyaṅgyārtha* :

BKB points out the distinction between the denotative and the suggestive sense where he again follows Ānandavardhana,[127] Mammaṭa[128] and Āśādhara.[129]

(i) **बोधभेद-Distinciton of apprehension:**—The denotative sense (वाच्यार्थ) is comprehended by those who have the knowledge of denotation, whereas the suggestive sense (व्यङ्ग्यार्थ) is understood by the connoisseurs (सहृदय).

(ii) **स्वरूपभेद-Difference of nature:**—The *abhidhā* may denote a negative sense, while the *vyañjanā* may suggest affirmative sense.

(iii) **संख्याभेद-Distinction of number:**—The denotative sense is only one. whereas the suggestive sense appears to be varied pertaining to each of the characters (i.e. listeners) etc.

(iv) **निमित्तभेद-Distinction of cause:**—The denotative sense is cognised at the very utterance of the word; while the suggested sense is realised by the clearness of intellect.

(v) **कार्यभेद-Distinction of effect:**—The denotative sense brings about simple cognition, the suggestive sense brings about a specific cognition which causes excellence of charm.

(vi) **प्रतीतिभेद:-Distinction of cognition:**—*vācyārtha* gives cognition while *vyaṅgyārtha* gives striking cognition.

(vii) **कालभेद-Distinction of time:**—The denotative sense is cognised first, the suggestive sense is cognised afterwards.

(viii) **आश्रयभेद-Distinction of resort:**—The denotation resorts to the words only, while the suggestion resort to a *pada,* its part, its meaning, the sentence and so on.

May it be added here that the denotative sense is meant for one listener and the suggestive sense may be meant for some other person. In the verse—कस्य न वा स्यात् रोषो.......etc. the denotative sense is for the heroine, while the suggestive meaning—'the lower lip is not bitten by the paramour but it is the bite of the bee in the lotus'-is suggested for the husband.

Such distinction leads to the conclusion that *vyañjanā,* suggestion must be accepted as an independent function of the poetic word. It is not, and cannot be included either in *abhidhā* or *lakṣaṇā,* or in inference.

(5) Nature of *rasa* :

Āśādhara has not touched the topic of *rasa* either in KND or in TRN. BKB who has written a fresh commentary on Bhānudatta's Rasataraṅgiṇī[130] states that the relish of *rasa* provides a sound footing for accepting *vyañjanā.* He cannot resist the temptation of treating though in brief, the topic of *rasa,* which has captured the attention of many scholars. As *rasa* is vyañgya, the cognition of *rasa* is attained through *vyañjanā* only, BKB incidentally describes the nature of *rasa.* He naturally quotes two *kārikās* from KP, describes the nature of *rasānubhūti,* 'relish of *rasa'* following the terminology used by Jagannātha in Rasagaṅgādhara and also enumerates the number or *rasas, sthāyibhāvas* and *vyabhicāribhāvas* citing from the Nāṭyaśāstra.

In a poetic or dramatic work, the characters like Sītā etc. are depicted with their specific details; but owing to the poetic genius they are cognised in a generalised form by the connoisseurs with clear intellect. The sentience of the connoisseurs involved in the process of this experience is demarcated by their own *rati* etc. because the whole import (विभावादि) is taken by them in a generalised form. The connoisseurs experience these emotions irrespective of any specific time, place or situation. this sentience (संविद्) of the connoisseurs becomes free from all such obstructions, and shines forth in the form of bliss. It dawns in the form of pure delight. It arises by the power of *vibhāvādi* but it is distinct from *vibhāvādi*. It is *rasa*.

Or in other words, the sentience demarcated by *rati* etc. is *rasa*. The nature of *rasa* is described by BKB after Abhinavagupta and Mammaṭa as quoted in Rasagaṅgādhara, cf. इत्थं चाभिनवगुप्तमम्मटभट्टादिग्रन्थस्वारस्येन भग्नावरणचिद्विशिष्टो रत्यादिः स्थायीभावो रस इति स्थितम्। वस्तुतस्तु वक्ष्यमाणश्रुतिस्वारस्येन रत्याद्यवच्छिन्ना भग्नावरणा चिदेव रसः।[131] To simplify, we can say, in the रसपदार्थ, there are two components viz. रत्यादि स्थायीभाव and चित्. Between these two, which is विशेषण qualifier and which is विशेष्य qualified, that may be the question of difference of opinion. Both the ways *rasa* is, विभावादिचर्वणावधि i.e. relish of *rasa* remains till the enjoyment of *vibhāvādi* remains.

Having described the nature of *rasa* thus, BKB incidentally, touches the issue of *śāntarasa*, of course, again, after Jagannātha. He has quoted the whole portion from Rasagaṅgādhara :

शान्तस्य शमसाध्यत्वान्नटे च तदसंभवात्।
अष्टावेव रसा नाट्ये न शान्तस्तत्र युज्यते॥

इत्याहुः। तच्चापरे न क्षमते। तथा हि-नटे शमाभावादिति हेतु-रसंगतः नटे रसाभिव्यक्तेरस्वीकारात्।[132]

Though Abhinavagupta established *śānta* as the ninth *rasa* on solid ground, some poeticians do not accept it, saying that *śāntarasa* is effected from *śama* and *śama* cannot be there in the *naṭa,* 'actor'. So in drama at least, only eight *rasas* should be accepted. *śānta* is not suitable in drama. This view, BKB states, does not seem to be admissible, this argument against *śāntarasa* is not justified. The reason is-as they say, *śama* cannot reside in *naṭa* but in fact, *rasa* is never manifested in *naṭa,* actor, it is not cognised or experienced by the actor. It is cognised by the connoisseur. The relish of *rasa* is associated with the connoisseur. Thus, *śama* may be intensified in *śāntarasa* that is the experience of the connoisseur.

BKB, then, enumerates nine *rasas, sthāyībhāvas* and thirty three *vyabhicāribhāvas* according to Bharata Nātyaśāstra. He names *rasa* as *asaṅlakṣyakramavyaṅgya dhvani,* a single type of *dhvani* in which Ānandavardhana includes the whole *rasa-prapañca.* vide

असंलक्ष्यक्रमोद्द्योतः क्रमेण द्योतितः परः।
विवक्षिताभिधेयस्य ध्वनेरात्मा द्विधा मतः॥
रसभावतदाभासतत्प्रशान्त्यादिरक्रमः।
ध्वनेरात्माङ्गिभावेन भासमानो व्यवस्थितः॥[133]

The author also brings out the distinction between *sthāyibhāva* and *rasa:* when the *rati* etc. are in a premature stage, they are called the *sthāyibhāva* and in a fully developed stage, they are called *rasas*. he also quotes the Bharata *Sūtra:* "From the combination of the *vibhāvas,* the *anubhāvas* and the *vyabhicāribhāvas rasa* arises." In real life, they are called कारण-कार्य-सहकारी, causes, effects and associative emotions. Bharata has named them as *vibhāvādi* in order to establish the transcendental nature of *rasa* in poetry.

Here, the clear mention of Nūtanatarī, the author's commentary on Bhānudatt's Rasataraṅgiṇī provides an important source for the documentation of BKB's personal details.[134]

(6) Examples of three types of poetry :

One of the arguments in support of *vyañjanā* was that the

scheme of three types of poetry would not be justified without it. BKB, gives definitions and illustrates these three kinds of poetry and explains each exemplary verse in detail.

(a) **ध्वनिकाव्य–The best poetry:**–कियत्त्यजन्नोदन.......This verse is quoted from Naiṣadhacaritam. The enquiry of a youth who has come as the bride groom's companion towards a young lady is suggested here. Under the pretext of his movement in the rice served in the plate, the youth enquires whether that young lady would come to see him, or he would have to go for a secret meeting. Her gesture of lowering the face under the pretext of shyness is suggestive of her reply. Thus *vyaṅgyārtha* is conveyed by the movements (चेष्टा) of the characters. BKB has quoted the famous verse निःशेषच्युत..........etc. also.

(b) **मध्यमकाव्य–Mediocre poetry:**–As defined by Mammaṭa, 'when the expressed sense surpasses the suggested meaning, the poem is of the mediocre type.' The example is from *prākṛta*—अम्ब गड्डुद्वयं मे..........etc. There is a dialogue between an adolescent girl and her mother. The implied (=*vyaṅgya)* sense is this: "You are unknown to youth now: so there is no agony but when you will experience young age, it will be there." The denotative sense here is "one who sees feels agony." In comparison to the suggestive one, it is more charming because of असङ्गति figure of speech in it. असङ्गति is defined in KP as follows :

भिन्नदेशतयात्यन्तं कार्यकारणभूतयोः।
युगपद् धर्मयोर्यत्र ख्यातिः सा स्यादसङ्गतिः॥[135]

"Where the two properties that are related to eachother as effect and cause, are presented as simultaneously residing in totally different places, that would be *asaṅgati*' incongruity', "In the verse अम्ब गड्डुद्वयं मे.........etc. the wound and the pain, the properties related as cause and effect, are described as residing in different places, the wound-the cause-in the girl's body and the pain-the effect-with the seer. Hence *asaṅgati* figure of speech, which creates charm in the verse. It is the *vācyārtha,* the denotative sense. The suggestive sense is not so charming as compared to the denotative one. Hence मध्यमकाव्य or गुणीभूतव्यङ्ग्य, the mediocre poem.

(c) **अधम (अवर) काव्य–The lowest type of poetry:** –Again, the definition and its explanation both are quoted from KP. The lowest poem is void of a distinct suggested sense. It is possessed of the excellences and figures of speech (अलङ्कार). The example is साटोपव्योम.........etc. This is the eulogy of the sun. The verse contains ओजस् गुण and both शब्दालङ्कार, i.e. वर्णानुप्रास and अर्थालङ्कार i.e. श्लिष्टरूपक. BKB gives a detailed and complete explanation of this verbous verse, in a commentary style. He refers to a certain judiciary system for detecting a thief. The person who is alleged of theft, is forced to draw out a serpent placed into a pot. If he is bitten by that serpent, the allegation against him is proved, and if he is not, he will be set free being innocent. This tradition is reflected in the metaphor used in the verse. The night is a merchant lady. The stars are her pearl-necklace. The sun is alleged of its theft. He wants to clear himself off the allegation. So he draws out the black serpent in the form of a series of black bees from the pot in the form of lotus, with his hands in the form of rays. It is a paranomastic metaphor, metaphor based on pun. The diction in the verse has ओजस् गुण. so it is an example of चित्रकाव्य. Another example—नयनरथचक्रमित्रम्........etc. of चित्रकाव्य contains यथासंख्य अलङ्कार which is defined as : यथासंख्यं क्रमेणैव क्रमिकाणां समन्वयः।[136] "यथासंख्य–Repective order is the connection in the same order of objects which are stated in some order." नयन-रथचक्र-मित्र, रूप-आहार-ध्वज, पद-अम्बर-गात्र

and हरि-हर-मदन—all these four groups of words are connected in order. The poet, however, desires to praise the beauty of the lady. The verse could not be traced out. It seems to be BKB's own creation. The author again, gives elarborate explanation of the same. Hari-Viṣṇu, Hara-Śiva and Madana-Kāmadeva are disputing among themselves on seeing the moon-like face of the beautiful lady. Viṣṇu claims that it is his left eye. Śiva claims that it is his chariot-wheel, Kāma says it is his friend. Thus the words, मुख, नयन-रथचक्र-मित्र and हरि-हर-मदन are connected in respective order. Again नयन-it is like fish (मीन). Viṣṇu claims that it is his own form-रूप in मत्स्यावतार-fish incarnation. Hara claims that it is his prey because he had taken the form of a hunter to chase Brahmā in the form of a deer as thus is described in शिवमहिम्नःस्तोत्रम् cf. :

प्रजानाथं नाथ! प्रसभमभिकं स्वाम् दुहितरम्
गतं रोहिद्भूतां रिरमयिषुमृष्यस्य वपुषा।
धनुष्पाणेर्यातं दिवमपि सपत्राकृतममुं
त्रसन्तं तेऽद्यापि त्यजति न मृगव्याधरभसः॥[137]

"O lord! Brahmā reached heaven in the form of a deer for an amorous sport with his own daughter in the form of a she-deer. You intended to teach him a lesson. You chase him to heaven, aimed an arrow at him, shot it. O Śiva! even today you do not release him who is frightened." The reference here actually, is, that of *mṛgaśirṣa* and *vyādha* constellation in the sky. Again, Kāma who is known as मकरध्वज, insists that the fish-like eye of the lady is his flag-staff as it is like fish. then the word-उदर—belly. It is as deep as the sky. Viṣṇu crossed the sky in a single step in his वामन-अवतार. So this belly, deep as the sky is his step. Śiva thinks it is his garment because he is called *digambara* 'whose garments are the sky'. Kāma claims that this belly is his limb, because he is अनङ्ग, सूक्ष्माङ्ग, having a very subtle body. BKB quotes from a number of classical literary works like Anagharāghava, Śiva-mahimnaḥ stotra and Naiṣadhacaritam to support his interpretation of the verse. The meaning involves many ellipses to be supplied. The comprehension of the verse becomes more difficult, because a number of mythological references are also involved. This elaborate verse does not contain any charming distinct suggestive meaning. Hence it is the example of the lowest type of poetry.

(7) Threefold suggested Meaning (त्रिविधव्यङ्ग्यार्थ) :

BKB describes three kinds of suggested meaning again after Mammaṭa. Sometimes the suggested meaning is concealed (गूढ), sometimes it is unconcealed (अगूढ) and sometimes it is partly concealed (गूढागूढ). He does not give the examples of all the three for the fear of expansion. Mammaṭa has, however, exemplified the first two, viz. गूढ[138] and अगूढ[139]. BKB quotes a famous verse to explain गूढागूढ—partially concealed suggested meaning.

"Not very obvious like the breasts of an Āndhra woman, not very concealed like the breasts of a woman from Gujarat, the meaning of words in the poems shines forth when partly covered and partly obvious like the breasts of a Marāṭhā woman.

(8) (a) Suggestion based on Meaning (अर्थनिष्ठा व्यञ्जना) :

आर्थी or अर्थनिष्ठा व्यञ्जना occurs in all those of suggestion, where the peculiar conditions, which are the foundations of शाब्दी व्यञ्जना are not present. अभिधामूलव्यञ्जना or शाब्दी व्यञ्जना requires the use of polysemic (अनेकार्थ) word, whereas आर्थी व्यञ्जना is based on the denotative meaning, it does not require the polysemic (अनेकार्थ) word. In the stanza-निः शेषच्युतचन्दनं स्तनतटं .....etc. the suggestive meaning shines forth from the denotative meaning. Therefore, it is an example of आर्थी व्यञ्जना which employs in specific sutuations, contexts or circumstances. These circums-tances are enumerated in a couple of stanzas by Mammaṭa,[140] which are quoted by BKB. These *kārikās* contain a definition of suggestion based on sense. The function of sense, which owing to the speciality of the speaker etc., causes to persons possessing poetic genieus, the apprehension of another sense is nothing but suggestion. These circumstances are: वक्तृवैशिष्ट्य speciality of the speaker, the speciality of the person addressed, modulation of voice, the proximity of some other sentence or expressed sense, the context, the place, the time and so on. BKB does not give illustrations for each of these. But he quotes a verse from the Naiṣadhacaritam which contains the speciality of the speaker, the person addressed and the intonation (काकु). In this stanza, Sarasvatī gives the introduction of all the four gods namely Indra, Agni, Yama and Varuṇa to Damayantī. The meaning of the verse applies to each of the four gods, in which case, the general construction of it would be like this:

"Wise maid! why do you not conclude this divine being to be Nala? Nor choose him as your consort? Certain it is, he is not the real Nala. It would be an overwhelming loss to you if you don't accept him; who else will be your spouse?"

The speaker of this verse is Sarasvatī, she is describing Nala before Damayantī, using such words as would be applicable to all the four gods, who are present in the guise of Nala. the expressive sense is limited to Nala by context, but by the speciality of the speaker (i.e. Sarasvatī), of the listener Damayantī (who is a *vidusī*) and of the tone, other senses pertaining to other gods also are suggested.

(b) Another example of शब्दशक्तिमूलाव्यञ्जना–suggestion based on the power of the word: – (सत्त्यासक्तमना: etc.)

BKB now quotes his own verse as an example of शब्दशक्ति-मूला व्यञ्जना; as Āśādhara has done in Triveṇikā[141] The verse सत्त्यासक्तमना: etc. contains at least five suggestive meanings due to the power of polysemic (अनेकार्थ) words. These meanings are applicable to Brahmā, Viṣṇu, Śiva, the sea and a brahmin named Gaṅgādhara. BKB elaborates all the senses in minute detail. His creative genius is also expressed here. The denotative sense of the verse is as follws:

"May that glorious Gaṅgādhara protect us, Gaṅgādhara, whose mind is attached to Satī, whose body is adorned with ashes, the lord of the senses, omniscient, whose body is adorned with the moon, endowed with *yogamāyā,* knower of the *vṛttis,* blissful, fulfiller of the wishes, giver of joy to good people, possessing innumerable eyes, engrossed in the worship of *brahman."*

Sense pertaining to Śiva: गङ्गाधर means one who holds the Gaṅgā. In Amarakośa word गङ्गाधर is given as a synonym to अन्धकरिपु i.e. Śiva. 'May Śiva protect us. The rest of the words are the qualifiers of Śiva. सत्यासक्तमनाः सती–the daughter of दक्ष. She was born as पार्वती in the second birth. Such is the well-known *purāṇa* story. Śiva is ever-attached to Satī. भूत्याविभूषिततनुः Śiva applies भस्म ashes on his body. गवामीश्वरः गो–विद्या i.e. learning. Śiva is described as the lord of all the branches of learning. BKB quotes ईशानः सर्वविद्यानाम्। from Taittirīya Āraṇyaka. Or गवाम्-दिशाम् रक्षिता—The protector of all the directions. Or Śiva is thought to be having five faces. So he has fifteen eyes with three on each. The word गो in neuter gender denotes the sense of 'eye'. सर्वज्ञः–omniscient. द्विजराज-राजितवपुः–Śiva holds the moon on his twisted hair, so looks beautiful. मायान्वितः–Śiva is always accompanied by Pārvatī, the *yogamāyā* incarnate. He is called अर्धनारीनटेश्वर, वृत्तिवित्-Śiva is a *yogin.* He is capable of knowing each and every thought and desire of beings. आनंदीप्सितपूरकः नन्दी is Śiva's carrier. He satisfies his desires. सुमनसाम् आनन्ददः–He gives joy to the gods by fulfilling their desires, by destroying demons. अनन्तदृक्– Ananta is the other name of the serpent Śeṣa=Śiva is said to be the worshipper of Viṣṇu who rests upon *śeṣa*. Therefore, he always sees him, i.e. *śeṣa* the bed of Viṣṇu. ब्रह्मोपासन–तत्परः–Śiva is ever-engrossed in the meditation of *brahman,* the supreme. qualified by all these qualifiers, Śiva, may protect us. Such is the prayer.

Sense pertaining to Viṣṇu-The Gaṅgā is said to have emerged from the feet of Viṣṇu in the *purāṇas*. Thus Viṣṇu holds the Gaṅgā. Hence गङ्गाधर, भगवान्–possessed of a variety of affluences. सत्यासक्तमनाः–whose mind is attached to Satyā i.e. Satyabhāmā because Kṛṣṇa is Viṣṇu himself. भूत्याविभूषिततनुः–whose body is adorned with riches. गवाम् ईश्वरः-controller of the cows. सर्वज्ञः–Omniscient. It is said in Muṇḍakopniṣad that he knows everything. द्विजराजराजितवपुः–The left eye of Viṣṇu is the moon itself. So his body is adorned with the moon. BKB quotes the description of the moonrise from BP:

तदोडुराजः ककुभः करैर्मुखं
प्राच्या विलिम्पन्नरुणेन शन्तमैः।
स चर्षणीनामुदगाच्छुचो मृजन्
प्रियः प्रियाया इव दीर्घदर्शनः॥[142]

"Then, the moon, the king of constellations smeared saffron on the face of the east by his hand-rays, as if a lover wished to please his beloved. The moon thus removed not only her pain but also the torment af all the creatures, the torment which has been increased due to the sun-rays in the autumn." This moon-rise is described to be the result of Lord Kṛiṣṇa's will. Thus the adjective द्विजराजराजितवपुः for Viṣṇu is suitable. मायान्वितः-Accompanied by Yogamāyā. In BP Viṣṇu is described thus:

भगवानपि ता रात्रीः शरदोत्फुल्लमल्लिकाः।
वीक्ष्य रन्तुं मनश्चक्रे योगमायामुपाश्रितः॥[143]

"On observing those nights with blossomed and fragrant flowers of *mallikā* in autumn, god, accompanied by *yogamāyā* determined to perform *rāsakrīdā.*" The adjective 'accompanied by *yogamāyā,* used for Kṛṣna here justifies the same for Viṣṇu. वृत्तिवत्-knower of the feelings of cowherdesses. Kṛṣna knew the inner feelings of the sixteen thousand princesses held in prison by Bhaumāsura at the time of marrying them. आनन्दी-Blissful. *Śruti* says that bliss is the nature of *brahman* and *viṣṇu* is *brahman* itself. ईप्सितपूरकः-Viṣṇu fulfils the desires of his devotees or the cowheredesses. सुमनसाम् आनन्ददः-He gives joy to those who are pure-minded. अनन्तदृक्-Viṣṇu with innumerable eyes because the supreme man परमपुरुष is described as सहस्राक्षः सहस्रपात्। He has thousand eyes and thousand feet.[144] ब्रह्मोपासनतत्परः- engrossed in the study of the Vedas. The word गङ्गाधर in the sense of Viṣṇu is यौगिक-etymological.

Sense pertaining to Brahmā:

All these qualifiers apply to Brahmā also. सत्यासक्तमनाः-His mind is attached to *śruti* and *smṛti*. vide:

त्र्यायुषञ्जमदग्नेः कश्यपस्य त्र्यायुषम्।
यद्येवेषुत्र्यायुषन्तन्नोऽस्तु त्र्यायुषम्॥[145]

"Three lives i.e. *sthūla, sukṣma* and *kāraṇa* which were attained by Jamadagni, Kaśyapa and the gods, may be attained by us!" and धार्यं भस्म etc....... Both the verses are quoted by BKB in support. गवाम् ईश्वरः—brahmā gives the fruits of sacrifices. BKB quotes a verse from the Bhagavadgitā which states that Brahmā created people alongwith these sacrifices and ordered them to multiply and to fulfil their desires by performing those sacrifices.

Incidentally, here BKB discusses about the reading

प्रसविष्यध्वम् in the stanza,[146] which is grammatically unjustified in his opinion. The discussion again reveals his *śāstraic and* grammatical approcah. he also cites a similar example from the BP where the reading प्राचीनमूलेषु is traditionally accepted in place of प्राचीनतूलेषु, which is justified even in view of Śrīdhara-swāmin's commentary upon it. This reading is also supported by Dharmaśāstra. BKB here plunges into a detailed description of Dharmaśāstra rituals which reveals his versatility and acumen. गवाम् ईश्वर:–Brahmā is the originator of the Vedas in the form of Sarasvatī. सर्वज्ञ:–Being the creator of the world, he knows everything about it. द्विजराजराजितवपु:–His body is adorned with austerities since *brahmaloka* is full of austerities, मायान्वित:–He (Brahmā is associated with *māyā* composed of *rajoguṇa* and is the creator of the universe. वृत्तिवित्–he knows the behaviour of the people. आनन्दी–He gives joy because he fulfils the desires of gods. अनन्तदृक्–He observes the infinite universes as the creator of them. ब्रह्मोपासनतत्पर:–He is always engrossed in the meditation of the supreme *brahman* through *prāṇāyāma*. Thus all the qualifiers apply to Brahmā also.

The sense pertaining to the ocean :

The word गङ्गाधर denotes the sense 'ocean' by etymology. All the other adjectives will qualify 'the ocean' also, thus: सत्यासक्तमना:–whose mind is engrossed in सत्य i.e. observing the boundaries. The ocean always observes its limits. भूत्याविभूषिततनु:–The ocean is adorned with the wealth of jewels, pearls etc. and so it is called रत्नाकर, the treasure of jewels. गवामीश्वर:– The lord of waters. सर्वज्ञ:–The ocean knows the dual forms of all the rivers. द्विजराजराजितवपु:–Shining with the moon, the ocean's son because the moon emerged from the ocean, when the gods and denons chrned it for wealth. मायान्वित:–मा means *lakṣmī* याति–acquires. Viṣṇu acquires Lakṣmī. The ocean is associated with Viṣṇu because he has his bed in the ocean. वृत्तिवित्–The ocean obeys the orders of his lord, knowing his attitudes. आनन्दी–joyful at the moon-rise. सुमनसां ईप्सितपूरकः–The ocean fulfils the desires of the sea-travellers who are expert in trade. So he gives them joy. अनन्तदृक्–The ocean sees the great serpent *śeṣa* or *ananta* who has formed himself into the coach of Viṣṇu. ब्रह्मोपासनतत्परः–The ocean is engaged as an escort to Brahmā, the creator. and again that Lord is with *nārāyaṇa,* Viṣṇu, *bhaga* who is everpresent in the ocean.

The sense pertaining to the brahmin named Gaṅgādhara Śāstrī: BKB has mentioned the name of Gaṅgādhara in the concluding verse[147] also. He may be some contemporary scholar for whom he cherished great honour, due to his scholarship and acumen. Thus the word Gaṅgādhara is a special noun, given by the guardians. The other qualifiers are explained thus: सत्या०......His mind is attached to speaking the truth. भूत्या०. ....He might be rich due to his scholarship and his esteem in the rich. Or, as a brahmin, he applied *bhasman* to his body. गवा० he must be the master of speech, an excellent orator, as he was well-versed in scriptures, he was called Bṛhaspati incarnate. सर्वज्ञः–He was versatile, having knowledge of all the *śāstras,* religious practices of castes and stages. द्विजराज०.....He was the king of Brahmins and had a luminous body. मायान्वितः–he was adjoined by auspicious rituals and prosperity. वृत्तिवित्–He had the knowledge of five *vṛttis* namely *kṛt, taddhita, samāsa, ekaśeṣa* and *sanādyanta dhātu*, or three *vṛttis* named *abhidhā. lakṣaṇā* and *vyañjanā,* the three functions of words. आनन्दी–joyful by nature. सुमनसाम् ईप्सितपूरकः–He fulfilled the desires of the learned and gave them joy. अनन्तदृक्........His knowledge was endless, or he visualised the infinite *brahman.* ब्रह्मोपासनतत्परः–He was always engrossed in the meditation of *gāyatrī, brahman* the absolute. भगवान् fortunate. This Gaṅgā-dhara Śāstrī was quite famous.

The word Gaṅgādhara also operates derivatively in the sense of a sage named Jahnu, because the Gaṅgā is described as the beautiful daughter of Jahnu. BKB quotes the verse आदावादि......etc. to support his opinion.

Thus the verse सत्यासक्तमना: etc. conveys at least five senses by the power of the words which are polysemic (अनेकार्थ). Among the senses described above, four senses are relevant (*prakṛta)* but the sense pertaining to the ocean is irrelevant (*aprakṛta*). There is paranomasia (*śleṣa)* of relevant and irrelevant here. Therefore, the verse is an illustration of suggestion based on words, शब्दशक्तिमूला व्यञ्जना, according to the opinion of the ancients. In *śleṣa* figure of speech, both the senses are relevant to the context and both are conveyed through *abhidhā,* while in शब्दशक्तिमूला व्यञ्जना, one sense is relevant (*prakṛta*) and the other senses are irrelevant (*aprakṛta*) and they are conveyed through *vyañjanā* because certain factors restrict the *abhidhā,* 'denotation'. The author has used the word भगवान् as a qualifier and it suggests the specific name of the writer of this work also. Therefore, the मुद्रालङ्कार is suggested here. where the intended sense is suggested in a verse, it is called a मुद्रालङ्कार.

(c) Suggestive sense conveyed by a specific utterance :

Sometimes the suggested sense is conveyed through a specific speech or utterance. It is conveyed in a concealed or hidden way. BKB states that such a suggestive sense is not understood by laymen. It is cognised by the connoisseurs having a specific genius or clear intellect; the persons who have cultivated an aesthetic taste by a constant approach to the best literary works. The author gives an example where the suggested sense is conveyed through a specific utterance in इयं सुरतरङ्गिणी ......etc. and explains the suggested meaning in detail. A lady has arrived at the bank of the river Gaṅgā to fetch water. She addresses a young traveller. Her address is suggestive due to the tone of her speech, and the suggestive sense is distinct from the explicit meaning: "She stays alone at home and the traveller can enjoy the close embrace of hers." The bold young lady thus invites the traveller for dalliance. The words used by her सुरतरङ्गिणी........(the river of gods, a lady who likes amorous sport), नौसङ्गमः (the availability of a boat, our meeting, विपुल चारु फुम्भद्वयं (two big, beautiful pots, large and beautiful breasts), and धनरस (thick waters, the intense sentiment of love) carry double meaning. The address is utterred in a specific tone by which it conveys the suggestive meaning.

(d) Suggestive meaning conveyed through a gesture :

BKB has quoted a *prākṛta* verse to illustrate the suggested meaning conveyed through a gesture. The verse describes an impudent deed of a wife who amuses hereself by an amorous sport with her paramour in the absence of her one-eyed husband who suddenly returns from outside. The wife wants to hide her shameless deed. So she displays false love for the husband, with a wonderful unique gesture. She covers both his ears so that he cannot hear her paramour's footsteps, simultaneously, she kisses his undamaged eye so that he cannot see him; she also makes the paramour a sign to leave the place without being frightened.

It should be noted here that while depicting the topic of *vyañjanā,* BKB elaborately explains each and every illustration in minutest details, supporting his explanations and interpretations by a number of quotations from classical texts or lexicons or scriptures revealing thereby his scholarship moving quite freely in each and every branch of Indian *śāstras,* whether it be grammar, or *nyāya* or *purāṇas* or *dharmaśāstra,* and even classical literature. BKB does not give anything new or original to the treatment of the topic, but his contribution lies in the *śāstraic* discussions he adds therein.

IV. x Concluding verses and the colophon :

BKB gives some personal details in six concluding verses composed in various metres. He states quite candidly that he depicted nothing original or new in the composition named Vicāradīpa. His humble aim was to remove the darkness of doubt from the hearts of the scholars about the debatable points associated with *śabdaśakti*. He expresses his expectation that this सद्ग्रन्थ, good work, may give pleasure to the scholars who are not jealous of others' achievements and who can simply appreciate them without hypocrisy. Here we can see that BKB himself is quite conscious of his diffculty in treating such a topic *śabdaśakti* as has been already depicted by his own *guru* *Āśā*dhara Bhaṭṭa in two works: and it provides us a clue to evaluate his composition accordingly. He also expresses esteem for his father Paṇḍita Ānandarāma Bhaṭṭa who himself was quite a learned man. For himself, he claims rightly that his prime interest is in making research and modifications into the meaning of the scriptures by hair-splitting analysis and debates. He employs the qualifier बुध: for himself, and we cannot deny the claim that he is a learned scholar in so many branches of learning viz. *śruti, smṛti, vyākaraṇa, nyāya, mimāṁsā, dharmaśāstra, purāṇa, alaṅkāraśāstra,* classical Sanskrit texts and so on and so forth. This scholarship has made him humble enough to apologize for any mistake committed in the work. he proivides information about his native place Lālīgrāma[148] some twenty five kilometres far from Ahmedabad. he clearly mentions the date of the composition of this treatise Vicāracīpa. He accomplished the work on Monday, *śukla panchmī* of Āśvina in 1860 V.S. i.e. in 1804 A.D. in the morning. Thus BKB's date can be fixed towards the latter half of the eighteenth and the former half of the ninetheenth century. In the colophon there is a mention of his caste also. He belonged to the Raikva Rāyakawāḷa brahmin caste. All these details are analogous to those he has given in the concluding verses of Nūtanatarī, his another work, a commentary or Rasataraṅgiṇī of Bhānudatta.[149]

FOOTNOTES

1. Patañjali's Vyākaraṇa Mahābhāṣya A.1. P.I, i, Paśpaśāhnika.
2. अधीताशाधरगुरोर्यथा रसतरङ्गिणी।
   तथैव रचिता तस्याष्टीकेयं कृतिनां मुदे।। Nūtanatarī Ms F_{97}o.
3. see note No.4 Ch. V.
4. see note No.5 Ch. V.
5. see note No.6 Ch. V.
6. There is no work called भाष्यवार्त्तिक available. the quotation-भवति.. ...वृत्तिः। etc. could not be traced to either वार्त्तिक (of K.) or भाष्य (of Pat.) There is a work called भाषावृत्ति written by one पुरुषोत्तम (12th cent.) but it could not be traced. The enigma of the quotation remains unresolved.
7. मल्लिनाथकृतसञ्जीविनीटीका on रघु० ६, २.
8. Vide note No.11. ch, V.
9. Vide note No.13. ch, V.
10. Vide note No.14. ch, V.
11. एवं निरूपितः सपरिकरो........स्यादित्याहुः। Rasavilāsa, Seventh Stabaka.
12. Vide note No.16. ch, V.
13. KND. III, 40 and commentary thereon.
14. वैयाकरणनागेशस्स्फोटायनऋषेर्मतम्।
    परिष्कृत्योक्तवांस्तत्र प्रियतां जगदीश्वरः।। स्फोटवादः p. 102.
15. एवम् स्फोटायनस्य। P. VI, i, 102.
16. Pāt. Mbh. Ip.181.
17. इदमेकं पदमेकं वाक्यमिति प्रत्ययस्स्फोटसत्त्वे तदेकत्वे च प्रमाणम्।–महाभाष्यप्रदीपोद्योत vol. I, p.ii.
18. प्रत्यक्षमेवात्र प्रमाणम्, गौरित्येकं पदमिति नानावर्णातिरिक्तैकपदवगतेस्सार्वजनीनत्वात्।–सर्वदर्शनसङ्ग्रह p.299.
19. स्फोटात्मा तु प्रत्यक्षवेदनीयः। स्फोटसिद्धिः p.171.
20. सार्वजनीनमपि पदमिति वाक्यमिति चैकविषयानुभवम्। तत्त्वबिन्दु p.23.
21. cf. तत्र रामो भवति इत्यादौ तत्तदानुपूर्व्यवच्छिन्नवर्णसमुदायरूपाः प्रकृतिप्रत्ययभागाः प्रयुज्यमानपदवाक्यादौ श्रूयमाणाः वाचकाः। न तु तैः स्मृता आदेशेन इति वर्णस्फोटपक्षः। 'सर', 'रसः' इत्यादावविशेषवारणाय तत्तदानुपूर्व्यवच्छिन्ना। (स्फोटवादः, नागेशभट्ट p.5.)
22. The discussion of the *sphoṭa* theory is based on 'Indian Theories of meaning', by Raja K.Kunjunni and on 'A study in the dialectics of *sphoṭa*' by Śāstrī Gaurīnāth.

23. Com. by Pūnyarāja on VP II, 252.
24. VP II, 253.
25. यौगपद्यमतिक्रम्य पर्याये व्यवतिष्ठते! ibid II, 251a.
26. अर्थप्रकरणाभ्याम् वा योगाच्छब्दान्तरेण वा। ibid II, 251 b.
27. एकत्वं तु स्वरूपत्वाच्छब्दयोर्गुणमुख्ययो:।
प्राहुरत्यन्तभेदेऽपि भेदमार्गानुसारिण:।। ibid II, 257.
28. शब्दार्था: प्रविभज्यन्ते न रूपादेव केवलात्।
भेदपक्षेऽपि सारूप्याद्भिन्नार्था: प्रतिपत्तिषु।
नियता यान्त्यभिव्यक्ति शब्दा: प्रकरणादिभि:। ibid II, 316, 317.
29. KND I-17.
30. वाच्यभेदेन भिन्ना यत् युगपद्भाषणस्पृश:।
श्लिष्यन्ति शब्दा: श्लेषोऽसौ.......KP IX, 84.
31. लघुशब्देन्दुशेखर, com. on. VP II, 478.
32. KND I, 22-23.
33. Vide note No 20 in ch. V.
34. Pāt. Mbh. on p. I,i, 3 Vārt, 6.
35. Vide note No 21 in ch. V.
36. PariŚek.p.126.
37. P. I, iv, 3. vide note No 25 in ch. V.
38. P. I, iv, 4. vide note No. 24 in ch. V.
39. P. VI, iv, 77.
40. P. VI, iii, 107. vide note No.26 in ch. V.
41. vide note No.25 ch. V.
42. The reading सुभ्रू: in place of सुभ्रु is found in some recension of BP.
43. सुभ्रुशब्दो ह्रस्व: प्रमादजो नदीसंज्ञानिषेधात्। पञ्जिका on KS V, 43.
44. सञ्जिवनी by Mallinātha on KS V, 43.
45. ऊकारान्तादप्यूङ्प्रवृत्ते:।। (V, ii, 48)।। उत ऊङ्विहित: ऊकारान्तादपि क्वचिद्भवति। आचार्यप्रवृत्ते:। क्वाऽसौ प्रवृत्ति:। अप्राणिजातेश्चारज्ज्वादीनाम् इति। अलाबू: कर्कन्धू-रित्युदाहरणम्। तेन, 'सुभ्रु किं संभ्रमेण।' अत्र सुभ्रुशब्द ऊङिसिद्धौ भवति। ऊङित्वसति सुभ्रूरिति स्यात्।। ४८।। Kāvyālaṅkārasūtravṛtti. p.226.
46. Vide note No.32 ch.V.
47. P.IV, i, 66,
48. Vide note No.31 ch.V.
49. Vide Pp. 38-39 ch.II.
50. Śrītharīṭikā on BP.X, Liii. 37.
51. Abhm. the beginning p.3.

52. वृत्तय: काव्यसरणावलङ्कारप्रबन्धृभि:।
अभिधालक्षणाव्यक्तिरिति तिस्रो निरूपिता:।
तत्र क्वचित्क्वचिद्वृद्धैर्विशेषानस्फुटीकृतान्।
निष्टङ्कयितुमस्माभि: क्रियते वृत्तिवार्तिकम्।। Vṛttivārttika. opening verses p.29.
53. TRN. p. 1-2 after the verse 1.
54. KND, 1, 2.
55. साहित्यदर्पणे तु वृत्तिशब्दस्थाने शक्तिशब्दो दृश्यते। TRN ch. I,1.
56. ....मुख्यलाक्षणिकयोरभिधाव्यापारयोरत्रविवेक: क्रियते। Abhm. p.3.
57. स मुख्योऽर्थस्तत्र मुख्यो व्यापारोऽस्याभिधोच्यते। KP I, 3.
58. KND, I, 46.
59. Nyāyasiddhāntamuktāvlī *Vṛtti* on Kārikā 81.p.265.
60. KP *Vṛtti* on II, ii.
61. Vākyapadīya, I, 56.
62. KND, I, 28-31.
63. ibid I 12-13.
64. ibid I, 47.
65. TRN I p.5.
66. ibid I p.5.
67. ibid I p.6.
68. Discussion based on 'Pāṇiniya Vyākaraṇa Vimarśa'. Bhaṭṭa Vasanta Kumara Pp. 189-191.
69. शक्तं पदम्। तच्चतुर्विधम्। क्वचिद्यौगिकं, क्वचिद्रूढं, क्वचिद्योगरूढं, क्वचिद्यौगिकरूढम्। Nyāyasiddhāntamuktāvalī, Śabdakhaṇḍa, Padavibhāgaḥ Pp.282.
70. Nyāyasiddhāntamuktāvalī, Śabdakhaṇḍa, Padavibhāgaḥ Pp.282-284.
71. Śrītharīṭīkā on BP III, i, 34.
72. Vide note No.48 ch.V.
73. लक्षणा शक्यसम्बन्ध: तात्पर्यानुपपत्तित:। Nyāyasiddhāntamuktāvalī K. 42, p. 285.
74. Vṛttivārttika ch.II.
75. KND II.v.
76. TRN ch.II.p.12.
77. VD. The text. ch. II.
78. 'गङ्गायां घोष:' इत्यत्र तटस्थघोषाधिकरणत्वसिद्धये गङ्गाशब्द: स्वार्थमर्पयति इत्येवमादौ लक्षणेनैषा लक्षणा। (KP.II.V.वृत्ति)
79. 'कुन्ता: प्रविशन्ति', 'यष्टय: प्रविशन्ति' इत्यादौ कुन्तादिभिरात्मन: प्रवेशसिद्ध्यर्थं स्वसंयोगिन: पुरुषा: आक्षिप्यन्ते, तत उपादानेनेयं लक्षणा। (KP.II.v.वृत्ति.)

80. तात्पर्यानुपपत्तिर्लक्षणाबीजम्। Tarkadīpikā on Tarkasaṅgraha sec. 59.
81. लक्षणा शक्यसंबन्धस्तात्पर्यानुपपत्तितः। Bhāṣāparichheda. 82.
82. TRN ch.II.p.20.
83. TRN ch.II.p.17.
84. Vedāntaparibhāṣā Pp.97-102.
85. Ibid Pp.98-99.
86. Arthasaṅgraha p.93.
87. Arthasaṅgrha p.77.
88. TRN Ch.II.p.23.
89. Ibid ch II Pp.23-24.
90. Vide Ch. II, the text
91. TRN ch.II.p.12.
92. Candrāloka, v,18.
93. Vide note No.56, ch V.
94. KND ch II. 21 and commentary on it.
95. KND autocommentary on II, iv.
96. cf. KND II, 22-26; TRN. II pp. 17-22.
97. TRN ch.IIp.18.
98. Vide note No.59 in ch. V.
99. Śrītharītīkā on BP x,iv, 23.
100. Siddhāntakaumudī, ekaśeṣa prakaraṇam, vā.
101. P. I,ii, 64.
102. P. VI, i, 102.
103. KND Ch.II.
104. TRN Ch.II.
105. KP II, 9, 10a.
106. KND Ch.III, 1.
107. TRN III P.25.
108. KP II 9, 10 and *vṛtti* thereon.
109. KND. III, 18.
110. TRN. IIIp.25.
111. KND III, 2.
112. KP. II, 2.
113. Ibid II, 9, 10a.
114. TRN III p.25.
115. TRN. III p.25.
116. KP II, ii, a.
117. Dhavanyāloka III, 33. *vṛtti*.
118. KPv.

119. KND III, 25.
120. ibid III, 26.
121. Ibid III, 27.
122. KND III, 25-35 and TRN III Pp.27-28.
123. KP. II, 17 onwords.
124. ibid VII, 60, 62.
125. cf. काव्यस्योत्तमादिभेदत्रयानुपपत्तेश्च। TRN III, p.28.
126. Rasavilāsa, the first *stabaka p.98.*
127. Dhvanyāloka. I, iv. *vṛtti.*
128. KP V, 47, *vṛtti*.
129. KND III 30-33.
130. Vide ch. VI, 'Nūtanatarī : His other work'.
131. Rasagaṅgādhara I, xi, vṛtti p.65.
132. Ibid I p.98.
133. Dhvanyāloka II, 2, 3.
134. vide ch. VI.
135. KP X, 38.
136. KP x, 22.
137. Śivamahimnaḥ stotram. 22.
138. गूढम् यथा-मुखं विकसितस्मितं.........etc. KP II *vṛtti* on 8.
139. अगूढम् यथा-श्रीपरिचयाज्जडा...........etc. KP II *vṛtti* on 8.
140. KP III 1-2.
141. प्रकृताप्रकृतश्लेषे शब्दशक्तिमूला व्यञ्जनेति प्राञ्चः। सा यथा-
आशाधरहृदुत्पन्ना विमला शुद्धिबुद्धिदा।
कोविदानन्दसहजाऽनुग्रहैषा त्रिवेणिका।। (TRN III, p.25.)
142. BP x, xxix, 2.
143. ibid x, xxix, 1.
144. Ṛgveda x, xc, i.
145. Śukla Yajurveda VI, 7.
146. Bhagavadgitā III, 10.
147. VD ch II
148. See the map
149. vide ch. VI.

CHAPTER - V

NOTES

1. गुरुचतुष्टयः

In the *Mantraśāstra,* there is a tradition of paying obeisance to immediately preceding *gurus.* They are called (1) स्वगुरु– One's direct teacher, (2) परमगुरु–The grand teacher, (3) परमेष्टिगुरु–The great grandteacher and (4) परात्परगुरु–The fourth *guru*------in the परंपरा. Thus the four preceding *gurus* of king Parīkṣit in the Bhāgavata will be sage Śuka, sage Vyāsa, sage Parāśara and sage Śakti.

2. उपपदविभक्तेर्कारकविभक्तिर्बलीयसी। (परिभाषेन्दुशेखर, 94)

This is a Paribhāṣa from the Paribhāṣendusekhara. It states that a kāraka case possesses greater force than an *upapada* case. उपपद case means a case termination added to a word on account of the presence of another word requiring the addition. The परिभाषा states that a कारक case is stronger than an उपपद case, e.g. the accusative case as required by the word नमस्कृत्य is stronger than the dative case required by the word नमः

Hence, पादयुगं प्रणम्य, and पादयुगाय प्रणम्य should be there in the first stanza.

3. क्रियार्थोपपदस्य कर्मणि स्थानिनः। (P.II, iii, 14)

According to this dictum, the fourth case affix is employed

to denote the object of that verb which is suppressed (स्थानिन्) in a sentence, and which has in construction (उपपद) therewith, another verb, denoting an action, performed for the sake of the future action. In other words, when the sense of an infinitive of purpose formed by '*tumun*' and '*ṇvul*' (III, iii, 10) is suppressed in a sentence, the object of this infinitive is put in the dative case. e.g. फलेभ्यो व्रजति।= फलानि आनेतुं व्रजति। He goes for fruits, i.e. to bring fruits. This debars the accusative case.

The author sates that in प्रणम्य शितिकण्ठाय........etc. Kālidāsa has used the dative case following the above dictum.

4. इवार्थे कन् विधानस्य तथा दर्शनात्। (P.V, iii, 96)

The affix कन् also means 'like this'; when the imitation of a thing is to be expressed. The word कन् is understood here. Thus अश्व इवायम् अश्वप्रतिकृतिः= अश्वकः–an imitation of a horse in wood or clay.

In the title विचारदीप, the word दीप is used and not the word दीपक to debar the meaning above, i.e. दीप इवायम् दीपकः।

5. साकाङ्क्षम् असमर्थवत् वाच्यम्।

The word साकाङ्क्ष accurs in Pāt. M. Bh. on P. III, ii, 114. साकाङ्क्ष means possessed of an expectancy in meaning. cf. भवेत् पूर्वं परमाकाङ्क्षतीति साकाङ्क्षं स्यात् परं तु कथं साकाङ्क्षम्? असमर्थ means syntactically not connected. e.g. राज्ञः and पुरुषः in the sentece – भार्या राज्ञः पुरुषो देवदत्तस्य। असमर्थ means unable to enter into a compound word. This term is used in connection with another word, although related in sense to it, and connected with it by apposition or by a suitable case-affix, the reason being that it is connected more closely with another word: cf: सापेक्षम् असमर्थं भवति। M. Bh. II, ii 1 e.g. the words कष्टं and श्रितः in the sentence महत् कष्टं श्रितः।

The author here renders the पूर्वपक्ष against the compound विचारदीप. As the word विचार is साकाङ्क्ष–possessed of an expectancey—with the word शास्त्र, it can not enter into a compound, hence the compound विचारदीप is not acceptable.

6. समर्थः पदविधिः। (P. II, i,1)

This rule relates to complete words. It is to be understood to apply only to those words senses of which are connected. Wherever in Pāṇinian grammar a पदविधि is found, that must be understood to apply to समर्थ words. A rule relating to पद or 'complete words' is called पदविधि, that which is ordained (विधीयते) is called विधि. The rules which are ordained with regard to complete words are as follows: (1) Rules relating to समास or compounding of words; (2) Rules relating to विभक्ति or the application of declensional and conjugational affixes; and (3) the rule by which one word is considered as if it had become a constituent member of another word (पराङ्गवद्भाव). The word समर्थ means capable, that is to say that which is capable of expressing the sense of a sentence on analysis, is called समर्थ, or the word समर्थ may mean that which depends upon words as connected in sense, that is to say, a rule, relating to words the senses of which are connected together.

The author quotes this rule in the पूर्वपक्ष which argues that the compound विचारदीप is not possible as the rule above does not apply in the case. As the word विचार is expectantly connected with the word शास्त्र, it is to be considered as असमर्थ and it cannot be compounded. So the compound विचारदीप is ungrammatical.

7. सम्बन्धिशब्दसापेक्षो नित्यं सर्वः प्रयुज्यते। (भाष्य प्रदीप Pāt. M. Bh. on P.II, i,1)

Every word related mutually, can be used in a compound

because, as it happens in a sentence, that व्यपेक्षा (mutual relationship in sense) is not rejected in compound also. व्यपेक्षा means, mutual relationship in sense between two different words which are connected with eachother in a sentence. This is contrasted with compositeness of sense as seen in two words joined into a compound word. (समास)

This means that व्यपेक्षा applies in compounds. The author replies to the argument of the पूर्वपक्ष that the words विचार, though it is connected with the word शास्त्र, it can be connected in compound विचारदीप as both the words are mutually related in sense.

8. सापेक्ष

सापेक्ष means some word with expectancy in sense. In grammar expectancy is at the root of, and forms a sort of, a connecting link for various kinds of relations which exist between different words in a sentence, which has to give a composite sense. Yet, if a word outside a compound is connected with a word inside a compound, especially with a second or further member, the sense becomes ambiguous. Expectancy in such cases is looked upon as a fault. When, however, inspite of the fault of expectancy, the sense is clear,the compound is admissible due to गमकत्व, i.e. clarity of the sense is clear, the compound is admissible due to गमकत्व, i.e. clarity of the sense, possessed by that particular compound.

9. अनुशासन

Traditional instruction, treatment of a topic. e.g. अथ शब्दानुशासनम्। (M.Bh. on I, i, 1) Here the word is explained as अनुशिष्यन्ते संस्क्रियन्ते व्युत्पाद्यन्ते अनेन इति अनुशासनम्।

10. मनोरमा

This is the popular name given to the commentary प्रौढमनोरमा

on the सिद्धान्तकौमुदी of भट्टोजी दीक्षित by the author himself. The commentary is a scholarly one and very extensive and its first portion only upto the end of कारक is generally read in the Sanskrit *pāṭhaśālās*. The author quotes from मनोरमा while explaining the word शास्त्र.

11. उणादयो बहुलम्। (P.III, iii,1)

The affixes उण् and the rest, with the force of the present and with sense simply appellative, are attached diversely. By using the word 'diversely', it is indicated that these affixes are, of course, applied after roots about which they are ordained, but they come also after roots about which they are not ordained. Sometimes we must infer their application by seeing actual words. Some affixes though there be no expressed injunction regarding them, are to be inferred to belong to this class. The maxim in regard to the उणादि affixes is that when, in appellatives, we find the forms of verbal roots and affixes coming after them we may know, from the result as presented in the word, what are the indicatory letters which the affix must be possessed of in order to produce the result. These affixes are not given in Pāṇini's work, but they have been separately collected. The affix उण् is the first of them.

The author quotes this maxim in order to explain the word शास्त्र derivatively: शास् + ष्ट्रन् (औणादिक) शास्त्र.

12. क्षीरस्वामी

He was a grammarian from Kashmir. He lived in the 11th century. He wrote the famous commentary क्षीरतरङ्गिणी on the धातुपाठ. He also wrote a commentary on the निघण्टु. The author quotes क्षीरस्वामी in support of करणार्थे ष्ट्रन् applying to the word शास्त्र. He has also quoted him several times in Nūtanatarī, his other work.

13. बाहुलक

This is a word used for the application of a grammatical rule as a necessity to arrive at some forms in literature especially in the Vedic literature as also in the works of standard writers, which cannot be explained easily by the regular application of the stated rules. The author explains the word शास्त्र from शास्त्र+ ष्ट्रन् by बाहुलक.

14. तास्थ्यात्ताच्छब्द्यम्। (Pāt.M. Bh. on P.V, iv, 50 Vārt.3)

A particular word can be used for the thing residing in some thing by indication (लक्षणा), or metaphorically. e.g. सुरभिषु फलेषु........Here सुरभि-fragrance reside in the fruits, so the word सुरभि is used as a qualifier of फल in the sense-'those in which fragrance is there.' In the present context, grammar is bound to exist in other *śāstras* like न्याय, मीमांसा, वेदान्त etc. grammar itself is a शास्त्र. The traditional instruction तात्स्थ्यात् ताच्छब्द्यम् is applied here and the word शास्त्र can be used for the other *śāstras* as grammar is there in all other ones.

15. ऊह

ऊह is the modification of a word in Vedic *mantra,* so as to suit the context in which the *mantra* is to be utilised, generally by change of case affixes, thus ऊह is an adaptation of a *mantra.* cf. ऊह खल्वपि। न सर्वैर्लिङ्गैर्न च सर्वाभिर्विभक्तिभिर्वेदे मन्त्राः निगदिताः। ते च अवश्यं यज्ञगतेन यथायथं विपरिणमयितव्याः। (M.BH. on Pl, i. Āhnika-1.)

16. अर्धजरतीयन्याय

It is very difficult to fix on the exact force of this saying. Authorities differ so far its sense is concerned. As expounded by Vardhamāna (iii, 195), it seems to imply indefiniteness; half-and-half-ness, being neither one thing nor another. He says: 'यथा स्त्री न तरुणी श्लथस्तनत्वात् कृष्णकेशत्वान्न जरती वक्तुं शक्यते तद्वत् सिद्धासिद्धं प्रयोजनम्।' This seems to accord with the meaning assigned to it by Marāṭhās shown by Molesworth in his Marāṭthī dictionary where he defines it as 'action of indeterminate character, speech vague and indefinite, a proceeding void of decided leaning or bearing. In short, अर्धजरतीय is a maxim applied in cases where impossibility of two opposite attributes combined in a single individual at the same time occurs. The author refers to it while refuting the Mimāṁsakas' argument against *sphoṭa* theory.*

17. प्रत्यभिज्ञा

Recognition of the object which was known in the past. We had seen or known something in the past. It is forgotten in the course of time. Due to some cue, we identify the thing that it is the same as been known to us in the past. This process of knowledge is called प्रत्यभिज्ञा. The word is used in support of स्फोट here.

18. वर्णो वर्णेन (P.II, i, 69.)

A case-inflected word denoting 'colour' is compounded with another case-inflected word which is in agreement with the former, and also denotes colour, and the compound is तत्पुरुष. e.g. कृष्णेन सारङ्गः कृष्णसारङ्गः। This rule is quoted in connection with the discussion of the compound सर्वगुणवान्. The question of the पूर्वपक्ष is: सर्वः गुणः इति सर्वगुणः (कर्मधारय) and the affix मत्वर्थीय वत् is added to the कर्मधारय compound, the result is सर्वगुणवान्. Here सर्वे गुणाः यस्य सः इति सर्वगुणः। The compound बहुव्रीहि thus conveys the meaning. Then why should we use both the कर्मधारय and the affix मत्वर्थीय? It will cause वृत्तिद्वयकल्पन-गौरवदोष. The author defies the argument thus: According to the *sūtra* वर्णो वर्णेन, कृष्णः सारङ्गः। and कृष्णेन सारङ्गः। both are possible. Then what is the difference? The भाष्यकार पतञ्जलि

---

* Based on लौकिकन्यायाञ्जलि-प्रथमोभागः। coll. by Col. G.A. Jacob

has solved the querry. विप्रतिषेध leads to बहुव्रीहि. To avoid वृत्तिद्वय-कल्पनगौरव, the affix मत्वर्थीय after the कर्मधारय is prohibited.

Inspite of this; the compound सर्वगुणवान् is justified, because the specified meanings भूमनिन्दादि, conveyed by मत्वर्थीय affixes, cannot be conveyed by बहुव्रीहि. If some specific meaning is to be conveyed, गौरव is not a blemish. The महाभाष्य itself has given such compounds like सर्वधनी, सर्वबीजी etc. in support.

19. विप्रतिषेध

विप्रतिषेध is conflict, opposition between two rules of equal strength, which become applicable simultaneously.

Here the dictum विप्रतिषेधे परं कार्यम् (P.I. iv-2) applies, and the rule mentioned later on or subsequently in the अष्टाध्यायी is allowed to apply. This applies only when and if the confliciting rules are of equal strength.

20. भूमनिन्दादयः [p.९]

भूमनिन्दाप्रशंसासु नित्ययोगेऽतिशायिने। तदस्यास्त्यस्मिन्निति मतुप्। (P.V, ii, 94)

The affix मतुप् (मत्, मन्त् f. ई) comes after a word in the first case in construction in the sense of 'whose it is' or 'in whom it is.' Thus गावोऽस्य सन्ति-गोमत्-गोमान् देवदत्तः। The use of मतुप् and cognate affiexe are restricted in their application. the signafications are (1) a large quantity, (2) when censure (निन्दा) is implied, (3) when praise (स्तुति) is meant, (4) when an inherent or permanent quality of a thing is meant (नित्ययोग) (5) when excellence is meant; (6) when accompaniment (संसर्ग) is meant (7) when the sense of to be (अस्ति) is denoted.

All of these seven specific senses are not conveyed by

बहुव्रीहि, hence मत्वर्थीय affix alongwith कर्मधारय to convey specified meanings is justified.

21. ज्ञापक

The word ज्ञापक is very commonly used in the sense of an indicatory statement. The *sūtras* of Pāṇini are very laconic and not a single word in them is devoid of purpose. the commentators always try to assign some specific purpose for the use of every word in the sūtras.Such a word or words or sometimes even sūtras are called ज्ञापक or indicator of a particular thing. the ज्ञापक is shown to be constituted of four parts namely वैयर्थ्य, ज्ञापक, स्वस्मिञ्चारितार्थ्य and अन्यत्रफल.

The author quotes 'कृष्णसर्पवान् वल्मीकः' as a ज्ञापक which occurs in Pāt. M.Bh. on II-i-68. while explaining the compound सर्वगुणवान्, he opines that here the मत्वर्थीय-वत् affix is सार्थक because of the ज्ञापकवचन कृष्णसर्पवान्.........etc. in the Mahābhāṣya.

22. ज्ञापकसिद्धं न सर्वत्र। (परि॰शे॰ Pl.26.)

The ज्ञापक sayings are not applied in *sūtras* in each and every case. Pāṇini has not given all these sayings as *sūtras*. He has suggested to use them by अर्थापत्ति or अनुमान or it is certain that he does not allow ज्ञापक s to be applicable as universally as the *sūtras*. No अनिष्ट-undesired consequence or result is permissible by applying ज्ञापक system in grammatical formations, ज्ञापकs may assist but in rare cases, their extensive application, (अतिव्याप्ति) will result into undesired-अनिष्ट formations. which are not permissible.

cf. ज्ञापकसिद्धं न सर्वत्र। स्पष्टमेव पठितव्येऽनुमानाद्बोधनम् असार्वत्रिकत्वार्थमित्यर्थः। तेन ज्ञापकसिद्धपरिभाषयाऽनिष्टं नापादनीयमिति तात्पर्यम्। (परि॰शे॰ Par. 126)

23. प्रामादिक

प्रामादिकप्रयोग is a faulty employment or use of a word in language and literature about which, laying down rules is looked upon as the purpose of grammar.

24. नेयङुवङ्स्थानावस्त्री। (P.I., iv, 4.)

Feminine words ending in ई and ऊ which admit the substitute इयङ् and उवङ् are not called नदी, except the word स्त्री (which is called नदी) notwithstanding its substituting इयङ्. The definition of नदी given in the *sūtra* यू नदी (I, iv. 3) is rather too wide. This *sūtra* delimits the scope.Thus श्री and भ्रू, admit the substitutes इयङ् and उवङ् respectively, and they are not called नदी (see below). Their vocative singular is हे श्रीः, हे भ्रूः etc., while the vocative singular of स्त्री is हे स्त्रि! इयङ्-substitute for the इ before a vowel, generally in the case of monosyllabic roots, ending in इ and the word स्त्री. e.g. स्त्रियम्। उवङ्-substitute for the vowel उ belonging to the विकरण श्नु, to roots and to the noun भ्रू under certain conditions. e.g. भ्रुवम्.

According to this rule the word सुभ्रू does not belong to the group नदी.

25. नदीसंज्ञा

This is a technical term applied in Pāṇini's grammar to words in the feminine gender ending in ई and ऊ excepting a few like स्त्री, श्री, भ्रू and others. It is optionally applied to words ending in इ and उ, of course in the feminine gender, before case-affixes of the dative, ablative, genitive and locative singular.

26. अम्बार्थनद्योर्ह्रस्वः। (P.VII,iii,107)

A short vowel is substituted in vocative singular for the आ

of the feminine in the sense of 'mother, mother-dear', as well as for the long vowel of the feminines called नदी (P.L, iv, 3).

This dictum is quoted in connection with the discussion about the vocative singular form सुभ्रु, found in many literary works.

27. सम्बुद्धि

This is the term used in Pāṇini grammar for the case-affix of the vocative singular, cf. एकवचनं संबुद्धिः। P-II, iii, 49. The vocative is, however, not looked upon as a separate case, the designation संबोधन is given to the nominative case having the sense of संबोधन-vocation.

28. शब्दान्तर-शब्दान्तरत्वम् [p. ११]

This is a different wording as it results from modifications such as *āgama* or *ādeśa* or *lopa. cf.* शब्दान्तरस्य प्राप्नुवन् विधिरनित्यः। (परि०शे०परि०३४)

The author quotes it while taking note of a different reading suggested in Kālidāsa's कुमारसंभवम् (V.43): सुभ्रूः कुतस्तातगृहेऽवमानना in place of विमानना सुभ्रु कुतः पितुर्गृहे।

29. अप्राणिजातेश्चारज्ज्वादीनाम्। (P.IV, i, 66. वा० १)

This is वार्त्तिक-1 on Pāṇini's *sūtra* IV, i.66-ऊङुतः। This *sūtra* guides to ordain feminine forms from उ-कारानत masculine names. The meaning of the rule is: after a nominal stem ending in उ, not having the letter य् as its penultimate letter, and being expressive of races of men, the affix in the feminine is ऊङ् i.e. ऊ.

The अनुवृत्ति of the words मनुष्यजाति and अयोपधात् should be read into the *sūtra* to complete it. Thus कुरूः='a female of the country of the Kurus.' The indicatory letter ङ् in ऊङ् is to distinguish this affix in *sūtras* like नोङ्धात्वोः। (VI. i. 175), for had the affix been enunciated merely as ऊ, then the *sūtra* would have run as नो धात्वोः। and the sense would have been ambiguous, for we could not have known what affix was particu larly meant there. The long ऊ is taught to debar the affix कप्, for a short उ would also have given the form कुरू (कुरु+उ=कुरू). The long ऊ, therefore, indicates that the affix कप्, enjoined by V. iv. 154 in बहुव्रीहि s, will not apply in the feminine forms ब्रह्मबन्धूः and the like, by the rule of विप्रतिषेध.

Why 'not having the letter य् as its penultinate? To exclude अध्वर्युब्राह्मणी, a woman of the class of Brāhmaṇas versed in the Yajurveda. Vārt:-अप्राणिजातेश्चारज्ज्वादीनाम्।........This *vārttika* means: The affix ऊङ् comes under similar conditions, afterwords denoting non-animate *jāti,* except the words रज्जु etc. Thus अलाबूः-the bottle gourd; कर्कन्धूः-the jujube tree. By the word-अरज्जुः, words like रज्जु, हनु etc. are excluded.

The *sūtra* ऊङुतः and the *vārttika* above are quoted to explain the formation सुभ्रु in vocative singular from the word सुभ्रू, and to prove that सुभ्रु (voc. sing.) is not a प्रामादिक प्रयोग-faulty formation.

30. वामन

वामन the famous poetician wrote काव्यालङ्कारसूत्रवृत्ति between 7th and 8th centuries. he has explained the word सुभ्रु in the words quoted by the author: ऊकारान्तात् अपि ऊङ् प्रवृत्तेः इति।.........(काव्यालङ्कारसूत्रवृत्ति-V, ii, 48.)

31. मण्डूकप्लुति

Literally मण्डूकप्लुति means the gait of a frog. or jump. In Pāṇinian grammar the word मण्डूकप्लुति stands for the continuation of a word from a preceding *sūtra* to the following one or ones like the jump of a frog, by omitting one or more *sūtras* in the middle. cf अथवा मण्डूकगतयोऽधिकाराः। यथा मण्डूकाः उत्प्लुत्योत्लुत्य गच्छन्ति तद्वदधिकाराः। (M.Bh. on P.I, ii, 3 Vārt.2)

The author suggests the अनुवृत्तिः of the word बहुव्रीहेः in the *sūtra* उङुतः by मण्डूकप्लुति in justifying the form सुभ्रु (voc.sing.)

32. योगविभाग

योगविभाग is the division of the words of a grammatical rule which has been traditionally given as a single rule. A rule is divided into two to explain the formation of certain words, which otherwise, are likely to be stamped as ungrammatical. The वार्त्तिककार and the महाभाष्यकार have very frequently taken recourse to योगविभाग.

The author, भगवत्कवि adopts योगविभाग in the *sūtra* ऊङुतः। to explain the form-सुभ्रु. He argues that the भाष्यकार has used योगविभाग as a ज्ञापकवचन.

33. तपरकरण

तपरकरण is addition of the mute letter त् after a vowel to signify the inclusion of only such varieties of the vowel as take the equal time for their utterance like the vowel marked with त्.

34. अतन्त्रत्वम्

अतन्त्र is that which implies no specific purpose; that which is not intended to indicate or suggest anything.

35. अनुक्त

अनुक्त means that which is not actually stated or expressed in a rule. cf. चकारोऽनुक्तसमुच्चयार्थः। काशिका on P.II, iv, 18.

The author makes three alternative guesses about the interpretation of the rule ऊङ् उतः-(1) whether त् in उतः implies no specific purpose; (2) whether उ कार has no अनुवृत्ति in the *vārttika*-अप्राणिजातेश्चारज्ज्वादीनाम् (3) च in that *vārttika* is not actually stated.

36. अवधारण

अवधारण is restriction. limitation, cf. अवधारणमियत्तापरिच्छेदः। (Kāśikā on P-II, i, 8.) एव in अस्य एव भार्या.......etc. restricts the meaning, in six different ways as explained there.

37. समभिव्याहृत-समभिव्याहार

समभिव्याहार means (1) mentioning together, (2) association, company, (3) proximity to or association with a word, the meaning of which is clearly ascertained or understood. The first meaning of the word समभिव्याहृत fits in the context. एव is constructed with the rest of the various words one after another (=not simultaneously) and conveys the sense of restriction.

38. च्विप्रत्यय

च्वि is a तद्धित affix. It signifies taking place of something which was not so before. After the word ending in च्वि the forms of the root कृ, भू or अस् have to be placed. e.g. शुक्लीकरोति, cf. P.V, iv, 50.

The author reads च्विरूप in भार्याभवितुम् in अस्यैव.........etc., the verse from the Bhāgavata.

39. चादिगण

चादिगण is a class of words headed by च. They are termed निपात by Pāṇini. e.g. च, वा, ह, एवम्, नूनम्, चेत् etc.

The word is used here in connection with the discussion of एवार्थ, which is in a way a diversion from the topic due to the author's allegiance to Pāṇinian grammar.

40. निपात

निपात is a particle which possesses neither gender nor number. The case termination after it, is dropped or elided. निपात is given as one of the four categories of words viz. नामन्, आख्यात, उपसर्ग and निपात by all the ancient writers of *prātiśākhya, vyākaraṇa* and *nirukta* works. The *nipātas* are looked upon as possessed of no sense, cf. निपातः पादपूरणः। (ऋक्प्रातिशाख्य-XII, 8)

Pāṇini has not defined the word निपात, but he has enumerated them as forming a class with च as their head in the rule चादयोऽसत्त्वे। (P.1, iv, 57) In this rule, the word असत्त्वे conveys an impression that they possess no sense, the sense being of two kinds-सत्त्व and भाव, and the *nipātas* do not possess any of the two. The impression is confirmed by the Vārttikakāra in-निपातस्यानर्थकस्य प्रातिपदिकत्वम्। (P.1, ii, 45 vārt-12.) So the question whether the *nipātas* convey any sense by themselves or not is a difficult one to be solved. Although the ऋक्प्रातिशाख्य (XII, 8) lays down that the *nipātas* are expletive, still in the next verse it says that some of them do possess sense; cf. निपातानामर्थवशान्निपातनादनर्थकानामितरे च सार्थकाः। On this, Uvvaṭa remarks: केचन निपाताः सार्थकाः केचन निरर्थकाः। The remark of Uvvaṭa appears to be a sound one as it is based on actual observation, and accordingly, the conflicting views are reconciled by Bhartṛhari. He lays down that the *nipātas* never directly convey the sense but they indicate the sense. Regarding the sense indicated by the *nipātas,* it is said that the sense is never सत्त्व or द्रव्य or substance as remarked by Pāṇini, it is a certain kind of relation and that, too, is not expressed directly by them; it is actually indicated. Bhoja in his Śṛṅgāra-prakāśa gives a very comprehensive definition of *nipātas* as–

जात्यादिप्रवृत्तिनिमित्तानुपग्राहित्वेनासत्त्वभूतार्थाभिधायिनः अलिङ्ग-संख्याशक्तयः उच्चावचेष्वर्थेषु निपतन्तीत्यव्ययविशेषाः एव चादयो निपाताः।

The *nipātas* are such distinguished indeclinables as convey various senses, excluding being or substance, they possess no gender or number, (they do not fall in the class जाति, गुण, क्रिया, द्रव्य, प्रवृत्तिनिमित). They are not applied by four causes such as जाति, गुण, क्रिया, द्रव्य.

Bhagavatkavi Bhaṭṭa starts a detailed debate on the controversy whether the *nipātas* denote or indicate the sense. This discussion is remotely related to the subject of शब्दशक्ति, and is not included by his teacher Āśādhara in his *prakaraṇa granthas* on *śabdaśakti*.

41. भूषण-वैयाकरणभूषण or वैयाकरणसिद्धान्तभूषण

This is a well-known work on the grammatical interpretation of words written by Koṇḍabhaṭṭa as an explanatory work (व्याख्यान) on the small work in verse consisting of only 72 Kārikās written by his uncle Bhaṭṭoji Dikṣita. The treatise is also named Bṛhadvaiyākaraṇabhūṣaṇa. Smaller work consisting of the same subject-matter but omitting discussions, is written by the author for facilitating the understanding of students to which he has given the name Vaiyākaraṇabhuṣaṇasāra.

42. क्तप्रत्यय

कृत् affix is called क्त. It is used in various senses called by the name निष्ठा in Pāṇini's grammar along with the affix क्तवत्. cf. क्तक्तवतू निष्ठा. (P.l, i, 26) क्त is prescribed to denote various senses but here in संपृक्तौ it is used to convey the sense of कर्तृ in the nominative case as suggested by the author.His interpretation seems to be quite unusual.

43. प्रवृत्तिनिमित्त

प्रवृत्तिनिमित्त means the cause of the application of a word which is shown by the word when the affix त्व or ता is added to it. There are given four such causes namely जाति, गुण, क्रिया and संज्ञा.

44. इवेन विभक्त्यलोपः पूर्वपदप्रकृतिस्वरत्वं च। (P.II, i, 4, Vā.1)

This is a Vārttika of Kātyāyana. It is explained thus: इव forms a necessary or permanent compound with a noun, that noun does not lose its case-termination, the same noun which forms the first member of the compound retains its natural or original accent. The author has quoted the Vārttika to explain the compound वागर्थाविव।

45. एकार्थीभाव

एकार्थीभाव is a union of meanings. It is one of the two ways in which the word सामर्थ्य is explained, cf. एकार्थीभावो वा सामर्थ्यं स्याद् व्यपेक्षा वा। (M.Bh. on II, i, 1,) In connection with the discussion of योगशक्ति the author quotes from वैयाकरणसिद्धान्त-कारिका. एकार्थीभाव is explained is detail in the fourth chapter.

46. जहत्स्वार्थावृत्ति

A composite expression where the constituent members give up their individual sense is called जहत्स्वार्थावृत्ति. In compound words as राजपुरुष in the sentence राजपुरुषमानय the word राजन् gives up its sense in as much as he, the king, is not brought, The word पुरुष also gives up its sense as every man is not brought. It is, of course, to be noted, that although the sense is given up by each word, it is not completely given up, cf. जहदप्यसौ स्वार्थं नात्यन्ताय जहाति। (Pāt M.Bh. on P.II, i, 1. Vārt. 2.)

47. सामर्थ्य

Literally सामर्थ्य means capacity of a word to express its sense. But the word is used rather technically as derived from समर्थ, in the sense of compositeness. cf. तत्र एकार्थीभावः व्यपेक्षा

वा सामर्थ्यम्। (Pāt M.Bh. on P.II, i, 1.) The word is also used in the sense of 'conformity in sense' or 'connectedness'. The word is used by the author while discussing उद्‌बाहुः इव। which is not a compound.

48. क्विपि शकन्ध्वादित्वात् पररूपं वाच्यम्। (P. VI, i, 94 वा-४)

क्विप् = कृत् affix zero, added to the roots सद्, सू, द्विष् and others with a preceding word as *upapada* or with a prefix or sometimes even without any word, as also to the root हन् preceded by the words ब्रह्मन्, भ्रूण and वृत्र and to the root कृ, preceded by सु, कर्मन, etc., and to the roots सु and चि under certain conditions e.g. उपसत्, सूः, प्रसूः पर्णध्वत्, ब्रह्महा, वृत्रहा, सोमसुत्, अग्निचित्. cf. P. III,ii, 61.

The meaning of the Vārttika: शकन्ध्वादिषु पररूपं वाच्यम्। (P.VI, i, 94 Vā.4) is this: for the अ or आ of the preposition - ए or ओ of a verbal root, the second vowel is the single substitute. The *pararūpa* substitution takes place in the case of शकन्धुः etc. As शक + अन्धुः-शकन्धुः, कुल + अटा-कुलटा, सीम+ अन्तः-सीमन्तः. The author explains the word सात्वत with the help of this Vārttika. सात्वान् अतन्ति इति सात्वतः। Thus सात्व + अत = सात्वत and not सात्वात.

49. आशाधरभट्ट

Āśādharabhaṭṭa was the teacher of Bhagavatkavi Bhaṭṭa He wrote two books on the *śabdāśakti* namely Kovidānanda and Triveṇikā.

50. त्रिवेणिका

The name of a small *prakaraṇa grantha* on *śabdāśakti*. It was written by Āśādharabhaṭṭa the teacher of Bhagavatkavi, who gives a number of quotations from the book here in the Vicāradīpa.

51. आधारोऽधिकरणम्। (P.I, iv, 45).

That which is related to the action as the site where the action is performed is आधार. It means the object being in that place is called अधिकरण or the location. That in which the action is supported or located is called *ādhāra*. The *adhikaraṇa* takes the seventh case-affix e.g. कटे शेते। He is sleeping on the mat.

The *sūtra* is quoted in connection with जहल्लक्षणा in गंगायाम् घोषः। The author gives the example 'वटे गावः सुशेरते।' for सामीपिक अधिकरण. The word *ādhāra* is explained thus: आध्रियन्ते अस्मिन् क्रियाः इत्याधारः। (Kāśikā on P.1, 4, 45). The Prakriyā Kaumudī mentions four kinds of *ādhāra:* cf. औपश्लेषिकः सामीपिको विषयो व्याप्त इत्याधारश्चतुर्धा। (Prakriyā Kaumudī on. II, 3,36).

52. तात्पर्यानुपपत्तिर्लक्षणाबीजम्। (तर्कदीपिका on तर्कसंग्रह Sec. 59)

The Naiyāyikas like Annambhaṭṭa lay stress on the incomprehensibility of the speaker's purport so far as operation of *lakṣaṇā* is concerned. In their opinion, *lakṣaṇa* occurs only with reference to the understanding of the general purport or the intention of the speaker. When the hearer fails to comprehend the speaker's import due to the use of some word in its primary sense, he takes recourse to some other meaning related in some way to that primary sense. Thus, the *tārkikas* say that it is only the incomprehensibility of the speaker's purport wherein lies the root of *lakṣaṇā*.

53. समुदाय।

समुदाय means aggregrate, totality, collection of individual members. In मुखचन्द्र there is no लक्षणा because both the words मुख and चन्द्र make a compound and convey the sense by attribution or imputation of properties. Both Āśādhara and BKB strongly believe that there can be no *lakṣaṇa* in metaphorical compound words. cf. मुखचन्द्रः इत्यादौ समस्तरूपके त्वारोपसत्त्वे तस्य समासोत्पन्नसमुदायशक्त्या निर्वाहाल्लक्षणाभावः। (त्रि० लक्षणाप्रकरणम्)

54. प्रातिपदिक

प्रातिपदिक literally means available in every word, but the term प्रातिपदिक can be explained as प्रतिपदं गृह्णाति तत् प्रातिपदिकम्। cf. P. IV, iv, 39, or पदं पदं प्रति प्रतिपदम्। प्रतिपदेषु भवम्। The original form of words.

The regular division of a word into the base (प्रकृति) and the affix (प्रत्यय) is available for the first time in the grammar of Pāṇini, who has given two kinds of bases, the noun-base and the verb-base. The noun-base is named *prātipadika* by him while the verb-base is called *dhātu*. The definition of *prātipadika* is given by him as a word which is possessed of sense, but which is neither a root nor suffix: अर्थवदधातुरप्रत्ययः प्रातिपदिकम्। (P.I, ii, 45)

The word is used here in the discussion of 'द्रोणो व्रीहिः' as an example of सारोपा लक्षणा.

55. शब्दकौस्तुभः It is a treatise on grammar, critically explaining and discussing the meaning of Pāṇini *sūtras* in the order of the author himself. The work is written by Bhaṭṭoji Dīkṣita. It is mainly based on the Mahābhāṣya of Patañjali.

56. मयूरव्यंसकादिसमासः

मयूरव्यंसकादि is a class of compounds of the type of मयूरव्यंसक which are somewhat irregular formations and hence mentioned as they are found in use. These compounds are called simple *tatpuruṣa* compounds. e.g. मयूरव्यंसक–a roguish peacock or a rogue of a peacock. The author says that the word शब्दकौस्तुभः is not a मयूरव्यंसकादि समास because the latter member- उत्तरपद is preponderant in मयूरव्यंसकादि समास while in शब्दकौस्तुभ the पूर्वपदशब्द is preponderant so far as the determination of sense depends upon the word शब्द and it is the पूर्वपद-anterior member.

57. लक्ष्यमाणगुणैर्योगाद्वृत्तेरिष्टा तु गौणता। (तन्त्रवार्त्तिक १, ४, १२, ३३, सूत्रभाष्य)

This is Kumārilabhaṭṭa's definition of गौणीवृत्ति, which is the same as Mammaṭa's गौणीलक्षणा. This should be explained in this way: लक्ष्यमाणगुणैः वाहीकगुणैः कृतात् योगात् वाच्यार्थलक्ष्यार्थ-सम्बन्धात्। वाच्यार्थो गौः लक्ष्यार्थो वाहीकश्च वाहीकगुणै सम्बद्धौ। Here योग-connection-is effected by वाहीकगुणः which are the same as गोगुणाः, As the वाच्यार्थ and लक्ष्यार्थ are connected by means of common qualities, their function is known as गौणी. The verse is quoted here in connection with the discussion of गौणी लक्षणा.

58. तद्वानासामुपधानो मन्त्र इतीष्टकासु लुक् च मतोः। (P.IV, iv, 125)

This *sūtra* is quoted to explain the formation स्वस्रोः in श्यालः स्वस्रोरथाग्रहीत्। (श्रीमद्भागवतपुराण 10, 4, 23)

The *sūtra* is explained thus:

The affix यवत् comes in the *chhandas* after a nominal stem, in the first case in construction, ending with the affix *'matup'* (मतुप्), when the sense is "This is their *mantra* of putting up" provided that the things put up are bricks and the affix *matup* is elided by *luk*.

This *sūtra* requires analysis: तद्वान् is formed by adding

मतुप् to तद् meaning 'having that', and refers to a noun formed by the affix मतुप्. The word आसाम् is genitive plural feminine of इदम् meaning 'of them', The prouonu refers to the word इष्टका. The word उपधान means 'putting up' and technically means 'used as a *mantra* in the putting up of sacrifical bricks, pots etc.' मन्त्र-sacred hymn. इष्टका-bricks.

The meaning of the whole *sūtra* is this : the affix 'यत्' is used with the force of a genitive-आसाम्, after a word which ends with मतुप् and denotes a *mantra* used in putting up of sacrifical objects. When such *mantra* refers to bricks; and when this affix यत् is added, the affix मतुप् is elided. Thus वर्चस्वान् is a *mantra* containing the word वर्चस्. The bricks put up or collected (उपधीयते) with the recitation of वर्चस्वान् *mantra* will be called वर्चस्या. (वर्चस्वत्+यत्=वर्चस्+यत्, the affix वत् (मतुप्) being elided=वर्चस्य) वर्चस्या-fem. (Thus वर्चस्या उपदधाति-'he collects *varcasyā* bricks i.e. on which *varcasvān mantra* has been pronounced).

This *sūtra* works in स्वस्रोः। and thus the word gives the meaning of 'the sister and her husband'.

59. एकशेषः

एकशेष is a kind of composite formation to which only one of the two or more words compounded together subsists, the other being elided. cf. एकः शिष्यते इतरे निवर्तन्ते वृक्षश्च वृक्षश्च वृक्षौ। Kāśikā on सरूपाणामेकशेष एकविभक्तौ। (P.I, ii, 64) cf. also:

सरूपसमुदायाद्धि विभक्तिर्या विधीयते।
एकस्तत्रार्थवान् सिद्धः समुदायस्य वाचकः॥
समानार्थानां च भिन्नरूपाणां क्वचिदेकशेषो वक्तव्यः।
वक्रदण्डश्च कुटिलदण्डश्च कुटिलदण्डौ वा॥

(Bhāṣāvṛtti on P.1, ii, 64)

There is a dictum of the grammarians that every individual object requires a separate expression to convey its presence. Hence, when there is a dual sense, the word has to be repeated, as also, the word has to be multiplied, when there is a plural sense. In current spoken language, however, in such cases, the word is used only once. To justify this single utterance for conveying the sense of plurality, Pāṇini has laid down a general rule: सरूपाणामेकशेष एकविभक्तौ। and many other similar rules to cover cases of plurality, not of one and the same object, but plurality caused by many objects, such as plurality caused by ideas going in pairs or relations such as parents, brothers and sisters, grand father and grand-son, male and female. For example, वृक्षश्च वृक्षश्च वृक्षौ, माता च पिता च पितरौ, देवी च देवः च देवौ। etc. Pāṇini has devoted ten *sūtras* to this topic of ekaseṣa. The *vārttikakāra has* also commented upon it at length.

The author refers to the word एकशेष in connection with the formation स्वस्रोः in the श्रीमद्भागवत. स्वसा च स्वसृपतिश्च स्वस्रौ। तयोः इति एकशेषः।

60. प्रथमयोः पूर्वसवर्णः। (P.VI, i, 102)

For the simple vowel of a nominal stem and for the vowel of the case-affixes of the nominative and the accusative in all numbers, there is the single substitution of a long vowel corresponding to the first vowel.

Thc words अकः and दीर्घः of the preceding *sūtra* are both understood here. The word प्रथमा here means the प्रथमा विभक्ति, i.e. the nominative case; and it includes here the द्वितीया विभक्ति also. This *sūtra* teaches the substitution of a पूर्वरूप or a homogeneous long vowel corresponding to the first vowel. Thus अग्नि+औ = अग्नी, वायु+औ = वायू.

The *sūtra* is quoted here as a ज्ञापक to support भिन्नार्थानां विरूपाणामप्येकशेषः।

प्रथमा च द्वितीया च–प्रथमे तयोः। Here the words प्रथमा and

द्वितीया are भिन्नार्थ–having different sense and विरूप–having different forms, yet they form एकशेष.

61. अनवस्था

अनवस्था is a fault of having no end. It means endlessness. cf अवश्यं ह्यनेन अर्थानादिशता केनचिच्छब्देन निर्देशः कर्तव्यः स्यात् तस्य च तावत्केन कृतो येनासौ क्रियते। अथ तस्य केनचित्कृतस्तस्य केन कृत इत्यनवस्था। (Pāt. M.Bh. on II,i,l) The word अनवस्था is used by the author in support of the व्यञ्जनावृत्ति after Mammaṭa.

62. नञोऽल्पार्थत्वम्

नञ् is the negative particle that possesses the six senses which are sketched as–

सादृश्यं तदभावश्च तदन्यत्वं तदल्पता।
अप्राशस्त्यं विरोधश्च नञर्थाः षट् प्रकीर्तिताः॥

These senses are respectively illustrated by the examples अनिक्षुः शरः, भूतले घटो नास्ति, अघटः पटः, अनुदरमुदरं तरुण्याः, अब्राह्मणो वार्धुषिकः and असुर दैत्यः।

The author quotes नञ् to support its अल्पार्थत्वम् in अनङ्ग, in the sense of अल्पाङ्ग.

63. राजाहः सखिभ्यष्टच्। (P. V, iv, 91)

The affix टच् (अ) is added to the words राजन्, अहन् and सखि when standing at the end of a *tatpuruṣaa* compound. Thus compounds like महाराजः, परमाहः, राजसखः etc. are formed.

The author quotes this *sūtra* in connection with the word द्विजराजः.

64. कृत्तद्धितसमासैकशेषसनाद्यन्तधातुरूपाः पञ्चवृत्तयः। (सिद्धान्त-कौमुदी-सर्वसमासशेषप्रकरणम्-२२)

वृत्ति is a compound word giving an aggregate sense different from the exact literal sense of the constituent words. There are mentioned five *vṛttis* of this kind: कृत्, तद्धित, समास, एकशेष, सनाद्यन्त धातु. कृत्–This is the term used in the grammars of Pāṇini and others for affixes applied to roots to form verbal derivatives. The *kṛt* affixes are given exhaustively by Pāṇini in *sūtras* III, i, 91 to III, iv, 117.

तद्धितः–The word तद्धित is used by the ancient grammarians in the sense of a word derived from a substantive (प्रातिपदिक) by the application of suffixes like अ, यत् etc. and not in the sense of words derived from roots by affixes like अन्, ति etc. which are termed नामकरण, as possibly contrasted with the word तद्धित used by Yāska in II, 5.

समासः–समास means placing together of two or more words so as to express a composite sense; It is a compound composition. cf. पृथगर्थानामेकार्थीभावः समासः।

एकशेषः–Refer to note No. 59.

सनाद्यन्तधातुः–

(1) सन् is desiderative affix स applied to any root in the sense of desire; e.g. चिकीर्षति, जिहीर्षति, बुभूषति; cf. धातोः कर्मणः समानकर्तृकादिच्छायायां वा। (P.III, i, 7.) (2) सन् is applied in the specific senses possessed by the root to the roots गुप्, तिज्, कित्, मान्, वध्, दान् and शान् e.g.जुगुप्सते, तितिक्षते, चिकित्सति, मीमांसते, बीभत्सते, दीदांसते, शीशांसते, cf. P. III, i, 5 and 6. The roots to which सन् is applied are reduplicated and the reduplicated form ending with सन् (स) is looked upon as a different root from the original one for purposes of conjugation, which takes, however, conjugational affixes of the same *pada* as the original root; cf सनाद्यन्ताः धातवः। (III, i, 32.)[1]

1. Most of the grammatical terms are explained with the help of 'The Dictionary of Sk. Grammar', ed. by K.V. Abhyankar. The Pāṇinian *śūtras* are explained after S.C. Vasu, (Aṣṭādhyāyī of Pāṇini, Vol. I-II).

CHAPTER - VI

NŪTANATARĪ : HIS OTHER WORK

Nūtanatarī (NT) of BKB is a commentary on the famous Rasataraṅgiṇī of Bhānudatta in eight *taraṅgas*. P.V.Kane[1] and S.K.De[2] just make a bare mention of it. New catalogus catalogorum[3] refers to the single manuscript of NT which is preserved in the Oriental Institute Baroda[4]. The commentary is not published so far.

Since NT is the only other work of BKB which has come down to us, we have thought it worthwhile to give a rather comprehensive (though brief) introduction to the work in a separate chapter on the basis of the *codex unicum* of the work.

The title given to the commentary is meaningful. If Bhānudatta calls his work, Rasataraṅgiṇī, 'the river of *rasa'*, BKB calls his commentary Nūtanatarī, 'a fresh boat,' to cross the river of *rasa,* as it were,. He calls it *nūtana,* fresh, because he is aware that the work Rasataraṅgiṇī is indeed very popular and a number of commentaries of various types on it already exist. His explanation of the title Rasataraṅgiṇī also reminds one of his exposition of the title of his other work Vicāradīpa. vide:

एतादृशाः रसा एव रसा इति श्लिष्टरूपकम्। तरङ्गिणी एव तरङ्गिणीत्युभत्रापि वृत्तौ साध्यवसाना लक्षणा।[5]

The commentary of BKB is of the type of gloss on the Rasataraṅgiṇī. It is divided into eight *taraṅgas* corresponding to the eight chapters of the original work. In the maṅgala śloka, BKB offers his salutations to, Gaurī and Śaṇkara:

गौरीं त्रिलोकजननीं जनकं जगत्याः
शम्भुं शशाङ्ककलया च विराजमानम्।
हृत्पुण्डरीककुहरेस्थिरभावयोग–
गम्यं नमामि भगवानहमर्थसिद्ध्यै।।[6]

(For the fulfilment of my objectives, I bow down to Gaurī, the mother of three worlds and Śambhu, the father of the universe, who is intelligible through steady meditation in the lotus of heart.)

Again, as in the case of the *maṅgala śloka* of VD, here also, he gives an expositary commentary on the *maṅgala śloka* of NT. As already stated in the first chapter, BKB's religious inclinations are suggested here. In the second verse, he has mentioned the name of his teacher Āśādharabhaṭṭa respectfully:

श्रीमदाशाधरगुरोः प्रसादात्क्रियते मया।
तरी रसतरङ्ङ्गिण्याष्टीकेयं नातिविस्तरा।।[6]

The colophons at the end of the eight chapters are all identical with only the titles of the respective chapters changing thus :

इतिश्री महोपाध्यायावटङ्कानन्दरामभट्टात्मजभगवद्भट्टविरचितायां रसतरङ्गिणीव्याख्यायां नूतनतरीसमाख्यायां स्थायिभावनिरूपणे प्रथमस्तरङ्गः।[7]

इतिश्री........विभावनिरूपणे द्वितीयस्तरङ्ग।[8]

इतिश्री.........अनुभावनिरूपणे तृतीयस्तरङ्गः।[9]

and so on.

Like his VD, BKB concludes, NT also with five verses. In the first verse, he confesses in a polite tone:

पाण्डित्यं प्रकटीकृतं न च मया निर्मूलमत्राधुना
नो वा भूरितरो वृथा विरचितो वादो वितण्डात्मकः।
कोशव्याकरणाद्यलङ्कृतिकृतां ज्ञात्वा मतं तत्त्वतः
संक्षिप्तैः प्रतिसंस्कृतैः रसतरङ्गिण्याः कृतेयं तरी।।१।।[10]

(I have not displayed my acumen here without sources now. Nor have I exercised fruitless, fallacious debate. I have written this NT (lit. prepared this 'boat') on the Rasataraṅgiṇī only after having studied the opinions of lexicographers, grammarians and poeticians and having modified them briefly in essence.)

He then mentions the name of his father Ānandarāma Mahopādhyāya Bhaṭṭa as a scholar, who was well-known among the connoisseurs of poetry and poetics:

आनन्दरामविबुधः प्रथितः परो यः
काव्याद्यलङ्कृतिरसादिविभावकेषु।
तत्सूनुना भगवता विदुषा कृतेयं
टीकाऽधुना रसविवेकवतां मुदे स्तात्॥२॥[11]

In the final verse, BKB clearly mentions the name of Āśādharabhaṭṭa as his *vidyāguru* :

अधीताऽऽशाधरगुरोर्यथा रसतरङ्गिणी।
तथैव रचिता तस्याष्टीकेयं कृतिनां मुदे॥५॥[12]

While explaining the word *hāsya* derivatively, BKB also mentions another important work of Āśādharabhaṭṭa namely Rasikānanda :

विशेषस्त्वाशाधरभट्टकृते रसिकानन्दे बोध्यः।[13]

The single ms. of Rasikānanda is with oriental Institue, Baroda. The work has been taken up for a critical edition by Prof. R. I. Nanavati, Director (now-ex) of the institute.

The value of NT also lies in the fact that BKB mentions some of the works of his versatile teacher Āśādharabhaṭṭa which, it appears, have not come down to us even in ms. form. Thus at one place, after quoting the *chhandaḥsūtra* for the definition of *vaitālīya* metre, BKB also cites Āśādhara's commentary thereon :

तथा च सूत्रम्–

वैतालीयं द्विःस्वरा अयुक्पादे युग्वसवोऽन्ते रलगति।* व्याख्यातं चैतदाशाधरभट्टैः। तथा हि–

प्रथमे च तृतीये च यत्र मात्रा चतुर्दश।
द्वितीये च चतुर्थे च पादे मात्रास्तु षोडश।।
पादान्तरे गणौ यत्र लघुर्गुरुरपि क्रमात्।
तच्छन्दः शास्त्रतत्त्वज्ञाः वैतालीयं प्रचक्षते।।

इति।[14]

It appears that Āśādhara either wrote a work on classical metres or commented upon the famous work of Piṅgala. The work, however, has not come down to us. In yet another significant reference, the commentary mentions the name of Yadurāmabhaṭṭa, the *guru* of Āśādhara also. In an elaborate explanation of *nirveda* BKB discusses the fallacy shown by his grandteacher thus:

अत्रश्लोके आशाधरभट्टगुरुयदुरामभट्टोक्तो दोषोद्धारप्रकारः प्रदृश्यते।[15]

The importance of NT, thus also lies in such references to personal details about its author.

So far as its other features are concerned, NT is a standard commentary on the Rasataraṅgiṇī. It fulfils all the requirements and expectations of good expository gloss. It reveals both his author's proper and clear understanding of the issues touched upon by the author of Rasataraṅgiṇī as well as his critical acumen.

BKB's equipment in various *śāstras* claimed by him in his first concluding verse[16] is not only confirmed but also fruitfully employed in this commentary. As a commentator, BKB explains systematically all the illustrations given by Bhānudatta. his concern for authentication of the meanings and synonyms given by him is well-observed in numerous quotations he has

---

* The actual *sūtra* in Piṅgal Chhandaḥsūtras is वैतालीयं द्विस्वराः अयुक्पादे युग्वसवोऽन्तेर्ल्गः (पिङ्गलनागविरचितम् छन्दःशास्त्रम्।।४,३२।।)

given from well-known lexicons like *Amarakośa*[17] *Haima,*[18] and sometimes even from the commentaries like *Vaijayantī*[19] and *Rāmāśramī.*[20] He unusually seeks confirmation even from *Nighaṇṭu*[21] once.

It is, of course, only natural that he should have a deeper and wider knowledge of traditional Sanskrit Poetics and poeticians and should refer to a number of works on Sanskrit poetics like Nāṭyaśāstra,[22] Kāvyaprakāśa,[23] Kuvalayānanda,[24] Rasavilāsa[25] and so on and so forth. What is more noteworthy is, he also quotes from some less referred to authors on poetics like Vāmana[26] and Daṇḍin,[27] This shows that his scholarship in the field of poetics is nor perfunctory or superficial or limited but is thorough and wide and qualifies him eminently to write a fresh commentary on a popular work like Rasataraṅgiṇī. It is also interesting to see that BKB takes note of the views of more than one rhetoricians in identifying the figures of speech in the case of the same verse. Here are a couple of examples:

पाषाणे यदि मार्दवं यदि पयोधाराहुताशोदरे
व्यालीनां वदने सुधा यदि रवेर्गर्भे हिमानी यदि।
स्थेमा किञ्च समीरणे यदि तदा स्वप्ने भवेत् सत्यता
किन्नामा स्मरभूमिपाल भगवन् क्रोधान्मुधा धावसि।।

The verse is quoted by Bhānudatta as an illustration of प्रणयात्मा उपालम्भ. BKB's comments on this verse are:

काव्यप्रकाशमतेऽतिशयोक्तिरियम् कुवलयानन्दमते तु संभावन-मलङ्कारः।[28] Another verse is given in the original work as an example of संशयात्मा उपालम्भः

सौन्दर्यस्य मनोभवेन गणनालेखा किमेका कृता
लावण्यस्य विलोकितुं त्रिजगतामेषा किमुद्ग्रीविका।
आनन्दद्रुमकन्दलीनयनयोः किं वासमुञ्जृम्भते
राधाया किमुवा स्वभावसुभगा रोमालिरुन्मीलति।।

In his comment, BKB refers to the two different opinions about the figure of speech in this verse as follows:

कुवलयानन्दमते उल्लेखालङ्कारः। काव्यप्रकाशमते तु रूपकमिति विवेक इति दिक्।[29] The commentator thus appears to have adopted even a comparative approach which seems to be somewhat ahead of his time.

Metrics is such another *śāstra,* as is closely connected with poetics. BKB does not disappoint his reader even on this score.He identifies the metres used in all those illustrative verses given by Bhānudatta, invariably. He quotes definitive aphorisms either from Piṅgala or from Vṛttaratnākara, or other sources. For examples, we have already referred to the definition of *vaitālīya* metre as quoted by him from Piṅgala above. Or the following definition of *śārdūlavikrīdita,* he quotes from Vṛttaratnākara:

सूर्याश्वैर्मसजस्तता स गुरवः शार्दूलविक्रीडितमिति लक्षणात्।[30]

We have already seen BKB's inclination towards grammar in his work VD where it assumes the nature of a *vādagrantha* only on the ground that it seeks to establish the *śabdaśakti* on the arguments of poetics and includes a number of discussions based on gammatical issues and observations. In NT, BKB takes liberty to explain words and grammatical formations often. Here is an example:

श्रीयते विद्वद्भिरिति शृङ्गारः। शृङ्गारभृङ्गारावित्युणादिसूत्रेण आरन् प्रत्यये श्रीधातोः शृ आदेशः। गुणाभावो नुकगुकौ चेति निपातनात् साधुः।[31]

He comments on the word धरणि on the same line: ध्रियन्ते प्राणिन इति धरणिः। धृङ् अवस्थाने इति धातोः मूर्तिसृधृ इत्युणादिसूत्रेण अनिप्रत्यये रूपम्।[32]

Among various schools of Sanskrit grammar BKB's clear allegiance is towards Pāṇinian System. This is explicit in his exposition wherein he, time and again, refers to the Pāṇinian *sūtras*[33] *vārttikas,*[34] Mahabhāṣya,[35] Manoramā,[36] Paribhāṣā,[37] etc. At times he even chooses to give names of the compounds in discussions of particular words: For example, commenting upon the compound word-पांसुलहेमकेतकदलद्रोणीदुरापश्रिय:।......

BKB explains: पांसुलानि रजोयुक्तानि हेमकेतकदलानि सुवर्णसदृशकेतकपत्राणि तानि द्रोण्य एवेत्युपमितसमास:।[38]

Occasionally, he identifies the figures of speech in the verse. Here is one such instance, Bhānudatta gives this verse as an example of *sāttvikabhāva sweda.*

कान्ते तव कुचप्रान्ते राजन्ति (राजन्ते) स्वेदबिन्दव:।
हृष्यता मदनेनेव (मन्मन्थेनेव) कृताः कुसुमवृष्टय:।।

BKB comments on the verse thus:

स्वेदं दर्शयति। कान्त इति। हे कान्ते। तव कुचप्रान्ते स्तनतटे स्वेदबिन्दव:। हृष्यता प्रसन्नेन। मन्मथेन। मनो मथ्नातीति। पृषोदरादित्वात्साधु:। मननं सत् मथ्नातीति मन्मथ इति वा। कामेन कृताः कुसुमवृष्टय: इव राजन्ते शोभन्ते। अत्रोपमानोपमेयवाचकसाधारणधर्माणामुपादानात् पूर्णोपमालङ्कार:।[39]

It is only to be expected that a writer of BKB's erudition should have more than casual knowledge of various other sciences, scientific and literary works of various classes of literature. Thus BKB reminds the reader of Nirukta when he explains some words by means of etymology. Here are two examples : श्रीयते विद्वद्भिरिति शृङ्गार:।[40] Again he explains the words सन्ध्या on the same line:

सम्यक् ध्यायन्त्यस्यां विप्रा इति सन्ध्या।[41] Or, विद्योतते इति विद्युत्।[42] BKB lucidly quotes from the Mahābhārata.[43] He is well-acquainted with *smṛtigranthas* like Yajñavalkyasmṛti.[44] He also refers knowledgeably to *upa-purāṇas* like Gaṇapatipurāṇa[45] and directs the reader to the original commentary of his classic predecessor Mallinātha on Kirātārjunīyam.[46]

A writer on poetics must, of course, have read the classic literary works closely and BKB fulfils our expectations on that score also as he has done in VD. Rasataraṅgiṇī quotes from number of works like Raghuvaṁśam, Kumārasambhavam, Kādambarī etc. and BKB perceptibly explains these illustrations alongwith the context they occur in. However, one strange fact seems to surface when we realize that the author of Rasataraṅgiṇī has not quoted from Naiṣadhakāvyam even once, whereas BKB seems to have a special liking for Naiṣadha. He has referred to it thrice in VD and evenwhen there was no occasion in NT, he brings in one quotation from Naiṣadha[47] on his own.

So far as his style of commenting upon the original text is concerned, he observes a systematic order. In the first place, he explains the context in which a particular illustration occurs; then he gives the *pratīka* word; then he explains words with the help of their synonyms for which he quotes from various lexicons; he also offers more than one interpretations wherever they are possible, he often throws light upon the propriety of using a particular word from among many of its synonyms; he also explains grammatical forms and usages; thereafter he identifies the figure or figures of speech in that verse; occasionally also explaining the charactristics thereof. Finally he defines and identifies the metre in that particular verse. This is thc system he has generally followed throughout his commentary. It will not be out of place to quote his commentary on one verse *in extenso* to illustrate how these characteristics actually operate in practice in his commentary. For this purpose, we quote below fully the text of RT on विबोध, one of the thirty three *vyabhicāri bhāvas,* its illustration given by Bhānudatta and BKB's commentary on this portion :

The text of Rasataraṅgiṇī-इन्द्रियाणां प्रथमः प्रकाशो विबोधः। निद्राच्छेदो विभावः। अनुभावाः अङ्गाकृष्टिजृम्भाक्षिमर्दनाङ्गुलीमोटनादयः। यथा–

राधाया सहसा दृशाकुवलयद्रोणीदरिद्रं नभः
कुर्वन्त्या कलकण्ठकण्ठनिनदैः सांकेतिकैर्जाग्रतः।
अङ्गाकृष्टिविवर्त्तमानवपुषो देवस्य कंसद्विषो
लोलापाङ्गतरङ्गभङ्गचतुरं नेत्राम्बुजं पातु वः॥

BKB's commentary upon the verse runs as follows:

विवाद (विबोध) मुदाहरति। राधाया इति। दृशा दृष्ट्या। नभोऽन्तरालम्। कुवलयद्रोण्यां विषये। दरिद्रं कुर्वन्त्याः। सुप्तायां इति यावत्। नेत्रसंकोचे नेत्रान्तरालाभावादित्यर्थः। यद्वा नभो दृशा संयुक्तां कुर्वन्त्याः प्रातः प्रबुद्धाया इति यावत्। रात्रौ कमलस्य दिवा पद्मस्य संकोचात् तदन्तर्वर्तिनभसो दरिद्रत्वमिति योजना। राधायाः सांकेतिकैः संकेतस्थले कुञ्जेभवैः कलकण्ठानां पिकानां कण्ठनिनदास्तैः। कण्ठग्रहणं माधुर्यातिशयद्योतनार्थम्। कलकण्ठः परभृतस्ताम्राक्षः कोकिलः पिकः इति हैमः। सहसा अकस्मात्। जाग्रतः अत एव अङ्गाकृष्ट्यै राधिकाङ्गाश्लेषाय विवर्त्तमानवपुषः। परिवर्त्तमान-स्वशरीरस्य। यद्वा अङ्गानामाकृष्टिश्छिरमोटनं (sic) यस्य तथाभूतं विवर्त्तमानं वपुर्यस्येति। कंसद्विषो देवस्य श्रीकृष्णस्य। लोलौ यावपाङ्गौ नेत्रप्रान्तौ तयोस्तरङ्गभङ्गचतुरं वीचिभङ्गिसुन्दरं नेत्राम्बुजम्। वो युष्माकं पातु रक्षतु। आशिषि लोट्। निद्राविच्छेदोऽत्र विभावः। अङ्गाकृष्टिरनुभावः। अत्र कण्ठकण्ठेति द्वयोः स्वरव्यञ्जनसमुदाययोः सकृदावृत्त्या च्छेकानुप्रासः। गकारस्य सकृदावृत्त्या वृत्त्यनुप्रास इत्येतयोः संसृष्टिः। अनुस्वारबाहुल्यान्माधुर्याख्यो गुणः। अनेकस्य व्यञ्जनस्य सकृत्सादृश्यं छेकानुप्रासः। एकस्यानेकस्य वा व्यञ्जनस्यद्विर्बहुकृत्वो वा सादृश्यं वृत्त्यनुप्रास (का०प्र० ९-७९ वृत्ति) इति काव्यप्रकाशलक्षणात्। तथा च किरातार्जुनीयकाव्यप्रारम्भश्लोके वने वनेचर इत्यत्र मल्लिनाथेन वृत्त्यनुप्रासो भवतीत्युक्तं तत्र मूलं मृग्यम्। सुप्ताया इति वक्तव्ये भङ्ग्यन्तरेण तत्कथनात् पर्यायोक्तमलङ्कारः। अङ्गाकृष्टिं प्रति निनदैर्जाग्रत इति वाक्यार्थस्य हेतुत्वात् काव्यलिङ्गमलङ्कार इत्यनयोरर्थालङ्कारयोः पूर्वं शब्दालङ्कारयोरिव तिलतण्डुलवत् संसृष्टिः। शार्दू०॥२५॥[48]

Towards the end of his work, BKB seems to overlap his

limits as a commentator. Bhānudatta has not attempted to show any distinction between *rasa* and *alaṅkāra*. BKB does this in his commentary and seeks to support his view from the Kāvyaprakāśa:

अथ रसालङ्कारयोः पृथक्लक्षणे। विभावानुभावव्यभिचारिव्यङ्ग्यत्वे सति पूर्णस्थायित्वं रससामान्यलक्षणम्। उक्तं च काव्यप्रकाशे-कारणान्यथ कार्याणि.....रसः स्मृतः इति। (का०प्र० ४) अथालङ्कारलक्षणम्रसात्मककाव्य-शरीराङ्ग भूतशब्दार्थान्यतरनिष्ठचमत्काराधायकत्वमलङ्कारसामान्यलक्षणम्। तत्रैव यथोक्तम्-पकुर्वन्ति........प्रासोपमादय इति। (का०प्र० ४, २७-२८)[49]

BKB also incidentally shows the defects in the definition of *alaṅkāra* given in the Alaṅkārachandrikā:

यत्तु अलङ्कारचन्द्रिकायामलङ्कारलक्षणमुक्तम् तन्मन्दमाभाति। तथा हि-अलङ्कारत्वं च रसादिभिन्नव्यङ्ग्यभिन्नत्वे सति शब्दार्थान्यतरनिष्ठा या विषयितासम्बन्धावच्छिन्ना चमत्कृतिजनकतावच्छेदकतावच्छेदकत्वम्। रसादिभिर्यद्व्यङ्ग्य वस्तुरूपमलङ्काररूपं च तद् भिन्नत्वे सति अत्यन्तम-युक्तम्। रसादिभिन्नव्यङ्ग्ययात् वस्तु-अलङ्काररूपात् भिन्नस्य रसादिव्यङ्ग्य-स्यैव ग्रहणापत्तेः। तथा च रसादिव्यङ्ग्यत्वे सतीत्यर्थः सिद्ध्यति। सत्येवं रसादिव्यङ्गयस्य नियतमलङ्कारत्वं प्राप्नोति। न हि रसादीनां सर्वकालिकम-लङ्काररूपत्वं किन्तु सजातीयस्य विजातीयस्य वा रसादेरङ्गभूतस्यैव न तु प्रधानीभूतस्य। तस्मादप्रधानीभूतेति रसादिविशेषणं योज्यं स्यादिति अन्येऽपिदोषाः प्रतिभान्तीत्यलमतिविस्तरेणेति।[50]

NT as a gloss, is, thus both explanatory as well as analytical. It reveals the stylistic peculiarities of its author. It also reveals the width and depth of his scholarship in various *śāstras,* his keen argumentative ability and acumen; in short, all the qualities expected of an expert commentator. All in all the commentary NT on Rasataraṅgiṇī gives a good account of BKB as a poetician, a commentator and a scholar. He is not only well-grounded in various branches of learning directly and distantly related to the field of his work, but he also evinces a systematic approach, a comparative outlook and even some independence of judgement. All these characteristics eminently qualify him to write a fresh commentary on a popular and even oft-commented work like Rasataraṅgiṇī.

FOOTNOTES :

1. Index of authors and works, 'History of Sanskrit Poetics.' Pp. 424, 431.
2. ibid Vol.I, P. 254.
3. C. Nūtanatarī By Bhagavadbhaṭṭa, Baroda II, 10842, K.100.
4. Acc. No. 10842; 98 Folios: 2000 *granthas.*
5. NT Ms. F_2o
6. ibid F_1o
7. ibid F_{11}o
8. ibid F_{20}R
9. ibid F_{30}o
10. ibid F_{97}o
11. ibid F_{97}o
12. ibid F_{97}o
13. ibid F_{13}o
14. ibid F_6o
15. ibid F_{36}R
16. ibid F_{97}o
17. खञ्जरीटस्तु खञ्जन इत्यमरः। ibid F_{57}o
19. कलकण्ठः परभृतस्ताम्राक्षः कोकिलः पिक इति हैमः। ibid F_{49}R
20. अङ्कः समीप उत्सङ्गे चिह्ने स्थानापराधयोरिति वैजयन्ती। ibid F_{11}o
21. पराक्रमोऽरिविजय इति रामाश्रमः। ibid F $_{26}$o
21. शतं सहस्रं कुविदिति बहोः संज्ञेति निघण्टौ। ibid F_{41}R
22. विभावानुभावव्यभिचारिसंयोगाद्रसनिष्पत्तिरिति भरतसूत्रोक्तेरिति। ibid F_{75}R
23. उक्तं च काव्यप्रकाशे-कारणान्यथ कार्याणि.......ibid F_{96}OR
24. कुवलयानन्दमते तु संभावनमलङ्कारः। ibid F_{53}O
25. विस्तरेणेदं स्फुटीकृतं काव्यप्रकाशे रसविलासे चेति। ibid F_{11}R
26. .....स्तथापि करिकलभकर्णावतंसादिषु प्रतिपत्तिविशेषकरेषु न दोष इति वामनवचनात्समा-धेयमिति। ibid F_{49}O
27. अत्र दण्डीमते विरोधालङ्कारः। ibid F_{52}O and also यथाह दण्डी-
    निष्ठ्यूतोद्गीर्णवान्तादिगौणवृत्तिव्यपश्रियात्।
    अतिसुन्दरमन्यत्र ग्राम्यकक्षां विगाहत इति। ibid F_{85}O
28. ibid F_{53}O
29. ibid F_{57}R

30. ibid $F_{10}R$
31. ibid $F_{12}R$
32. ibid $F_{11}R$
33. आशिषि लिङ्। ibid $F_{83}R$
34. अधिकार्थे द्वे वाच्य इति वार्त्तिकस्यापि नात्र प्रवृत्तिः। ibid $F_{9}O$
35. गुणवचनेभ्यो मतुपो लुगिष्ट इति भाष्यकारोक्तेः। ibid $F_{86}O$
36. समासेनैवाधिकार्थावगतेः। विस्तरस्तु मनोरमायां द्रष्टव्यः। ibid $F_{9}O$
37. कृद्वृत्तेस्तद्धितवृत्तिर्बलीयसीति परिभाषानुरोधात्। ibid $F_{12}O$
38. ibid $F_{21}R$
39. ibid $F_{31}R$
40. ibid $F_{12}R$
41. ibid $F_{12}R$
42. ibid $F_{20}O$
43. तेनैव नाम्ना तं देशं वाच्यमाहुर्मनीषिण इति महाभारतवचनादवगन्तव्यम्। ibid $F_{39}R$
44. अध्वनीनोऽतिथिर्ज्ञेय इति याज्ञवल्क्योक्तेः। ibid $F_{16}O$
45. कस्मिंश्चित्कल्पे गणपतिर्देवीगर्भादुत्पन्न इति गणपतिपुराणे उत्तरखण्डे वर्णनमवगन्तव्यम्। ibid $F_{40}O$
46. तथा च-किरातार्जुनीयकाव्यप्रारम्भश्लोके वने वनेचर इत्यत्र मल्लिनाथेन वृत्त्यनुप्रासो भवतीत्युक्तं तत्र मूलं मृग्यम्। ibid $F_{50}O$
47. नैषधे मनोरथेन स्वपतीकृतं नलमित्यादौ तथा वर्णनाच्चेति भावः। ibid $F_{60}R$
48. ibid $F_{49}R$ and $F_{50}O$
49. ibid $F_{96}O$ and $F_{96}R$
50. ibid $F_{96}R$

CHAPTER - VII

CONCLUSION

As is obvious from the contents of the Vicāradīpa (VD), the subject depicted by Bhagavat Kavi Bhaṭṭa (BKB) in the work is *śabdaśakti,* the functions or powers of the word, namely *abhidhā, lakṣaṇā* and *vyañjanā.* The same topic is discussed by BKB's teacher Āśādhara Bhaṭṭa (AB) in a couple of works, one named Triveṇikā (TRN), for the commoners and the other named Kovidānanda (KND), rightly meant for the scholars. AB includes all the minutest details related to the topic of *śabdaśakti* in KND written in verse, and to fulfil the requirements of his average students, he softens the subtle technicalities and treats the same subject in prose in a more comprehensive but simple style in TRN. Within themselves, both these works treat the subject fully, in all the details, both for a scholar and one not-so-scholar. A comparative study of the VD, KND and TRN taken up in the preceding pages (Ch.IV) shows that BKB states almost nothing new so far as the theoretical aspect of the subject is concerned, of course, no scholar can add anything original to the topic after what has been already said by the preceding scholars like Ānandavardhana, Mammaṭa,AB, etc. Moreover, BKB gives definitions illustrations and sometimes even discussions almost in the same words as those in the works of his teacher! As has been seen, the discussion about *śakti (=abhidhā), lakṣaṇā* and the classifications thereof are picked up often verbatim from either of his teacher's works. BKB has sometimes omitted subtopics. For example, he does not give the definitions of *śakti,yoga, rūḍhi, yogarūḍhi* etc. Again,he finds no need to treat the topics like various views on *saṅketa, śaktigrāhakas* and relations of *śakti* with *lakṣaṇā* already treated by his teacher in detail. He has not shown various relations between the denotative and indicative meanings as has been done by AB in TRN in detail. In this connection, it is important to note that in the interpretation of some examples of *lakṣaṇā* like न जातु ब्राह्मणं हन्यात्।, सोऽयं देवदत्तः।, तत्त्वमसि। etc. BKB differs from his teacher. Even in the treatment of *vyañjanā,* his only contribution is the addition of a few more examples and their fresh interpretations. He has hardly anything to add to the theoretical part of the topic.

The question, then, should naturally arise, why one more work on the same topic. What if at all, was BKB's specific purpose behind the composition of this work when two of his teacher's works were already there giving full justice to the topic?

In order to find an answer to this question, one must focus one's attention upon some salient points and features of this work.

In the very *pratijñā* verse of the treatise BKB states:

शास्त्रेति शब्दस्य विचारदीपं कुर्वे विवादं भगवान् सुबोधम्।

"I compose, a work named *vicāradīpa* as the science of word, in the form of comprehensive discussion about the subject."

This implies that BKB proposes to present debates connected with the science of the word; or in other words, his intention is to compose a *vādagrantha* whereas the purposes of his teacher AB in composing his works are (i) to present the views of the ancients on the topic in KND, cf:

प्राचां वाचां शब्दव्यापारनिर्णयम्।
करोमि कोविदानन्दं लक्ष्यलक्षणलक्षितम्।।

> "I, following the views of the ancients, compose KND, as a combination of illustrations and definitions, which depicts the function of the Word." (KND.I, ii)

and (ii) to present the topic in an easily comprehensible way for the novice. vide:

> प्रणम्य पार्वतीपुत्रं कोविदानन्दकारिणा॥
> आशाधरेण क्रियते पुनर्वृत्तिविवेचना॥

> "Bowing down to the son of Pārvatī, the author of KND, Āśādhara, again starts the explanation of the *vṛttis* i.e. the functions of the word." (TRN. I, i.)

The distinction lies in the fact that while both the works of AB can be called *prakaraṇa granthas* (for different levels of readers), the author of VD himself calls his work a *vādagrantha*. (cf. कुर्वे विवादं भगवान् सुबोधम्।)

From this point of view it is only natural that he should include a number of debates even in this small work.They are:

(1) how the science of the poetic word in considered to be *śāstra,*

(2) how a polysemic word like *śāstra* conveys its different meanings,

(3) why *sphoṭa* theory should be accepted,

(4) how the vocative singular form सुभ्रु is justified from grammatical point of view,

(5) whether the *nipātas* are denotative or suggestive,

(6) how *yogaśakti* and the expressive power of totality *samudāyaśakti* in compounds are different,

(7) from the Mīmāṁsā point of view, whether the sentence-न जातु ब्राह्मणं हन्यात्। is a *vidhi* 'injunction', or a *niyama* 'specification' or a *parisaṅkhyā* 'exclusion',

(8) how some readings like क्षत्रस्य शब्दो भुवनेषु रूढः। (रघु० २/५३), अनेन प्रसविष्यध्वमेष (भगवद्गीता. ३/१० p.३५) etc. in well-known texts are doubtful. He seems to be keen on exploring whether a poetic word is also capable of standing a close *śāstraic* scrutiny.

These, of course, would not have formed part of a systematic exposition of the powers of the word. They are specifically brought in by BKB justifying his nomenclature as a *vādagrantha* for his work. Thus while supporting the *sphoṭa* theory, he examines it from the *mīmāṁsaka* and the *naiyāyika* points of view and refutes their arguments against *sphoṭa* stating that their basic conceptions like *pratyabhijñā* of the Vedic *mantras* (*mīmāṁsā*) and logical hypotheses like शक्तं पदम्। (*nyāya*) would be harmed unless the *sphoṭa* theory is accepted. Of course, such hair-splitting analysis demands a very subtlelevel acumen and scholarship. This also makes it clear that BKB does not merely want to duplicate the work of his teacher, though he does state whatever is necessary to make the subject complete and explicit.

This naturally leads to another question: what is BKB's contribution to Sanskrit literature? As mentioned above, the *śabdaśakti* forms an important topic in *alaṅkāraśāstra* and the writers writing *prakaraṇagranthas* on this topic must follow the tradition closely, meaning that there is hardly any scope for any original contribution in its exposition. There is no possiblility of a new principle being founded. This is the case with BKB also. He can hardly add anything new so far as the topic of *śabdaśakti* is concerned. That is true even in the case of his *guru* AB also, and yet he has given two books on the same topic! What is his contribution then? To do him justice, we must say that in KND, AB has treated the subject technically for the scholars in a separate and independent work for the first time. It is a text-book, a *prakaraṇagrantha* written in verse form, which introduces the topic of *śabdaśakti* with all its depth and width, whereas TRN is a very simple text-book on the same topic written in lucid prose to make the subject easily comprehensive for the pupils.AB does not plunge into subtle and minute technicalities of grammar except touching them here and there. The third aspect of the topic, i.e. its *śāstraic* treatment is fulfilled by BKB. He has minutely observed the gaps which are left out in the preceding works and which can be treated systematically and *śāstraically.* thus, he is writing a sort of complementary *vādagrantha* to KND and TRN; on the other hand, he is particularly concentrating his attention on grammatical aspects, vide: the compound in सर्वगुणवान्, the vocative singular in सुभ्रु, the denotativensess or the suggestiveness of *nipātas,* the indication in द्रोणो व्रीहिः। and so on and so forth. these minutiae, niceties and subtle distinctions of fine hair-splitting relations are discursions in which lies BKB's contribution.His emphasis on the grammatical aspect of *śabdaśakti* seems to be the result of his intention to give the subject of *śabdaśakti* a status of *śāstra.* In order to achieve this purpose-to raise the topic to the dignity of a *śāstra*-he treats his subject in a *śāstraic* style[1] and expounds a number of arguments[2] and marshals a host of supportive statements from various sources.[3] He seems to have been prompted into this by a statement of his *guru* in his KND,[4] where he has shown the importance of the knowledge of *śabda* leading to the realisation of *brahma,* the supreme reality. He might have taken the clue from the famous statement of Patañjali (again quoted by AB in his commentary on KND towards the end of it) viz.

एकः शब्द सुष्ठुप्रयुक्तः स्वर्गे लोके कामधुग्भवति।[5] From this small incentive, BKB tries to spin out a substantial statement to claim the *śāstraic* status for his subject. He tries to do it in a number of ways. He compares *kāvya* to *the purāṇa* and establishes it as a *śāstra* refuting the arguments against its *śāstraic* character. The ultimate goal of any *śāstra* is *mokṣa* and if a *naiyāyika* can attain *mokṣa* by the knowledge of entities, if a *paurāṇika* can emancipate himself by reciting the *purāṇas,* a grammarian also can achieve that goal by realising the power of the word.[6] The germ of the argument lay in the work of his *guru* 'teacher'; the structure of arguments has been built up by the *śiṣya* 'the pupil'.

Again, BKB is aware of the difficulty of his situation. He is fully conscious of his *guru's* learned and skilful treatment of the subject. He, therefore, carefully avoids unnecessary repetitions. For instance, AB has shown the causes of *saṅketa* (सङ्केत-ग्रहणहेतवः)[7]. He has also discussed various views on establishing *saṅketa* 'convention', the denotation of a word.[8] He has also touched upon the *tātparyavṛtti* of the *mīmāṁsakas.*[9] He has discussed in detail the relationships between the denotative and the indicative meanings which cause *lakṣaṇā.*[10] BKB does not touch these points at all. Instead, he picks up the topic of the theory of *sphoṭa*, renders detailed treatment to it, poses arguments of the opposite block and then refutes them systematically. In the same way, BKB has filled up the lacuna left by his teacher so far as the treatment of polysemic words (like *śāstra)* and their meanings are concerned. He also incidentally indulges into the dispute whether these polysemic words convey all the senses simultaneously or consecutively.[11]

There are also instances where BKB seeks to detail upon the cursory treatment given to some discussions by AB bringing in some more elaborations from other sources such as Siddhāntakaumudī, Manorama, Śrīdharī commentary on Bhāgavata Purāṇa and also Vaṁśīdharī thereon. the discussion on *lakṣaṇā* in द्रोणो व्रीहिः।[12] and in श्यालः स्वस्रोरथाग्रहीत्।[13] are such examples. BKB discusses these points which have been left out by AB. While offering an interpetation to the operation of *lakṣaṇā* different from one given by his *guru* in the example- न जातु ब्राह्मणं हन्यात्। BKB also incidentally brings in the *mīmāṁsaic* discussion whether the statement can be called a *vidhi,* a *niyama* or a *parisaṅkhyā.*[14]

To conclude, we can say that in the treatment of *śakti* i.e.

abhidhā, BKB brings in all the sciences which deal with epistemology-*nyāya*, *mīmāṁsā, vyākaraṇa* etc. Thus it becomes an important major topic. BKB there clarifies the fundamentals of epistemological ultimata, the entities-the word and its meaning. Coming to *lakṣaṇā,* the scope for originality becomes limited to that of interpreting various examples, and of refuting the opinion of the *vaiyākraṇas*. Same is the case with *vyañjanā,* where he repeats the arguments of Ānandavardhana, Mammaṭa and Āśādhara in support of *dhvani,* ·*vyañjanā*-suggestion. What he adds is his own verse-सत्यासक्तमना:..........etc. and its fivefold interpretation in detail. However, he has added the description of *rasa* theory almost verbatim from the predecessors. To do him justice, we must say that nothing original or new can be said or is left out to be said so far as the subject of *śabdaśakti* is concerned.

But what is remarkable, appreciable and outstanding about the work is, how BKB renders the subject, how he gives it the form of a *śāstra* by his argumentative-*bhāsya* style and with so much spontaneity and lucidity, he moves into various *śāstras*. In the sweep of the topic under discussion, he sometimes enters into such subtlties of theoretical hairsplitting as would at once be a pointer to the excellent scholarship of the author as well as the delight for the learned connoiseurs. One would be prompted to say that these discussions are only remotely connected with the central topic of the work (and perhaps for that reason only, have been omitted by AB.). But let us again not forget the *pratijñā* he has made in the very first verse to make this into a *vādagrantha*. He is entering upon the deliberations of *śabda* as a matter of *śāstra*. That is the guideline. (cf: शास्त्रेति शब्दस्य विचारदीपं कुर्वे विवादं भगवान् सुबोधम्।) He does not think merely of *śabdaśaktis,* he thinks of *śabda* as *śāstra*-the science of *śabda* in the form of *brahma*. That provides a proper and correct angle both to view the content of the book and to decide upon the contribution of BKB to Sanskrit *śabdaśāstra*. The content which is primarily connected with poetics may not necessarily limit itself to it. The topic might enjoy the *śāstraic* excursions into different *śāstras,* at one moment it is *vyākaraṇa,* at another we may pass through the forest of *mīmāṁsā* or even we may have a dip into philosophy and so on. In fact VD is a delightful excursion of a learned scholar into various *śāstras* and this was not possible without an exemplary freedom of mind which BKB shows not only in his differences from his *guru* (of course. not without respect) but also in his discussions about the readings which have long-standing acceptance in the most popular texts like Reghuvaṁśam and Śrīmadbhagavadgītā. One point must be taken into note here: this worthy student of AB has been inspired and trained by his *guru* who himself has given some four/five important works on Sanskrit grammar.[15] BKB is so thoroughly steeped in the *śāstras* that not only the discussible words come to him handy from any of the well-known floating exuberance of *śāstras,* but even the discussions upon these words very easily and naturally glide into our traditionally accepted *śāstraic* style. That perhaps may be taken as BKB's strong point in his work. A strange but appropriate counterpart of his love for *śāstras* is apparent when we find at least five of his own illustrations (i.e. those which are not traditionally handed down in the previous works) from the Naiṣadhacaritam and two from the Śiśupāla-vadham both of which are called *śāstra-kāvyas*: This profusion of illustrations from the Naiṣadha (also in Nūtanatarī) and the Śiśupālavadham shows his *śāstraic* tendency.

Any region could have been proud of such a learned scholar versatile in various *śāstras*. We are happy to realise that not only Āśādhara himself, an excellent scholar of wide range of knowledge, but also BKB, a worthy student of this well-known *pandit* hailed from Gujarat which is often accused of little acumen and lack of versatility. That AB was from Gujarat is an established fact and BKB leaves fingerprints of his *gujaratiness* at one or two places in VD and clearly mentions *lālīgrāma* in the central part of Gujarat near Ahmedabad. (cf. ch. I) Thus, this learned pair of the teacher and the taught makes

Gujarat proud by their important contribution to *śāstra* literature in Sanskrit. [Incidentally, we must mention that BKB could have compose at least some poetic verses since he has quoted one (viz. सत्यासक्तमना:........) as an example of *abhidhāmūlā vyañjanā,* and Āśādhara has also given his own verse as an example of *śabdaśaktimūlā*[16] *Vyañjanā.* Such a pandit with a rare scholarship was moving about among us in Gujarat some two hundred years ago. And that is a matter of great pride and honour for us all.

The lacunae that have been left in the text leave the reader sometimes helpless and one wishes the editor could have availed herself of the help of at least one more manuscript of this work since the corrupt readings often leave one in doubt whether the emendations made in the text are correct or appropriate. A *codex unicum* makes the editor sometimes face such problems as have no solution. However, it is hoped that the critical edition of this manuscript may show some sound guidelines to the problems of manuscriptology.

FOOTNOTES:

1. Such a style is evident throughtout the work.
2. निदेशग्रन्थयोः शास्त्रमित्यमरव्याख्याने। and so on.
3. शब्दशास्त्रमनधीत्य......(सु०र०भा०वैयाकरणप्रशंसा, श्लो. ८)
   नाञ्जसा निगदितं.......(शिशु० १४, २३) and so on.
4. शब्दब्रह्मविचारेण परं ब्रह्मावगम्यते।
   शब्दवृत्तिविचारेण कृतस्तेऽस्माच्छिवप्रदः। (KND. III, 41)
5. महाभाष्यप्रदीप-पस्पशाह्निक, p.७
6. Vide p.5-7.
7. Vide KND I, 12, 13.
8. KNDI I, 28, 38.
9. KND I, 39.
10. TRN II.
11. VD, pp. 43-44.
12. Vide : यथा द्रोणो व्रीहिरिति। अत्र यत्परिमाणं तत्परिच्छिन्नो व्रीहित्यिर्थः। प्रत्ययार्थे

परिमाणे प्रकृत्यर्थोऽभेदेन संसर्गेण विशेषणम्। प्रत्ययार्थस्तु परिच्छेद्यपरिच्छेकभावेन व्रीहौ विशेषणमिति। (VD p. 20-21) and :.........वस्तुतस्तु सामान्याकारेण परिमाणं शक्योऽर्थः। द्रोणरूपविशेषाकारेण लक्ष्यार्थ एवेति। (त्रि. १६-१७)

13. Vide : किञ्च-श्यालः स्वस्रोरथाग्रहीदित्यत्र.......श्रीधरस्वामिनस्तु लिङ्गसमवायेन प्राणभृत उपदधातीतिवत् स्वसृशब्देन द्विवचनानुपपत्त्या मिथुनगुणद्वारा मिथुनलक्षणया स्वसृतत्पत्योरभिधानमित्याहु:। and श्यालः स्वस्रोरथाग्रहीत् इत्यत्र स्वसा च स्वसा च स्वसारौ तयोः। अत्र द्वितीयस्वसृशब्देन तत्पतिर्लक्ष्यते। यज्ञादिषु साहचर्यात्। एवं 'प्रथमयो पूर्वसवर्णः' अत्रापरेण प्रथमाशब्देन द्वितीया लक्ष्यते साहचर्यात् शब्दस्य द्रव्यत्वाच्च। (त्रि० २. पृ० १८)
14. Vide : किञ्च न जातु ब्राह्मणं हन्यादत्र विधिनियमः परिसंख्या वेति विचार्यते। (VDp. १९-२०).
15. The mss. of these works are traced out from oriental institute, Baroda, and Chunilal Gandhi Vidyabhavan Surat. Dr. R.I. Nanavati (Ex-director, ORI, Baroda. is working on the same.
16. आशाधरसमुत्पन्ना विमला बुद्धिशुद्धिदा।
    कोविदानन्दसहजाऽनुग्राह्यैषा त्रिवेणिका।। (त्रि. ३, पृ. २५).

APPENDIX - I

Xerox copy of the Manuscript

F_1O

F

F_1R

धिशब्दः सापेक्षोनित्यं सवः समस्यते॥ वाक्यवशाद्व्यपेक्षा हि वृत्तावपि न हीयत इति॥ समभिनाये
नाप्येतदभिप्रायेण सापेक्षत्वेपि गमकत्वात्समास इति उक्तं भवति॥ तेन वरतेर्गृहीतानुनयेन कामचै
त्रस्य शिष्यकुलं मैत्रस्य गुरुकुलमिति माख्याते॥ दृश्यं चक्षुस्तस्य शब्दोभुवने दुरे ठ इति पाठमं
नादृत्य अत्रेति शब्दोभुवनेष्विति पाठोगी कार्यः॥ कुर्वदृत्युक्तेन मधुकपरत्वहमिस ध्याहारेण बोध्यः॥
वाक्ये ह्याकांक्षितैकदेशपूरणमध्याहारः॥ आकांक्षितत्वं चार्थस्यैवान्वयस्यार्थ निष्ठत्वात्॥ यथा
भवानपीदं परवानेवेमीत्यत्र युष्मच्छब्दार्थस्याध्याहार इति अन्यथा शब्दाध्याहारे वेतीत्यत्र प्रथ
मपुरुषो न स्यात् युष्मच्छब्दस्य विशेष्येण प्रधान्यात् भवच्छब्दस्य तु न प्रधान्यं भातीति भवानिति
व्युत्पत्ते विशेषणत्वानुगमात्॥ तेन तत्वं निवृत्तस्त्वबिहाय कोऽत्रांछेरे भवान् द्विधिति शिष्याक्ति विस
त्रन पुनरुक्तिः॥ भवति भिक्षां देहीत्यादौ तु युष्मच्छब्दस्यैवाध्याहारः भवच्छब्दस्य संबोध्यतया च
रितार्थत्वात् अन्यथा देहीत्यत्र मध्यमपुरुषो न स्यात्। नन्वर्थनामे वान्वये शब्दाध्याहारो न्यु
क्त इति चेन्न शाब्दबोधे शब्दो पि भासत इति पक्षे शब्दहारे नैवार्थानामन्वयस्वीकारात् तोयमा
त्रस्येव पिपासते पि कलशाहारेवत दानयनवदिति अत्रावोनि विघ्नमप्यादि दोषपरिसन्नार्थेश्री श
ब्दप्रयोगः कृतो भवति॥ प्रथमे तावच्छिष्टसंप्रदायार्थनमस्क्रिया रूपं मंगलं निबध्नन् कुर्भिष्ट प्रति
जानीते वेदस्तु भगवान्साक्षात्तस्य व्याकरणं मुखं॥ यत्नयोर्वचनं शास्त्रं तास्थ्यात् त्वं परं घटु य
तु॥ द्वौ चक्रे द्वि चमी मांसे द्वौ योगाविति षड्बुध्या॥ वेदार्थदर्शकत्वेन दर्शनानि प्रचक्षते इति कर्तादि

F_2O

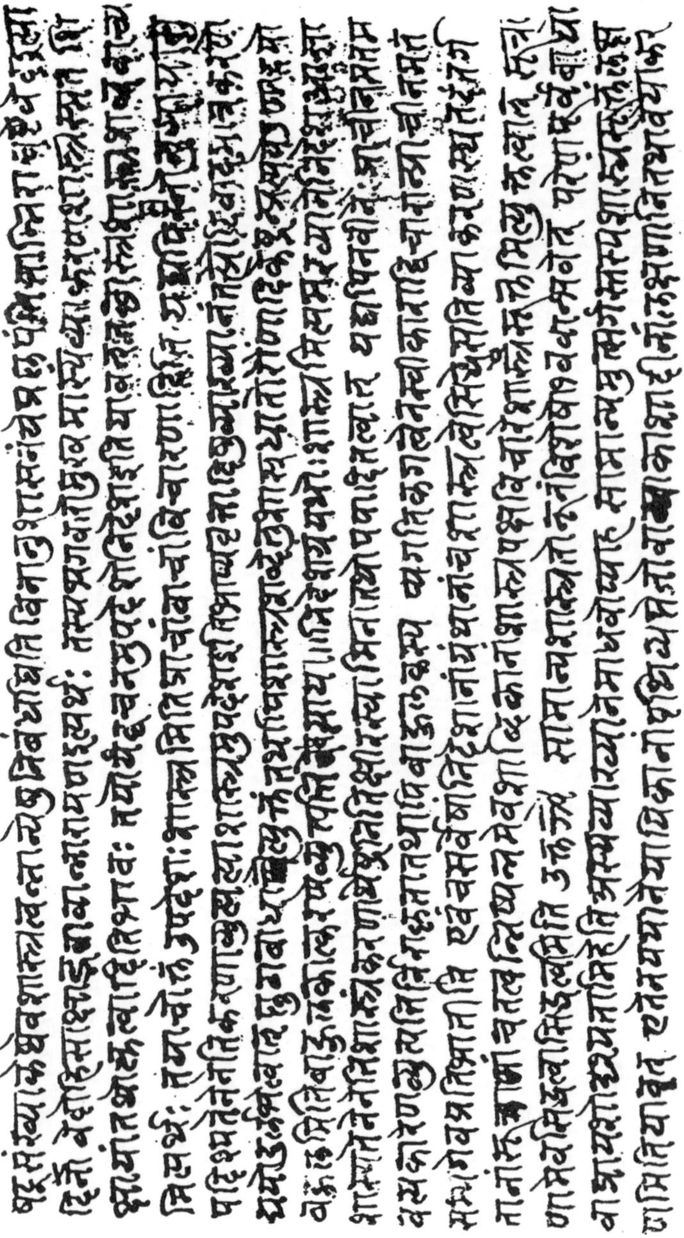

F_2R

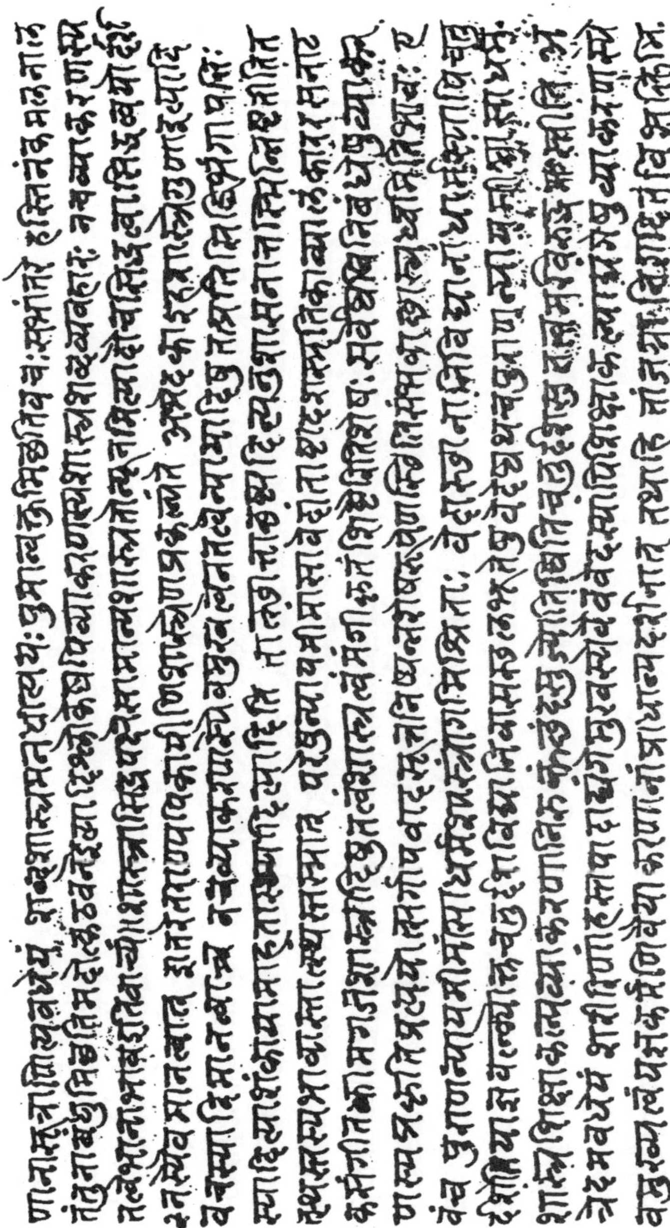

F_3O

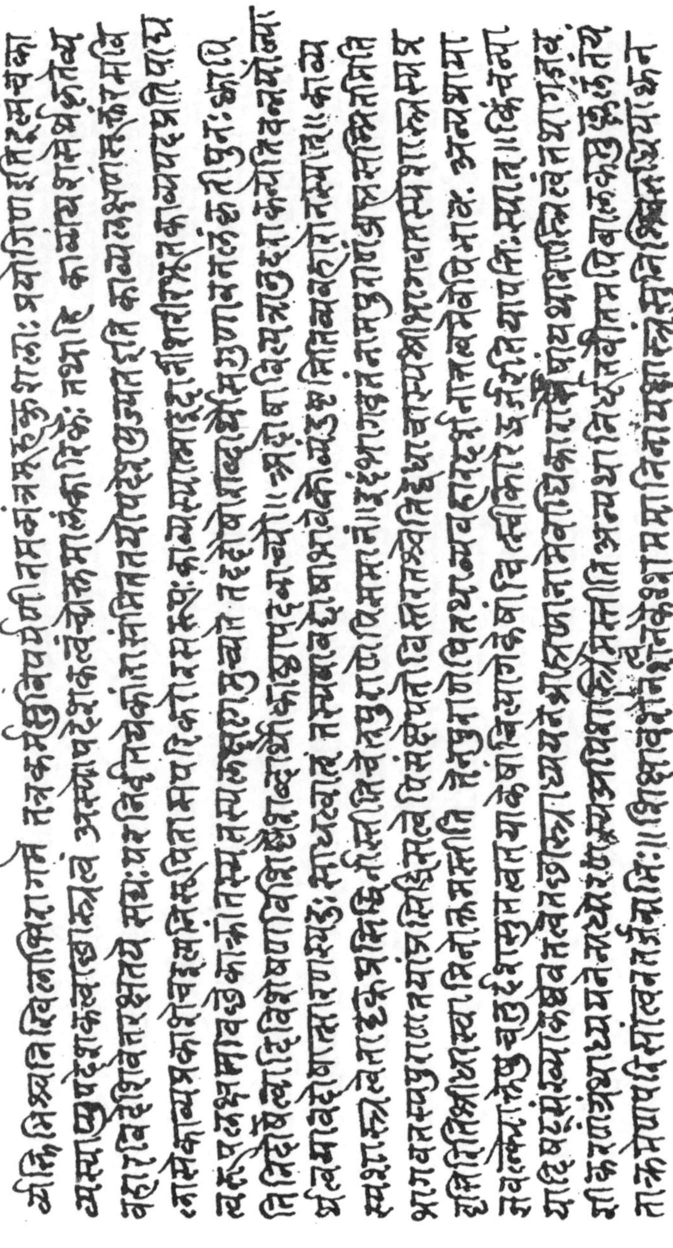

F_3R

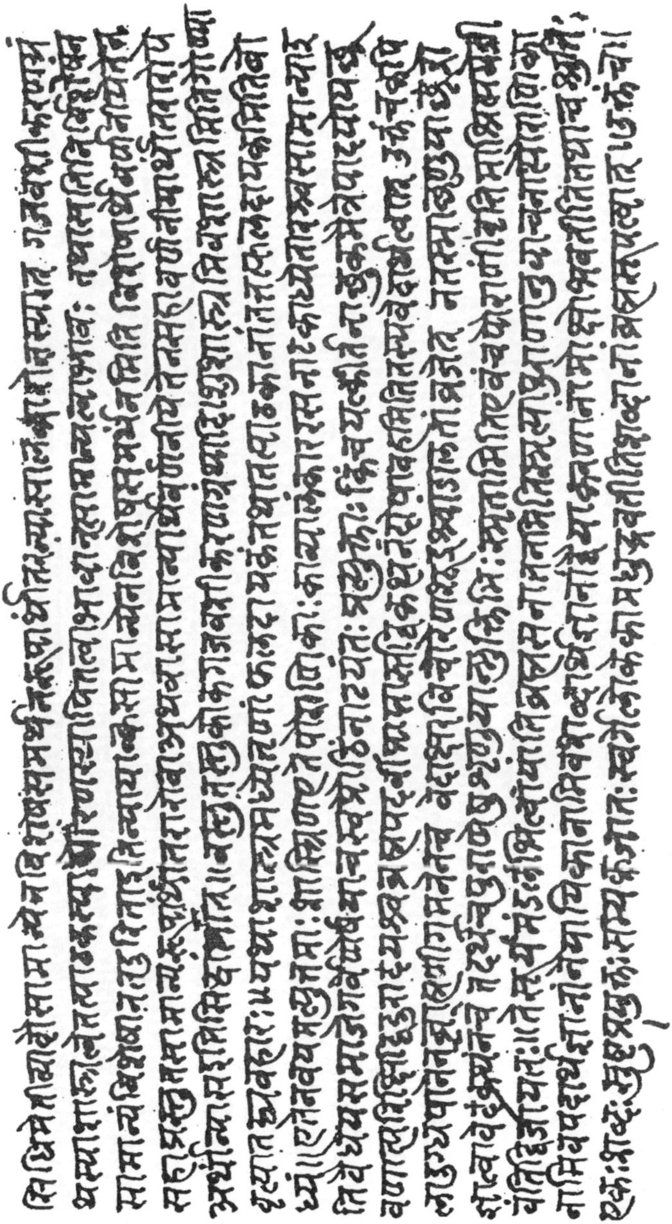

F$_4$O

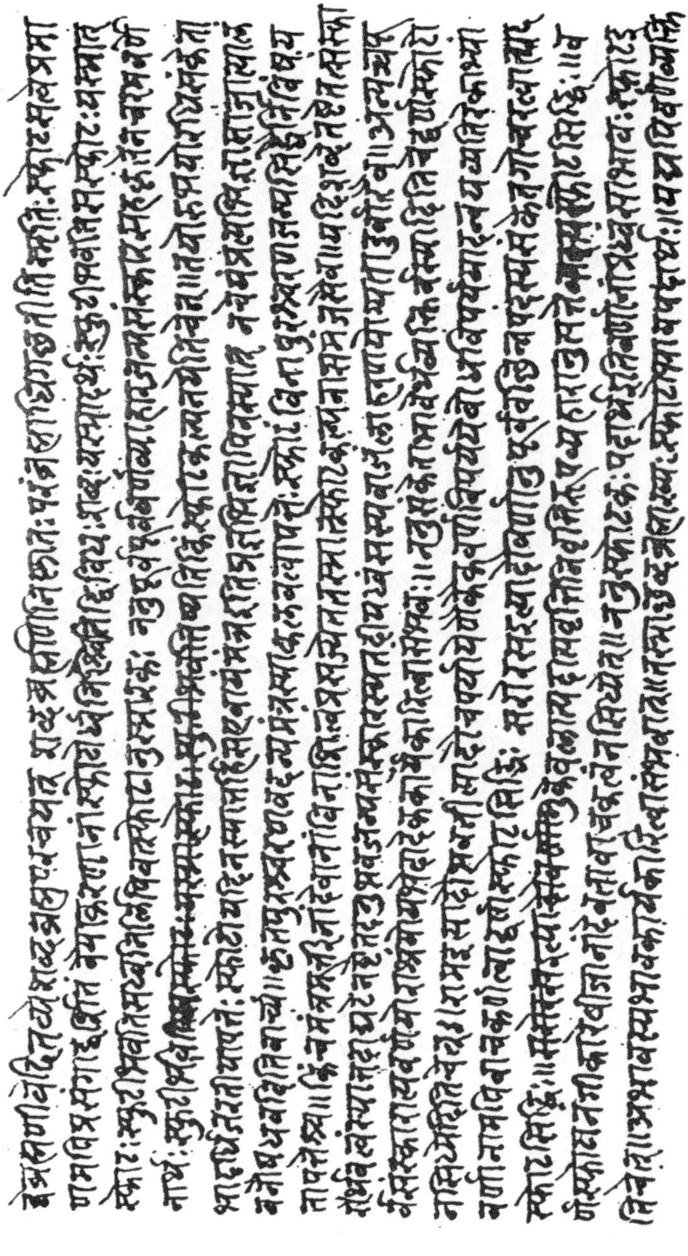

F$_4$R

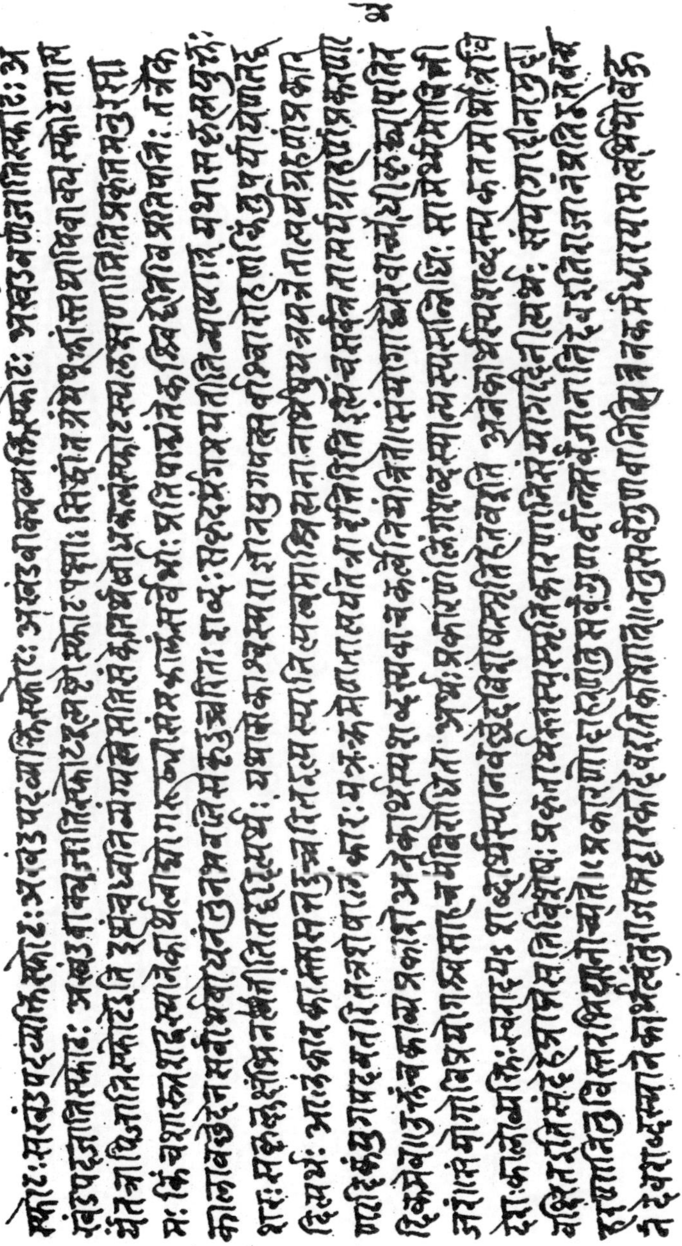

F_5O

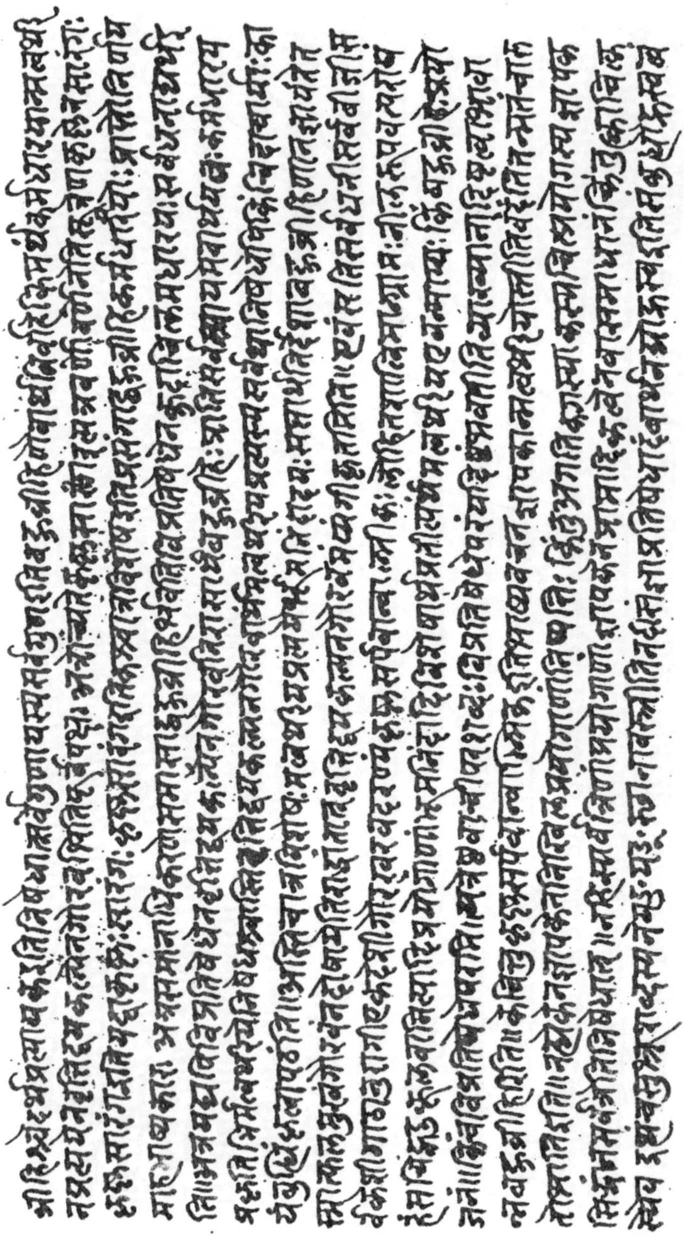

F_5R

F_6O

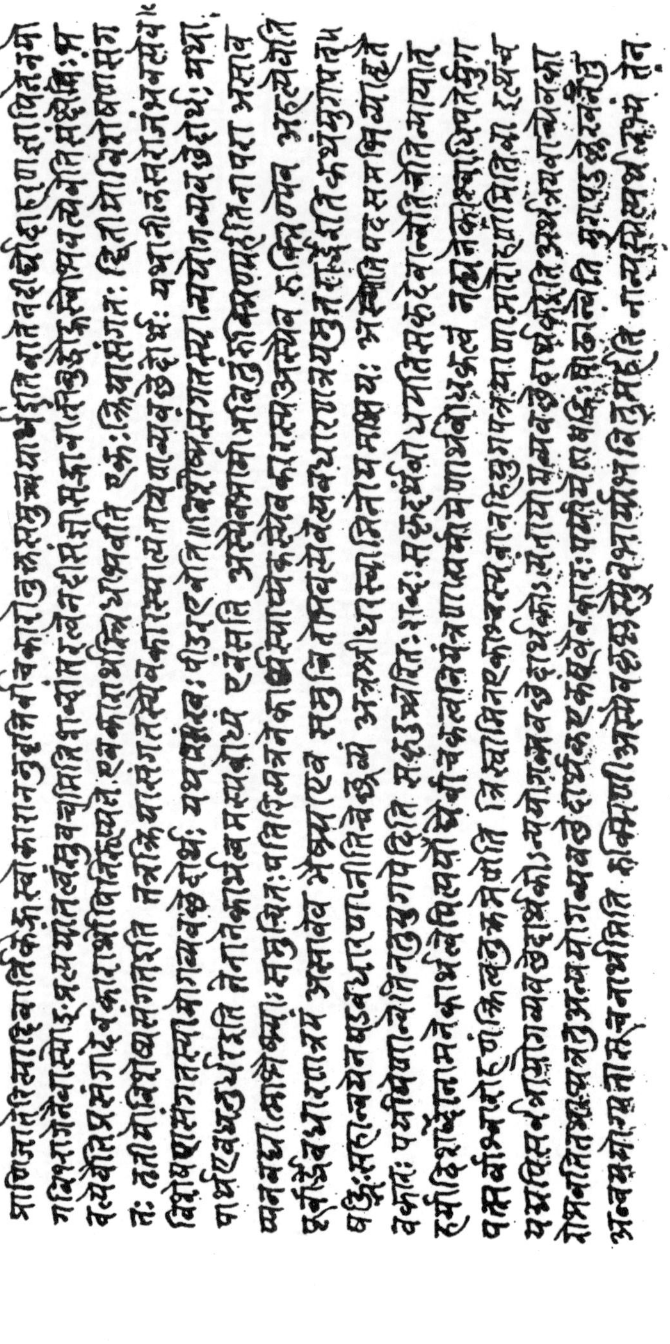

F_6R

श्रीकृष्णादन्यस्य चेयादैवेनकारेणान्ययोगव्यवच्छेदो बोध्यः॥ कुतइत्यपेक्षायामाह नापरेति इयं अपरा न भवतीति किं
तु राघवस्यैव सीता रुक्मिणी कृष्णजन्मनीति विष्णुपुराणवचनात् या पूर्वजन्मनि सीता सैव रुक्मिणीत्यायाति
सुज्ञानामयमाशयः यद्वा नास्ति अपरः श्रीकृष्णादन्यो वरणीयत्वेन यस्याः इति स्वस्य श्रीकृष्णसाधारण
गुणश्रवणात् यद्वा नास्ति आसमंतात्परा उत्कृष्टा यस्याः सकाशात् इति किं वास्य श्रीकृष्णस्य रुक्मिण्येव
भार्या भवितुमर्हतीति नापरेति रुक्मिणीपदसमभिव्याहृतैवकारेणान्ययोगव्यवच्छेदः यद्यपि सत्य
भामादीनां योग्यतास्ति तथापि पौरजनानां भविष्यज्ज्ञानाभावात् तादृक् विकल्पः पूर्वव्याख्याने तु अस्येति
समयपदसमभिव्याहृतैवकारेणान्ययोगव्यवच्छेदार्थमवधारणमत्र तु शाब्दमिति भेदः किं च रुक्मिणी अस्य
भार्या भवितुं यद्वा अभार्या भार्या न तथा संपद्यमाना भवितुमिति सप्तम्यंतमेव समस्तं पदं अर्हतीत्येवेति किं
यापदसमभिव्याहृतैवकारेण योग्यतायाः अत्यंताभावव्यवच्छेदात् योग्यतावधारणमिति त्रिधा व्याख्या
नेन भैष्म्याः सकलगुणसंपन्नत्वं पूर्वार्द्धेन व्यज्यते अथोत्तरार्द्धं व्याख्या अपि इष्टार्थे च परं अनवद्या
त्मा स्तुत्यविग्रहः स्तुत्यस्वभावो वा आत्मा देहे धृतौ जीवे स्वभावे परमात्मनि इत्यमरः असावैव भैष्म्याः पति
र्वरः सम्यगुचितः समुचितः योग्योस्तीत्यर्थः सकलगुणसंपन्नत्वेन स्पृहणीयगुणत्वादित्यर्थः उक्तं च कन्या
वरयते रूपं माता वित्तं पिता श्रुतं बांधवाः कुलमिच्छंति मिष्टान्नमितरे जना इति किं च भैष्म्या एव अन्यन
द्यात्मासौ पतिः समुचितोतिसमीचीनः सप्तवरगुणसंपन्नत्वाच्छस्त्रशास्त्रप्रवीणत्वाच्चेत्यर्थः उक्तं च कुलं
च शीलं च सनाथता च विद्या च वित्तं च वपुर्वयश्च एते गुणा सप्त वरे भवेयुः समीक्ष्य देया जनकेन पुत्रीति अथ च॥८

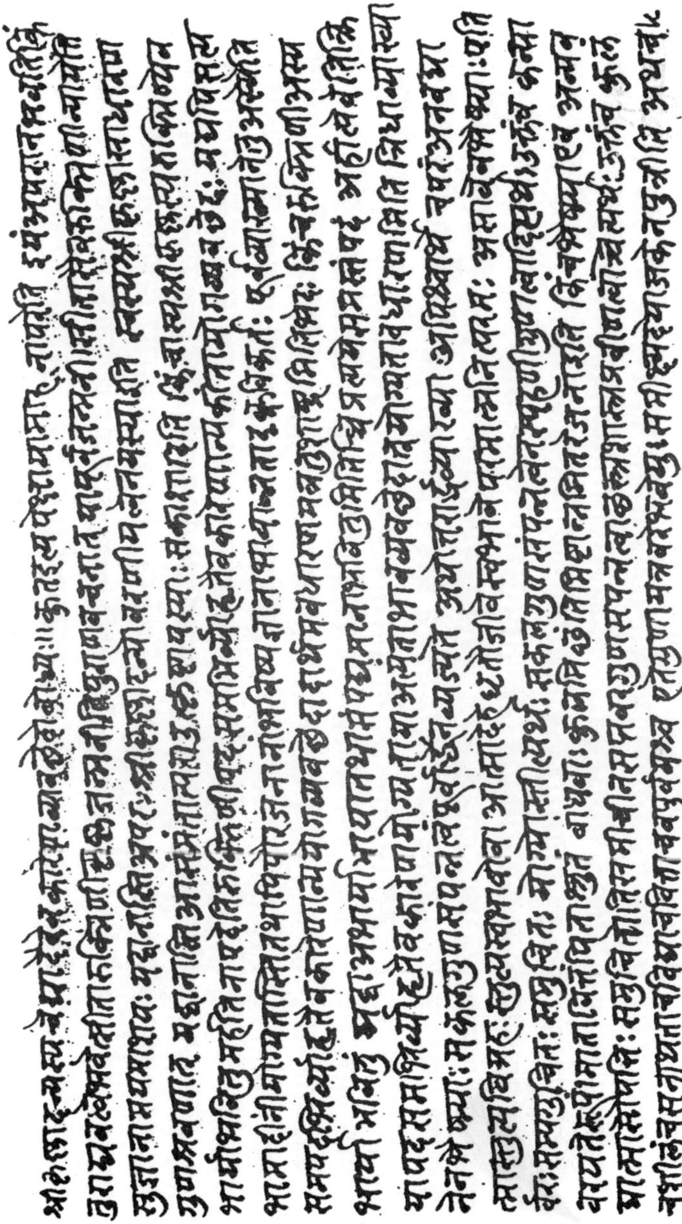

F$_7$O

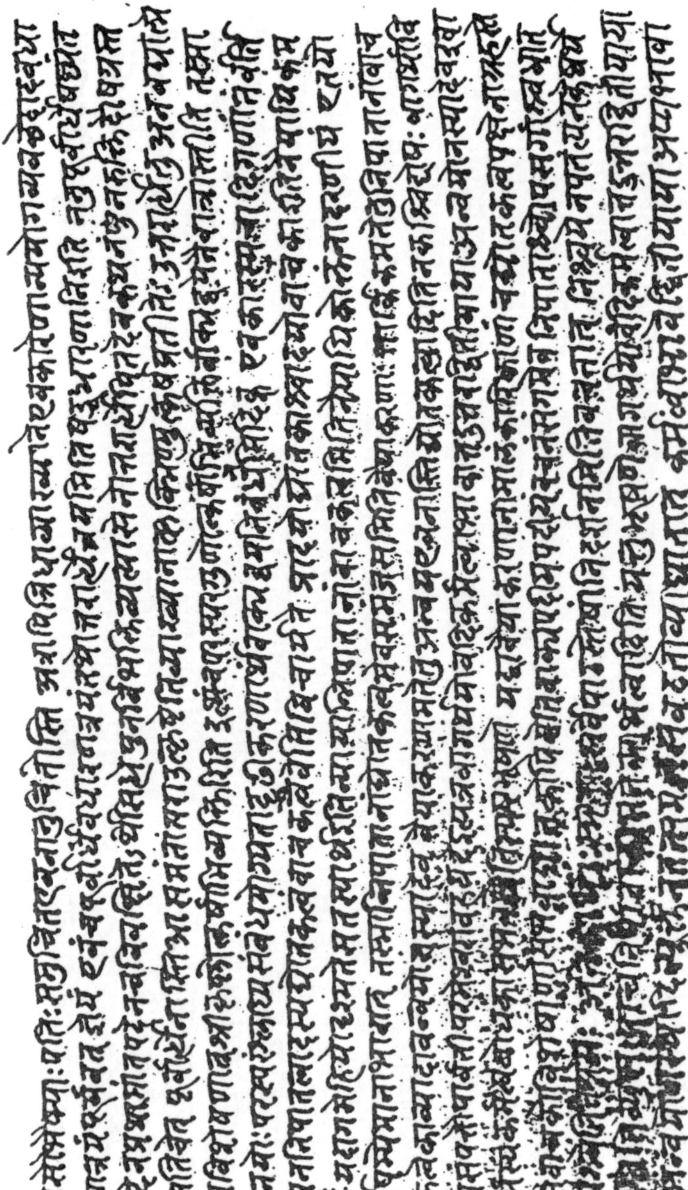

F_7R

केनसमर्थः प्रहितेयौविधानप्रमितेति पूर्वपक्षः वस्तुतस्तु अहितेत्येवं वक्तुं नार्हतीति किंतु प्रथममेवोक्त तथा
हि वागर्थाविवेत्यत्र शब्दस्य सादृश्यवाचकत्वं केन प्रकारेणाऽविवक्षितामिति चेदुच्यते वागर्थावि
ववागार्थौ यथा नित्यसंबद्धौ न संपृक्तौ संश्लेषैकीभूतौ नित्यः शब्दार्थसंबंध इति मीमांसकोक्तेः तथा
तेन प्रकारेण संपृक्तौ पार्वतीपरमेश्वरौ इत्यन्वयः संपृच्यतेनौ संपृक्तौ व्यतिकर्तरिक्तप्रत्ययः कर्तृकृताद्वो
त्कत्वात्स्वधर्मेव न द्वितीयेति सुधितादृक्षमयादृशावधातव्यमित्यालंकारिकाः किंच शब्दार्थयोर्बोध्यबोधक
भावलक्षणः संबंधो धर्मः सा च शब्दनिष्ठा अर्थविषया च हेतुमयधर्मः शक्तिलक्षणाव्यंजनाभेदात्त्रिधा
सेत्याहुः तत्र चास्मात्पदादयमर्थो बोद्धव्य इति प्रवर्तकोपदेशः संकेतः स एव शक्तिरिति तार्किकाः त
दतिरिक्ता तत्सहकारिणीत्यालंकारिकाः सर्वशब्दानां याथात्म्यग्राहकत्वरूपे देशाक्तीति वैयाकरणाः वृत्तिवि
षयभूतोऽर्थस्तथा च शब्दा अपि त्रिविधाः तत्राद्यः शक्यो द्वितीयो लाक्षणिकस्तृतीयो व्यंजकश्चेति वृ
त्तित्रयमध्ये संकेतसहकारिणी शक्तिः सा च शक्तिस्त्रिधा योगो रूढिर्योगरूढिश्चेति जातिगुणक्रियायदृ
दृच्छेति तु प्रवृत्तिनिमित्तानि एवं सति वागर्थाविति प्रथमोपवया इवेति च द्वितीयस्तयोर्द्विवेन विभक्त्यं
लोपः सर्वपदप्रकृतिस्वरत्वं चेति वक्तव्यमिति वार्तिकेन समासे सति या शक्तिः संपद्यते सा समस्तशब्दनिष्ठा य
गशक्तिः ननु समासे खलु भिन्नैव शक्तिः पंकजशब्दवत् बहूनां वृत्तिधर्माणां वचनेनैव साधने स्यान्मते और
वं तस्मादेकार्थीभावआश्रितइति सिद्धांतादत्र अवयवविभागकल्पनाभावाद्योगार्थ केन स्यादिति वा
च्यं जहत्स्वार्थावृत्तिपक्षे विभागानंगीकारेपि अजहत्स्वार्थावृत्तिपक्षस्यापि व्यवहारोपयोगेन स्वीकारात्
उद्धाकृरिवेमत्र तु इवशब्दस्य विशेष्यवामनपदेन सहान्वयस्य विवक्षा शब्दाङ्कशब्देन सामाध्यंशा

F_8O

F8R

सुशब्दं करोतीति तुंबुरुः तुंबधातोरुरुन्प्रत्यय इति हेमकोशे देवजातिगंधर्ववर्गप्रकारेण व्याख्यानेत
थाव्युत्पत्तिदर्शनात् तेन संज्ञारूढोयमेकार्थवाचकः शब्दस्तत्कारत्रयविशिष्टस्तस्य बोधेयं अथ लक्षणा ॥
शक्यसंबंधो लक्षणेति तार्किकाः संबंधस्योभयनिष्ठत्वान्मुख्ये शब्देपीयं प्रवर्तते । तस्माच्छक्यसंबंधे
नाशक्यार्थप्रतिपादनी वृत्तिर्लक्षणेत्यालंकारिकाः मम्मटेन त्विद्धलक्षणतामनुसृत्योक्तं भेदितो बाणोव
मेछेदमुदोभेदं प्राणापहरणंच करोति तथैकाभिधाख्यव्यापारवतः शब्दस्य पदार्थोपस्थितिरिति
लक्षणान्चनांगीकार्यास्याद्दीर्घदीर्घाभिधाव्यापारेणातीतादिप्रसिद्धेरिति वैयाकरणाः साचलक्ष
णावृत्तिः शब्दव्यापारत्वाच्छब्दनिष्ठा मुख्यार्थबोधे सति तत्संबंधिनमर्थं विषयी करोति उक्तंच मुख्या
र्थबाधे तद्योगे रूढितोथ प्रयोजनात् अन्योर्थो लक्ष्यते यत्सा लक्षणारोपित क्रियते मुख्यार्थबाधे
सति मुख्यार्थयोगे सति रूढेः प्रयोजनाद्वा यया वृत्त्या अन्योर्थो लक्ष्यते सा लक्षणेत्यन्वयः ॥ प्र
थमं तावल्लक्षणा त्रिविधा भवति जहल्लक्षणा अजहल्लक्षणा जहदजहल्लक्षणा चेति यत्र
सति मुख्यार्थबाधे शब्दः शक्यार्थं जहाति तत्र जहल्लक्षणा यत्र तमर्थं न जहाति तत्राजहल्लक्षणा
यत्र तदुभयं तत्र जहदजहल्लक्षणा पुनरपि द्विविधापीयं द्विविधा निरूढा फलवती च ॥ ॥
निरूढलक्षणीयाः शक्तितुल्यत्वात्कोशादिप्रसिद्धा इयं तु शक्तितुल्यापि मुख्यार्थ
बाधे सति स्यात्तेन शक्तितोस्या विशेषः अनादिलक्षणा चैषेत्याहुः यत्र फलवती ल
क्षणा तत्र फलं तु व्यंजनाख्यव्यापारगम्यमेव न शक्तिलक्षणागम्यमिति व्यंजनावृत्तिनिरूपणमुरीकर
व्यामइति

F$_9$O

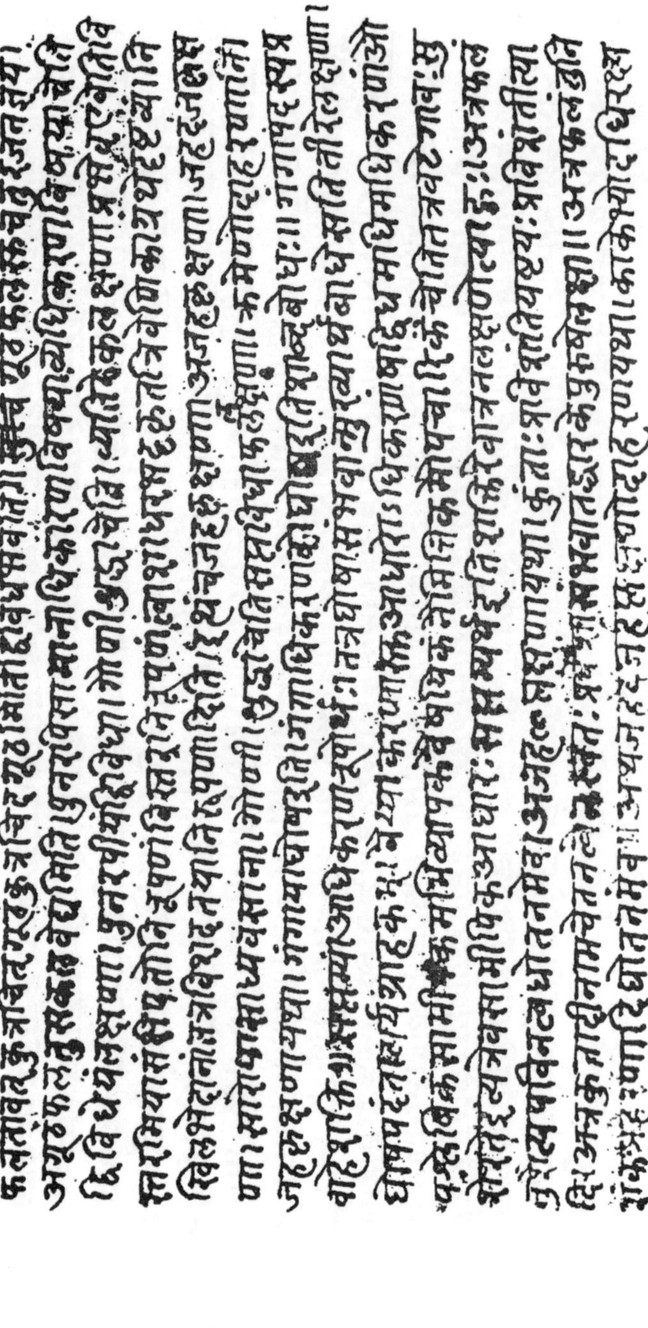

त्रामिति। अत्र शक्यकाकत्वपरित्यागेनाशक्यदध्युपघातकत्वपुरस्कारेण काकशब्दस्य दध्यु
पघातकत्वमात्रे जहदजहल्लक्षणेति। काकस्येतुच्छताप्रतीतिश्चात्र फलम्। यदा तु केनचि
द्रासिद्धं तस्य दधिपात्रस्यान्यथा तु केशकाकाभावात्तास्ययेपि पात्रिसत्वेन लक्षणा
न भवति। सर्वत्र तात्पर्यानुपपत्तिर्लक्षणाबीजमिति सिद्धान्तात्। उदाहरणान्तरमाह। न
नातु ब्राह्मणं हन्यादिति॥ अत्र शक्य ब्राह्मणशब्दो नरद्वितीयैकवचपरित्यागेनाश=
क्यद्वितीयाबहुवचनपुरस्कारेणैकवचनस्य बहुवचने लक्षणा। अन्यथा सर्वेषां ब्रा
ह्मणानामवध्यत्वं न स्यात्। यत्तु त्रिवेणीकायां नञा तु ब्राह्मणं नन्यादित्यत्र व्यक्तिपरेण
ब्राह्मणशब्देन तत्संभवे तो जातिर्लक्ष्यत इति प्राचीनमतानुसारेणोक्तं भूर्भविष्यतिपरं
तु न तत्संभवसंभवति भाति। तथाहि। अत्र लक्षणया व्यक्त्या जातिबोधाभ्युपगमे निन्ना
ते हननायोगात्पुनरपि व्यक्तौ लक्षणापेक्षा॥ यथा क्षत्रजादि रुदयायभुजाभ्यां यस्तवै
हस्त्वजतो मुखेन प्राग्निस्त्रजातिशब्देन तदाश्रयीभूताव्यक्तयो लक्ष्यं नरू तस्य भावे
मुख्यार्थं बाधत्वा नेहहदिहापीति तद्दोषता दवस्य मे व। तस्मात् ब्राह्मणशब्दो नर
द्वितीयैकवचनाशपरित्यागेनाशक्यद्वितीयाबहुवचस्वीकारेण लक्षणायाः प्रवृत्ते

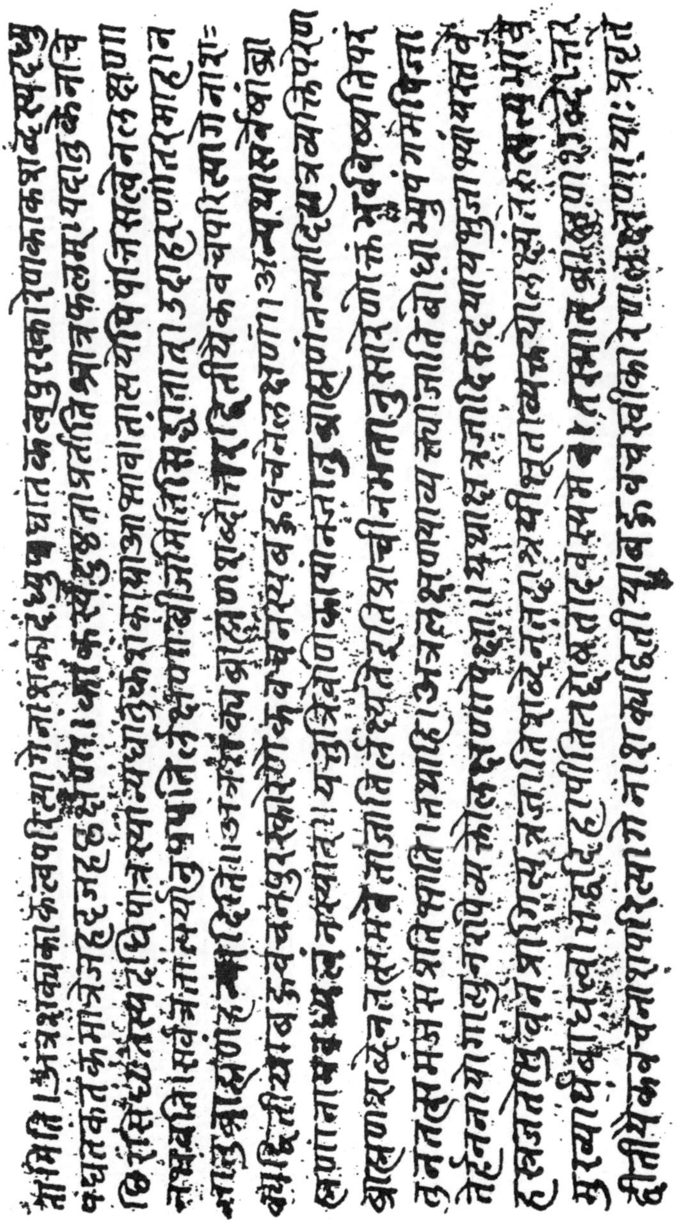

$F_{10}O$

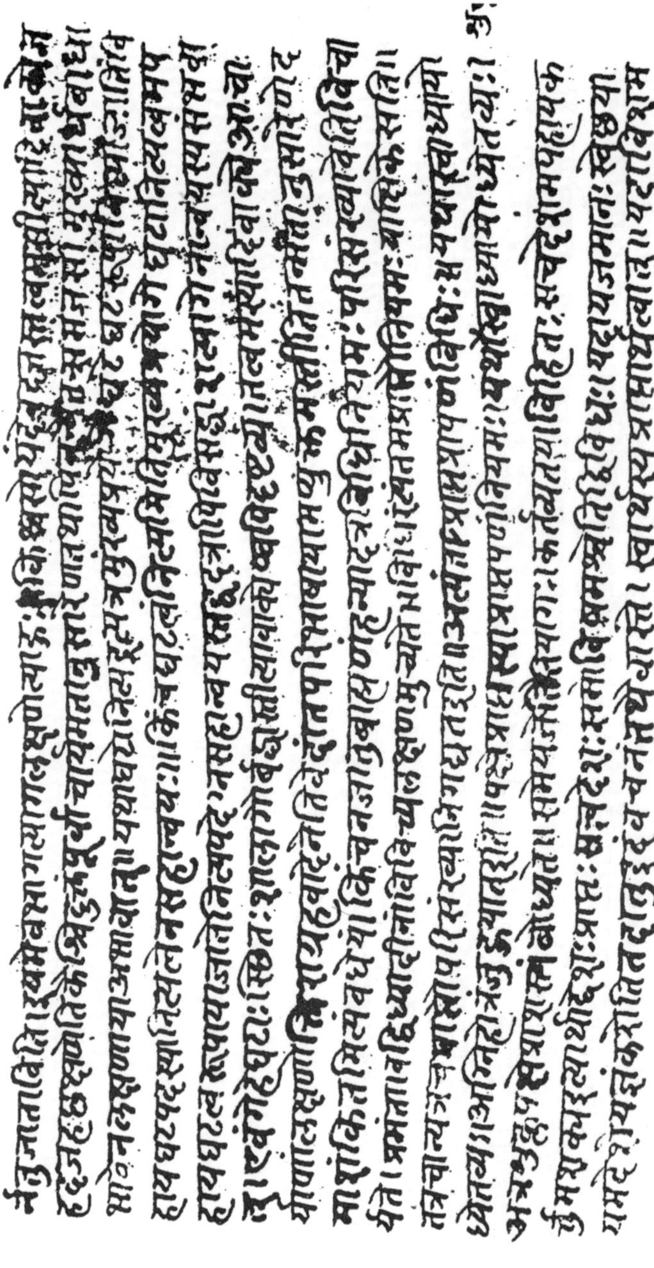

F$_{10}$R

देशे यजेत तदा तिदं वचनं स्वार्थं विधत्ते ॥ स्वार्थस्य तदानीमप्राप्तार्थत्वात् ॥ अन्यथा ऽशास्त्रीयं यागो
नुष्ठितः स्यात् ॥ एवं प्राङ्मुखोऽन्नानि भुंजीतेति स्मार्तमुदाहरणं व्याख्यातं ॥ एकस्यानेकत्र प्राप्त
स्यान्यतो निवृत्त्यर्थमेकत्र प्राप्त्यर्थं पुनर्वचनं परिसंख्या ॥ तथोदाः ॥ तिस्रो भार्या ब्राह्मणस्ये
ति ॥ अत्र विवाहविधिना चतुर्ष्वपि वर्णेषु संग्रहः प्राप्तः परिसंख्यया शूद्रानिषेधो बाध्यते ॥
यथा वा ॥ इमामगृभ्णन् रशनामृतस्येत्यश्वाभिधानीमादत्त इति मंत्रः ॥ स्वसामर्थ्यादश्वा
भिधान्या गार्दभाभिधान्यश्च रशनाया ग्रहणे विनियुक्तः पुनरश्वाभिधानीमादत्त इति
वचनेनाश्वाभिधान्यां विनियुज्यमानो गर्दभाभिधान्या विनिवर्तत इति ॥ एवं पंच पंचनखा
भक्ष्या इति । अत्र हि यदृच्छया शशादिषु श्वादिषु च भक्षणं प्राप्तं पुनः शशादिषु श्रूयमाणं
श्वादिभ्यो निवर्तत इति ॥ इत्थं च किमत्र ब्राह्मणावधनिषेधवाक्यं विधिरूपं किं वा नियम
मरूपं परिसंख्यारूपं वा । अत्रोच्यते न तावन्नियमविधिः पक्षे प्राप्तस्याप्राप्तत्वाभा
वात् ॥ नापि परिसंख्या । स्वार्थहानिः परार्थकल्पना प्राप्तबाधलक्षणदोषत्रयसमास
क्तेः । तस्मादपूर्वविधिरेवेत्याहुः ॥ किंच शुक्लपक्षे स्वाध्यायोऽध्येतव्य इति नियमवि
ध्युदाहरणे प्राशस्त्यमात्रं न तु तदकरणे दोष इति ॥ परिसंख्यायां तु शशादिभक्षणे न
दोषप्राशस्त्यं । श्वादिभक्षणे तु दोषश्रवणेन प्रायश्चित्तविधानमिति नियमविधेः सका

$F_{11}O$

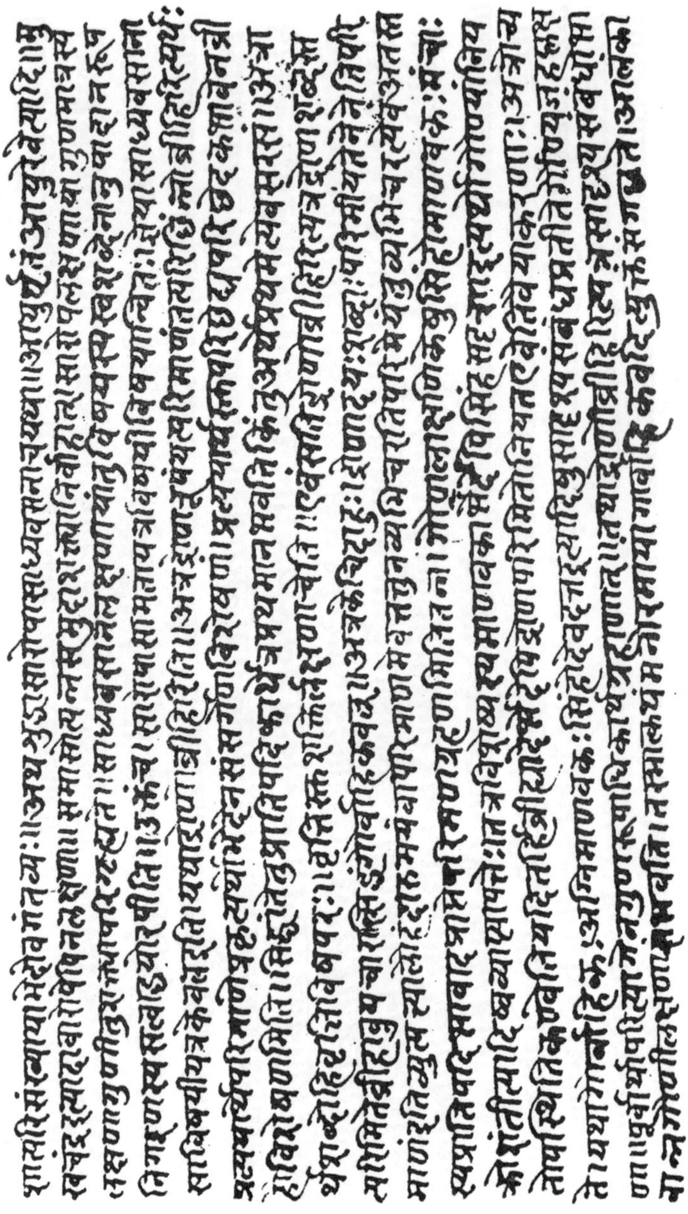

$F_{11}R$

रिकमतेत्वत्रशुद्धाफलवतीजहल्लक्षणातथासतिनकिंचिदूषणमिति।यथाआयुर्घृतंआयुरेवेदमित्यत्र
सामानाधिकरणविषयासारोपासाध्यवसानीचलक्षणाशुद्धास्तितद्वत्द्रोणोव्रीहिरित्यत्रापिद्रोणात्मप
मानपात्रेणपरिछिन्नेव्रीहौद्रोणशब्दोलाक्षणिकः।वस्तुतस्तुसामान्याकारेणपरिमाणंशक्योर्थः।।द्रोण
त्वपविशेषाकारेणलक्ष्यार्थएवेतिसिद्धांतएवेति।।अथसाध्यवसानोदाहरणं।।यथासिद्धांतकौमुदी
तिशब्दकौस्तुभइतिच।।अत्रकौमुदीशब्देनकौस्तुभशब्देनचद्वत्तौसाध्यवसानालक्षणा।।अथ न्यथा
इवार्थेकल्पविधानस्यदर्शनात्कौमुदीइवकौमुदिकाकौस्तुभइवकौस्तुभकइतिस्यात्।।किंचात्रशब्दभूतःकौस्तुभः
शब्दकौस्तुभइतिमध्यपदलोपीसमासःशब्दरूपेणपरिणतइत्यर्थः।।तेनपरिणामालंकारःशब्दत्वेनपरिणत
स्यकौस्तुभस्यार्थनिर्णयक्रियाहेतुत्वोक्तिःसामंजस्यात्।।नचोपमितसमासः।।उद्धतइतिसाधारणधर्म
प्रयोगात्।।नापिमयूरव्यंसकादिसमासः।।तत्रोत्तरपदार्थस्यप्राधान्यात्।।अत्रत्वर्थनिर्णयहेतुतयापूर्व
पदार्थप्राधान्यापेक्षणात्।।अर्थनिर्णयोहिशब्दैरेवजायतेनतुकौस्तुभेनमणिनेति।।नचोद्धतशब्दा
र्थानुरोधेनोत्तरपदार्थप्राधान्यंशक्यम्।।उद्धतइत्यस्योभयान्वयित्वात्।।भाष्योद्धतानांशब्दानांनिर्म
लत्वद्योतनायकौस्तुभपरिणामोक्तिरिति।।अत्रेदमवधेयंव्यस्तरूपकोदाहरणेसारोपालक्षणा।।रूपकातिश
योक्त्युदाहरणेसाध्यवसानालक्षणेति।।व्यतिरेकलक्षणातुसाधुरितिपुनःसाधुकर्त्तव्यंकिंमतःपरमित्यादि
षुद्रष्टव्या।।गौर्वाहीकइत्यादौजाड्यमांद्यादिगुणसाम्याद्गौणीलक्षणा।।उक्तंचलक्ष्यमाणगुणैर्योगाद्वृत्तेरि
ष्टातुगौणतेति।।शोणोधावतीत्यत्रशोणगुणविशिष्टेगुणिन्यश्वेलक्षणा।।नरवैर्युतंगर्भिणीनामधेयं
बाणेरश्वैस्त्र्यहायनेरित्यादिषुचनखगतविंशतिसंख्यारूपेगुणेलक्षणा।।नखादीनांविंशतिसंख्या

$F_{12}O$

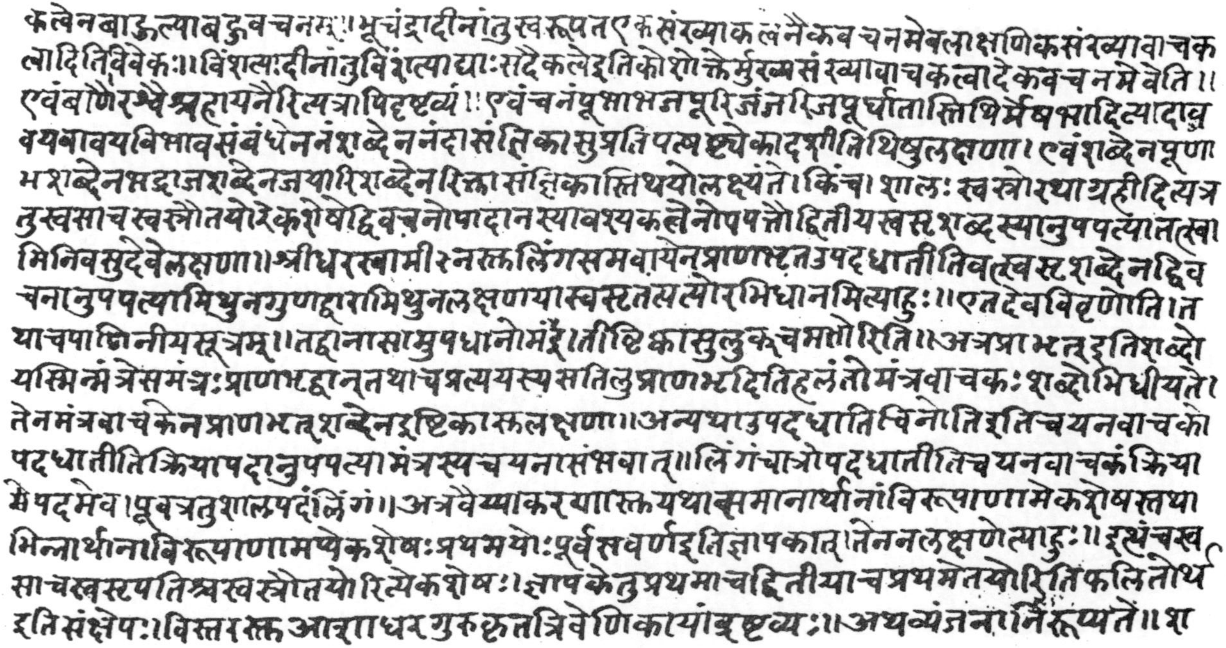

कत्वेन बाहुल्याद् बहुवचनम् ॥ भूचंद्रादीनां तु स्वरूपत एकसंख्याकत्वेनैकवचनमेव लाक्षणिकसंख्यावाचक
त्वादिति विवेकः ॥ विंशत्यादीनां तु विंशत्याद्याः सदैकत्वे इति कोशोक्तेर्मुख्यसंख्यावाचकत्वादेकवचनमेवेति ॥
एवं बाणैरश्वैश्च हायनैरित्यत्रापि द्रष्टव्यं ॥ एवं च नंपूर्भाभज भूरिजं नरिजपूर्णाता स्तिथिर्मेषभाद्दित्यादावु
वयवावयविभावसंबंधेन नंशब्देन नंदासंज्ञिका सुप्रतिपत्स्यष्ठ्येकादश्यस्तिथिषु लक्षणा । एवं शब्देन पूर्णा
भशब्देन भद्रा जशब्देन जया रिशब्देन रिक्ता संज्ञिकास्तिथयो लक्ष्यंते । किंच । शालः स्वस्त्रोरथा ग्रहीदित्यत्र
तु स्वसा च स्वस्त्रीतयोरेकशेषे द्विवचनोपादानस्यावश्यकत्वेनोपपत्तौ द्वितीयस्वसृशब्दस्यानुपपत्त्या तत्स्वा
मिनि वसुदेवे लक्षणा ॥ श्रीधरस्वामी स्वनस्त्रलिंगसमवायेन प्राणभृत उपदधातीतिवत् स्वसृशब्देन द्विव
चनानुपपत्त्या मिथुनगुणद्वारा मिथुनलक्षणया स्वसृतत्स्वस्त्रोरभिधानमित्याहुः ॥ एतदेव विवृणोति । त
या च पाणिनीयसूत्रम् ॥ तद्धानासामुपधानो मंत्र इतीष्टकासु लुक् च मतोरिति ॥ अत्र प्राणभृत् इति शब्दो
यस्मिन्मंत्रे स मंत्रः प्राणभृद्वान् तथा च प्रत्ययस्य सति लुप्राणभृदिति हलंतो मंत्रवाचकः शब्दोभिधीयते ।
तेन मंत्रवाचकेन प्राणभृत् शब्देन दृष्टिकास्त्र लक्षणा ॥ अन्यथा उपदधाति चिनोति इति चयनवाचको
पदधातीति क्रियापदानुपपत्त्या मंत्रस्य चयनासंभवात् ॥ लिंगं चात्रोपदधातीति चयनवाचकं क्रिया
से पदमेव । पूर्वत्र तु शालपदं लिंगं ॥ अत्र वैयाकरणास्तु यथा समानार्थानां विरूपाणामेकशेषस्तथा
भिन्नार्थानां विरूपाणामप्येकशेषः प्रथमयोः पूर्वसवर्ण इति ज्ञापकात् तेन न लक्षणेत्याहुः ॥ इत्थं च स्व
सा च स्वसृपतिश्च स्वस्त्रीतयोरित्येकशेषः ॥ ज्ञापके तु प्रथमा च द्वितीया च प्रथमे तयोरिति फलितोर्थ
इति संक्षेपः ॥ विस्तरस्तु आशाधरगुरुकृतत्रिवेणिकायां द्रष्टव्यः ॥ अथ व्यंजना निरूप्यते ॥ शा

F$_{12}$R

शक्यार्थलक्ष्यार्थातिरिक्तप्रकारेणोपयोग्यन्यार्थबोधिका वृत्तिर्व्यंजना॥ उक्तंच काव्यप्र
काशे॥ अनेकार्थस्य शब्दस्य वाचकत्वे नियंत्रिते॥ संयोगाद्यैरवाच्यार्थधीकृद्व्यापृतिरंजनं॥ इति॥ नानावि
धार्थस्य शब्दस्य वाचकत्वे संयोगाद्यैर्नियामकैर्नियंत्रिते सति प्रकृतार्थोपयोग्यन्यार्थबोधजनको व्यापारोऽं
जनं व्यंजनाख्या वृत्तिरित्यर्थः॥ इयं च व्यंजना त्रिविधा॥ शब्दशक्तिमूला॥ लक्षणामूला॥ व्यंजनमूला चेति।
शब्दशक्तिमूला यथा॥ तत्कारदायद्वदनस्य तत्क्वाबदेस्य शक्तिः कथमन्यथा ते॥ पत्रं कुदातुं गुणशालिपूग
कवादतः खंडयितुं प्रभुत्वं। अत्र यद्वदनस्य सरस्वतीवदनस्य रदा दंता स्तर्कास्तर्कैः शास्त्ररूपास्तर्काविचारणीयाः॥
चारणीयाः॥ अन्यथैवं नो चेदस्य वदनस्य वादे वादविषये शक्तिः सामर्थ्यं कथं स्यात्। न्यायशास्त्राध्य
यनं विना वादं कर्तुं न शक्यते इत्यर्थः॥ चतुर्विंशति गुणाशालिनां पदार्थानां पूगः समूहो यस्मिन्नेतादृ
शं पत्रं दातुं च परं वादाः खंडयितुं सामर्थ्यं कुत इति॥ वाद्यर्थितिद्वितीया प्रकृतार्थे॥ नास्ति दंता यस्य स अदन् तस्या
दतः दंतविहीनस्य तैर्दंतै[illegible]र्विना वादे॥ वश्च दश्च तानयोः समाहारो वादं तस्मिन्वादे। वकारदकारोच्चारणे कुतः श
क्तिः॥ वंकारस्य दंतोष्ठ्यत्वाद्दकारस्य दंत्यत्वाच्चेत्यर्थः॥ किंचास्य गुणाशालीपूगः क्रमुको यस्मिन्नेतादृशं पत्रं
नागवल्लीदलं तांबूलमिति यावत्। दंतैर्विना दातुं खंडनं कर्तुं दोबखंडते। कुः शक्तिः॥ हि यस्माद्दंतरहितस्य
पत्रमात्रमपि खंडयितुं प्रभुत्वं कुः स्यात्। न कदापीत्यर्थः॥ अत्र प्रकृत सरस्वतीवदनेव वर्णने प्रकृत दंतर
हितपुरुषप्रतीतेरियं शब्दशक्तिमूला व्यंजना। प्रकृताप्रकृत श्लेषे शब्दशक्तिमूला व्यंजनेति प्राचीनानां म
तं॥ लक्षणामूला यथा॥ साहेंती सहि सुहअं खणे खणे दूमि आसि मज्झकएर॥ सब्भाव नेह करणिज्ज सरि
स अं दाव विरइअं तुम एर॥ साधयंती सखि सुभगं क्षणे क्षणे दूनासि मम कृते॥ सद्भावस्नेहकरणीयसदृ

$F_{13}O$

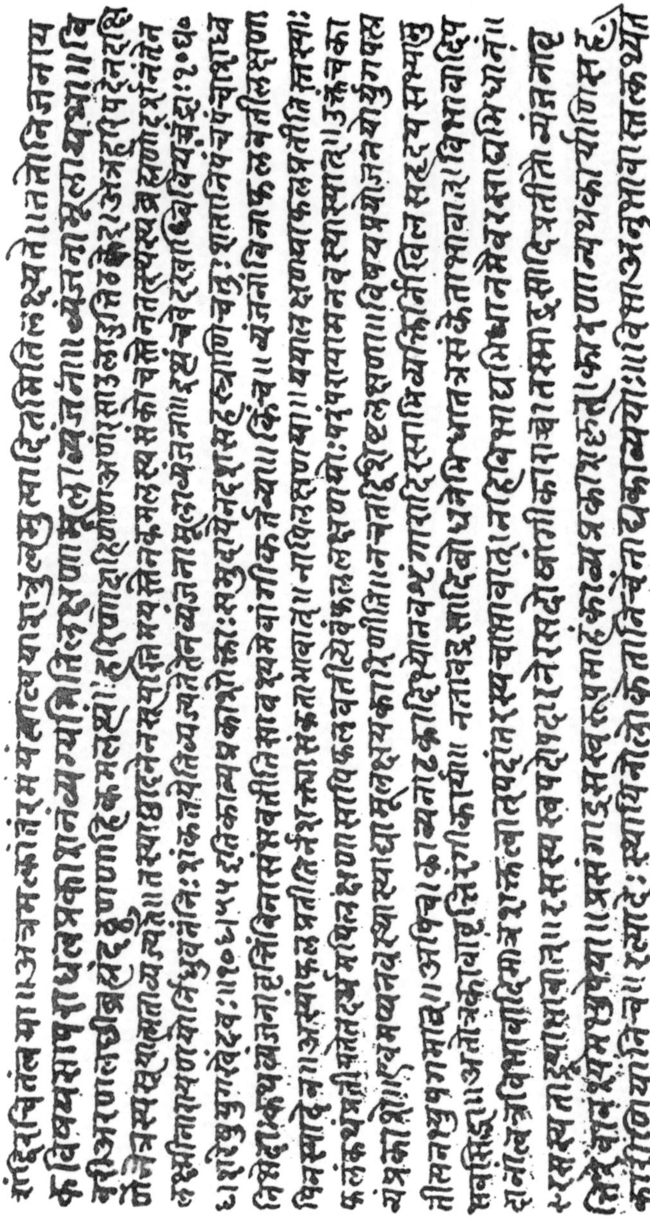

F$_{13}$R

व्यभिचारिणः। व्यक्तः स तैर्विभावाद्यैः स्थायिभावो रसः स्मृत इति। इत्थं च काव्योपनिबंधमहिम्ना परिगृहीतसीतात्वादिवि
शेषैः साधारण्येन प्रतीतैर्विभावादिभिर्व्यंजितं तं वर्णनीयसाधारण्येन गृहीत सामाजिकरत्याद्यवछिन्नमानंदांशं भग्ना
वरणमानंद रूपतयाप्रकाशमानं विभावादिसंभिन्नं चैतन्यं रस इति॥ यद्वा रत्याद्यवछिन्नं चैतन्यं रसः॥ यद्यपि शृंगारहा
स्यकरुणरौद्र वीरभयानकाः॥ बीभत्साद्भुतसंज्ञौ चेत्यष्टौ नाट्ये रसाः स्मृताः॥ अन्ये तु शांतस्य शमस्थायिनो न्न्टे
चनदसंभावात्॥ अष्टावेव रसा नाट्येन शांतस्तत्र युज्यत इत्याहुस्तन्न॥ नटे शमाभावादिति हेतुरसंगतः नटे रसा
भिव्यक्तेरस्वीकारात् सामाजिकानामेव रसास्वाद इति। तथा रतिर्हासश्च शोकश्च क्रोधोत्साहौ भयं तथा॥ जुगुप्सा
विस्मयश्चैव निर्वेदश्चेति ते नव ते स्थायिभावाः॥ तथा निर्वेद ग्लानि शंकाख्यास्तथासूयामदश्रमाः॥ आल
स्यं चैव दैन्यं च चिंता मोहः स्मृतिर्धृतिः॥ व्रीडा चपलता हर्ष आवेगो जडता तथा॥ गर्वो विषाद औत्सुक्यं निद्रा
पस्मार एव च॥ स्वप्नो विबोधोमर्षश्चाप्यवहित्थमथोग्रता॥ मतिर्व्याधिस्तथोन्मादस्तथा मरणमेव च॥
त्रासश्चैव वितर्कश्च विज्ञेया व्यभिचारिणः॥ त्रयस्त्रिंशदमी भावाः समाख्यातास्तु नामत इति शृंगारादिरसा
नामनेकत्वं तथापि ध्वनिभेदेष्वसंलक्ष्यक्रमरूपो रसध्वनिरेक एव स्वीकृत इत्यवधेयं। किंच सादीनामपूर्णत्वे
स्थायित्वं संपूर्णपरिपुष्टत्वे रसत्वमिति रसस्थायिभावयोर्भेदः॥ तथा च भरतसूत्रं॥ विभावानुभावव्य
भिचारिसंयोगाद्रसनिष्पत्तिरिति॥ सर्वत्र कार्यकारणसहकारिसंज्ञे ये व्यवहारसंभवे विभावादिसंज्ञां
तरकरणं रसस्यालौकिकत्वप्रतिपादनार्थमिति। विस्तरस्तु मत्कृते रसतरंगिणीव्याख्यानरूपनूत
नतरीयनाम्नि ग्रंथे द्रष्टव्यः॥ अथ व्यंजनायास्वीकारे काव्यस्योत्तमम ध्यमाधमत्वव्यवस्थापि न
स्यादेव व्यंग्याधिक्ये नैवोत्तमत्वमिति॥ उक्तं च॥ इदं उत्तममतिशयिनि व्यंगे वाच्याद् ध्वनिर्बुधैः कः

$F_{14}O$

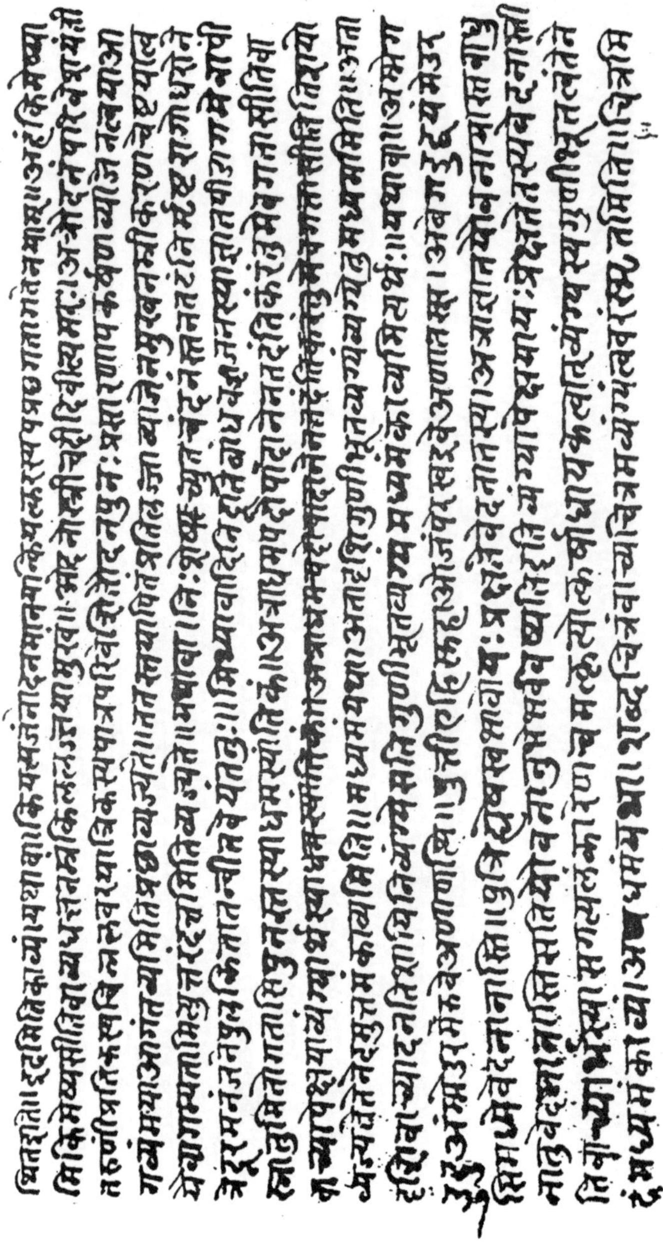

F$_{14}$R

८

ति गुणालंकारसहितं॥ अव्यंग्यमितिस्फुटप्रतीमानार्थरहितं अवरमधममित्यर्थः॥ यथा वा॥ साक्षेपव्योमह
ट्टोपितरजनिरमणिग्नायिको नमुक्ता रामुक्ताहारापहारात्तरलखगरवप्रोद्घताकीर्तिशांत्यै। कर्षन्नंभोज
कुंभोदरकुहरबहिर्निस्सरत्षट्पदालिकालव्योम्नी करेणाकलयतु दिनकृत्कल्मषोन्मूलनं वः॥ अत्र व्यो
मरूपहट्टो पितायारजनिरूपायावाणिग्नायिकाया हट्टस्थापिततारारूपो मुक्ताहारस्तस्यापहारो चौर्या
त्तरलायेखगाः पक्षिणस्तेषामारवः शब्दस्तेनोत्क्तांयाअकीर्तिस्तस्याः शांत्यर्थं कमलरूपकुंभोदर
मध्यान्निस्सरंतीभ्रमरपंक्तिरूपांकृष्णवर्णांसार्पिणीं करेण हस्तेन किरणेन॥ कर एव करइति श्लेषरू
पकं। कलयन्नाकर्षयन्नू दिनकृत्सूर्यः कल्मषोन्मूलनं वो युष्माकं करोत्वित्यन्वयः॥ कस्मिंश्चिद्देशे
तत्रत्यानामियं रीतिः॥ यस्य चौर्याद्यभिशापः प्राप्तस्तेन कुंभमध्ये प्रवेशितसर्पस्य स्वहस्तेन निष्का
सनं कर्तव्यं। यदि तस्य सर्पो दशति तर्हि स एव चोरो नो दशति चेत् शुद्ध इति॥ आर्त्रौ जो गुणेन शब्दा
र्थालंकाराभ्यां च चित्रं ज्ञेयं॥ यथा द्वा॥ नमन रथ च क्रमित्रं रूपाहारध्वजं स्कवदनायाः॥ वीक्ष्य पदां
बरगात्रं हारि हरमदनाः कथं न विवदंते॥ स्फुटवदनं यस्याः सा तस्याः सुवदनायाः शुभांग्याः॥ अत्र व
दनशब्दे नांगसामान्ये लक्षणा॥ प्रथमं मुखचंद्रं वीक्ष्येत्यध्याहारेण योजना। अयं मुखचंद्रो
मदीयं नयनं वामनेत्रं इति हर विवादः॥ निश्रेयसमहमुपास्महे भगवतः कौमोदकीलक्ष्मणः कोक
प्रीतिं च कोरपारणपटू ज्योतिष्मती लोचने॥ याभ्यामर्द्धविबोधमुग्धमधुरश्रीरर्द्धनिद्रायितो ना
भिपल्वलपुंडरीकमुकुलः कं बोसपत्नीकृत इति मुरारिनाम्नके हरिवामनेत्रस्य चंद्रात्मकतया व

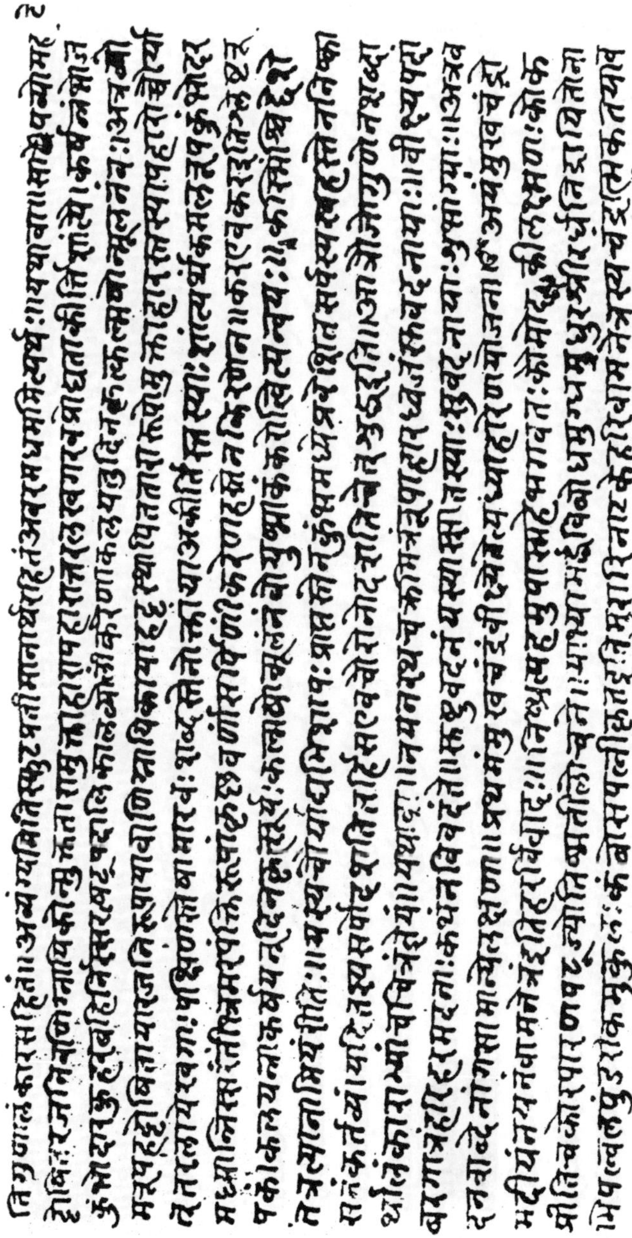

F$_{15}$O

र्णनात्॥ अस्या अयं मुखचंद्रो मदीयं र [illegible] थांगं चक्रमिति हरस्य विवादः। रथांगे चंद्र [illegible] कौ [illegible] स्थ [illegible] पापिः
शरदिति महिम्नस्तोत्रे तथा वर्णनात्॥ अयं मुखेंदुः कमादीपकत्वान्मदीयं मित्रमिति [illegible] स्य विवादः।
इति प्रथमं मुखं वीक्ष्य नयनरूप चक्रं मित्रमिति त्रयाणां योजना॥ अथास्या नयने वीक्ष्य [illegible] हि [illegible]
योजना॥ अस्या नयनं मीनसादृश्यान्मीनरूपं। तेन मे मत्स्यावतारत्वान्मत्स्वरूपमेवेति हरेर्विवादः।
ए तस्या नस्या नयनमीनोयं मम आहारो भक्ष्यमिति हरविवादः। त्यजति नमगव्याधरभस्मेति वर्णने
नात्शिवस्य व्याधरूपत्वात्। नयनमीनोयं मदीयध्वजरूपइति मदनविवादः। कामस्य [illegible] ध्वजे
प्रसिद्धेः। सुवत्तनाय्या उदरं वीक्ष्येति योजना। उदरस्य गगनसाम्यादुदरस्वरूपं गगनं वीक्ष्य मन्नाव
ताराक्रांतमिदं मदीयं पदमिति हरेर्विवादः। इदं मदीयमंबरं वसनमिति हरविवादः। शिवस्य दिगंबर
त्वात्। अनुदराया अस्याइदं अत्योदरं मदीयं गात्रमिति मदनविवादः॥ मारेनैस्य [illegible] गत्वा [illegible]
गत्वादिस्सर्पः। अत्रनञोल्यार्थत्वमनुदराकन्येति वचनात्॥ स द स [illegible] संसयगो [illegible] दर्शितो [illegible]
यंस्यास्तथा वर्णनात्। अत्र मुखनयनोदराणां त्रयाणां मध्या हारेणयोजनेत्या [illegible] टित्यर्थे [illegible]
भावेन व्यंग्यहितत्वाच्चाधमत्वं। इत्थं चोत्तम मध्यमाधमेति त्रयाणामपि काव्यानां [illegible] स्यां व्यंजना [illegible]
तिं विना न संभवतीत्यवश्यमेव सांगीकार्या॥ तथा चेषूदाहरणेषु सर्वत्रार्थमात्रे व्यंजनेत्यभिधातो
भिन्ना। वाच्योर्थः शक्तिज्ञानवद्भिरेव गम्यते व्यंग्यस्तु सहृदयैरेवेति बोधभेदो व्यंजनायाः॥ निःशे
षच्युतचंदनमित्यत्र तदंतिकं नगतासीति निषेधः शाब्दार्थः। तदंतिकं तु गतासीति विधिश्च

व्यंग्यत्वस्यार्थस्वरूपभेदोप्यभिधाव्यंजनयोः॥ किञ्च गतोस्तमर्क इत्यादौ शक्योर्थस्त्वेकरूप एव प्रतीयते व्यंग्यस्तु तत्र
प्रतिपात्राद्यद्भेदेन नानैव भासते॥ तथाहि॥ आपणिकानां भक्त्या प्रतिविक्रेयवस्तूनि संह्रियतामिति॥ दूती
नां नाभिसारिकां प्रति अभिसरणमुपक्रम्यतामिति॥ शिष्यस्य गुरुं प्रति सांध्योविधिरुपक्रम्यतामिति॥ नागतो द्यो प्रे
यानिति॥ दूरं मा गा इति॥ प्राप्तप्रायस्ते प्रेयानिति निरवधिर्व्यंग्योर्थः प्रकाशते वाच्यस्त्वेकरूप एवेत्यभिधाव्यंजनयो
र्थसंख्याभेदाद्भेदः॥ वाच्योर्थः शब्दोच्चारणमात्रादेव प्रतीयते व्यंग्यस्तु प्रतिभानैर्मल्यादिविकलिनिमित्तभेदः॥ वाच्यो
र्थस्तु चमत्कारकारी व्यंग्यस्तु प्रतीतिमात्रं चमत्कारकारीति कार्यभेदः॥ वाच्यः केवलं प्रतीतिकृत् व्यंग्यस्तु चम ति
त्कारिप्रतीतिकृदिति प्रतीतिभेदः॥ वाच्यः पूर्वं व्यंग्यः पश्चात्प्रतीयते इति कालभेदः॥ अभिधाश्रया व्यंजना
नानुपदं तदेकदेशात् तदर्थवाच्याद्याश्रयादित्याश्रयभेदः॥ कस्स ण व होइ रोसो दट्ठूण पिआए सव्वणं अहरं। सभ
मरपउमग्घाइरि वारिअवामे सहसु एण्हिं॥ कस्य न वा स्यात् रोषो दृष्ट्वा प्रियायाः सव्रणम
दामधरं॥ सभ्रमरपद्माघ्रायिणि वारितवामे सहस्वेदानीं॥ अत्र नेदं उपपत्तिकृतमधरदंश
नं किंतु सभ्रमरपद्माघ्राणजनितमिति व्यंग्यस्य कांतो विषयः॥ अतः परं त्वयानेतादृश
कर्म कर्तव्यमिदं तु मया यथा कथंचिदाच्छादितमिति व्यंग्यस्य कांता विषयः प्रतिपाद्य
इति विषयभेदः॥ अपि च भम धम्मिअ वीसद्धो सो सुणहो अज्ज मारिओ देण। गोलाण
ईकच्छकुडंगवासिणा दरिअसीहेण॥ भ्रम धार्मिक विश्रब्धः स शुनकोद्य मारितस्तेन। गोदानदीकच्छकुञ्जवासिना
दृप्तसिंहेन॥ अत्र गृहे श्वनिवृत्त्या भ्रमणं विहितं गोदावरीतीरे सिंहोपलब्धेरभ्रमणमनुमापयति। यद्यपि
रभ्रमणं तत्र इत्यनेकरूपानि हेतुपलंभपूर्वकं भवति॥ व्यतिरेकत्तिमाह। गोदावरीतीरे भीरुभ्रमणा

$F_{16}O$

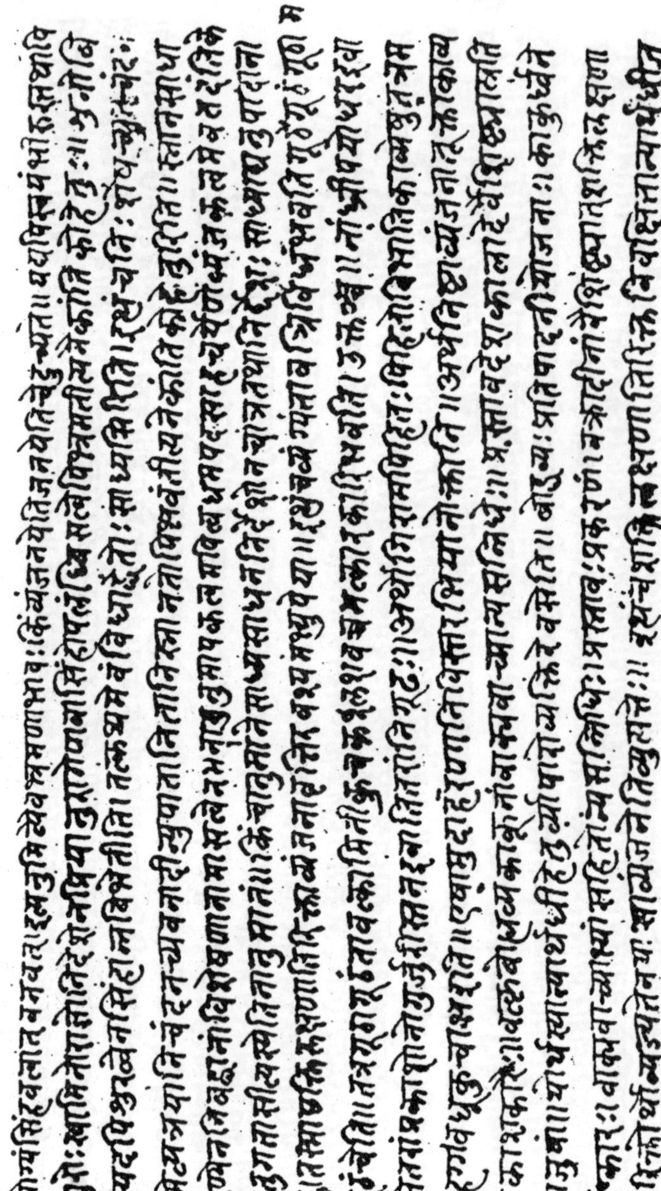

$F_{16}R$

नकोऽप्यापारोऽस्यं जैनेतिडुं॥ दिग्मात्रमुदाहृीयते। वस्तुवैशिष्ट्याद्यथा॥ देवः पततिर्विदुषि नैषधराज
गत्यानिर्णीयते न किमुनिर्ग्रियते सवत्सा॥ नालं नलः खलु तवांति महानलाभो यद्यैन मुञ्चसि वरः कतरः प
रस्ते। अत्र वत्सा सरस्वत्या दमयंतीं प्रति कृते नलवर्णने श्लेषमहिम्ना खं उत्काग्निसमवरुणानां भैमीप
रिणामन रूपकार्याथेन नलवेशधारिणां चतुर्णामपि संसूचनं व्यंग्यमर्यादयैव कृतमस्तीत्यवधेयं। अ
स्यंनलोऽस्यैतेन नलवेशधारिणो देवा इति प्रकाशतया वर्णने तु सजातीयैर्देवैः सहास्याः सरस्वत्याः
शत्रुत्वं स्यादिति। अत्र विदुषीत्यनेन श्लोकोक्ति परिज्ञानचातुर्यं दमयंत्याः सपादितमस्तीति॥ अत्र
वक्त्याः सरस्वत्यास्तथा बोद्धव्यस्य प्रतिपादनीयस्येंद्रादेस्तथा त्वया किमु न निर्णीयते किमु न म्रियते इति को कोम्बे
तित्र याप्यामपि वैशिष्ट्यं ज्ञेयं॥ यथा वा मम॥ सत्पात्रक्रमनाविभूषिततनुर्भूत्या गवामीश्वरः स
र्वज्ञो द्विजराजराजितवपुर्मायान्वितो वृत्तिवित्॥ आनंदी क्षितपूरकः सुमनसां मानंददो नंतर
कृब्रह्मोपासनतत्परः सपन्नगान् गंगाधरः पातु नः॥ अत्र श्लेषवशात् व्यंजना वृत्त्या प्रतीमाने ब्रुप्र
थमं शिवपक्षे व्याख्यात्, माह॥ धरतीति धरः पचाद्यच्। गंगायाः धरो गंगाधरः शिवः॥ शंगा
धरोंधकरिपुरिस्मरवन्धनात् योगरूढोयं शब्दः॥ नः पात्वित्यन्वयः॥ स कीदृशः सत्या
यां दाक्षिण्यामासक्तमनाः॥ तथा भूत्या भस्मना॥ भूतिर्भस्मनि संपत्स्मरं विभूषिततनुः शोभितो देहः॥ तथा ग
वां सर्वविद्या

$F_{17}O$

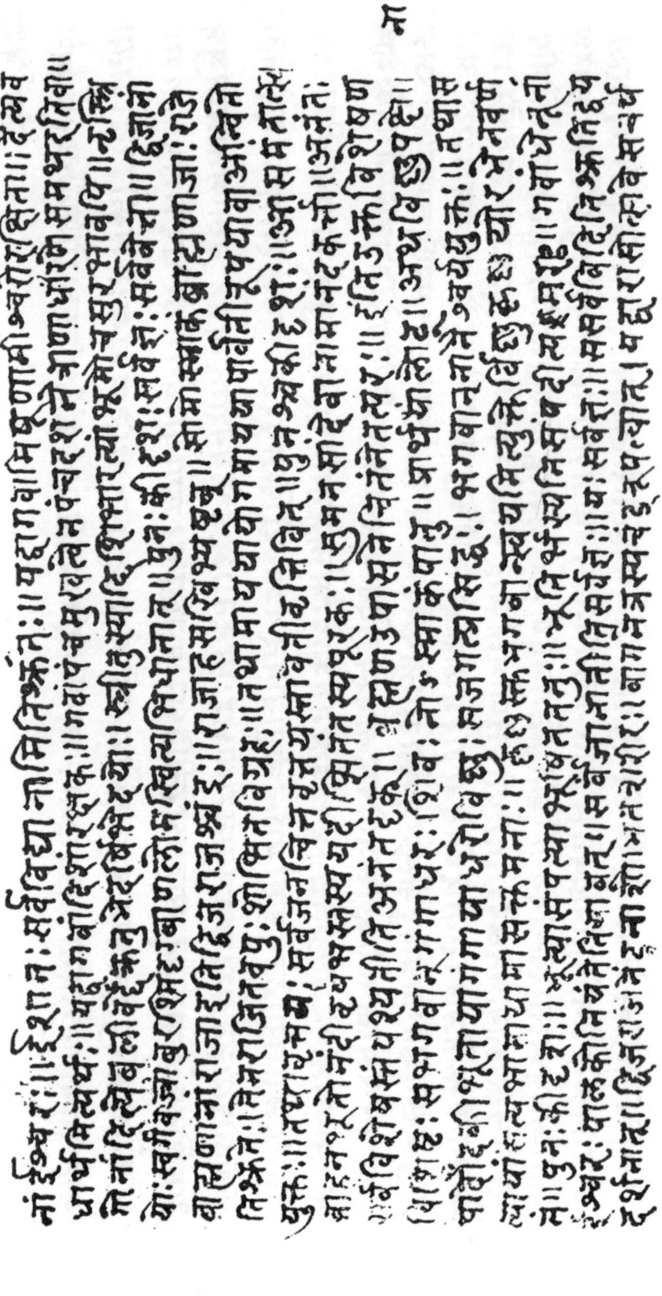

F$_{17}$R

णीनामुदगाच्छचोमदन्निति चंद्रोदयस्यसत्वात्तेन शोभितदेहः॥ तथामाययायोगमायया अन्वितः॥
योगमाययामुपाश्रित इतिभागवते तथावर्णनात्॥ रत्निरिति॥ गोपिकानांमाश्रित्तत्वतनयस्त्वा सांवेत्ता॥
महाराङ्गाडशसहस्रराजकन्यानांयुगपत्स्ववरणविषयेयाश्रित्तत्वतनयस्तासांवेत्ता॥ तथाआनंदी॥आ
नंदवान्॥ आनंदंब्रह्मणोरूपमितिश्रुतेः॥ भक्तजनानां गोपिकानांवाईप्सितपूरकः॥ तथासुमसांदेवाना
मानंददः॥ शुद्धचित्तानां वा॥ अनंतदृक् बहुनेत्रः॥ सहस्राक्षः सहस्रपादितिश्रुतेः॥ पुनः कीदृशः॥ ब्रह्मो
पासनेवेदाध्ययनेतत्परः॥ मद्ब्रह्मउपसमीपेयदासनंकमलंतदस्ति अस्येतिब्रह्मोपासनः पद्मयो
भइत्यर्थः॥ तत्परशांतपाद्यंयस्येति विशेषणसमासः॥ अस्मिन्विष्णुपक्षे गंगाधरशब्दो यौगिकः॥
अथब्रह्मपक्षे योजना॥ किंच॥ सत्ये सत्यलोके आसक्तमना॥ तथाभूत्वा भस्मना भव्यमूर्त्तिः॥ सर्व
दासंध्योपासनविधौ भस्मधारणस्य श्रुतिस्मृतिविहितत्वात्तस्य शस्त्वं बोध्यं॥ त्र्यायुषमितिश्रुतिः॥
स्मृतिरपि॥ धार्यंभस्मत्रिसंध्यंतु गृहिणा जलसंयुतं॥ वानप्रस्थयतीनांतु सायाह्ने जलवर्जितंतु
ति॥ तथागर्भा ऋतूनां ईश्वरः फलदाता॥ यद्यपि गोशब्दस्य ऋतुविशेषवाचित्वं नैकवचनसंभवस्त
थापि ऋत्वंगकर्मणामनेकत्वेन बहुवचनं॥ ब्रह्मणः ऋतूनां फलदातृत्वं चोक्तं भगवद्गीतायां॥
सहयज्ञाः प्रजाः सृष्ट्वापुरोवाचप्रजापतिः॥ अनेन प्रसविष्यध्वमेष वोऽस्त्विष्टकामधुगि
ति॥ प्रसविष्यध्वमिति सार्वत्रिकः पातस्तु चिंत्यः॥ स्यप्रत्यये लोटोऽसंभवात्॥ लुङि अडाग
मणभस्य दुर्वारत्वाच्च॥ यथाभागवते प्राचीनतूलेषु कुशेषु धीरतद्गति प्राचीनयथार्थपा
वेतदर्थबोधानवगमात्केनचिद्विदुषाभासे न प्राचीनमूले षिति कल्पितः पातोले

$F_{18}O$

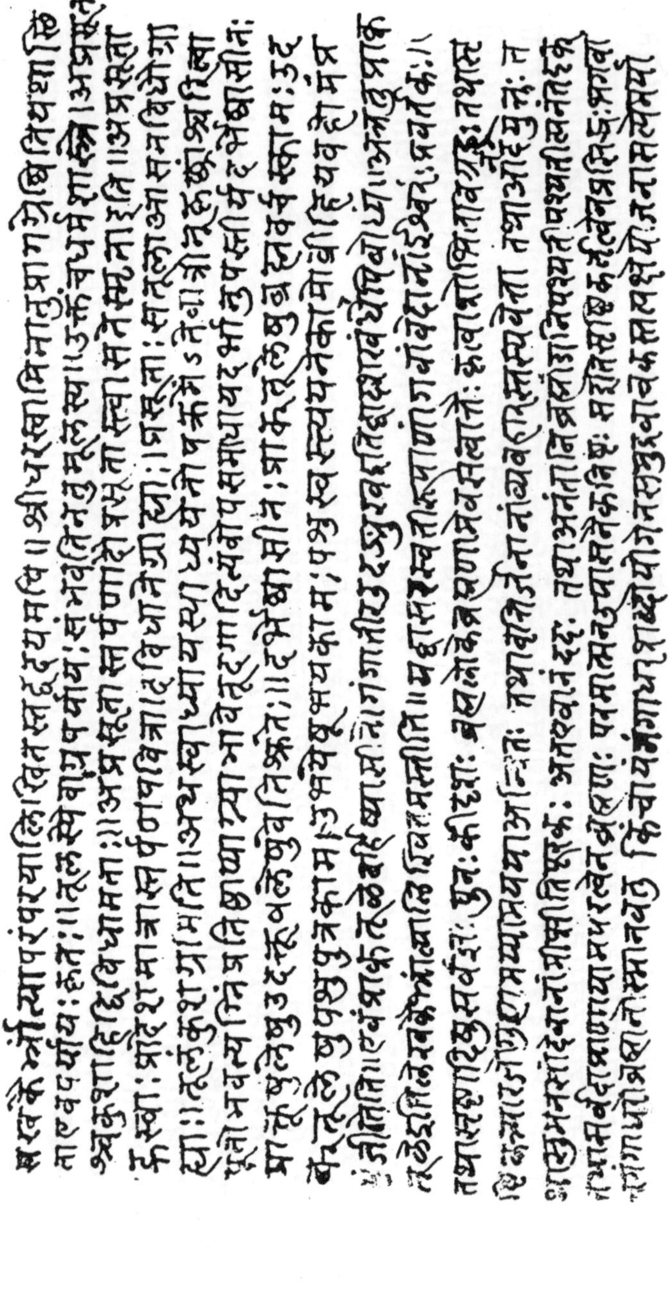

F$_{18}$R

दापात्मने आसक्तचित्तः भूत्या रत्नमुक्तादिसंपत्त्या भूषितवपुः तथा गवां जलानामीश्वरोधिपतिः
उळयोरभेदाज्जडाधिपतिरपि सर्वेशः नदीपर्वतादीनां ह्रदसमूहानां स्वामित्वात् द्विजराजेन सुपुत्रेण चंद्रेण
विराजित इत्यर्थः पुनः कीदृशः मां लक्ष्मीं याति प्राप्नोतीति मायो विष्णुस्तेनान्वितो युक्तः तथा दुग्धिरीश्व
रस्य चित्तवृत्तिस्तस्या वेत्ता ईश्वराज्ञापरिपालक इत्यर्थः तथा आनंदी चंद्रोदये सतीत्यर्थः पुनः किंल
क्षणः सुमनसां कियदि कार्ये प्रशस्तचित्तानां नेयाभिलाषपूरकः अत एवानंदजनकः॥८
अनंतं शेषणागं पश्यतीति अनंतदृक् प्रतिक्षणं पर्यंकतापन्नस्य तस्य स्वभिन्नसर्वदावर्तमानत्वात् अस्य
लोकेऽस्मिन् उपसमीपे आसनं रक्षणं तस्मिन् तत्परः उद्युक्तः तथा स भगवान् नारायणः हितः प्रियस
सुहृत्पक्षे योजना अथ गंगाधरनामा शास्त्री द्विजस्तत्पक्षे योजना यदृच्छया प्रोक्तं यं पित्रादिकृतसंकेत
त्वेन संज्ञात्वात् द्विजविशेषेरुक्तः सलोकः सत्यभाषणे आसक्तचित्तः पुनः किंविशेषणविशिष्टः भूत्या
संपत्त्या भस्मना वा भूषितविग्रहः गवां वाचां ईश्वरोधिपतिः साक्षाद्बृहस्पतिरेवायमित्यारोपः अ
थो ज्ञास्यतीति निपुण इत्यर्थः अत एव सर्वज्ञः सर्ववेत्ता यद्वा सर्वाणि शास्त्राणि सर्वलोकव्यवहारान्वा
सकलवर्णाश्रमधर्माचारान्वा जानातीति तादृशः पुनः कीदृशः द्विजानां ब्राह्मणानां राजेति द्विजराजः
स चासौ राजितवपुश्चेति विशेषणसमासः यद्वा द्विजाश्च राजानश्च तैः राजितवपुः पुनश्च मा लक्ष्मीः
अयः शुभावहो विधिः ताभ्यामन्वितो युक्तः पुनश्च यतियति कृतनिषित समासे कशेषसानामंतथा

$F_{19}O$

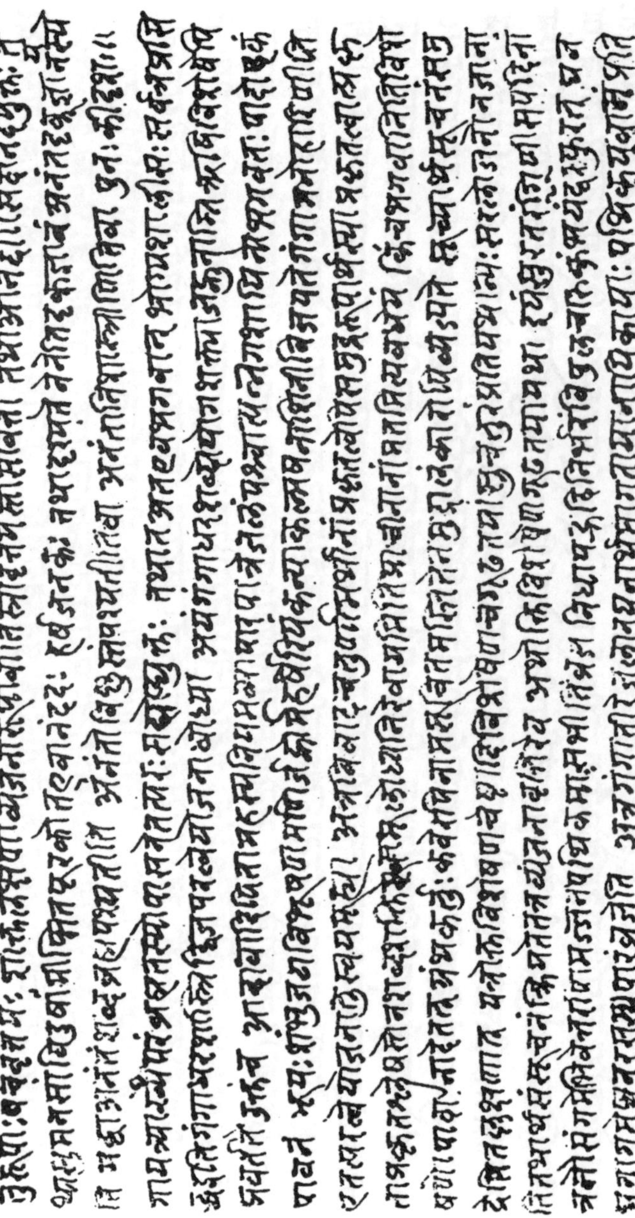

$F_{19}R$

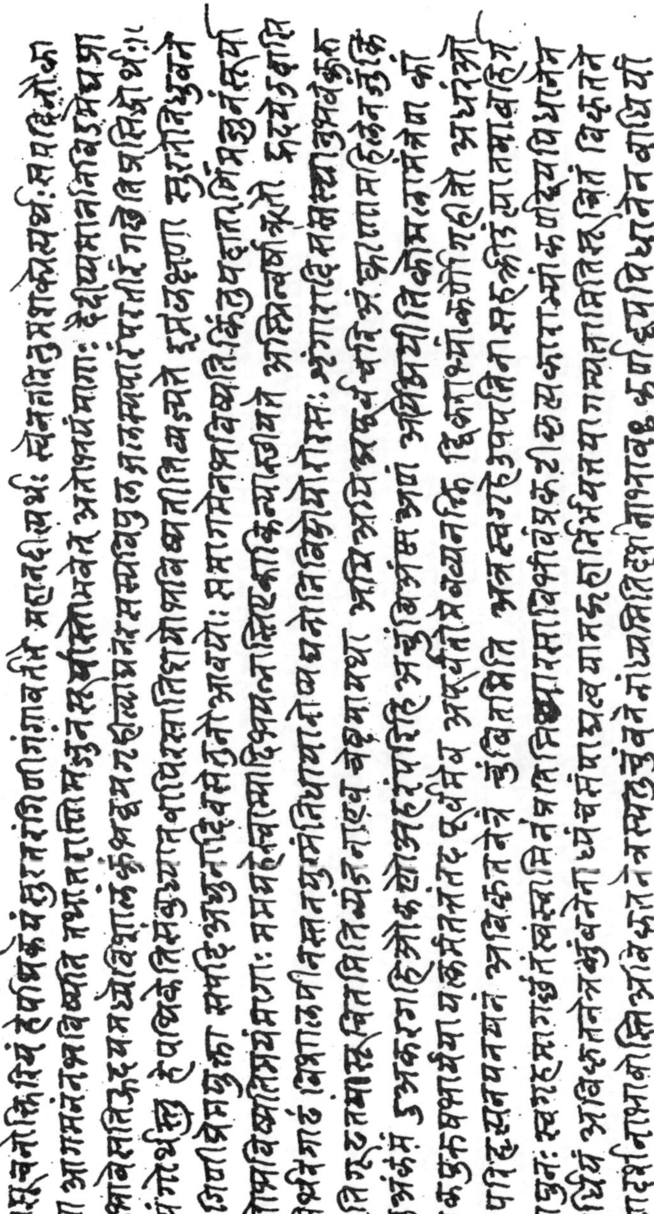

$F_{20}O$

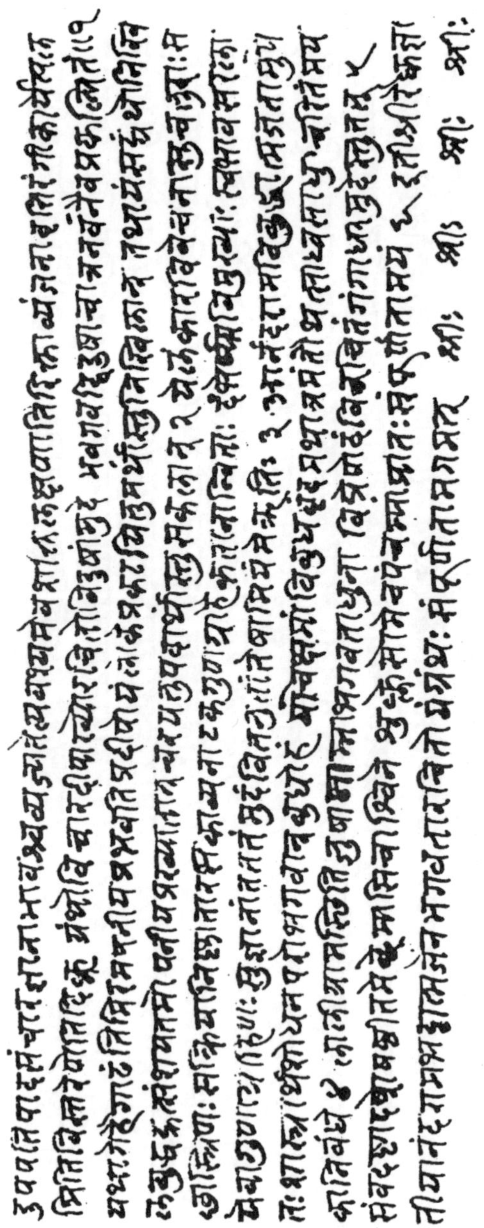

APPENDIX - II

Verses Quoted in the Text

Verses	Source	Page No.
अत एव गवित्याह.....	वै०सि०का० २७.	३२
अतादृशि गुणीभूतव्यङ्ग्यं.....	का०प्र० १-५.	७२
अनेकार्थस्य शब्दस्य.....	" २-१९.	४४,६६
अप्रसूताः प्रसूताश्च.....	?	८३
अपि स्विदास्ते.....	श्री०भ०पु० ३, १, ३४.	५५
अम्मे गुड्डुअम्मे.....	?	७३
अयि अयि अपूर्वचरिअं.....	?	८७
अस्यैव भार्या भवितुं.....	श्री०भा०पु० १०, ५३, ३७.	४९
आत्मा देहे धृतौ जीवे.....	अमर० ३, ३, १०९ रामाश्रमीटीका	५१
आदावादिपितामहस्य.....	महासुभाषितसंग्रह Vol. III P. 1143	८६
आस्थिताः पदवीं सुभ्रु.....	श्री०भा०पु० १०, ६०, १३.	४७
इदं भागवतं नाम पुराणं.....	श्री०भा०पु० १, ३, ४०; २, १, ८.	३९
इदमुत्तममतिशयिनि.....	का०प्र० १-४.	७१
इमामगृभ्णन् रशनामृतस्य.....	यजुर्वेद २२-२.	६१
इयं सुरतरङ्गिणी.....	सु०र०भा० (असतीचरित्रम्) ६, ८१, पृ० ३३४	८६
ईशानः सर्वविद्यानाम्.....	तै० आ० १०-४७-१	८०
उद्बाहुरिव वामनः.....	रघुवंशम्-१, ३.	५४
एकः शब्दः सुष्ठु प्रयुक्त.....	पा०म०भा०प्र० on पस्पशाह्निक p.२७.	४१

Verses	**Source**	**Page No.**
एवमप्यनवस्था स्यात्.....	का०प्र० २, १७.	६९
ओदनोऽस्त्री सदीदिवि.....	अमर० २-९-४८.	७२
कच्चित्सुखं सात्वत.....	श्री०भा०पु० ३, १, २९.	५५
कन्या वरयते रूपम्.....	सु०र०भा० पृ० ३८७, पद्य. ४०१.	५१
कपिलादुग्धपानेन.....	from रसविलास.	४०
कस्स न व......(कस्य न वा.....)	Q. from ध्वन्यालोक १-४ वृत्ति.	७६
कारणान्यथ कार्याणि.....	का०प्र० ४-२७.	६९
काव्यं यशसेऽर्थकृते.....	" १-२.	३८
कियत्त्यजन्नोदन.....	नै०म० १६-७९.	७१
कुलं च शीलं च.....	(शब्दान्तरेण) सुभाषितार्णव ५, ६, पृ० २८५६.	५१
क्षत्रजातिरुदियाय भुजाभ्यां.....	नै०म० २१-६३.	५९
क्षत्रस्य शब्दो भुवनेषु रूढ.....	रघुवंशम्-२, ५३	३३
गङ्गाधरोऽन्धकरिपु.....	अमर. १, १, ३४.	८०
गोर्नादित्ये बलीवर्दे.....	" ३, ३, २५. रामाश्रमीटीकायाम्	८०
जतौ तु वंशस्थ.....	वृत्तरत्नाकर-३, १३२.	४७
ज्ञेया साध्यवसाना सा.....	कोविदानन्द- २,११.	३२
तत्त्वं निवर्तस्व विहाय.....	रघुवंशम्-२, ४०.	३४
तददोषौ शब्दार्थौ.....	का०प्र० १, ४.	३८
तर्का रदा यद्वदनस्य तर्क्या....	नै०म० १०, ८३.	६६
...त्यजति न मृगव्याधरभसः...	शिवमहिम्नः स्तोत्रम्-२२	७५
त्र्यायुषम्.....	शुक्लयजु० ३, ६२.	८२
देवः पतिर्विदुषि नैषध.....	नै०म० १३, ३३.	७९
द्वे ब्रह्मणी वेदितव्ये.....	मैत्रायण्युपनिषद्-६, २२.	४१
द्वौ तर्कौ द्वे च मीमांसे.....	?	३४

Verses	Source	Page No.
धार्यं भस्मत्रिसन्ध्यं.....	प्रयोगपारिजात–आह्निकसूत्रावलि.	८२
न जातु ब्राह्मणं हन्यात्.....	मनुस्मृतिः ८–३८०.	५९
नमो नमस्तेऽस्त्वृषभाय.....	श्री०भा०पु०. २, ४, १४.	५५
नयनरथचक्रमित्रं.....	?	७४
नाञ्जसा निगदितं.....	शिशु० १४,२३.	३८
नान्ध्रीपयोधर इवा.....	सु०र०भा० ३९, ३९.	७८
निदेशग्रन्थयोःशास्त्रम्	अमर. ३, ३, ९.	३५
निपाताश्चोपसर्गाश्च	?	५२
निर्धूतवीतमपि.....	शिशु० ५, ४७.	३९
निर्विशेषं न सामान्यं.....	श्लोकवार्त्तिक–आकृति–१०– Q. by न्यायभूषण–p. २१७– स्वामीयोगीन्द्रानन्दजी and by त्रिवेणिका.	४०
निर्वेदग्लानिशङ्काख्या.....	भरत०ना०शा० ६, १८–२१.	७०
निष्प्रत्यूहमुपास्महे.....	अनर्घराघव–१, १.	७४
निःशेषच्युतचन्दनं.....	अमरुशतकम्–६१.	७२
नंपूभाभजपूरिजंजरि.....	?	६४
पञ्च पञ्चनखा भक्ष्या.....	वा०रा० ४, १७, ३९.	६१
पुराणन्यायमीमांसा.....	याज्ञवल्क्यस्मृतिः १, ३.	३७
पौराणीं वृत्तिमाश्रित्य.....	?	४०
प्रणम्य शितिकण्ठाय.....	कुमारसंभवम्–६–८१.	३२
प्राक्तूले बर्हिष्यासीनो	श्री०भा०पु० १२–६–१०.	८४
प्राचीनतूलेषु कुशेषु धीरः.....	" १–१९–१७.	८३
बहूनां वृत्तिधर्माणां वचनैरेव....	वै०सि०का० ३१.	
बाणैरश्वैश्च हायनैः.....	Q. in त्रिवेणिका. पृ. १६.	६४
भम धम्मिअ..... (भ्रम धार्मिक.....)	Q. in ध्वन्यालोक–१–४ वृत्ति	७७
भवानपीदं परवानवैति.....	रघुवंशम्–२, ५६.	३४

Verses	Source	Page No.
भूतिर्भस्मनि संपदि.....	अमर० ३, ३, ६९.	८०,८१
मुख्यार्थबाधे तद्योगे.....	का०प्र० २-९.	५७
यः सर्वज्ञः स सर्वविद्.....	मुण्डकोपनिषद्-१-९.	८१
योगमायामुपाश्रितः.....	श्री०भा०पु० १०-२९-१.	८१
रतिर्हासश्च शोकश्च.....	भरत०ना०शा० ६-१७.	७०
रतेर्गृहीतानुनयेन कामं.....	रघुवंशम्-६-२.	३३
रथाङ्गे चन्द्रार्कौ.....	शिवमहिम्नः स्तोत्रम्-१८.	७४
राघवत्वेऽभवत्सीता.....	विष्णुपुराण १-९-१४४.	५०
राजभ्यो बिभ्यतः सुभ्रु.....	श्री०भा०पु० १०-६०-१२.	४७
राजा भट्टारको देवः.....	अमर. १-७-१३.	४४
रामेति लोकरमणात्.....	श्री०भा०पु० १०-२-१३.	३२
लक्ष्यमाणगुणैर्योगात्.....	तन्त्रवार्त्तिक १, ४, १२, २२ (सूत्रभाष्य)	६४
वक्तृबोद्धव्यकाकूनां.....	का०प्र० ३, २१, २२.	७९
वयं कलादा इव.....	नै०म० ८-९९.	४७
वागर्थाविव संपृक्तौ.....	रघुवंशम् १-१.	५२
विधिरत्यन्तमप्राप्तौ.....	तन्त्रवार्त्तिक-३-२-४.	६०
विपरीतरमणे लक्ष्मी (विवरीअमणं लच्छी).	का०प्र० ५. उदा. १३७.	६८
विभावा अनुभावास्तत्.....	" ४-२८	६९
विमानना सुभ्रु कुतः पितुर्गृहे.....	कुमारसंभवम्-५-४३.	४७
विंशत्याद्याः सदैकत्वे.....	अमर० २-९-८३	६४
वेदखाष्छिवियच्चन्द्रा...........	का०प्र० ४-४४.	६८
शब्दचित्रं वाच्यचित्रमव्यङ्ग्यं...	" १-५.	७३
शब्दशास्त्रमनधीत्य.....	सु०र०भा० पृ० ४२ श्लो०८.	३६
शान्तस्य शमसाध्यत्वान्नटे.....	संगीतरत्नाकर-७-१३१७ Q.in रसविलासः	७०

Verses	Source	Page No.
श्यालः स्वस्रोरथाग्रहीत्	श्री०भा०पु० १०, ४, २३.	६५
शृङ्गारहास्यकरुणरौद्र.....	भरत ना०शा० ६-१५.	७०
स चर्षणीनामुदगाच्छुचो.....	श्री०भा०पु० १०, २९, २.	८१
सदसत्संशयगोचरोदरी.....	नै० म० २-४०.	७५
सम्बन्धिशब्दसापेक्षो.....	पा०म०भा०प्र० on. P. २-१-१.	३३
स वाचको विशेषाणाम्.....	वाक्यपदीय० २, १८८.	५२
सहयज्ञाः प्रजाः सृष्ट्वा.....	श्रीमद्भगवद्गीता-३-१०.	८२
सहस्राक्षः सहस्रपात्.....	ऋग्वेदः १०-९०-१.	८२
संयोगो विप्रयोगश्च.....	वाक्यपदीय २-३१५-३१६.	४४
साटोपव्योमहट्टोषित.....	सु०र०भा० पृ० २७. श्लो० १३.	७३
साधयन्ती सखि सुभगं.....	गाथासप्तशती ८६०.	६७
साधु दूति पुनः साधु.....	कुवलयानन्द उदा०७१.	६४
सामान्यशास्त्रतो नूनं विशेषो...	?	३६
सारोपा सा मता यत्र.....	कोविदानन्दः २-११.	६२
सुभ्रु त्वं कुपितेत्यपास्तमशनं...	चौरपञ्चाशिका-बिल्हणचरित-७६.	४७
सूच्यार्थसूचनं स मुद्रा.....	कुवलयानन्द का० १३९ पृ० ७३.	८६
सोमोऽस्माकं ब्राह्मणानां.....	शुक्लयजुर्वेद-१०, १८/९, ४०.	८१
हा पितः क्वासि हे सुभ्रु.....	भट्टिकाव्य ६-११.	४६

APPENDIX - III

Pāṇiniya Sūtras Quoted in the Text

Sutras		Page No.
अम्बार्थनद्योर्ह्स्वः।	७, ३, १०७.	४६,४८
आधारोऽधिकरणम्।	१, ४, ४५.	५८
उणादयो बहुलम्।	३, ३, १.	३५
ऊङुतः।	४, १, ६६.	४८
क्रियार्थोपपदस्य च कर्मणि स्थानिनः।	२, ३, १४.	३२
तद्वानासामुपधानो मन्त्र इतीष्टकासु लुक् च मतोः।	४, ४, १२५.	६५
नेयङुवङ्स्थानावस्त्री।	१, ४, ४.	४६
प्रथमयोः पूर्वसवर्णः।	६, १, १०२.	६५
राजाहः सखिभ्यष्टच्।	५, ४, ९१.	८१
वर्णो वर्णेन।	२, १, ६८.	४४
विप्रतिषेधे परम्।	१, ४, २.	४६
समर्थः पदविधिः।	२, १, १.	३३

APPENDIX - IV

Vārttikādi Quoted in the Text

		Page No.
अप्राणिजातेश्चारज्ज्वादीनाम्।	वा० १ ४, १, ६६	४८
इवेन विभक्त्यलोपः पूर्वपदप्रकृति-स्वरत्वं च।	वा० २ २, १, ४	५४
कदाचित्कर्मधारयः सर्वधनाद्यर्थः।	वा० ५ २, १, ६८	४५
शकन्ध्वादित्वात्पररूपम्	वा० ४ ६, १, ६४	५६
समानाधिकरणसमासाद्बहुव्रीहिर्भवति विप्रतिषेधेन।	वा० ४ २, १, ६८	४५
चकारोऽनुक्तसमुच्चयार्थः।	काशिका २, ४, १८	४८
कृत्तद्धितसमासैकशेषसनाद्यन्तधातुरूपाः पञ्चवृत्तयः।	ल०सि०कौ० वृत्ति २, १, ४	८५

Paribhāṣā quoted in the Text

उपपदविभक्तेर्कारकविभक्तिर्बलीयसी।	परि०शे०प० ९४.	३१
ज्ञापकसिद्धं न सर्वत्र।	परि०शे०प. १२६.	४६

APPENDIX - V

Works Mentioned in the Text

	Page No.
काव्यप्रकाशः	३८,४३,४७,६६,६८,६९
कुमारसंभवम्	४७
त्रिवेणिका	६६
नूतनतरी	७१
नैषध (चरितम्)	४७,७५
पाणिनीयसूत्रम्	३३
भगवद्गीता	८२
मनोरमा	३५
मुरारिनाटकम् (अनर्घराघवम्)	७४
रसतरङ्गिणी	७१
रसविलासः	३८,४७
वाक्यपदीयः	५२
वृत्तरत्नाकर	४७
वेदान्तपरिभाषा	६०
(वैयाकरण) भूषण (सार)	५२
शब्दकौस्तुभ	६३
(शिव) महिम्नः स्तोत्रम्	७५
(श्रीमद्)भागवत	३९,४७,८१,८३,८४
सिद्धान्तकौमुदी	६३

APPENDIX - VI

Authors Mentioned in the Text

	Page No.
अमर (कोशकारः)	५१,७२,८०,८१
आशाधरभट्ट	६६
कालिदास	४७
काव्यप्रकाशकृत् (काव्यप्रकाशकारः)	६९,७८
कैयट	३३
क्षीरस्वामिन्	३५
भट्टि (कवि)	४६
भाष्यकार	४५,४८
मल्लिनाथ	३३
माधव	३६
मुरारि	७४
याज्ञवल्क्य	३९
वामन (काव्यालङ्कारसूत्रवृत्तिकारः)	४८
श्रीधरस्वामिन्	३९,४९,६५,८३

CONSPECTUS
TOPICS DISCUSSED IN THE WORK

	Page No. (Text) (Discussion)
maṅgala śloka	31-148
the title Vicāradīpa	32-152
discussion of *śabda* 'the word' as a śāstra	34-156
etymology of the word *śāstra*	35-156
the view of the grammarians about *śāstra*	36-157
the theory of *sphoṭa*	41-160
the opposition against the theory of *sphoṭa*	41-162
reply to the opposition	42-162
classification of *sphoṭa*	43-164
the word *śāstra*-a polysemic word	43-166
factors restricting the sense of a polysemic word	44-168
the compound सर्वगुणवान्-a *bahuvrīhi* or a *karmadhāraya* with *matvarthīya* affix ?	44-168
acceptability of ज्ञापक and justifiablitiy of the form सुभ्रु (voc.sing.)	46-169
the multiple meaning of एव	49-173
evakārārtha in अस्यैव भार्या.......and its explanation	49-174
vācakatva or *dyotakatva* of the *nipātas*	52-175
vṛtti-the definition etc.	53-177
śakti (abhidhā)	54-179
threefold *śakti*	54-180
yogaśakti in compounds—a view	54-181
sātvata and *sātvat-two* examples of रूढ and योगरूढ words respectively	55-183
lakṣaṇā: definition and nature	56-185

dīrgha-dīrghatarā-vyāpāravāda	56-187
comparison of *lakṣaṇā* as depicted in TRN and VD	57-188
classification of *lakṣaṇā*	57-190
elaboration of the classification of *lakṣaṇā*	58-190
problem of the reading-क्षत्रजातिरुदियाय.....प्राक् (नै०च० २१. ६३)	59-194
lakṣaṇā in the examples-सोऽयं देवदत्तः।, तत्त्वमसि। etc.	59-195
vidhi, niyama, parisaṅkhyā and the statement-न जातु ब्राह्मणं हन्यात्।	60-198
śuddhā sāropā lakṣaṇā in द्रोणो व्रीहिः।	62-202
gauṇī sādhyavasānā lakṣaṇā-examples	63-205
vyatireka lakṣaṇā	64-206
gauṇī lakṣaṇā and *gauṇī vṛtti*	64-206
(*lakṣaṇā* in) *śyālaḥ svasro—, rathāgrahīt*	65-208
vyañjanā-definition	66-210
classification of *vyañjanā*	66-212
arguments in suppport of *vyañjanāvṛtti*	68-216
nature of *rasa*	69-222
three types of poetry-their examples	71-224
threefold suggested meaning	71-228
distinction between the *vācyārtha* and the *vyaṅgyārtha*	75-221
suggestion based on meaning-*arthaniṣṭhā vyañjanā*	78-228
śabdaśaktimūlā vyañjanā in सत्यासक्तमनाः etc.	80-229
suggestive sense conveyed by a specific utterance	86-235
suggestive sense conveyed through a gesture	87-236
concluding verses and the colophon	88-236

General Index

	Page No. (Text) (Discussion)

acceptability of ज्ञापक and justifiability of the
form सुभ्रु (voc.sing.) 46-169
arguments in support of *vyañjanā-vṛtti* 68-216
classification of *lakṣaṇā* 57-190
classification of *sphoṭa* 43-164
classification of *vyañjanā* 66-212
comparison of *lakṣaṇā* as depicted in TRN
and VD 57-188
concluding verses and the colophon 88-236
concluding verses and the colophon 56-187
distinction between *vācyārtha* and *vyaṅgyārtha* 75-221
elaboration of the classification of *lakṣaṇā* 58-190
etymology of the word *śāstra* 35-156
evakārārtha in अस्यैव भार्या.......and its explanation 49-174
factors restricting the sense of a polysemic word 44-168
gauṇī lakṣaṇā and gauṇī *vṛtti* 64-206
gauṇī sādhyavasānā lakṣaṇā-examples 63-205
grammarians' view about *śāstra* 36-157
lakṣaṇā in the examples-सोऽयं देवदत्तः,
तत्त्वमसि etc. 59-195

maṅgala śloka 31-148
multiple meaning of एव 49-173
nature of *rasa* 69-222
opposition against the theory of *sphoṭa* 41-162
problem of the reading-क्षत्रजातिरुदियाय......प्राक्।
(नै०च० २१, ६३) 59-194
reply to the opposition of *sphoṭa* 42-162
śabda 'the word' as a *śāstra* 34-156
śabdaśaktimūlā vyañjanā in सत्यासक्तमना:......etc. 80-229
śakti (abhidhā) 54-179
sarvaguṇavān-a *bahuvrīhi* or a *karmadhāraya* compound with *matvarthīya* affix 44-168
śāstra-a polysemic word 43-166
sātvata and *sātvat*-रूढ and योगरूढ words respectively 55-183
śuddhā sāropā lakṣaṇā in द्रोणो व्रीहि:। 62-202
suggestive sense conveyed by a specific utterance 86-235
suggestive sense conveyed through a gesture 87-236
suggestion based on meaning-*arthaniṣṭhā vyañjanā* 78-228
śyālah svasro ruthāgrahīt and *lakṣaṇā* 65-208
the title Vicāradīpa 32-152
the theory of *sphoṭa* 41-160
threefold *śakti* 54-180
threefold suggested meaning 71-228
three types of poetry: their examples 71-224
vācakatva or *dyotakatva* of the *nipātas* 52-175
vidhi, niyama, parisaṅkhyā and the statement-
न जातु ब्राह्मणं हन्यात्। 60-198

vṛtti-definition etc. 53-177
vyañjanā-definition 66-210
vyatireka lakṣaṇā 64-206
yogaśakti in compounds—a view 54-181

GLOSSARY

adhikaraṇa	location
adhyāhāra	elipsis, supplementation
anuvṛtti	continuity
anuśāsana	traditional knowledge
anekārtha	polysemic
anaikāntika	multi-pronged
anvaya	logical continuance, prose-order, construe
apavāda	exception
abhidhā	denotation
abhedasañsarga	inseparable contact, connection of unity
arthāntaranyāsa	corroboration
ardhajaratīya	semi-acceptability
avadhāraṇa	*restriction,* determination
avayava-avayavī-bhāva	part and whole relationship
ādhāra	substratum
utsarga	rule
upacāra	secondary usage
upapatti	coherence
kārya-kāraṇa-bhāva	cause and effect relationship
gamakatva	comprehensibility
guṇa	*attribute*, quality, excellence
gauṇī	qualitative
gaurava	prolixity, cumbrousness
graha	premise
grahaṇa	mention, utterance, acceptance

jāti	genus, class
jñāpaka	indicatory statement
tātparya	purport, intended meaning
doṣa	blemish, defect, fault
dyotaka	suggestive
parichhedya-pari-chhedaka-bhāva	measurable and measurer relationship
prakaraṇa	context
prakṛti	stem, original word
pratīti	cognition, perception
pratyaya	affix, suffix
prasaṅga	contingency
prātipadika	noun-base
prādhānya	predominance
prāśastya	admirability, praise, pre-eminence
prauḍhivāda	persistence
phala	fruit,purpose, motive
bodha	apprehension
bodhya-bodhaka-bhāva	signification
mukhya	denotative, expressive, primary
yoga	etymology
yoga-rūḍha	etymologico-conventional
yaugika	etymological
yaugika-rūḍha	etymological-conventional
rūḍha	conventional
rūḍhi	convention
lakṣaṇā	indication
vṛtti	compound, function, process
viśeṣa	distinction, specific
viśeṣaṇa	adjective, qualifier
viśeṣya	substantive
viṣaya	object, scope
vyakti	individual, suggestion
vyañjanā	suggestion
vyatireka	logical discontinuance

vyatireka lakṣaṇā	indication by contrareity
vyāpāra	function, process
vyāpti	scope
vyutpatti	derivation, etymology
śakti	denotation
śakyārtha	denotative, expressive sense
śuddhā	pure
saṅyoga	conjunction
saṅketa	convention
samānādhikaraṇya	apposition
samāsa	compound
samudāya	totality
sādhya	conclusion, major term
sādhyavasāna	introsusceptive
sāpekṣa	possessed of expectancy
sāropā	super-imposed
sārvatrika	universal
hetu	cause

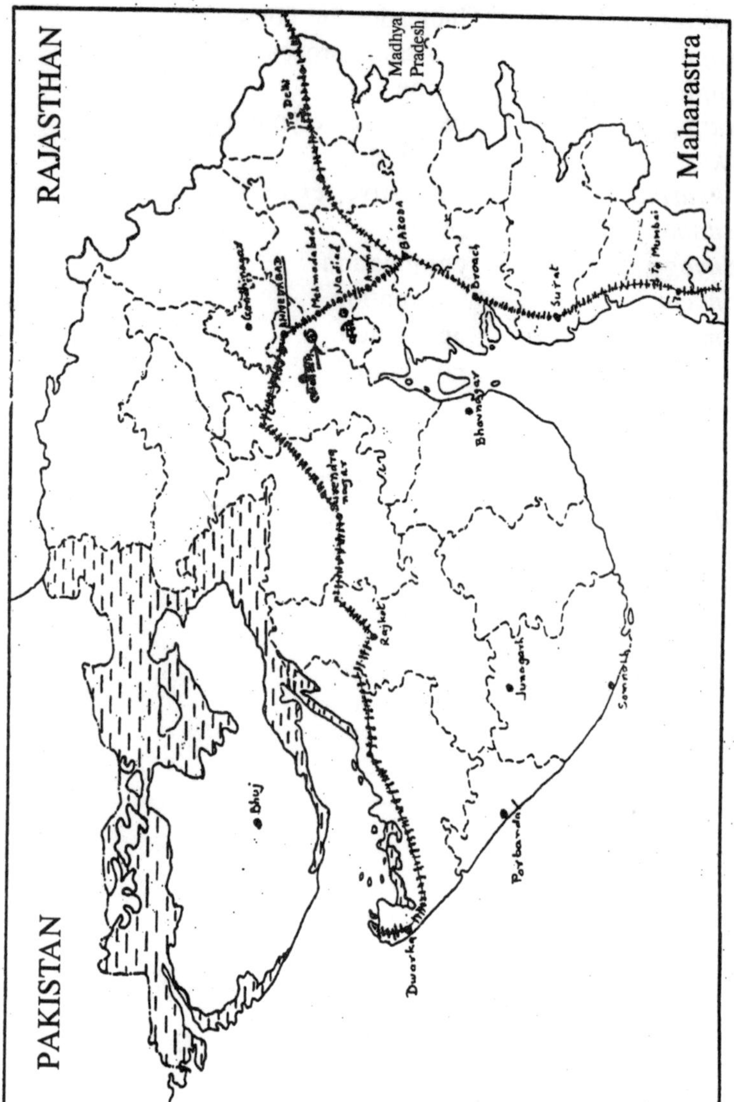

Map : The Map of Gujarat showing Lālīgrāma, the place Bhagavatkavi hails from and Vaso, the place of his teacher Āśādhara Bhaṭṭa.

BIBLIOGRAPHY

SANSKRIT WORKS (WORKWISE)

VEDIC

(1) *Ṛgveda-Saṃhitā*
pub. Vaidic Saṁśodhana Maṇḍaḷa, Poona, 1933

(2) *Taittirīya-Āraṇyaka*
Ed. Apte Harinārāyaṇa.
Anandashram Mudraṇalaya, 1897

(3) *Muṇḍaka-Upaniṣad*
Ed. Bhide S.S. Tr. Bhatt M.C.
Gujarat Vernacular Society, I[st] Ed. 1936

(4) *Śukla-Yajurveda-Saṁhitā.*
Ed. Pt Mishra Ramsakal.
Chaukhamba Sanskrit Book Depot, Benares.

EPICS-PURĀṆAS

(5) *Padmapurāṇa*
Epics-Purāṇas

(6) *Vālmīki Rāmāyaṇa.*
Critical Text Only, 1992
Oriental Institute, Baroda.

(7) *Viṣṇupurāṇa-Vol. I & II*
Critical Edition, (1997, 2000)
Oriental Institute, Baroda.

(8) *Śrīmad-Bhāgavata-Purāṇa-Vol I-II*
Chaukhamba Sanskrit Pratiṣṭhān, Delhi.

SCIENTIFIC

(9) *Amarakośa*
Tr. Shastri K.K. (Guj.)
Uni. Grantha Nirmana Board, Ahmedabad, IInd Edition, 1998

(10) *Aṣṭādhyāyī of pāṇini-Vol. I-II*
Ed. Vasu. S.C.
MBD. 1962

(11) *Kārikāvalī-Muktāvalī* by Pañcānana Viśvanātha
Ed.Shukla Hariram.
Chaukhamba Sanskrit Series, Benares, 1951

(12) *Kāvyaprakāśa of Mammaṭa*
Ed. Gajendragadkar A.B.
Popular Book Depot, Bombay-7. IInd Edition 1959.

(13) *Kāvyānkāra-sūtra-vṛtti of Vāmana*
Ed. Dr. Jha Bechan Chaukhamba Sanskrit Series, Benares, 1971

(14) *Kuvalayānanda of Appaya Dīkṣita*
Ed. Paṇaśikar Vāsudeva Lakṣmaṇa
Nirnayasagar IVth Ed. 1917

(15) *Tarkasaṅgraha of Annambhaṭṭa*
Ed. Sukthankar S.S.
The Bombay Book Deopt, 1930

(16) *Triveṇikā of Āśādharabhaṭṭa*
Ed. Kaviraja Gopinatha
The Princess of Wales Sarasvati Bhavan Text-14 Benares, 1925

(17) *Triveṇikā of Āśādharabhaṭṭa*
Ed. Shukla Kalikaprasad
Bharatiya Sahitya Vidyalaya, Varanasi, 1957.

(18) *Dhvanyāloka of Ānandavardhana*
Ed. & Tr. Parekh Nagindas (Guj.)
Gujarati Sahitya Parishad, Ahmedabad, 1981.

(19) *Dhvanyāloka of Ānandavardhana*
Tr. Dr. Krishnamoorthy K. (Eng.)
Oriental Book Agency, Poona, 1955,

(20) *Nāṭyaśāstra of Bharata.* Vol. I
Ed. Krishnamoorthy K.
G. O. Series-36, Oriental Institute, Baroda. IVth Edition, 1992.

(21) *Nūtanatarīṭīkā on Rasataraṅgiṇī*
Ms. Acc. No. 10842.
Oriental Institute, Baroda.

(22) *Paribhāṣenduśekhara of Nāgeśabhaṭṭa*
Ed. Pt Śāstrī Sādaśiva
Kashi Sanskrit Series-31. Benares. 1931

(23) *Prauḍhamanoramā or Bhaṭṭoji Dīkṣita*
Ed. Pt. Mānavallī Rāmaśāstrī
Messr. Braj B.Das & Co. Benares., 1888.

(24) *Manusmṛti*
Ed. Jha. Ganganath
Parimal Publications, Delhi.

(25) *Mahābhāṣya of Patañjali*-Vol. I to III
Motilal Banarasidas. 1967.

(26) *Yājñavalkyasmṛti*
Ed. Apte Harinārāyaṇa.
Anandashram Mudranalaya, 1903

(27) *Rasagaṅgādhara of Jagannātha-Vol, I-II* 1974, 1976
Ed. Athavale R.B. Tr. parekh Nagindas (Guj.)
Uni. Grantha Nirmana Board, Ahmedabad.

(28) *Rasavilāsa of Bhudeva Śukla*
Ed. Sharma Prem Lata.
Poona Oriental Book House, 1952

(29) *Laukika-Nyāyāñjaliḥ*
Ed. Jacob G.A. Vol. I,
Nirnaya Sagar Press, Bombay-1907

(30) *Vākyapadīya of Bhartṛhari*
Tr. & Notes by Shukla. J.M. (Guj.)
L.D. Institute of Indology, Ahmedabad, 1984.

(31) *Vedāntaparibhāṣā of Mādhavānanda*
Tr. by Adhvarīndra Dharmarāja (Eng.)
The Ramakrishna Mission, Śārdāpīṭha
Belur Maṭh, Howrah IVth Ed. 1972.

(32) *Vaiyākaraṇa-Bhūṣaṇa of Koṇḍabhaṭṭa*
Ed. Pt. Shastri Nandkishor
Bhargava Pustakalaya, 1934.

(33) *Vaiyākaraṇa-siddhānta-kārikā of Bhattoji Dīkṣita*
Ed. Apte Harinārāyaṇa
Anandashrama Mudranalaya. 1901.

(34) *Vṛttaratnākara of Kedārabhaṭṭa*
Ed. Sharma-Deshpande
Sanskrit Parishad, Usmania Viśvavidyālaya, Haidrabad.

(35) *Vṛttisamuccaya Vol. I part I &II*
Ed. Dr. Avasthi Brahmanand Mitra
Indu Prakashan, Delhi-7.

(36) *Siddhāntakaumudi of Bhattoji Dīkṣita*
Chaukhamba Sanskrit Pratishthan, Delhi- 1985.

(37) *Sphoṭavādaḥ of Nāgeśabhaṭṭa*
Ed. Krishnamacharya V.
The Adyar Library, madras. 1946

(38) *Sphoṭasiddhiḥ of Maṇḍana miśra*
Ed. Shastri Ramanath
Madras University, 1931

CLASSICAL

(39) *Anargharāghavam of Murāri.*
Ed. Mishra Ramachandra
Chaukhamba Vidyabhavan, Varanasi. 1960.

(40) *Amaruśatakam*
Ed. Devadhar C.R.
Oriented Book Agency, Poona, 1959.

(41) *Kumārasambhavam of Kālidāsa*
Ed. & Pub. Dr. Patel Gautam. Ahmedabad, 1986.

(42) *Caurapañcaśikā of Bilhaṇa*
Ed. Shrivastava. V.C.
Chaukhamba Sanskrit Samsthan, Varanasi. 1971.

(43) *Naiṣadhīyacaritam of Śrīharṣa*
Ed. & Tr. Handiqui Krishna Kanta
Motilal Banarsi Dass, Lahore, 1934.

(44) *Naiṣadhīyacaritam of Śrīharṣa*
Ed. Shukla Chandikaprasad Acharya
Sahityasadan, Dehradoon I[st] Ed. 1951.

(45) *Bhaṭṭikāvyam of Bhaṭṭi*
Vol. I & II. Ed. Trivedi K.P.
Govt. Central Book Depot, Bombay, Ist Ed. 1898.

(46) *Raghuvaṁśam of Kālidāsa*
Ed. Mishra Haragovind
Chaukhamba Sanskrit Series, Varanasi, 1961.

(47) *Śiva-mahimnaḥ-stotra of Puṣpadanta*
Ed. Dr. Joshi Jagadishbhai (Guj.)
Dhananjaya Publication, Himmatnagar, IInd Ed., 1999.

(48) *Śiśupālavadham of Māgha*
Ed. Shastri Haragovind
Chaukhamba Vidyabhavan, Varanasi, 1961.

(49) *Suktimuktāvalī of Jalhaṇa*
Ed. Bhaṭṭacharya B.
G. O. Series-82 Oriental institute, Baroda, 1991

(50) *Subhāṣitaratnabhāṇḍāgāra*
Ed. Acharya Narayana Ram
Nirnayasagar Press, Bombay, 1952

ENGLISH (AUTHORWISE)

(1) Abhyankar K. V. & Shukla J.M.
A Dictionary of Sanskrit Grammar (G.O.S. No. 134)
1986, Baroda, Oriental Institute.

(2) De. S. K., *Studies in the History of Sanskrit poetics.*, Vol. I & II, 1923-1925, Luzac & Co.

(3) Kane P. V., *History of Sanskrit Poetics,* IVth Edition. 1971, Delhi, Motilal Banarasidas.

(4) Katre S. M., *Introduction to Indian Textual Criticism,* 1941, Bombay, Karnatak Publishing House

(5) Raja K. Kunjunni, *Indian Theories of Meaning*, 1963, Madras, The Adyar Libary and Research Centre.

(6) Sadhale Gajanan Shambhu (Ed.) *Upaniṣad-vākya-mahākośa,* Vol. I & II, 1991, Jaipur, Roopa Book Pt. Lt.

(7) Śāstri Gaurīnāth, *A Study in the Dialectics of Sphoṭa*, 1980, Delhi, Motilal Banarasidas.

HINDI/GUJARATI

(8) Bhaṭṭa Vasantkumar, *Pāṇiniya Vyākaraṇa Vimarśa (Guj.)* I[st] Edition. 1994.

(9) Mishra Jagadishprasad, Āśādharabhaṭṭa (Hindi), I[st] Edition, 1987, Delhi, Eastern Book linkers.

(10) Pariyawala Hansa J., *Mammaṭano śabdaśaktivicāra,* (Guj.), Dissertation for M.Phil degree, S.G. Uni. Surat, 1978